LTC CHARLES J.

THANKS FOR YOUR DEDICATED
SERVICE TO MI AND OUR GREAT
ARMY.

Robert W. Noonan Jr.
MG, USA
CG, INSCOM

Chas —

Please continue to consider that knowledge
and study of history will contribute to our
remaining "ALWAYS OUT FRONT." Thank you
for everything. Let's keep in touch. Your friend
and comrade-in-arms....
A Fellow Former "SCIFite" and "DIACer"

— Mark

Mark Benedict
MAJ, MI, USAR
19 May 2000

MILITARY INTELLIGENCE

Military Intelligence Corps
Regimental Insignia

ARMY LINEAGE SERIES

MILITARY INTELLIGENCE

John Patrick Finnegan

Lineages Compiled by
Romana Danysh

MILITARY INSTRVCTION

Center of Military History
United States Army
Washington, D.C., 1998

Library of Congress Cataloging-in-Publication Data

Finnegan, John Patrick.
    Military intelligence / John Patrick Finnegan : lineages compiled by
Romana Danysh.
          p. cm. — (Army lineage series)
    Includes bibliographical references and index.
    1. Military intelligence—United States—History. 2. United States.
Army—History. I. Danysh, Romana, 1940– . II. Title. III. Series.
UB256.U6F56   1997
355.3'432'0973—dc21   96–44554
                                                    CIP

CMH Pub 60–13

For sale by the U.S. Government Printing Office
Superintendent of Documents, Mail Stop: SSOP, Washington, DC 20402-9328
ISBN 0-16-048828-1

Foreword

Intelligence has been defined as the art of "knowing one's enemies," and military intelligence is as old as war itself. However, the development of an intelligence organization within the United States Army is comparatively recent. The Army did not acquire a permanent peacetime intelligence organization until 1885, and the oldest of today's military intelligence units can trace its lineage only back to the eve of World War II. The Army did not formally recognize intelligence as a distinct professional discipline until 1962, when it finally created the Army Intelligence and Security Branch, the predecessor of today's Military Intelligence Branch. The Military Intelligence Corps, which incorporated all military intelligence personnel and units into a single large regiment, did not come into existence until 1987.

Although the intelligence organization within the U.S. Army was slow to develop, it has become increasingly important both as a combat multiplier in war and as a source of information for the nation's decision makers in peace. As the nation and its Army move into an information age, military intelligence will assume an even greater significance.

To tell the military intelligence story in as much detail as security regulations currently in force allow, the U.S. Army Center of Military History has worked in collaboration with the U.S. Army Intelligence and Security Command (INSCOM) to produce this volume of the Army Lineage Series. It is intended both to bring a relatively unknown part of the Army heritage to the attention of the general public and to foster unit esprit de corps among the thousands of military intelligence specialists now serving in the ranks of America's Army.

ROBERT W. NOONAN, Jr.
Major General, USA
Commanding
U.S. Army Intelligence and
  Security Command

JOHN W. MOUNTCASTLE
Brigadier General, USA
Chief of Military History

The Authors

John Patrick Finnegan graduated magna cum laude from Boston College in 1957 with an A.B. in English Literature. After a period of civilian employment with the National Security Agency and military service in the U.S. Army Counter Intelligence Corps, he went on to receive a Ph.D. in Twentieth Century American History from the University of Wisconsin–Madison. Before accepting his present position as historian with the U.S. Army Intelligence and Security Command, Dr. Finnegan taught at several American universities and at the University of Ibadan, Nigeria, and worked as a military historian at the U.S. Army Center of Military History. He is the author of *Against the Specter of a Dragon: The Campaign for American Military Preparedness, 1914–1917*, *Military Intelligence: A Picture History*, and *The Military Intelligence Story: A Photo History*, as well as coeditor of *U.S. Army Signals Intelligence in World War II: A Documentary History*.

Romana Danysh graduated from Barnard College in 1962 and received her M.A. degree in history from Stanford University in 1963. Since 1964 she has served as a historian at the U.S. Army Center of Military History. Ms. Danysh is coauthor of *Infantry, Part I: Regular Army*, a volume in the Army Lineage Series.

Preface

This book attempts to present an organizational history of Military Intelligence in the United States Army from its beginnings to the present. It makes no pretense at discussing the operational aspects of intelligence in detail, partially due to the continuing need to safeguard intelligence sources and methods. Furthermore, the book focuses its attention on the Army and necessarily slights the complex interrelationships between Army intelligence and other organizations in the intelligence community. Finally, although the book includes the lineages and heraldic items of military intelligence brigades, groups, and battalions organized under tables of organization and equipment (TOEs), it does not cover the numerous intelligence units, past and present, organized for one-of-a-kind missions under tables of distribution and allowances (TDAs).

Preparation of this volume has been a collaborative effort between the U.S. Army Center of Military History (CMH) and the U.S. Army Intelligence and Security Command (INSCOM). John Patrick Finnegan, Military History Office, INSCOM, wrote the narrative text. Romana Danysh, Organizational History Branch, CMH, compiled the lineages.

Both authors owe large debts to numerous individuals. The idea of preparing an organizational history was conceived by James L. Gilbert, INSCOM Command Historian; Janice E. McKenney, Chief of the Organizational History Branch, CMH, was instrumental in bringing about its publication as part of the Army Lineage Series. The introductory text owes much to those who took the time and trouble to compose unit histories, as well as to the former historians of the U.S. Army Intelligence Center, the U.S. Army Security Agency, the U.S. Army Intelligence Command, and the Office of the Assistant Chief of Staff for Intelligence. Lt. Col. Marc Powe's thesis on the evolution of the Military Intelligence Division from 1885 to 1917 served as a basic building block for the monograph, as did Col. Bruce Bidwell's unpublished eight-volume manuscript on the development of military intelligence from the founding of the republic to 1953. The unpublished thirty-volume history of the Counter Intelligence Corps which Maj. Ann Bray and others prepared in the late 1950s also contained a wealth of information. Finally, preparation of the narrative would have been impossible without the research assistance provided by the library and archival staffs of the National Archives and Records Administration, the U.S. Army Military History Institute, the Library of Congress, the National Security Agency, the U.S. Army Cryptologic Records Center, the Pentagon Library, and the Center of Military History.

Special thanks are due to the individuals who served on the panel that reviewed and commented on the first draft of the narrative. These include Brig. Gen. James L. Collins, U.S. Army (Retired), former Chief of Military History; Romana Danysh, Morris J. MacGregor, Jr., Janice E. McKenney, and John B. Wilson of CMH; Dianne Putney of the U.S. Air Force History Office; and Col. James W. Dunn, U.S. Army (Retired), of the Corps of Engineers History Office. Others who provided a valuable critique include David F. Trask and Robert K. Wright, Jr., of CMH; Dean Allen of the Defense Intelligence Agency History Office; Bruce Saunders, formerly with the History Office, U.S. Army Intelligence Center and School; and Henry Schorreck, formerly with the National Security Agency's History Office. Jeffrey J. Clarke, the Army's present Chief Historian, devoted considerable time and energy to polishing the final version of the manuscript. Over the years, a succession of INSCOM commanders have encouraged the project of compiling an organizational history, while former INSCOM Chief of Staff Malcolm L. Hollingsworth provided steady support.

In addition to the narrative history, this volume features lineages and heraldic data for 108 military intelligence units—13 brigades, 10 groups, and 85 battalions. They comprise all active and inactive Regular Army and Army Reserve TOE units as well as all federally recognized Army National Guard TOE units as of 30 June 1996. We did not include smaller units, such as companies and detachments, because they are not authorized their own heraldic items. However, former separate companies and detachments perpetuated by brigades, groups, or battalions are covered in the relevant lineages. No TDA units of any size are included because, in accordance with longstanding Army policy, lineage and honors are determined for TOE units only.

The Organizational History Branch of CMH is responsible for determining and publishing the official lineage and honors of Army units. The lineages in this volume are the result of research done by many past and present members of the branch, including John Finnegan. Romana Danysh prepared all the lineages for publication and updated them to reflect significant organizational changes, campaign participation credit, and unit decorations through 30 June 1996.

Each lineage is adapted from the unit's official Lineage and Honors Certificate, which outlines the history of the unit in a highly stylized format and constitutes its birth certificate, its deed to organizational properties, and verification of its service record. Although we have compressed the lineage and honors data in this book to save space, the information is the same as that on the certificates, which accounts for the technical language used. The glossary at the end of the volume will assist readers unfamiliar with lineage terms. The parenthetical entries after each unit decoration refer to the general orders announcing the awards.

Descriptions of coats of arms, shoulder sleeve insignia, and distinctive unit insignia approved for the units appear with the lineages. These descriptions as well as the color illustrations and the brief account of heraldic items were furnished by The Institute of Heraldry (TIOH). The authors are particularly grateful to Gerald T. Luchino, Thomas B. Proffitt, Nuala Barry, and James M. Hammond for their expert assistance in providing the heraldic material for this book. We also want to express our very special thanks to the late Ronald E. Dudley, an alumnus of both TIOH and CMH, who volunteered to type the heraldic data in the appropriate format for publication. In some instances, the text relating to the heraldic items is not as comprehensive as in the original letters of approval, amendment, or redesignation sent to the units. Minor changes have been made to meet the need for brevity.

Although previous volumes in the Army Lineage Series had individual unit bibliographies, the scarcity of open-source literature on military intelligence units made such an approach impracticable. Very few histories of intelligence units have been published, and historical reports submitted by intelligence organizations generally have been classified. The files of the INSCOM History Office contain information on selected units and installations. Some intelligence histories are also included in the large unit history collection maintained by the U.S. Army Military History Institute at Carlisle Barracks, Pennsylvania. In addition, the *Military Intelligence Professional Bulletin*, a quarterly publication of the U.S. Army Intelligence Center and Fort Huachuca, regularly features thumbnail sketches of various military intelligence units.

Photographic support for this volume was provided by T. Gardner, Sr., and Robert J. Bills, contractors working for the Assistant Chief of Staff, G–6, INSCOM. At CMH, John W. Elsberg, Arthur S. Hardyman, Catherine A. Heerin, Diane M. Donovan, the late Rae Panella, Joycelyn M. Canery, and John Birmingham all participated in the various aspects of producing the book.

As indicated, the efforts of a great many people contributed to the production of this volume of the Army Lineage Series. However, any mistakes, errors, or omissions are solely the responsibility of the authors.

JOHN PATRICK FINNEGAN
U.S. Army Intelligence and
   Security Command

ROMANA DANYSH
U.S. Army Center of
Military History

Contents

Illustrations

The following photographs appear between pages 60 and 61:

Nineteenth century intelligence collectors
New quarters for the War Department's intelligence organization, 1908
Pioneers of Military Intelligence
Interrogation of German prisoners of war during World War I
Technology at the service of intelligence: an Army aerial photographer
Herbert O. Yardley, intelligence hero and villain
Group photograph of the Signal Intelligence Service
The new location of the SIS in Arlington, Virginia, 1942
Signal Security Agency personnel decrypting Japanese diplomatic traffic
Cipher machines like SIGABAs guarded the security of Army communications.
Officers of Security Detachment D in the European Theater of Operations
A Counter Intelligence Corps agent questioning a source in the ETO
Soldiers of the elite Alamo Scouts in the Southwest Pacific Area
Postwar headquarters of Army Security Agency, Europe, in Frankfurt
A Nisei Counter Intelligence Corps agent during the occupation of Japan

The following photographs appear between pages 144 and 145:

Antenna field during the Korean War
Photointerpreters of the 45th ("Thunderbird") Infantry Division
The sphinx, historically identified with Military Intelligence
Antenna array at an overseas site
The durable Mohawk
Maj. Gen. Alva Fitch
Members of a military intelligence detachment during the Vietnam conflict
An intelligence officer interrogating a suspected member of the Viet Cong
A Special Forces team operating an AN/PRD–1 radio direction finder
Operations room at the Intelligence Command during the Vietnam era
A soldier demonstrating a PRD–11 radio direction finder
Guardrail Common Sensor mounted aboard the RC–12 platform
Organization Day ceremonies for the Military Intelligence Corps
New headquarters building of the Intelligence and Security Command
Use of automation and communications systems after the Cold War

A color illustration of the regimental insignia of the Military Intelligence Corps appears as the frontispiece. Color illustrations of heraldic items approved for military intelligence brigades, groups, and battalions appear between pages 214 and 215.

MILITARY INTELLIGENCE

Introduction

Military Intelligence—the collection of information by commanders on the enemy and the battlefield environment they must confront—has existed since the beginnings of armies and of wars. However, the emergence of professional Military Intelligence organizations and the definition of the functions they most appropriately performed are comparatively recent developments. Until the nineteenth century, Military Intelligence was practiced only in wartime; methods of collection were rudimentary; and the conduct of Military Intelligence was considered a function of command, one which any professional officer could perform. Furthermore, commanders tended to be skeptical about the reliability of the information they received from spies, scouts, and their own troops. In his monumental treatise *On War*, Clausewitz commented only that "many intelligence reports in war are contradictory, even more are false, and most are uncertain."[1]

The powers of continental Europe developed military staff organizations during the nineteenth century and provided a peacetime institutional locus for Military Intelligence organization. Staffs developed an intelligence element that collected maps and military statistics and dispatched attaches. Ultimately, these developments were replicated in the United States, although not without some delay. The U.S. Army was small, it had no general staff, and there were no pressing military threats to drive intelligence collection. And although George Washington had been a masterful practitioner of intelligence while serving as commander in chief of the Continental Army, this aspect of his experience has never become part of the national heritage. A small Division of Military Information was finally set up within the Adjutant General's Office twenty years after the American Civil War had ended. A few years later the Army dispatched its first military attaches abroad to provide general information on worldwide military affairs. When the Army at last gained a General Staff in 1903, the Military Information Division was transformed into the General Staff's Second Section.

---

1 Karl Von Clausewitz, *On War*, ed. and trans. Michael Howard and Peter Paret (Princeton: Princeton University Press, 1976), p. 117.

At the time, the Army's fledgling General Staff was groping to define its own appropriate mission, and these beginnings were never fully developed. A subsequent reorganization effectively eliminated the intelligence function of the staff, and it took America's entry into World War I to reverse the situation. To fight a land campaign on the continent of Europe, the Army was compelled to remodel itself along continental lines. An intelligence division was re-created within the War Department General Staff, and staffs that included intelligence officers were introduced at all units down to the level of battalion. Military Intelligence expanded to become a "shield" as well as a "sword," as the Army became heavily involved in counterintelligence.

In the field, technology helped to rationalize intelligence collection at the tactical and operational levels. Under combat conditions, intelligence gathering was accomplished not only by Military Intelligence specialists but also by the line troops themselves. As S. L. A. Marshall later stated, "Infantry . . . is the antenna of the mechanism of combat intelligence."[2] Increasingly, these sources were augmented by what were later called "special information services" that engaged in various types of technical collection activities.[3] World War I exposed the Army to a dazzling new array of technological enhancements to the collection process: aerial photography and reconnaissance, radio intercept, and optical and acoustical sensors used to detect aircraft and artillery. One secondary effect was that much of the Army's practical intelligence work was carried out by nonintelligence personnel: the intercept personnel of the Signal Corps; technicians manning artillery targeting devices; topographic specialists in the Corps of Engineers; and aviators. This situation in turn tended to block or delay the further centralization of the intelligence function.

In the long years of peace following the Armistice, Army Intelligence continued to search for an appropriate place within an Army the size of which had again been greatly reduced. A basic problem of Army Intelligence remained conceptual: defining what an intelligence organization should do. Army Intelligence offices, in fact, continued to be regarded as clearing houses for all manner of information functions unrelated to intelligence. During the interwar years, for example, intelligence staffs managed the Army's public affairs programs; later they were tasked with conducting psychological warfare and writing the Army's history. It took a surprisingly long time—until the end of World War II—for Army Intelligence to shake off such extraneous functions and concentrate on its primary task, "knowing one's enemies."[4] At the War Department level, the Army's intelligence organization tended to act more as a reference library than as

---

2 Quoted in Eliot A. Cohen and John Gooch, *Military Misfortunes: The Anatomy of Failure in War* (New York: Free Press, 1990), p. 181.

3 Robert R. Glass and Phillip B. Davidson, *Intelligence is for Commanders* (Harrisburg: Military Service Publishing Co., 1946), p. 25.

4 This useful definition is taken from the title of Ernest May's *Knowing One's Enemies: Intelligence Assessments Before the Two World Wars* (Princeton: Princeton University Press, 1986).

a positive directing force. Not until May 1945 did the War Department's Military Intelligence Division (MID) acquire an organization to establish intelligence priorities and requirements, missions that finally allowed it to put into practice all components of the modern intelligence cycle: determining requirements, collecting the appropriate information, processing the acquired data into finished intelligence, and disseminating the results, a circular process that often generates a new set of requirements, initiating the cycle again.[5]

Military Intelligence also labored under other handicaps in the years between the wars. Under garrison conditions, unit intelligence officers found themselves with little to do. Battlefield collection mechanisms seemed to have little utility in peace. The Military Intelligence Division maintained a small counterintelligence element and for a time funded a small cryptanalytic unit; but the latter function subsequently passed over to the Signal Corps. Military attaches continued to report, but their purpose was somewhat anomalous— government parsimony and expensive representational demands made it impossible for officers without private incomes to serve in overseas posts, and their function seemed more political and social than military.

These factors, along with the perceived absence of any real threat in times of peace, effectively marginalized intelligence work within the Army. Intelligence seemed unrelated to the real life of the Army, and intelligence assignments were viewed as curiosities at best. General of the Army Dwight D. Eisenhower later commented, "I think that officers of ability in all our services shied away from the intelligence branch in the fear that they would be forming dimples in their knees by holding teacups in Buenos Aires or Timbuctoo."[6] At the same time, if intelligence was peripheral, the Army still assumed that any officer could fulfill its functions.[7]

In World War II these attitudes began to change. Military and political leaders alike recognized that intelligence was crucial to military success. To meet its information needs, the Army was forced to create a large intelligence structure, manned largely by draftees and officers commissioned into the Reserves. Acting through its wartime operating arm, the Military Intelligence Service, the Military Intelligence Division instituted formal training for intelligence personnel in a diversity of disciplines. By the end of the war, various types of intelligence teams and counterintelligence detachments were supporting the intelligence

---

[5] Military Intelligence Division, A History of the Military Intelligence Division, 7 December 1941–2 September 1945, unpublished Ms, U.S. Army Center of Military History, 1946, p. 72, copy in INSCOM History Office files.

[6] Dwight D. Eisenhower, "Command in War," lecture presented to the National War College, Washington, D.C., 30 Oct 50.

[7] The author of one of the earliest books on Military Intelligence in the U.S. Army stated, "If things are not going right between G–2 and G–3 . . . then a switching of the duties of these is recommended. If the G–2 is not competent to be a G–3, he is not competent to be a G–2 and should be retired from the General Staff." Walter Campbell Sweeney, Military Intelligence: A New Weapon in War (New York: Frederick A. Stokes Co., 1924), p. 135.

staffs of all tactical units in the field. Meanwhile, the Signal Corps conducted its own intelligence and security war, entering the field of radar, which was at once a collection technology, a new intelligence target, and a subject of possible countermeasures. More important, the Signal Corps provided cryptologic support to the War Department through its Signal Security Agency and furnished theater commanders with tactical signals intelligence units. The growing importance of communications intelligence ultimately resulted in the transfer of responsibility for the function from the Signal Corps to Military Intelligence. The Army emerged from World War II with an intelligence structure that in some ways prefigured that of the present. Most of the lineages of today's intelligence units trace back to the second World War. However, this structure was departmentally oriented, fragmented, and less than fully articulated. Following the postwar reorganization of the Army in 1946, the Military Intelligence Division again emerged as the dominant institution in the whole architecture, providing overall direction, producing intelligence, and engaging in a diversity of operational activities. As part of its mandate, the Division commanded a vertically organized signals intelligence and security apparatus, the Army Security Agency (ASA), and an administratively centralized counterintelligence element, the Counter Intelligence Corps (CIC). Both ASA and CIC were organized into sizable units. However, the Army's other intelligence disciplines—human intelligence and imagery intelligence—continued to be essentially orphans, their personnel grouped into small teams supporting tactical commanders and their training base neglected. Electronic warfare remained the province of the Signal Corps. The system continued to be manned by a mix of detailed Regular Army officers and reserve officer specialists who chose to remain in uniform when the war came to an end.

During the next forty years, these arrangements were reshaped by several diverse influences. The Cold War, advances in technology, and imperatives of bureaucracy were perhaps the most significant. To meet evolving challenges, the structure of Army Intelligence was repeatedly reorganized. Military Intelligence was professionalized, its disciplines integrated, and the scope of its operations enhanced. As a result, Military Intelligence became a branch in the U.S. Army, and Military Intelligence professionals were affiliated with the Army's regimental system through the creation of the Military Intelligence Corps. Intelligence staff sections, present at all Army levels, were supplemented by specialized intelligence units up to brigade level. This book attempts to trace the long and complicated organizational history that characterized this evolution.

1

The Beginnings

In 1885 the Division of Military Information was established as part of the Military Reservations Division, Miscellaneous Branch, of the Adjutant General's Office. This step gave the U.S. Army a permanent intelligence organization for the first time in a century.

The long delay in giving recognition to the importance of Military Intelligence stemmed from various factors. One of these was the marginal position that the Army itself occupied in American society. The American tradition was one of liberty, democracy, and commercialism; except in time of war the country tended to neglect all the Army's needs. The professional Army was there to perform constabulary work against scattered Indian tribes in the vastness of the American West, to man coast defenses against the implausible threat of a foreign attack, and to serve as a continuing nucleus of professional expertise. Should a real threat to the Republic appear, citizens would rally to the flag, as they had in all of America's past wars, and some kind of mechanism for collecting intelligence would eventually be improvised to meet the crisis.

Another factor retarding the development of a permanent intelligence organization until 1885 was the general backwardness of the Army. On the European Continent, armies had been forced to create systematic staff organizations dealing with both operations and intelligence since the beginning of the nineteenth century. The Prussian Great General Staff provided the model for all of Europe's armies. In the United States, with its distrust of militarism, the idea of such a super army headquarters was repellent. Collecting intelligence and laying out detailed war plans were not in the American tradition. The U.S. Army's central staff consisted mainly of bureaus dealing with questions of administration and supply, and these reported directly to the secretary of war, not to the commanding general of the Army.

Without any organizational support, each U.S. commander served as his own intelligence officer, and the intelligence function was limited to simple reconnaissance in time of war or during an Indian campaign. In the field, units set up security patrols in tactical arrangements described in a now-quaint vocabulary of pickets, vedettes, and Cossack posts.[1] During major deployments, such as those which took place in the Civil War, cavalry served its traditional function as the eyes of the Army.

Army topographic engineers and other officers trained under the U.S. Military Academy's engineer-oriented curriculum also made important contributions to intelligence, continuing an Army tradition that dated back to the explorations of Lewis and Clark. In 1814 the War Department created a unit of topographic engineers to help with the military effort against Great Britain. From 1818 on, the Army maintained a topographic bureau and from 1838 to 1863 a separate Corps of Topographic Engineers. West Point–trained engineers helped lead Maj. Gen. Winfield Scott's army to the conquest of Mexico City in 1847.[2] Reconnaissance efforts carried out by troops were often supplemented by civilian auxiliaries. Indian and civilian scouts brought their special expertise to bear on the frontier. During the Mexican War, General Scott had even employed a group of locally hired Mexican bandits and deserters, the "Mexican Spy Company," to gather specific tactical intelligence.

Limiting Military Intelligence to tactical collection had led to numerous disasters in the past. In the War of 1812 American troops had crossed the Canadian border without maps in an abortive invasion attempt that ended in a fiasco. A generation later, the Army's quartermaster general found himself with no idea whether or not wagons could be used to support the advance of Maj. Gen. Zachary Taylor's forces into Mexico. In a classic breach of security, the Army then sent a courier to Taylor carrying unenciphered secret orders that stripped the general of most of his regulars. The orders were captured on the way, and Taylor's lack of reconnaissance allowed his depleted forces to be taken by surprise at Buena Vista. Buena Vista turned out to be an American victory only due to the fighting prowess of Taylor's volunteer troops. With luck on its side, the Republic managed to muddle through the Mexican War just as it had through the War of 1812. In both cases, the ultimate triumph of largely improvised forces encouraged a casual approach toward Military Intelligence, an attitude that fit well with the longstanding American tradition of subordinating military concerns to other, more immediate interests.

The nature and scope of the Civil War provided unusual opportunities for intelligence collection.[3] Because the North and South were physically proximate

---

1 See Arthur L. Wagner, *The Service of Security and Information* (Kansas City: Hudson-Kimberley Publishing, 1893), pp. 55–67.

2 The services of the topographical engineers are documented in William H. Goetzman, *Army Exploration in the American West, 1803–1863* (Lincoln: University of Nebraska Press, 1979); Guy C. Swan III et al., "Scott's Engineers," *Military Review* (March 1983): 61–68, deals with reconnaissance in the Mexican War.

3 An excellent treatment of Civil War intelligence can be found in Peter Maslowski, "Military Intelligence Sources During the American Civil War," in *The Intelligence Revolution: An Historical Perspective; Proceedings of the Thirteenth Military History Symposium, United States Air Force Academy*, ed. Walter T. Hitchcock (Washington, D.C.: Office of Air Force History, 1991), pp. 39–70.

and loyalties were desperately intermixed, both sides made extensive use of spies as well as the military information cheerfully turned over by an uncensored press. In the field the rival armies often used civilian guides, willingly or unwillingly recruited from the population. This was an American adaptation of Napoleon's succinctly brutal advice on intelligence collection: "You order the major to put a peasant at your disposal, arrest his wife as a hostage, have a soldier dress himself as the man's farm hand. This system always succeeds."[4] Cavalry once again proved its indispensability. For the first part of the war, lack of an effective cavalry organization left the Union armies blinded in the presence of their enemies. During the Gettysburg campaign, however, the situation was reversed. Maj. Gen. J. E. B. Stuart's decision to raid rather than scout led directly to the Confederates' accepting battle on unfavorable terms.

Increased use of technology also contributed to innovations in the intelligence and security arena during the Civil War. The Union Army used both free and tethered balloons to watch over enemy dispositions in the early stages of the conflict. Manned by civilian aeronauts, the balloons were successively assigned to the Corps of Topographic Engineers, the Quartermaster Corps, and the Corps of Engineers.[5] The Army Signal Corps, first set up in 1863, also came to play an intelligence role. Signal Corps communications troops posted on high ground often provided valuable field intelligence.[6] However, their messages, transmitted by "wig-wagged" signal flags, could be intercepted. Similarly, the increased use of the telegraph by each side created opportunities both for communications intercept and communications deception. This quickly led to the employment of rudimentary field codes and ciphers in tactical situations.

Most commanders on both sides continued to serve as their own intelligence officers. Confederate Lt. Gen. Thomas "Stonewall" Jackson directly supervised the mapping of the Shenandoah Valley.[7] Another Confederate corps commander, Lt. Gen. James A. Longstreet, personally debriefed the spy who provided the first indications that the Union Army was on the move to Gettysburg.

---

4 Martin Van Creveld, *Command in War* (Cambridge: Harvard University Press, 1985), p. 67.

5 Army balloon activities in the Civil War and later periods are covered in Tom D. Crouch, *The Eagle Aloft: Two Centuries of the Balloon in America* (Washington, D.C.: Smithsonian Institute Press, 1983). The Confederates were able to field only one balloon during the course of the conflict, but its performance impressed at least one rebel officer. "My experience with this gave me a high idea of the possible efficiency of balloons in active campaigns. Especially did we find, too, that the balloons of the enemy forced upon us constant troublesome precautions in efforts to conceal our marches." General E. P. Alexander, *Military Memoirs of a Confederate* (Bloomington: Indiana University Press, 1962), pp. 172–73.

6 The Union Signal Corps operated both "stations of observation" and "stations of communication." J. Willard Brown, *The Signal Corps, U.S.A. in the War of the Rebellion* (New York: Arno Press, 1974), p. 125. The Confederate Signal Corps was even more involved in intelligence work. See William A. Tidwell et al., *Come Retribution: The Confederate Secret Service and the Assassination of Lincoln* (Jackson: University Press of Mississippi, 1988), pp. 80–104.

7 This is documented in *Make Me a Map of the Valley: The Civil War Journal of Stonewall Jackson's Topographer*, ed. Archie P. McDonald (Dallas: Southern Methodist University Press, 1973).

However, there were some attempts to designate intelligence officers and to establish rudimentary intelligence organizations. During the opening days of the Bull Run campaign, Maj. Gen. Pierre Beauregard's assistant adjutant general was able to provide the Confederate Army with early warning of incipient Union moves through a well-connected spy network he ran in Washington, D.C. Shortly afterward, Maj. Gen. George McClellan, the newly appointed head of the Union Armies, employed private detective Alan Pinkerton as his intelligence chief. However, Pinkerton's untutored and exaggerated evaluation of Confederate strength virtually paralyzed Union operations for a time.8 But amateurishness in the field of intelligence at this point was not confined to civilians: after Pinkerton's return to private life, McClellan's cavalry chief, Maj. Gen. Alfred Pleasanton, provided equally misleading information regarding the enemy's numbers.9

Union forces did not acquire a professional intelligence officer until the spring of 1863, when Maj. Gen. Joseph Hooker, commander of the Army of the Potomac, directed Col. George V. Sharpe of the 120th New York Volunteer Infantry to set up a bureau of information. Sharpe, a lawyer and diplomat in civilian life, devised an effective system making use of civilian scouts, behind-the-lines agents, and interrogation reports from deserters and prisoners of war to build up an accurate picture of Confederate order of battle and intentions. By the end of the war, Sharpe was a brevet brigadier general and assistant provost marshal assigned to Headquarters, Armies of the United States.10

Counterintelligence organizations also made an appearance. In one of their few successes, Pinkerton and his operatives rolled up the Rosa Greenhow spy network that had funneled information to the Confederates from the nation's capital. At the beginning of 1862 the War Department took over the rather elaborate nationwide counterintelligence organization built up by Secretary of State William Henry Seward and placed it under Lafayette Baker, a civilian who subsequently operated a "secret service" of detectives that engaged in both positive collection and counterintelligence. In addition, Baker supervised investigations of graft and fraud and still found time to organize his own cavalry regiment, thus acquiring

---

8 To the end, Pinkerton was convinced he was right. See his autobiographical work, *The Spy of the Rebellion: Being a True History of the Spy System of the United States Army During the Late Rebellion* (New York: G. W. Carleton and Co., 1883), p. 588. The best evaluation of his performance is in Edwin C. Fishel, "Pinkerton and McClellan: Who Deceived Whom?" *Civil War History* 24 (June 1988): 115–42.

9 Stephen V. Sears discusses the "singular ineptitude" of Pleasanton as an intelligence officer in *George B. McClellan: The Young Napoleon* (New York: Ticknor and Fields, 1988), p. 274. Pleasanton continued to serve as cavalry chief of the Army of the Potomac even after McClellan stepped down. His reports continued to be "remarkably unreliable." Russell F. Weigley, *History of the United States Army, Enlarged Edition* (Bloomington: Indiana University Press, 1984), p. 242.

10 Maslowski, "Intelligence Sources," p. 40. It should be noted that Sharpe's organization was known as a "bureau of information," not an intelligence office. In nineteenth-century usage, the word "intelligence" equated with today's "news." The Army Intelligence Office, which the Confederates established in 1862, was headed by a chaplain with the mission to inform the families of wounded Southern soldiers about their care and disposition.

the rank of colonel. As a result of his work in tracking down Lincoln's assassins, Baker also ended his Civil War service as a brevet brigadier general.[11]

After the Civil War, older habits reasserted themselves. The vast armies were hastily demobilized, and the wartime arrangements for gathering intelligence discontinued. Sharpe returned to civilian life; Baker was fired by President Andrew Johnson, who disagreed both with his methods and, more to the point, his suspicions that unregenerate Confederates were regaining power and influence under the Johnson administration. Once Reconstruction had ended, the Army was scaled back to a force of some 25,000 men, thinly scattered over the empty spaces of the American West. Once again, each commander served as his own intelligence officer. Under typical conditions of Indian warfare, cavalry regiments were broken up into penny-packets and employed as standing garrisons or mobile strike forces. In the West, commanders relied on Indian scouts and civilians like Buffalo Bill Cody to fulfill their intelligence needs. Indians had been used in this role since the beginning of the Republic, and Congress had authorized a permanent Corps of Indian Scouts in 1866. Although the legislation provided for a force of 1,000 scouts, budgetary factors allowed no more than 300 scouts to be employed at any one time.[12]

Despite its occasional wartime accomplishments, Army Intelligence had been a matter of improvisation. There had been no institutional structure to give it historical continuity. Expertise gained in wartime had quickly dissipated. However, by the 1880s the tide began to turn. American society itself was rapidly changing from a loosely knit aggregation of agriculturalists into an industrial unit of large corporations bound together in a national market. This in turn led to a new emphasis on professional expertise.[13] At the same time, similar developments were taking place in the major nations overseas, which began to exhibit a renewed interest in imperial expansion, a fact of some concern to the United States. The U.S. preoccupation with the Civil War had already encouraged French intervention in Mexico. As the steamship and the international cable continued to draw the world closer together, the actions of foreign powers impinged on the American popular consciousness in a way that had not been the case in the past.

Slowly, America's military institutions began to respond to these pressures for greater professionalization and greater access to information concerning events abroad. In 1881 the Army created a professional school at Fort Leavenworth, Kansas, to give advanced instruction to infantry and cavalry officers. In 1882 the U.S. Navy set up the Office of Naval Intelligence with the primary mission of observing and reporting on new developments in maritime technology overseas.

---

[11] Baker told his own story, possibly with some improvements, in *History of the United States Secret Service* (Philadelphia: L. C. Baker, 1867).

[12] Robert M. Utley, *Frontier Regulars: The United States Army and the Indian, 1866–1890* (New York: MacMillan Co., 1973), p. 53.

[13] This interpretation owes much to Robert G. Wiebe.

The establishment of the Division of Military Information by the Army in 1885 was thus part of a larger pattern of historical developments.

Military Intelligence in Place

The Army's Intelligence organization underwent a steady evolution between 1885 and the beginning of the war with Spain. Initially, the Division of Military Information appears to have been seen as simply a passive repository for information on military-related developments at home and abroad. Its domestic responsibilities led to its location in the Military Reservations Division of the Adjutant General's Office. Initial collection requirements were disarmingly simple. The adjutant general requested that the Army's geographical departments and technical services "whenever practicable, make report on anything which it may be desirable for the Government to know in case of sudden war." Just what sort of information this was, however, was "almost impossible to specify in detail . . . but this can well be left to the intelligence and discretion of the officers."[14]

In 1889 the division took a first step toward taking on a more positive role when the Army dispatched military attaches to the capitals of the five major European powers: Great Britain, France, Germany, Russia, and Austria-Hungary. Since the attaches were charged with performing intelligence-gathering tasks in addition to diplomatic representational duties, they provided the division with its own professional collection arm. About the same time, the division became a separate body, directly subordinate to the adjutant general, and access to its files was restricted to the commanding general of the Army and the bureau chiefs.[15]

Although the introduction of attaches improved the Army's foreign intelligence capabilities, it also resulted in the Army's first intelligence scandal. In 1892 Capt. Henry T. Borup, the American attache posted to France, was expelled from the country for attempting to purchase the plans for the fortifications of Toulon from a disgruntled employee of the French Ministry of Marine. This event caused some consternation, especially to Jefferson Coolidge, the American minister to France. Coolidge pointed out that Borup's action had been "perfectly useless"; not only was America at peace with France, but the small American navy could not attack Toulon.[16] However, the captain's behavior, while indiscreet, was not totally irrational; the United States had recently embarked on a program to upgrade its own coastal defenses, and Borup, an

---

14 Ltr, Brig Gen R. C. Drum to Chief of Engineers, 23 Nov 1886; George W. Auxier, Historical Manuscript File: Materials on the History of Military Intelligence in the U.S., 1884–1944, U.S. Army Center of Military History, Washington, D.C., hereafter cited as MID Documents.

15 A succinct account of the organization can be found in Elizabeth Bethel, "The Military Information Division: Origin of the Intelligence Division," *Military Affairs* 11 (Spring 1971): 17–24.

16 Alfred Vagts, *The Military Attache* (Princeton: Princeton University Press, 1967), p. 222.

ordnance officer, presumably believed that any information gleaned from abroad would be helpful. At any rate, this minor embarrassment did not interfere with the growth of the attache system. By 1894 five additional attache posts had been set up at other European capitals, Japan, and Mexico.

Meanwhile, the functions of the Military Information Division expanded further. In 1892 the secretary of war reorganized the division, assigning it a wide spectrum of duties that nearly transformed it into a combined operational and intelligence staff. The division was tasked to collect information on both the United States and foreign countries, to direct the attache system, and to disseminate intelligence products and maps to the Army. In addition, it was to monitor the militia mobilization base, prepare instructions to the militia inspectors, and formulate mobilization plans. As if all of this were not enough, the division was also directed to "have charge of a museum . . . for the care and preservation of military relics."[17]

By 1893 the Military Information Division was large enough to be organized into four branches. The Progress in Military Arts Branch collected scientific and technical intelligence from the various attaches. The Northern Frontier Branch focused on the Canadian border: Great Britain was still thought of as a possible, though not probable, enemy, and Army officers were encouraged to take "hunting and fishing" leaves to reconnoiter and map certain areas of Canada. The Spanish-American Branch monitored developments in the troubled Caribbean, where Cuban revolutionaries were already plotting insurrection against Spain. Finally, the Militia and Volunteer Branch kept track of the various state National Guard organizations and performed whatever rudimentary mobilization planning was possible in peacetime.

As a result, when the war with Spain began in April 1898, the Army for once entered upon a conflict with at least a semblance of intelligence preparation. Eleven officers were on duty with the Military Information Division at the State, War, and Navy Building in Washington; 6 additional attaches went to join the 10 already abroad, and another 40 officers provided status reports on the nation's militia.[18] The Military Information Division had already collected a good deal of intelligence on conditions in Cuba and soon collected more using Army officers on undercover assignments in Cuba and Puerto Rico. The clandestine collection mission of Lt. Albert Rowan in Cuba was later both popularized and distorted in Elbert Hubbard's famous story, "A Message to Garcia."[19]

---

17 Orders, Secretary of War S. B. Elkins, 12 Mar 1892, MID Documents.

18 Marc B. Powe, *The Emergence of the War Department Intelligence Agency, 1885-1918* (Manhattan, Kans.: MA/AH Publishing, 1974), p. 29. The head of the Military Information Division at the time was Col. Arthur S. Wagner, author of *The Service of Security and Information* and the leading expert on intelligence in the Army.

19 For the true story, see Rowan's own account in *Military Intelligence: Its Heroes and Legends*, comp. Diane Hamm (Arlington, Va.: U.S. Army Intelligence and Security Command, 1987), pp. 1–19.

Unfortunately, the war would reveal much about the weaknesses of both the Army and its Military Intelligence organization. The 25,000-man Regular Army was increased in strength, but concomitantly 140,000 militiamen and volunteers were placed under arms, creating intolerable strains on the country's mobilization capacities. The dispatch of the main Spanish fleet to Santiago, Cuba, first discovered by a Signal Corps wiretap of the Spanish cable, led to the hasty deployment of elements of the Army's newly organized V Corps to that island. This expeditionary force was pulled together amid conditions of chaos and then committed to action under a slothful commander of dubious tactical skills. Eventual victory in Cuba owed much to the valor of regular and volunteer troops, but little to planning or to the effective use of intelligence, since the expedition's commander had refused the War Department's offer to set up a Military Information Division in the field to support the campaign.

Meanwhile, mobilization effectively disrupted the workings of the Military Information Division. The natural desire of officers for field service, coupled with the need to stiffen the volunteer troops with regulars, drained the Military Information Division of its uniformed personnel; only 2 officers and 10 civilian clerks were left on duty in Washington when the war came to a close, and all but 5 attaches had returned from their posts abroad. But during the same period the Army's intelligence needs had grown immensely. Following Dewey's victory at Manila, troops had been committed to the Philippines. An intelligence officer accompanied the expedition, but he labored under severe handicaps because the Military Information Division had never made any study of the Far East. Once a Filipino insurrection against American occupiers broke out, the Army in the Philippines was forced to expand its intelligence activities. In 1899 it set up its own independent counterintelligence center, the Bureau of Insurgent Records. Redesignated a year later as the Bureau of Military Information, this organization was not subordinated to the War Department's Military Information Division until 1902.

The lessons of the war with Spain and the imperatives of maintaining a 100,000-man Army to secure America's new empire led to a complete reorganization of the War Department in 1903. As a result, the Army finally acquired a General Staff organization to carry out administrative, intelligence, and planning functions. Six of the forty-four officers on the new War Department General Staff were assigned to its Second Division, which absorbed the Adjutant General's Military Information Division and was given the exclusive mission of collecting foreign intelligence. The arrangement allowed the Army's military information organization to focus its attention on intelligence rather than on the diversity of operational assignments that the Military Information Division had been given in 1892. In 1904 Great Britain belatedly organized its own Army General Staff, adopting precisely the opposite solution: the British combined intelligence with operations in the same staff element.[20]

Four major duties were assigned to the U.S. General Staff's Second Division: collecting and disseminating information on foreign countries; directing the work of the attache system and managing contacts with foreign military attaches in the United States; supervising mapping; and maintaining a reference collection. However, even under the new arrangements, the military information unit still could not perform certain vital intelligence staff functions. First, it had not been given the responsibility for planning Army Intelligence organization and operations in the field; it simply acted as a central point for intelligence-gathering at the War Department level. Second, the organization had no responsibility for security or counterintelligence within the Army. Moreover, the division's small staff was hard pressed to cope with its existing functions, and the War Department General Staff could not give the subject the attention it deemed necessary. Nevertheless, at least some officers had come to realize that the criterion for staffing the new organization should have been the size of the world rather than the size of the Army.

Military Intelligence in the Twentieth Century

The first decade of the twentieth century furnished Army Intelligence with new challenges. Formerly, intelligence officers had concerned themselves with procuring information on the neighboring states in the Western Hemisphere and collecting, on a more or less academic basis, technical intelligence on military developments in Europe. The acquisition of the Philippines had forced the Army to develop a counterintelligence capability in that area. The Army soon realized that the Philippine involvement, together with a growing American commercial and military presence in China, had a wider intelligence impact. America was now a Far Eastern power. This meant that the Army now had to evaluate the military threat of the expanding Japanese Empire. Prejudice against Asian immigrants on the West Coast, which repeatedly jeopardized American-Japanese relations, only reinforced this need. Military observers thus went abroad to supplement attache coverage of the Russo-Japanese War of 1904–1905. In 1907 the Army began to assign officers to Japan for language training and shortly thereafter to China for the same purpose.

Paradoxically, as the Army's need for intelligence increased, the Army's capacity to meet it declined. Between 1903 and America's entry into World War I, the Army's new General Staff strove to find an identity and a suitable role. The Army's intelligence organization was caught up in this bureaucratic maneuvering with unfortunate results. In 1907 the incumbent adjutant general, the autocratic Maj.

---

[20] Thomas G. Fergusson, *British Military Intelligence, 1870–1914: The Development of a Modern Intelligence Organization* (Frederick, Md.: University Publications of America, 1984), p. 202.

Gen. Frederick Ainsworth, restricted the authority of the Second Division to communicate directly with the attaches overseas, insisting that certain categories of correspondence pass through his office. Then, in 1908 the Third Division of the General Staff, which dealt with contingency and operational planning and was a principal consumer of the Second Division's products, relocated to Washington Barracks (now Fort McNair). Unfortunately, its new and spacious quarters were some miles away from the Second Division's offices in downtown Washington, D.C. This soon caused coordination problems, since the Third Division had only one automobile at its disposal. To satisfy the Third Division's information requirements, the Second Division was in turn moved from its own centrally located offices and banished to Washington Barracks. Incumbent Chief of Staff Maj. Gen. J. Franklin Bell then decided that it was impracticable to have two separate General Staff elements in the same place and directed that the two divisions be merged. The Army's intelligence staff element thereby lost its separate identity.[21]

The result of this reorganization was an unqualified disaster for the intelligence function at the General Staff level. Intelligence was now assigned to the Military Information Committee, all of whose members were preoccupied with numerous other duties. Intelligence was no longer produced for the Army as a whole, but for the War College Division (as the Third Division was later redesignated), and soon it ceased to be produced at all. A few years later, the chief of the War College Division had to confess that because of the press of business, "the collecting, digesting, and filing of military information of foreign countries . . . appears never to have been carried on continuously," and that "the work of attaches is without proper supervision and guidance, and therefore, to a large extent, the value of their work is lost."[22]

The outbreak of revolution in Mexico in 1911 did little to end this situation, although two War College Division captains were eventually detailed to monitor developments and compile what information about the country was available.[23] Still, when American forces landed at Vera Cruz in 1914 they were essentially without intelligence support. Sent down to investigate the situation, Capt. Douglas MacArthur reported back to his superior that "the Intelligence

---

21 Maj. Gen. Ralph Van Deman, who headed War Department Military Intelligence for most of World War I, commented that "had there been sufficient automobile transportation it is possible that the disastrous incident . . . would not have occurred." *The Final Memoranda: Major General Ralph Van Deman, U.S.A. Ret., 1865–1952: Father of Military Intelligence*, ed. Ralph J. Weber (Wilmington: Scholarly Resources, 1988), p. 15.

22 Memo, Brig Gen M. M. Macomb for Chief of Staff, 13 Jul 14, sub: Employment of a Monograph Clerk, Record Group (RG) 165, ser. 5, National Archives and Records Administration (NARA), Washington, D.C. A contemporary observer attributed the eclipse of the intelligence function to a personnel shortage. "The reduction of the General Staff by 12 officers in 1912 had made it impossible for an Intelligence division of any strength to be maintained." Maj Gen Dennis E. Nolan, Memoirs, ch. 4, p. 4, Dennis Nolan Ms, U.S. Army Military History Institute, Carlisle Barracks, Pa.

23 Ltr, Brig Gen M. M. Macomb to Brig Gen Tasker H. Bliss, 26 Oct 14, Tasker Bliss Ms, Library of Congress (LC), Washington, D.C.

Office established by the Brigade was practically useless for my purpose. There seems to be no logical conception of just what information is needed and as a result its efforts consist largely in accumulating wild and exaggerated reports from a lot of scared and lying American refugees."[24]

The outbreak of general war in Europe also failed to revive the Army's intelligence program, even though the United States was soon on the verge of breaking diplomatic relations with Imperial Germany over the sinking of the *Lusitania*. Although the attache system was now extensive—historian Alfred Vagts has pointed out that only Imperial Russia had as many military attaches as the United States—and although additional military observers were sent to Europe to watch the fighting there, the mechanism for analyzing the reports submitted from overseas was lacking.[25] After 1915 the Military Information Committee was used simply as a bookkeeping device. Congressional appropriations listed the committee as a budget line item, but its membership comprised all War College Division officers engaged in "current General Staff work" as opposed to war plans.[26]

The state of intelligence work in the Army was demonstrated graphically when the War Department was called upon to produce a preparedness plan for Army reorganization in 1915. Preparation of the threat estimate justifying the plan was assigned to Capt. Dennis E. Nolan of the War College Division, who assembled his data from three open source references: a 1914 almanac of the world's armies, a shipping register from the same year, and the Army's own Field Service Regulations. In the interest of simplicity, Nolan decided to ignore the fact that the outbreak of World War I had rendered the information contained in these documents obsolete and changed the whole strategic situation. But by using this material creatively, Nolan demonstrated that Germany, to use only one of his examples, could deploy a force of 435,000 men and 91,457 animals in the United States within 15.8 days of the start of hostilities. Although this estimate served to justify the War Department's plans for a greatly expanded Army, it ignored so many other factors as to pass beyond the bounds of reality.[27]

Although Army Intelligence was collapsing at the center in the period just before American entry into World War I, there were other, more positive developments taking place in the field. These were mostly brought about by Signal Corps initiatives in the areas of communications intelligence, aerial reconnaissance, and communications security. A growing Signal Corps involvement in the

---

24 Ltr, Capt Douglas MacArthur to Maj Gen Leonard Wood, 7 May 14, Leonard Wood Ms, LC.

25 Vagts, *The Military Attache*, p. 34.

26 *The Final Memoranda*, p. 147.

27 However, the Epitome of Military Policy produced by the War Department General Staff in 1915 concluded that "the accomplishment of the plan outlined above for the invading force instead of being a noteworthy military achievement would be a commonplace military operation ridiculously easy of accomplishment." John P. Finnegan, *Against the Specter of a Dragon: The Campaign for American Military Preparedness, 1914–1917* (Westport, Conn.: Greenwood Press, 1974), p. 50.

intelligence arena came about by a circuitous route. The Signal Corps had used balloons for meteorological purposes when it had the mission of operating the U.S. Weather Bureau. After the Signal Corps turned over all but the military aspects of the weather function to the Department of Agriculture in 1890, it redirected its aeronautical expertise toward the development of a manned observation balloon. A Signal Corps balloon, the *Santiago*, took part in the fighting in Cuba, where it served chiefly to draw enemy fire. Undeterred, the Signal Corps persevered in this line of development and continued to experiment with the possibilities of aerial observation from a variety of platforms.28 In the early years of the twentieth century, it made trials of traditional tethered observation balloons, a small powered dirigible, and the new airplane invented by the Wright brothers. In 1909 the Army purchased its first aircraft and by 1915 had a whole squadron.

Similarly, the Signal Corps pioneered the development of wireless for military uses. In 1914 it acquired three "radio tractors," actually White Company motortrucks equipped with radio sets. Although this equipment was procured for communications work, it could easily be adapted to intelligence purposes. Finally, in the field of security, Capt. Parker Hitt became the first Army officer to undertake research in the exotic field of codes and ciphers. In 1916 Hitt produced the first work on cryptology ever published in the United States.29

About the same time, other signs of renewed interest in Army Intelligence began to emerge. In March 1916 Maj. Ralph Van Deman, an infantry officer on detail to the War College Division, submitted to his superiors two multipage memorandums on the subject. Van Deman had served with the former Military Information Division both in Washington and in the Philippines, performed undercover work in China, and held an intelligence position on his previous General Staff assignment from 1907 to 1910. Upon returning to Washington, he expressed his dismay at the extent to which the General Staff had allowed its intelligence function to lapse. Van Deman pointed out that information was no longer "collected—it just comes in. . . . But even such information as does come in, is not studied and checked. . . . As far as any benefit to the Government is concerned, the mass of this information might just as well be in Timbuctoo. It will remain in the Record Section unavailable to the end of time."30 What the Army needed, Van Deman felt, was a separate division of the General Staff to deal exclusively with military information.31 Although this report had no immediate effect, in April the acting chief of staff

---

28 In the 1903 revised edition of his book, *The Service of Security and Information*, Colonel Wagner included an extensive treatment on the employment of observation balloons for reconnaissance. I am indebted to Dr. Edward Raines of the U.S. Army Center of Military History for this piece of information.

29 Parker Hitt, *Manual for the Solution of Military Ciphers* (Fort Leavenworth: Press of the Army Service Schools, 1916).

30 *The Final Memoranda*, p. 104.

31 Ibid., pp. 113–14.

of the Army ordered intelligence officers to be posted in the Army's four continental United States and two overseas geographic departments. In addition to supporting their own commanders, these officers would report back to the Military Intelligence Committee. Even before this step had been taken, the Army found it had new requirements for intelligence.

In March 1916 the forces of Mexican bandit leader Pancho Villa raided Columbus, New Mexico, inflicting loss on troopers of the 13th Cavalry and causing civilian casualties. In response, the Wilson administration ordered Brig. Gen. John J. Pershing to lead a punitive expedition into Mexico to hunt down Villa's guerrilla band. Subsequently Pershing's forces deployed the widest range of intelligence assets which the Army had yet managed to field.

During the American foray into Mexico, traditional collection mechanisms were augmented by newly emerging technologies. Pershing's intelligence officer, Maj. James A. Ryan, organized a highly effective "service of information" that gave Pershing a good knowledge of northern Mexico. Ryan made use of local informants, supplemented by the Army's own reconnaissance capabilities. These were extensive. A large part of the force consisted of horse cavalry, and for the last time in its history the Army fielded a force of twenty Apache Indian scouts. In addition, the Punitive Expedition was accompanied by the aircraft of the Army's 1st Aero Squadron, commanded by Maj. Benjamin Foulois, the first Army officer to learn to fly. The squadron attempted aerial reconnaissance and even brought along an aerial camera, although little came of these efforts. The planes were too underpowered to fly over the mountain ranges of Mexico and all eight initially assigned to the expedition crashed within two months.[32]

Finally, motor vehicles appeared in an intelligence role for the first time in the Army's history. Pershing's expedition was not only supported logistically by trucks, but also used a few for intelligence collection. Although rugged Mexican terrain and the limitations of the early motor vehicle meant that ground reconnaissance still depended on horse cavalry, the "radio tractors" of the Signal Corps deployed with Pershing's forces monitored Mexican government communications as Mexican authorities became increasingly alarmed at the American probe, which soon extended 500 miles into their sovereign territory. Although the Punitive Expedition was a limited success—Villa's troops were engaged and scattered, but the leader himself escaped, and war with Mexico almost ensued—it was a milestone in the Army's use of multisource intelligence.

On 1 February 1917, the Mexican problem was suddenly eclipsed by the German decision to wage unrestricted warfare against all vessels carrying supplies to the Allied Powers. In addition to threatening America's capacity to export, this act defied the principles of neutral rights, which the Wilson admin-

---

[32] Clarence C. Clendenen gives a good account of the Punitive Expedition in *Blood on the Border: The United States Army and the Mexican Irregulars* (London: MacMillan Co., 1969). Chapter 17 of the book is devoted to "Airplanes and Motors."

istration had upheld since the beginning of World War I. As the United States
teetered on the brink of war, all War College students were relieved of their normal duties and instructed to familiarize themselves with attache reports relating
to the war in Europe. At the same time, Secretary of War Newton Baker recommended that each state appoint a National Guard officer to receive intelligence
training.[33] However, when Congress finally declared war against Germany on 6
April 1917, the U.S. Army still had no intelligence organization. The Army
essentially was moving blindly into the greatest foreign conflict in its history.

---

[33] Powe, *The Emergence of the War Department Intelligence Agency*, pp. 81–82.

2

World War I

The United States entered World War I almost completely unprepared: the National Defense Act which Congress had passed in 1916 had provided the basis of a mobilization plan, not an actual army. In early 1917 the country had only 210,000 men under arms, a third of them National Guardsmen who had been called up the previous summer to serve on the Mexican border. The Army had no permanent tactical organization above the level of the regiment and lacked adequate quantities of artillery, machine guns, tanks, modern aircraft, and even gas masks. Its General Staff organization was not designed to cope with the logistical and operational problems presented by a major conflict, and at the direction of the Wilson administration it had made no war plans. The Army had no intelligence organization.

Within seventeen months, however, the country had transformed itself into a fighting machine. With the help of the draft, the United States raised an Army of 4 million men; half of this great force was transported to France, where it provided the decisive margin that led to victory over Imperial Germany and its allies. American industry was also mobilized for war, but not soon enough, forcing Britain and France to supply the American Expeditionary Forces (AEF) in France with almost all required tanks, planes, and artillery. The General Staff was repeatedly restructured and finally became an effective instrument of control. And under the pressures of war, the Army was forced to develop new intelligence capabilities.

The development of Army Intelligence in World War I proceeded along two parallel but more or less separate tracks. At the War Department level, intelligence work was revived; by the end of the war, Military Intelligence had become a full-fledged staff element as one of four operating divisions of the General Staff. Concurrently, General John J. Pershing, commander of the AEF, built up his own field intelligence organization, structured along rather different lines to meet tactical needs. Pershing's ideas on Army reorganization and on the need for an intelligence apparatus were adopted by the War Department in organizing troop units and ultimately provided the basis for reorganization of the General Staff itself.

Van Deman and Military Intelligence

At the War Department level, the individual most responsible for rebuilding an intelligence apparatus was Maj. Ralph Van Deman, the General Staff officer who had lobbied vigorously but unproductively in the years before the war to re-create the Army's capabilities in this area. In 1917, with the United States at war, Van Deman tried again. He submitted a formal recommendation to Maj. Gen. Hugh Scott, the Army's chief of staff, urging the War Department to establish a Military Intelligence Division. This initiative was strongly supported by Van Deman's immediate superior, Brig. Gen. Joseph Kuhn, chief of the War College Division.[1] Unfortunately, the chief of staff was not receptive. Scott was an old-time cavalryman with an encyclopedic knowledge of Indian sign languages and a deep interest in packsaddles, but his former commander in chief, President William Howard Taft, had described his intellectual abilities as "wood to the middle of his head." By 1917 he was demonstrating a disconcerting tendency to fall asleep at Cabinet meetings.[2] Scott simply believed that the Army had no need for an intelligence organization: since America was now fighting a war as an ally of Great Britain and France, the United States could acquire whatever intelligence it needed from them.

Undeterred, Van Deman decided to adopt different tactics, employing what British military analyst Basil Liddell Hart would later describe in another context as the "indirect approach."[3] Using such diverse contacts as a lady novelist and the police chief of Washington, D.C., as intermediaries, Van Deman discreetly lobbied Secretary of War Newton D. Baker. Baker proved to be more receptive to the major's ideas, and on 3 May 1917, the War College Division replaced its moribund Military Information Committee with the Military Information Section headed by Van Deman.[4] Although far from an ideal organizational setup, with Military Intelligence subordinated to what was essentially a planning organization, it was at least a beginning.

The Military Intelligence Section began modestly, with Van Deman, two other officers (one retired), and two civilian clerks. Initially, its office space was confined to a balcony overlooking the War College Division's library. At first it had no data files, since the information collected by the old Military Information Division had been merged into the War College Division's general files and remained there, effectively lost. Its responsibilities, however, were considerable. In addition to supervising the existing Army attache system and

---

1 Powe, *The Emergence of the War Department Intelligence Agency*, pp. 82–84.

2 Finnegan, *Against the Specter of a Dragon*, p. 45.

3 Sir Basil Liddell Hart, *Strategy* (New York: New American Library, 1974), p. 6.

4 In his memoirs, Van Deman highlights his own role in bringing about the rebirth of Army Intelligence. *The Final Memoranda*, pp. 21–23. Marc Powe finds substantial continuities between the old Military Information Division and Van Deman's organization. *The Emergence of the War Department Intelligence Agency*, pp. 77–81, 102–03.

developing policies and plans for Army Intelligence activities, Van Deman's organization was charged with "the supervision and control of such system of military espionage and counterespionage as shall be established . . . during the continuance of the present war."5 The section was thus not only to serve as a staff element but was also to perform operating functions.

In the beginning, Van Deman's organization depended heavily on the British and the French, who supplied it with watch lists of suspected enemy sympathizers and basic organizational concepts. From the British, Van Deman borrowed the fundamental division of intelligence into "positive" and "negative." Positive intelligence consisted of collecting information from the enemy; negative intelligence consisted of denying the enemy intelligence about one's own forces. An important part of negative intelligence was "counterespionage," another new word in the Army's growing intelligence vocabulary, this one borrowed from the French.

Doctrine and data could be borrowed from abroad, but personnel could not. Because of the demand for regular officers in combat assignments, no more than six regulars were available for intelligence duties at the General Staff during the whole war. To obtain additional competent personnel for his own organization, Van Deman used an informal "old boys" network that recommended civilians for direct commissions, a practice not uncommon in the World War I Army. Initially, many of these men were commissioned in the Signal Corps, since there were unused officer billets in the Aviation Section of that branch. Later, intelligence officers were hastily commissioned in whatever Army branch could afford to give up a few of its slots.

The buildup of the Military Intelligence element of the War Department General Staff took place at the same time that hundreds of additional intelligence officers had to be found for the Army's divisions and subordinate units. In July 1917 Pershing and the War Department agreed that intelligence staffs had to be provided to units down to the battalion level. Logically, this was an area in which the General Staff's intelligence organization should have had an interest. However, the Military Intelligence Section was too small to supervise the procurement and training of intelligence personnel for the field army. Instead, this was accomplished through normal Army channels. The process began in July 1917, when the adjutant general directed departmental commanders to select 160 specially qualified men from the newly established officer training camps for intelligence assignments. The ideal individual, the adjutant general advised, was a "young college instructor" with language ability.6 The Signal Corps trained intercept operators and photo interpreters, and the Corps of Engineers trained topographic personnel. The Military Intelligence Section did process

---

5 History of the Counterintelligence Corps, vol. 3, U.S. Army Intelligence Center, Fort Holabird, Md., 1959, p. 1.

6 Ibid., p. 4.

applications for the Corps of Interpreters, a new Army organization of officers and noncommissioned officers set up in July 1917 to handle the Army's language functions. Later, it procured enlisted counterintelligence specialists.

Intelligence Operations

The General Staff's former Second Division had confined its efforts to gathering positive intelligence, employing the Army's military attache system to collect scientific, technical, and geographic data from abroad. Although the Military Intelligence Section was responsible for the lapsed functions of the older organization, it got off to a curiously slow start in collecting foreign intelligence. Until the end of 1917, only one officer was assigned to the task, and the principal target was Mexico. However, as his organization enlarged Van Deman was able to direct greater resources to this area. In doing so, Military Intelligence gained a broader definition. In addition to accumulating data on the military situation abroad, the Army began to collect information on economic, social, political, and even psychological factors worldwide. World War I was a global conflict fought between entire industrialized societies, where victory depended on more than military factors; the fighting armies were only the cutting edges of much larger swords. The War Department's Military Intelligence staff element thus became the functional equivalent of today's Central Intelligence Agency.

However, the War Department's efforts at collecting foreign intelligence were somewhat overshadowed by the fact that the AEF's general headquarters (GHQ) in France was 3,000 miles nearer the enemy and in a much better position to gather information on the European theater. Pershing had already established his own intelligence staff element, and this functioned almost autonomously. The great distances between the two separate organizations discouraged collaboration, as did Pershing's belief that he was responsible for the conduct of the war and that the only function of the War Department was to furnish him with the troops and supplies he needed.

Because of this, Van Deman directed much of his attention to the new field of negative intelligence, or counterintelligence.[7] This was an area in which the Army had little previous experience. Although the Army had conducted counterintelligence work during the Philippine insurrection, not since the Civil War had it contended with the problems of espionage, sabotage, or subversion in the continental United States. However, when the United States joined the war against Germany in 1917, it appeared that the country confronted a substantial threat from within. The America that entered World War I was still a nation of

---

[7] It should be noted that Van Deman's first intelligence assignment, in the Philippines, had been as a counterintelligence officer fighting insurrectos. There, he had "synthesized reports, analyzed captured documents, and provided pictures and descriptions of known revolutionaries." Brian McAllister Lynn, *The U.S. Army and Counterinsurgency in the Philippine War, 1899–1902* (Charlotte: University of North Carolina Press, 1989), p. 155.

immigrants, many newly arrived. German Americans were particularly suspect, but the War Department was also concerned about the loyalties of Irish Americans, Scandinavian Americans, and African Americans. In addition to the problems that might be posed by unassimilated ethnics, there was a substantial antiwar movement. Finally, opinion-makers at the outbreak of war had exaggerated ideas about the scope and power of the German espionage and sabotage organization within the country.

In 1917 the United States seemed almost defenseless against these perceived enemies from within. The Treasury Department had a Secret Service, but it was confined by law to narrowly circumscribed duties. The Department of Justice maintained the Bureau of Investigation, but the bureau's duties before the outbreak of war had largely consisted of investigating cases of fraud against the government. A few major cities had organized police "bomb squads" to deal with the anarchist threat of the period. The almost total lack of civilian resources in the field spurred the Army to launch its own major and wide-sweeping counterintelligence program.

In June 1917 Van Deman took his first step, setting up a War Department security force of civilian investigators drawn from the ranks of the New York Police Department's Neutrality and Bomb Squad. Its operations were cloaked in secrecy, with members working from a private office building in Washington, D.C., under the enigmatic designation "Personnel Improvement Bureau." At first intended as a guard force, the unit soon began screening military personnel and applicants for government employment. A month later, the Military Intelligence Section opened its first field office in New York City, also staffed by former New York City policemen. Six additional field offices were subsequently set up in other major cities and embarkation points to provide counterintelligence coverage.

This was only the beginning. The Military Intelligence Section was concerned particularly with the problem of possible subversion within the vast new citizen forces being raised by the draft. The draft act which Congress passed in May 1917 had been designed to tap as much of the national manpower pool as possible. Granting few exemptions, the act impartially swept up American citizens and resident foreign nationals, including citizens of enemy countries. Regarding this heterogeneous force as posing a serious threat to national security, Van Deman believed that the newly forming National Guard and National Army divisions were infested with German agents and sympathizers.[8] In October 1917 he ordered the divisional intelligence officers just assigned to these units to come to Washington, D.C., under tight security. Upon reporting, the officers were instructed to set up a secret surveillance program within their

---

8 Intelligence officers professed to fear that "unless we proceed on an extensive and thorough scale, the enemy, with his existing system in the United States, will be stronger than we are right in our own army and we will be helpless." War Department General Staff, War College Division (WCD), MI–3, Provisional Counter Espionage Instructions, WCD 10148–37, INSCOM archives, Fort Belvoir, Va., Feb 1918, p. 3.

divisions. The program was later extended to Regular Army divisions and fixed installations with the assistance of a confidential pamphlet, "Provisional Counter-Espionage Instructions," drawn up by Van Deman's staff.

Van Deman conceived a comprehensive counterespionage program. It envisaged the creation of a clandestine agent network extending throughout the Army down to company level. Nets in each division would be managed by an assistant to the divisional intelligence officer. He would work through a system of anonymous collection managers known only to himself and to their own immediate superiors and subordinates within the apparatus. At the bottom of this secret pyramid, "operatives" placed in every company would submit intelligence reports on their fellow soldiers. At least two operatives, mutually unknown to one another, would be recruited from each company.[9] Reports emanating from this organization would be relayed by the divisional intelligence officer to the Military Intelligence staff in Washington for investigation.

Once this system was in place, it produced a growing stream of incident reports that drove the relentless expansion of the War Department's counterintelligence organization. To supplement the efforts of his overextended force of intelligence officers, Van Deman hired additional civilian detectives, recruited unpaid volunteers, and soon found a fresh source of investigative manpower in the enlisted counterintelligence specialists of a completely new military organization, the Corps of Intelligence Police.

The Corps of Intelligence Police (CIP)

The stimulus for the creation of this corps of enlisted investigators had originally come from the AEF. Soon after his arrival in Europe, Maj. Dennis E. Nolan, Pershing's intelligence officer, had become concerned about the possible security problems faced by American troops fighting on foreign soil. In 1915 Nolan had written alarmingly about the possibilities of German invasion; now his work took on a more concrete form. In early July 1917 he requested that the adjutant general provide him fifty company grade officers proficient in foreign languages. In addition, Nolan asked for "fifty secret service men who have had training in police work [and] speak French fluently."[10] This called for a category of intelligence personnel not previously imagined by anybody in the War Department, but in August the acting chief of staff authorized the creation of a fifty-man Corps of Intelligence Police made up of enlisted soldiers who would serve with the "rank, pay, and allowances" of sergeants of infantry.[11]

---

9 Ibid.

10 History of the Counter Intelligence Corps, vol. 3, p. 3.

11 As was later pointed out, the title of the organization was a little anomalous. "It was a 'Corps' that was not a 'Corps.' It was a 'counterintelligence' organization but called an 'Intelligence' organization and it was called 'Police' when it had no interest in crime, as such, and no police power." History of the Counter Intelligence Corps, vol. 3, p. 114.

Tasked with furnishing the appropriate personnel, Van Deman ran into difficulties. Private detective agencies seemed a likely source at first, but when told of the Army's requirements for French-speaking investigators, the head of the Pinkerton Agency countered, "There ain't no such animal."[12] The War Department was reduced to recruiting the first CIP agents through newspaper advertisements. The first contingent was assembled at Fort Jay in New York Harbor, given a month's training as infantry, outfitted with distinctive green-corded campaign hats, and shipped to France without civilian clothes or any instruction in intelligence work. Once overseas, the group was screened by French authorities, who rejected many as undesirables. Those who passed muster were then bustled off to Le Havre for instruction by veteran Allied counterintelligence officers.[13]

The initial group was not promising, but the need for enlisted counterintelligence specialists remained, and the formation of the CIP had set a precedent. The Military Intelligence Section found it increasingly difficult to staff its headquarters and expanding network of field offices with the existing mix of freshly commissioned reserve officers, civilian volunteers, and hired detectives. Officers were a scarce commodity, and competent civilian investigators were hard to find, especially since the War Department paid them only $4 a day plus expenses. Thus it seemed logical for Van Deman's organization to turn to the enlisted ranks of the Army to solve the personnel problems in the counterintelligence arena. The iron broom of the draft had swept highly qualified people into the ranks of the Army; men experienced in law, teaching, or insurance investigation were especially fit for counterintelligence work. Additionally, the military thought that investigations of Army personnel could be carried out most appropriately by other soldiers. In November the Military Intelligence Section requested that it be allotted 250 CIP agents to assist its counterintelligence program. Many of the civilians previously employed by Van Deman promptly enlisted in the Corps of Intelligence Police, including the twenty-three former policemen in the New York Field Office.

Expansion

The expansion of Van Deman's organization, largely driven by operational responsibilities in the counterintelligence field, in turn forced a growing specialization within the Military Intelligence staff. It was no longer possible for Van Deman and a small group of assistants to deal interchangeably with all aspects of positive and negative intelligence. The whole operation had to be put under a

---

12 *The Final Memoranda*, p. 37.

13 The commander of the Corps of Intelligence Police in France was Lt. Royden Williamson. His recollections, "As It Was in the Beginning with the Corps of Intelligence Police," 11 Aug 53, are in RG 319, NARA.

bureaucratic regimen. Between December 1917 and January 1918, Van Deman divided his organization into functional subsections, all according to the British practice with which he was now familiar. As the organization grew larger and more complex, it achieved a position of greater prominence within the War Department. In February, following a reorganization of the General Staff, the Military Intelligence Section was upgraded in status, becoming a branch of the newly established Executive Division. Since the Executive Division was burdened with diverse responsibilities, the reorganization was less than perfect. As one knowledgeable officer put it, its chief "could not know and would not know what MI was doing . . . when MI papers came up to him, they were like Greek to him."[14] In March the Military Intelligence Branch, overcrowded at the War College, moved to a seven-story apartment building in downtown Washington, D.C., where it was at least in closer proximity to the Army's center of administrative power.

The Military Intelligence Branch initially consisted of eight numbered sections. MI–1, MI–5, MI–6, and MI–7 were responsible for carrying out general support functions in the respective areas of administration, publications, translation, and management of confidential files. Later, MI–7 assumed responsibility for graphics. At first there was only one section, MI–2, exclusively dedicated to collating foreign intelligence, although MI–5 soon received the new mission of coordinating the collection efforts of the attaches. Two other sections were set up to manage aspects of counterintelligence: MI–3, which handled counterespionage in the military services, and MI–4, which dealt with civilian subversion.[15] MI–3 worked closely with over 400 divisional and installation intelligence officers who supervised the clandestine counterespionage system. Other subelements served specialized needs: administering the District of Columbia field office, dealing with the specific counterintelligence problems presented by foreign-born draftees, and overseeing programs that dealt with particularly sensitive Army branches such as the Air Service and the Chemical Corps. Thousands of investigations were conducted, but contrary to early fears, only a relatively small number of troops had to be removed. The draft-raised Army was loyal.

In addition to policing the Army's own ranks, Van Deman was concerned that spies and agitators in the civilian community might also threaten the Army or at least its mobilization base. At the same time that MI–3 was created, MI–4 came into existence to handle counterintelligence in the civilian sector. This section sought to cope with broad and ill-defined threats, initially concerning itself with labor unrest in the West, racial disturbances in the South and Southwest, and foreign disaffection in the polyglot cities of the East. Its operative premise

---

14 Lt Col Frank Moorman, "Lecture Delivered to the Officers of the Military Intelligence Division, General Staff—Concluding Remarks by Brigadier General Churchill," 13 Feb 20, p. 16, Army Cryptologic Records, INSCOM.

15 Bruce W. Bidwell, *History of the Military Intelligence Division, Department of the Army General Staff, 1775–1941* (Frederick, Md.: University Publications of America, 1986), p. 123.

was that "the misbehavior, disloyalty, or indifference of native Americans is as important a material of military intelligence as any other."[16] At one time or another, the organization involved itself in deportation cases, sabotage by organized labor, enemy finance and trade, and counterespionage work abroad.

To carry out its duties, MI–4 had to conduct an active liaison with many other government agencies, especially the Department of Justice, which alone had powers of arrest and prosecution in cases of civilian offenses against the military. MI–4 also relied on two civilian auxiliaries, the Plant Protective Service and the American Protective League. The Plant Protective Service was an organization of undercover civilian operatives originally established by the chief signal officer to protect the country's new aircraft industry. Subsequently it spread to other private plants working under government contract. Almost inevitably, the organization came under the aegis of Military Intelligence.

The American Protective League, larger and less official in character, comprised several vigilante groups originally put together to help the Department of Justice uncover spies. Once in place, it also began to assist local authorities in enforcing the draft act, and its activities brought it into a close working relationship with MI–4. The Army sought to curb the organization's excesses while still making use of its thousands of members: estimates of the league's strength ranged between 60,000 and 200,000, with the organization itself favoring the latter number. Ultimately, top American Protective League leaders were commissioned as officers in MI–4 to enhance military control over the league's activities. Although such paramilitary organizations appear alien to the American tradition, similar organizations existed in Great Britain and France, reflecting the intense and sometimes excessive nationalism of the period.

In addition to his pioneering work in establishing an Army counterintelligence organization, Van Deman also involved Army Intelligence in the exotic world of codes and ciphers. This was an area in which the Army as a whole already had some experience. Ciphers had been used in the Civil War, and the War Department had employed a telegraph code since 1885. More recently, in 1916, the Signal Corps' Capt. Parker Hitt had published a manual on military cryptography. However, it was Van Deman who made cryptology an adjunct of Military Intelligence. One of his first acts after setting up the Military Intelligence Section was to secure a commission for a youngish State Department code clerk, Herbert O. Yardley, so Yardley could head up a Cipher Bureau for Van Deman's organization. Although Hitt and a few other Regular Army officers possessed the necessary expertise in this field, all of them were needed for other duties when war broke out.

The Cipher Bureau, later redesignated MI–8, soon found itself caught up in a multiplicity of projects. Van Deman quickly saw that the Army had no means

---

16 War Department General Staff, Military Intelligence Division, *The Functions of the Military Intelligence Division, General Staff* (Washington, D.C.: Government Printing Office, 1918), p. 18.

of secure communications. The War Department Telegraph Code of 1915 in use for Army administrative communications was a cumbrous work designed to save telegraph costs rather than to provide security, and in any case, it was probable that the Germans already possessed a copy of the code book. Yardley's bureau was hastily directed to devise new enciphering tables for the code that once more made it practical for secret messages. MI–8 then prepared a completely new code that Military Intelligence as well as the rest of the Army could use. Regrettably, this was compromised as soon as it was issued, and a new code could not be prepared before Armistice Day. However, MI–8's own communications system, which made use of the new enciphering tables, remained secure and was used throughout the war as a channel to transmit messages from the secretary of war and the chief of staff to the field.

MI–8 was to have more success in breaking codes than in making them. It soon began to attack agent communications. This led Yardley's unit into the arcane world of secret inks, regarding which the British provided help and advice. It was forced also to learn to read the diverse systems of shorthand employed in the United States and abroad.[17]

MI–8's increasing responsibilities, together with the AEF's anticipated requirements in the area of codes, soon created a demand for trained cryptologic personnel. To meet the need, the Army turned to the only organization in the United States with cryptanalytic expertise. This was Riverbank Laboratories, a private research foundation set up by the eccentric philanthropist George Fabyan in Geneva, Illinois.[18] One of Fabyan's hobbies was attempting to prove that Shakespeare's plays contained hidden cipher messages revealing that the works had actually been written by Sir Francis Bacon. Fabyan was wrong—no such cipher existed—but his obsession had led to the creation of a center for cryptanalysis at Riverbank. This organization trained three classes of Army cryptanalysts in late 1917 and early 1918. The arrangement ended only when MI–8 developed its own training program. Ultimately, two Riverbank instructors accepted Army commissions and went to France as cryptanalysts with the AEF.

The cryptanalytic side of its work soon led MI–8 into other fields. To supplement physical interception of German messages, it established a radio intelligence service using selected Signal Corps personnel. These specialists monitored German diplomatic and agent communications, initially employing a chain of fourteen "radio tractors" strung out along the Mexican border and later using fixed intercept sites in the same locations. The radio intelligence service also had a large fixed station at Houlton, Maine, that monitored transatlantic German diplomatic communications.

---

17 David Kahn, *The Codebreakers: The Story of Secret Writing* (New York: MacMillan Co., 1967), pp. 352–54.

18 Special Research History (SRH) 29, A Brief History of the Signal Intelligence Service, p. 1, RG 457, NARA (hereafter, these documents will be cited by SRH number).

The Military Intelligence Division

In April 1918 General Peyton C. March was recalled from France to become the new Army chief of staff. In June he ordered Van Deman, now a colonel, to go to Europe to inspect the intelligence operations of the AEF. Van Deman left behind a functioning Military Intelligence organization that had a strength of 170 officers and hundreds of enlisted agents and civilians and was still growing. The expansion forced the War Department to again move its intelligence headquarters, this time to the Hooe Building in Washington, D.C. However, the full development of the wartime Army Intelligence organization was not yet complete. Military Intelligence reached its final organizational development in World War I as a result of March's experiences with Pershing's AEF.

In August 1918 March restructured the General Staff, in the process raising the intelligence function to the status it enjoyed in France. He established the Military Intelligence Division (MID) as one of the four principal divisions of the War Department General Staff. The new division's enhanced prestige and responsibilities meant that Van Deman's successor, a Field Artillery lieutenant colonel from the AEF with the glorious name of Marlborough Churchill, was advanced to the rank of brigadier general. With these changes Military Intelligence had finally reached the position of institutional equality on the Army Staff that Van Deman had long advocated. In turn, this elevation in status permitted a more elaborate form of organization, with Positive and Negative Branches now controlling the various numbered sections.

One of the motives for the establishment of MID was March's desire to create an organization that could bring Army Intelligence training in the continental United States into line with the needs of the AEF. Military Intelligence had heretofore neglected this area for a number of reasons, including its limited charter, its concentration on counterintelligence activities, and its lack of jurisdiction over training. The perceived deficiencies of training in the United States had previously led Pershing to demand that all commanders and staff officers, including intelligence officers, spend a lengthy period in France prior to the arrival of their divisions. To help rectify this situation, MID recalled an experienced intelligence officer from France to head a new Field Intelligence Section, MI–9, that would provide MID input to the training camps. However, the war ended before the plans devised by the new element could be put into effect.

In the meantime, MID's counterintelligence operations underwent a further expansion. The Negative Branch extended the scope of its operations across the seas in September 1918, taking over supervision of the counterintelligence operations of military attaches. It also created a new section to handle passport control duties previously shared jointly by MI–3 and MI–4. The State Department had primary jurisdiction over foreign travel by American citizens, but MID also wanted to screen all individuals traveling to Europe. Military Intelligence was particularly interested in checking the backgrounds of the large numbers of welfare workers sent overseas to support the AEF by the Red Cross, the YMCA, the Salvation Army, and other organizations.

The same month, MID also gained control over military censorship within the continental United States, setting up another new section, MI–10, to handle the assignment. Originally, Army censorship had been regarded as an independent function under a chief military censor, partially out of deference to the American tradition of freedom of speech. However, the general Army reorganization of August 1918 had made this an intelligence responsibility. MI–10's activities soon encompassed a wide variety of fields—in addition to censoring military mail and Army photographs, the organization also supervised a system of voluntary press censorship, ran a newspaper clipping bureau, accredited newspaper correspondents, monitored telephone and telegraph lines running into neutral Mexico, assumed direction of the radio intelligence service, and maintained liaison with other government departments. All this demanded a heavy commitment of personnel, and by the end of the war 300 people were on duty with MI–10.

In two areas the Negative Branch ventured completely beyond the normally defined boundaries of intelligence activity. The branch became involved in investigating graft and fraud within the Army and in finding ways to enhance military morale. In both cases, the transfer of these functions to intelligence came by default. Although the quartermaster general was originally assigned to deal with cases of graft and fraud, he had no trained investigative personnel. As a result, MI–13 was organized in August 1918 to assume the mission. The problem of Army morale was added to the MID agenda when Corps of Intelligence Police investigators included instances of low morale in their intelligence reports. Since MID had discovered the problem, it seemed appropriate to some members of the Army Staff that the division find a way to counter it. In this case, however, MID was able to reassign the function to a separate Military Morale Section of the General Staff in November 1918.

The armistice finally ended the headlong and rather undisciplined expansion of MID's activities. By this time, 282 officers, 250 CIP agents, and 1,100 civilians were on its staff. Van Deman's labors had succeeded in building up a massive intelligence organization that doubtless surpassed his wildest expectations. The establishment of MID had restored the intelligence function to the level of the General Staff, where it would remain from then on. However, in the process it had acquired broad ancillary functions the precise boundaries of which had yet to be defined rationally.

The American Expeditionary Forces in France

The American Expeditionary Forces in France built up an intelligence organization parallel, but not completely similar, to MID. When Pershing took command of the AEF, he designated Maj. Dennis E. Nolan as his intelligence officer.

Once in Europe, Pershing decided to adopt the French staff system throughout the AEF. Intelligence became the second section, or "G–2," of Pershing's head-quarters staff. Intelligence thus achieved a position of equality with other func-tional areas in the AEF a year before it would do so at the General Staff level in the continental United States, and Nolan ultimately became a brigadier general.

Pershing arrived in France in June 1917 with a small headquarters and a hastily formed division of infantry. By November 1918 the AEF had grown to a force of twenty-nine combat divisions and had opened its own front against the armies of Imperial Germany. The expansion and elaboration of the Army Intelligence structure ran hand in hand with the growth of the AEF it support-ed.[19] Initially the AEF heavily depended on help from the British and French in this field as in many others. Intelligence officers assigned to document exploita-tion and prisoner-of-war interrogation were trained at the British intelligence school at Harrow until August 1918, when the AEF finally opened its own intelli-gence school at Langres, France. Students at Langres were provided with the unique opportunity to interrogate real prisoners of war as part of their training. From the start, the AEF trained its own photo interpreters and intercept operators.

By the end of the war, G–2 at Pershing's Chaumont headquarters had grown to a full-fledged theater intelligence center, engaging in a span of activities that was even broader than that of the Military Intelligence Division in Washington, since it also supervised deception operations and actively managed a propagan-da campaign. In contrast, the work of MID's "psychological" subsection concen-trated on coordination and training. The intelligence operations of Pershing's G–2 staff also overlapped and duplicated those of MID, because it produced its own political and economic intelligence as well as dealing in combat intelli-gence. Pershing considered that as a theater commander, his legitimate intelli-gence interests extended beyond the immediate Western front to cover develop-ments on the Eastern, Macedonian, and Italian fronts. In Pershing's mind, any overlap with the activities of MID in the continental United States was justified because MID was an ocean away from the main battle and the transatlantic cable system had limited capacities.

The capstone of the intelligence pyramid, the Military Information Division, or G–2–A, produced finished intelligence reports and studies from the mass of information available from the AEF's tactical units and the other divisions of G–2.[20] The division was able to draw upon the full range of intelligence disci-plines (human, photographic, and signals) to supply combat intelligence, and it also produced political and economic intelligence, mostly from open sources. The production activities of G–2–A had the result of involving the organization

---

[19] There has never been a scholarly study of intelligence work in the AEF. British Military Intelligence in World War I has been better served. See Michael Occleshaw, *Armour Against Fate: British Military Intelligence in the First World War* (London: Columbus Books, 1990).

[20] Reminiscences of the order of battle specialist on Pershing's G–2 staff are contained in Samuel T. Hubbard, *Memoirs of a Staff Officer* (Tuckahoe, N.Y.: Cardinal Associates, Inc., 1959).

in areas outside the field of pure intelligence: by the summer of 1918 G–2–A was also releasing the Army's daily public affairs communique and furnishing the War Department with a daily informational cable.

The base of this intelligence pyramid within the AEF began at the level of the battalion, the smallest unit with an intelligence staff officer, the S–2, and dedicated intelligence collection personnel.21 In addition to its S–2, each infantry battalion had a reconnaissance element consisting initially of 1 officer and 28 enlisted men, including 15 scouts, 11 observation post personnel, and 2 snipers. At the next level of the command structure was a regimental intelligence officer, with 8 additional observers at his disposal. Brigades were not authorized intelligence officers under the original scheme of organization, but in practice intelligence personnel were frequently detailed to these commands.

At the division level, there was a small intelligence section headed by the divisional G–2, who was assisted by a deputy for combat intelligence, a commissioned interpreter, a topographic officer, and various enlisted personnel. This was the initial level for interrogating prisoners of war and collecting enemy documents. Ground observation at this echelon was supplemented by spotting reports from Army Air Service balloons forwarded through division artillery channels. Under World War I conditions, divisions were responsible for keeping watch over the section of enemy front opposite them for a depth of two miles. In practice, however, the length and breadth of a division's span of interest was often much larger.

Balloons were used primarily for observing artillery fire, but balloon units also provided intelligence, especially under the static conditions of trench warfare that prevailed on the Western front.22 The main disadvantages of balloons were their vulnerability and their requirement for support personnel. A balloon in combat had an estimated life expectancy of fifteen minutes; although fliers did not wear parachutes in World War I, balloonists did. It took a full company of 178 men to service a single balloon, because it took many hands to deploy a balloon in a breeze and because each company was also responsible for manning six antiaircraft machine guns to defend its fragile aerial asset.

The intelligence officer at corps level used a wider array of resources that allowed him to take responsibility for surveillance of the area between two and five miles beyond the enemy's forward line of troops. In addition to observation posts and balloons, he used aero squadrons equipped for visual and photo-

---

21 *United States Army in the World War, 1917–1919,* vol. 13, *Reports of the Commander in Chief AEF, Staff Sections and Services* (Washington, D.C.: Government Printing Office, 1990), pp. 1–10; Maj Gen Dennis E. Nolan, Dictation of March 2, 1935: Echelons of Intelligence from the Front Line Back to G.H.Q., Nolan Ms, U.S. Army Military History Institute; Intelligence Regulations, American Expeditionary Forces, Aug 1918.

22 Balloons could ascend to an altitude of 4,500 feet, allowing observers to watch enemy positions eight miles away. Richard P. Weinert, *A History of Army Aviation, 1950–1962: Phase I: 1950–1954* (Fort Monroe, Va.: U.S. Army Continental Army Command, 1971), p. 2.

graphic reconnaissance and sometimes even flash- and sound-ranging troops who detected and targeted enemy batteries. These were under the command of the corps artillery headquarters but under the staff supervision of G–2. Five of the seven corps that the AEF committed to combat were supported by such troops.[23] The corps also had its own dedicated counterintelligence element consisting of twelve Corps of Intelligence Police sergeants.

The most sophisticated intelligence resources were concentrated in the field armies formed in mid-1918 and at GHQ, Chaumont. Each of the two field armies in the AEF had additional aerial reconnaissance units, including some that could operate at night.[24] A topographic battalion allowed the army-level intelligence staff to draw up large-scale war maps, termed *plans directeurs* in the jargon of the day. Each Army Intelligence staff also contained a radio intelligence section that translated intercepted enemy messages. A larger radio intelligence element at GHQ engaged in cryptanalysis and supplied the subordinate Army sections with the necessary keying material to decode the messages. Intercept was provided by Signal Corps personnel who operated direction-finding and intercept equipment and manned listening posts directed against low-level enemy telephone and ground telegraph communications, a task facilitated by the use of induction coils rather than by direct wiretaps.[25]

Pershing's radio intelligence organization not only monitored enemy ground communications, but also could track the movements of enemy spotter aircraft through their transmissions. Searchlight platoons of the 56th Engineers attached to the AEF's Antiaircraft Service provided early warning of night air attacks. These units were equipped with multihorn and parabolic acoustical detectors that alerted crews to the approach of aircraft before they were in visual range.[26]

At the top of this layered intelligence structure was G–2–A at Chaumont, which processed and analyzed the information sent up from lower levels. Its efforts were supplemented by those of three other, more specialized, divisions of G–2. The "secret service," G–2–B, supervised both undercover collection operations and counterintelligence. Although most of the intelligence obtained by Pershing's headquarters about political and economic develop-

---

[23] A participant documented this specialized technical activity in Edward A. Trueblood, *Observations of an American Soldier During His Service with the AEF in France in the Flash Ranging Service* (Sacramento, Calif.: News Publishing, 1919).

[24] The AEF experience produced the first clash between ground commanders and airmen over the priority to be given aerial reconnaissance. It would not be the last. Interestingly enough, the recalcitrant aviator was Col. William Mitchell. See Maj Gen Dennis E. Nolan, Dictation 38, p. 17 (1–31–36), Nolan Ms, U.S. Army Military History Institute.

[25] War Department, Office of the Chief Signal Officer, *Final Report of the Radio Intelligence Section, General Staff, General Headquarters, American Expeditionary Forces* (Washington, D.C.: Office of the Chief Signal Officer, 1935). An anecdotal treatment of these activities can be found in E. Alexander Powell, *The Army Behind the Army* (New York: Charles Scribner's Sons, 1919), pp. 16–22.

[26] William Barclay Parson, *The American Engineers in France* (New York: D. Appleton and Co., 1920), pp. 256–61.

ments in Germany came from open sources, G–2–B did set up "information centers" in Switzerland, Denmark, and Holland that ran agent nets behind the enemy lines. The most valuable contribution of clandestine intelligence probably came from the reports of the "trainwatchers" who monitored rail movements of the German army.[27] G–2–B's information centers competed directly with the MID-directed activities of the military attache offices in the same neutral countries and depended heavily on British and French assistance. The British and the French were also called upon for assistance in counterintelligence. However, the development of the Corps of Intelligence Police gave G–2–B an instrument of its own in this field. By Armistice Day some 450 sergeant investigators were on duty with the AEF, not only supporting the rear communications zone, but also providing intelligence coverage to corps and divisions at the fighting front.

Mapping was normally a function of the Corps of Engineers. But under combat conditions in France, it fell under the supervision of the intelligence staff, since battle maps included information about enemy as well as friendly forces. G–2–C, the Topographic, Map Supply, and Sound- and Flash-Ranging Division of G–2, essentially served to coordinate the activities of the 29th Engineers, a bizarrely structured regiment without a headquarters that provided the AEF with both topographic and sound- and flash-ranging personnel. One battalion of the 29th manned the AEF's large map-printing facility at Langres; another supplied topographic troops to the field armies; ranging companies from two additional battalions supported the targeting needs of the field artillery while providing collateral intelligence.

Finally, a fourth division, G–2–D, handled press and censorship matters. Censorship operations were an intelligence function within the AEF from the very beginning. While mail was censored at the unit level, a base censor's office in Paris conducted spot checks of regimental mail, operated a secret-ink laboratory, and censored mail written in foreign languages. Internally, the section was able to translate mail written in forty-nine languages, requesting outside help only for messages written in Chinese or Japanese. One additional function of this office was to censor letters containing information that servicemen did not want their immediate superiors to see. Such correspondence was mailed in specially issued blue envelopes.

Managing press relations was the division's second principal function. This included supervising the accreditation of war correspondents, censoring their dispatches, and making arrangements for their transportation and billeting. In view of practices in later wars, correspondents were held on a fairly tight rein.

---

27 Bidwell, *History of the Military Intelligence Division*, p. 139. General Nolan felt that no more than 15 percent of his intelligence requirements were filled by secret agents, but felt that reports by the network of trainwatchers tracking German rail movements across the bridges over the Rhine were most useful. Memoirs, ch. 4, p. 9, Dennis Nolan Ms, U.S. Army Military History Institute.

Censorship principles insisted on accuracy; forbade releasing military informa-tion useful to the enemy; and prohibited news stories which would "injure morale in our forces here, or at home, or among our Allies" or "embarrass the United States or her Allies in neutral countries."28 On the other hand, corre-spondents had free access to the troops, and G–2–D refrained from using them for propaganda.

In addition, G–2–D carried out a wide spectrum of other information-relat-ed activities. It was charged with preparing propaganda to undermine German morale—by the fall of 1918 a rain of 3 million propaganda leaflets from G–2–D was blanketing German lines, distributed by plane and balloon and even by rifle grenade and patrol. And while it sought to undercut German morale, the divi-sion tried to preserve that of the AEF. The famous troop newspaper, *Stars and Stripes*, was published in Paris under G–2 auspices. Finally, straying even fur-ther from any conceivable intelligence functions, the division supervised the Army art program, employing the services of eight soldier-painters, and was tasked with taking photographs for historical purposes and verifying the accura-cy of their captions.

Communications Security in the AEF

Communications security within the American Expeditionary Forces in France was primarily a Signal Corps responsibility. Although MI–8 was responsible for preparing the War Department's codes, in France this task was assigned in December 1917 to the Signal Corps' Code Compilation Section, a small group located at the GHQ at Chaumont. This organization found itself confronted by an immense task. The Army entered World War I with few effective arrangements for secure tactical communications. The insecure and cumbersome War Department Telegraph Code was intended for administra-tive use, not battlefield communications. The Signal Corps' existing cipher disk was a simple celluloid device designed on principles as uncomplicated as those of the toy code-rings that once appeared in cereal boxes. When used with a running key, however, at first it seemed to offer unbreakable security. However, cryptanalysts at Riverbank and at MI–8 quickly discovered that messages encrypted this way could be broken faster than they could be enci-phered. The British introduced the U.S. Army to the Playfair cipher, but this too was easy prey for cryptanalysts.

As a result, the AEF decided to devise a completely new system. The first efforts were unsuccessful. The Code Compilation Section produced a one-part trench code and a set of enciphering tables, but these proved to be impractica-ble for use in combat situations. What was needed was a method of encryption that would place as little burden as possible on communicators operating under

---

28 *United States Army in the World War*, vol. 13, p. 86.

battlefield conditions.29 The solution finally adopted was the creation of a set of two-part codes with separate tables for encoding and decoding. In June 1918 the section produced the "Potomac Code," the first in a series of codes named after major American rivers. The "river" codes were issued to the First Army when it became active in August 1918. When the Second Army took the field in October, a separate "lake" series of codes was introduced to meet its needs. These codes, distributed down to regimental level through intelligence channels, carried the main burden of Army traffic, supplemented as necessary by a small number of more specialized codes. To ensure security, individual code books were replaced about every two weeks or upon evidence that they had been compromised.

Regrettably, the sophistication of the AEF's cryptographic systems did not equate with good communications security. The mere fact that codes were available did not mean that they were used. Communicators unfamiliar with codes showed a marked disinclination to employ them, and tactical units evolved various private, unsanctioned codes of their own. Moreover, the AEF relied on the telephone rather than the radio for the bulk of its communications, and officers repeatedly sent plain-language messages on tactical matters over unsecured telephone lines. To eliminate such problems, the AEF's general headquarters issued security guidelines for Army communications and established its own Security Service. Signal Corps personnel assigned to the Security Service monitored radio and telephone communications and reported violations of established procedures to control officers at the radio intelligence sections within the headquarters of the field armies. The G–2 then reported security breaches to commanders, but little could actually be done to punish offenders.30

Sideshows

The bulk of American forces committed overseas in World War I went to France. However, it is sometimes forgotten that there were some peripheral ventures. An infantry regiment and support troops were hastily deployed to the Italian front to help shore up the morale of the flagging Italian Army after its disastrous defeat at Caporetto in the fall of 1917. More importantly, two separate American Expeditionary Forces, miniatures of the larger AEF in France, were sent respectively to Murmansk and Siberia in the summer of 1918 as a result of the Bolshevik Revolution, which had forced Russia out of the war and

---

29 "In view of the fact that code work is frequently done under heavy bombardment and gas or in the critical moments of an advance, it does not seem advisable to add any additional burdens to code operators." War Department, Office of the Chief Signal Officer, *Report of the Code Compilation Section, American Expeditionary Forces, December 1917–November 1918* (Washington, D.C.: Office of the Chief Signal Officer, 1935), p. 1.

30 James L. Gilbert, "U.S. Army COMSEC in World War I," *Military Intelligence* 14 (January 1988): 19–21.

created conditions of chaos in Eastern Europe. Both expeditions were launched on ill-defined missions and given little background intelligence.

The reinforced regiment ordered to North Russia, originally assigned the limited mission of keeping a large store of war supplies from German hands, became involved in operations against the Bolsheviks as part of a much larger Allied effort and only evolved a G–2 section of its own shortly before the force was withdrawn in early 1919. However, Bolshevik propaganda and war-weariness after the armistice did confront the unit with serious problems of subversion.

A larger force under Maj. Gen. William S. Graves went to Siberia to help rescue former Czechoslovakian prisoners of war from the Bolsheviks and incidentally to keep an eye on the Japanese intervention force sent on a similar mission. Since the initial American contingent deployed from the Philippines and included elements from the Philippine Department's Military Intelligence Division, it incorporated an intelligence section from the beginning. Additional intelligence personnel from the continental United States joined the force later. Unfortunately, intelligence efforts were largely stultified by a conflict between General Graves and his G–2 concerning the nature of the latter's responsibilities. Graves pursued a policy of strict neutrality towards the Bolsheviks and vetoed any attempt to gather intelligence by using the services of the anti-Bolshevik "White" forces.[31]

Conclusion

World War I was the watershed in the evolution of U.S. Army Intelligence. Both in the War Department and in the field intelligence work was revitalized and placed on a footing of organizational equality with other major functions. The Army ventured into new fields of counterintelligence and cryptology and made use of the full spectrum of intelligence sources. Although some of these— such as prisoner of war interrogation, captured document exploitation, and ground reconnaissance—were traditional, the newer disciplines of signals intelligence, aerial photography, and collection through sensing devices were not. At both the War Department and theater levels, the definition of Military Intelligence was enlarged to include the collection of political, economic, and social data. Finally, intelligence activities were expanded to include the allied fields of deception and propaganda.

The professional intelligence field was still, however, in its infancy. Intelligence was still considered essentially a staff-level activity within the Army. No intelligence units as such were fielded, although the Army did deploy a topographic engineer regiment and aerial observation groups to France. A table of

---

[31] The prominent historical novelist Kenneth Roberts served on the intelligence staff of the Graves Expedition. His recollections of the experience can be found in his autobiography, *I Wanted to Write* (Garden City, N.Y.: Doubleday and Co., Inc., 1949), pp. 98–112. I am indebted to Col. William Strobridge, U.S. Army (Ret.), for calling my attention to this fact.

organization for a field-army radio section—a communications intelligence unit—was drawn up, but never implemented, as Pershing chose to keep his limited intercept assets under direct GHQ control. Moreover, Army Intelligence was not yet considered an official career field. After the war, both Van Deman and Nolan became major generals, but they achieved their stars as tactical commanders, not as intelligence officers. Still, compared with the past, much had been accomplished. For Army Intelligence, World War I represented a great leap forward.

As an Army Intelligence organization was put together from nothing in the space of seventeen hectic months, many mistakes were made. MID largely concentrated its efforts on counterintelligence operations directed at a threat that proved to be largely imaginary.[32] Yet its concern, however misplaced, reflected widespread perception among American leaders. The year before war broke out, even President Wilson's closest confidant, Colonel House, fretted that "there are more German reservists here [in the United States] than I thought."[33] More telling is the criticism that MID spread itself too thinly by venturing into areas like fraud investigation and morale enhancement. Even some of its foreign intelligence efforts could be questioned. MID maintained files on areas as remote from the war effort as the Antarctic islands and on topics as broad as "Christendom."[34] Similarly, G–2 in the AEF became deeply involved in press relations, a precedent which confused the duties of intelligence with those of public information in a way that would have an adverse application for Army Intelligence in the twenty years of peacetime following the armistice.

Nevertheless, the Army had at last established a permanent structure for meeting its intelligence needs. After 1918 the evolution of Army Intelligence would follow a twisted road, but it would never return to the marginal position it had occupied prior to World War I.

---

[32] There were also questions as to the efficacy of the whole effort. On the eve of America's entry into World War II, the officer who then headed the Corps of Intelligence Police provided a scathing evaluation of the World War I counterintelligence program. "In the United States the Corps of Intelligence Police was composed of many well-meaning but inexperienced officers, enlisted men, and civilians and their unorganized efforts accomplished practically nothing. It is said the organization in the United States may have caught one spy." History of the Counter Intelligence Corps, vol. 4, p. 122.

[33] Finnegan, *Against the Specter of a Dragon*, p. 149.

[34] Memo for Acting Director, Military Intelligence Division, 24 Apr 20, MID Documents.

3

Military Intelligence Between Wars

Woodrow Wilson had declared that America entered World War I to make the world safe for democracy. The effort had not succeeded. Four great empires had collapsed in Central and Eastern Europe, creating a revolutionary battleground for many disparate and competing political ideologies. Novelist John Dos Passos later described the year 1919 as a time for "machinegunfire and arson, starvation, lice, cholera, and typhus."[1] The peace process went awry. The victors at Versailles saddled the new republican government of Germany with great territorial losses and reparations payments while allowing it to remain the strongest and most industrialized power on the European Continent. Meanwhile, the growing problems posed by the widening revolution in Russia went unaddressed, and animosities developed rapidly among the victors. Wilson had hoped that the peace settlement, however flawed, would be redeemed by the establishment of a collective security organization, the League of Nations. But his own Senate refused to ratify the measure as America retreated toward isolationism.

Within the United States, there was also unrest as the bonds that had held the nation together during the war began to dissolve. Motivated by wartime idealism, pundits had spoken vaguely of a postwar era of "reconstruction" that would lay the basis for an "industrial democracy" in which the American economic cornucopia would be shared more equitably by all.[2] Instead, the end of the war brought unemployment, inflation, and labor unrest. Alarmed by revolution abroad and radical labor agitators at home, the country was swept by a "Red Scare" leading to thousands of arrests. In the end, a fatigued American people, weary of wartime idealism and stress, voted for Warren G. Harding and a return to "normalcy."

Military Intelligence was intimately involved in these events, both at home and abroad. Twenty MID officers accompanied President Woodrow Wilson and

---

1 John Dos Passos, *U.S.A.: Nineteen Nineteen* (Cambridge: Houghton Mifflin, 1946), p. 281.

2 For example, see William Leavitt Stoddard, "The Shop Committee—Some Implications," The *Dial* 67 (12 July 1919): 7–8; "Reconstruction Miscellany," The *Survey* 42 (31 May 1919): 375.

the American delegation to the Paris Peace Conference. Sixty CIP agents, direct-
ed by Van Deman, provided security for the American party, and Maj. Herbert
O. Yardley of MI–8 furnished cryptologic support.[3] Meanwhile, Army
Intelligence personnel accompanied the new Third Army, the American occupa-
tion force that marched into the Rhineland under provisions of the armistice.
On the domestic front, Bolshevik agents replaced German spies as the focus for
MID's counterintelligence efforts. In the fall of 1919 a naive MID officer warned
that "the situation in the United States [was] . . . verging on revolution."[4]
However exaggerated the estimate, it accurately reflected the fears of many
Americans who found the world changing too fast for America ever to recover
her lost innocence.

Military Intelligence at Peace

Normalcy meant a return to a peacetime Army, a process that had begun
almost as soon as the fighting ended. The vast conscript armies that had won the
war were hastily demobilized, and a new volunteer force enlisted. Subsequently,
the National Defense Act of 1920 provided for a Regular Army of 280,000,
backed up by Organized Reserves and a 475,000-man National Guard. The command and control of this force would be exercised through nine corps areas in the
continental United States and through three overseas departments in Hawaii, the
Philippines, and Panama. Under the terms of this legislation, MID retained its
place as one of the four principal divisions within the Army Staff. Among its
numerous duties were administering the attache system, supervising military
drawings and maps, writing regulations for tactical intelligence personnel, performing liaison with other intelligence agencies, approving codes and ciphers, and
planning censorship operations. As one of the four assistants to the chief of staff
authorized by law, MID's director was given the rank of brigadier general.

Unfortunately for the Army, the economy-minded Congress never provided
the necessary appropriations to maintain the authorized force. By 1929 the
Regular Army had thus shrunk to a strength of 137,000, with four skeleton
combat divisions in the continental United States and three more in the overseas
departments. That part of the force assigned to the continental United States
was scattered over a multitude of tiny posts inherited from the Indian Wars. The
subsequent Great Depression made Congress even more parsimonious, forcing
the Army to make do with the large but increasingly obsolescent stockpile of
weapons left over from World War I. The Military Intelligence Division was
directly affected by these policies, dwindling from a peak strength of 80 officers

---

3 Some of the CIP agents in Paris questioned the utility of their assignments. Apart from the
men detailed to guard President Wilson, one wrote, they were employed as "a species of bell boys,
ladies maids, and hallmen." Gilbert Elliott Ms, p. 7, RG 319, NARA.

4 Memo, Col C. H. Mason for Brig Gen Marlborough Churchill, 31 Oct 19, sub: Sinister
Inertia in Present United States Situation, MID Documents.

and about 160 civilians in 1920 to a cadre of 20 officers and fewer than 50 civilians by 1934, and undergoing repeated internal realignments.[5]

The reorganization of the Army Staff under General John J. Pershing also weakened Military Intelligence. After becoming chief of staff in 1921, Pershing imposed the AEF's wartime model of a five-part General Staff on the Army, directing that separate divisions be established for personnel, intelligence, operations and training, supply, and war plans. However, congressional legislation had provided for only four brigadier generals on the staff, and in the savage competition for general officer slots the intelligence staff often lost. Of the seven directors of the Military Intelligence Division who served between 1922 and 1939, only two were brigadier generals.[6] Military Intelligence thus became a second-class citizen, since its lesser position on the Army Staff was reflected throughout the rest of the Army. Implicitly, U.S. military leaders seem to have accepted the dictum of British Field Marshal Sir Douglas Haig that "intelligence is rather a special kind of work and has a very small place in the army in peacetime."[7]

This trend was reinforced by Pershing's insistence that G–2 undertake public relations duties as it had done in the AEF. Under peacetime conditions, these responsibilities became one of the Military Intelligence Division's principal functions. Intelligence officers at corps level and below also spent much of their time in this secondary area. As a result, intelligence work often became a dumping ground for officers incapable of performing any more demanding activities, and astute officers regarded intelligence assignments as detrimental to their military careers. According to intelligence historian Thomas Troy, "intelligence was neither a profession [n]or a career; at best, it was a one-time activity in an army or navy officer's service. Hence, when closely scrutinized, the intelligence services [were] small, weak stepchildren of their parent organizations."[8]

The weakness and lack of professionalism of Army Intelligence during this period was reinforced by the decline in its capabilities for intelligence collection. The attache system remained MID's principal means for collecting foreign intelligence, irregularly supplemented by arrangements made with American businessmen working abroad. General George Marshall would write later that interwar military intelligence was "little more than what a military attache could

---

5 From 1920 on, MID strength was affected by the provisions of the National Defense Act of 1920, which limited the number of General Staff officers on duty in Washington, D.C., to 93. This meant that MID would be allotted 14 to 16 General Staff officers. When the law took effect, Brig. Gen. Dennis Nolan, assistant chief of staff, G–2, hoped that 31 more officers could be detailed from the line to keep MID up to what he regarded as minimum strength. In this, he was disappointed. Memo, Nolan for Chief of Staff, 28 Jul 21, sub: Relief of Thirteen Line Officers on Duty with Military Intelligence Division To Date, MID Documents.

6 Memo for Chief of Staff, 19 Jun 37, sub: Increase in Number of Assistants to the Chief of Staff, MID Documents.

7 Maj. Gen. Sir Kenneth Strong, *Men of Intelligence* (New York: St. Martin's Press, 1972), p. 34.

8 Thomas F. Troy, *Donovan and the CIA: A History of the Establishment of the Central Intelligence Agency* (Frederick, Md.: University Publications of America, 1984), p. 6.

learn . . . at a dinner, more or less, over the coffee cups."9 Even here the limitations were severe. Postwar economies forced the abandonment of a number of minor attache posts, and the scarcity of funds dictated that attache assignments be restricted to officers with private means of support, irrespective of their professional qualifications. Finally, the interwar years saw the rise of totalitarian governments and controlled and closed societies. Military attaches were allowed increasingly less freedom to collect useful intelligence in precisely those countries that posed the most dangerous threat to American security.10

Army Intelligence in the domestic arena was equally weak. This was partially the result of a general public reaction to some of the excessive actions of the Wilson administration against dissidents, both in World War I and during the postwar "Red Scare." Fortunately the impoverished peacetime volunteer Army had little to worry about in the way of threats posed by espionage, sabotage, and subversion. Thus the Army discontinued its countersubversive system in 1920 and recalled all MID regulations on the subject from the field. With only six agents on duty, the Corps of Intelligence Police narrowly escaped extinction when wartime emergency legislation expired that same year, but MID managed to keep the organization alive by detailing personnel to CIP duties from the Army's Detached Enlisted Men's List. The Negative Branch of MID, which had supervised the War Department's counterintelligence work, was less fortunate and closed shop in 1921.

All attempts to collect domestic intelligence ended soon afterward. This was caused by the rash actions of Lt. W. D. Long, an intelligence officer at Vancouver Barracks, who sent a circular letter to the county sheriffs of Oregon asking them to maintain a surveillance of suspect organizations. Included on the lieutenant's list were veterans' groups, the Nonpartisan League, and the American Federation of Labor. This list caused a considerable uproar when inevitably it was made public. The secretary of war ordered that all intelligence posts in the Army not authorized by tables of organization be discontinued, and that intelligence officers confine themselves to instructing troops in combat intelligence techniques. This left most of the forty-five CIP agents authorized in 1920 with little to do, and the force was repeatedly scaled back. By 1934 the Corps of Intelligence Police consisted of just sixteen noncommissioned officers, and a subsequent survey found that most of them were used as classified file clerks rather than as investigators. Only in the overseas departments and in the Eighth Corps Area on the Mexican border did the Corps of Intelligence Police still provide useful services.11

---

9 Ibid., p. 15.

10 One especially aggressive attache was Maj. Truman Smith. Posted to Nazi Germany, Smith obtained intelligence reports on the *Luftwaffe* from the American aviator and popular hero Charles Lindbergh, who repeatedly toured German aircraft factories as a guest of Reichsmarshal Hermann Goering and other Nazi top brass. *Washington Post*, 4 Nov 84, p. A–3.

11 Of the 16 CIP agents surveyed, 10 were acting as confidential clerks for G–2s in the various corps areas, 5 were engaged in investigative work, and 1 was unfit. History of the Counter Intelligence Corps, vol. 4, p. 87.

If the Military Intelligence Division was collecting little foreign and less domestic intelligence over most of this period, it was not overly active in other areas. Although one section of MID was charged with intelligence training, it had no statutory responsibility to supervise such work, and the assistant chief of staff for operations and training refused to acknowledge its authority. As a result, in 1931 the head of the section was forced to confess that "the state and extent of combat intelligence training in the Army is not known to this branch, as it makes no inspections and receives no training reports."[12]

Another section of MID was charged with supervising the Military Intelligence Officers Reserve Corps (MIORC), which had been formed in 1921 to use the services of the large number of officers who had served in intelligence positions throughout the wartime Army. In theory this organization of reservists should have given the Army a trained and experienced mobilization base, but many reserve officers were in fact journalists who had served G–2 in public affairs positions, and by the time they were ultimately needed, they were too old and too high ranking to fill the positions the Army required. The younger reservists in MIORC had never served on active duty. Perhaps the only lasting contribution of MIORC was the adoption of the sphinx as its insignia, an action which had the effect of permanently associating this somewhat bizarre heraldic item with the field of Military Intelligence.[13]

Not everything was completely bleak in the intelligence field between the wars. Although hobbled by budgetary restraints, the Army began to take advantage of new technological developments that expanded the possibilities of intelligence collection. Advances in motorized transport significantly enhanced the Army's ground reconnaissance. By 1931 an Experimental Mechanized Force had been created—its scout element had armored cars and radio-equipped vehicles—and the cavalry began to field mechanized units in addition to its traditional horse troops. The Army Signal Corps experimented with methods of detecting aircraft and ships through thermal and electronic means, and by 1937 the Army had a pilot model of a mobile radar set. Although limited to short-range targeting functions, the principles it embodied would apply to more powerful sets that could perform an early-warning function, filling a critical gap in Army capabilities after the increased speed of aircraft had rendered acoustical techniques almost useless.[14]

The growth of the Army Air Corps also affected intelligence. Air Corps officers were incorporated into MID, and Air attaches supplemented the work of the regular military attaches abroad. At the technical level, aircraft development

---

12 Bidwell, *History of the Military Intelligence Division*, p. 362.

13 Ltr with Incl, ACSI–DO, 25 Feb 63, Organization Day for Military Intelligence file, INSCOM History Office.

14 Radar developments in the Army up to 1941 are covered in Dulany Terrett, *The Signal Corps: The Emergency*, United States Army in World War II (Washington, D.C.: U.S. Army Center of Military History, 1956). For early experiments, see pp. 44, 46–47.

was steady, since this was the one part of the Army that Congress was willing to fund. The Air Corps made significant advances in aerial photography, including night photography, and in aerial mapping techniques, all of which potentially enhanced intelligence gathering. Much of the pioneering work in this area was done by Lt. George Goddard, who would ultimately go on to become an Air Force brigadier general.[15]

In practice, the technological advancement of the Army Air Corps was a two-edged sword. The observation squadrons of World War I had flown in flimsy biplanes, and these aircraft could take off from grassy strips and work in close support of tactical commanders. But the sophisticated high-speed monoplanes with ample "greenhouse" canopies which the Air Corps developed in the 1930s for observation work, otherwise advanced machines with greatly improved performance, no longer could operate from unimproved airstrips. Furthermore, aeronautical progress encouraged Air Corps leaders to aspire to an independent role. The Air Corps became increasingly interested in fighting an air war of its own, instead of providing ground support. Aerial reconnaissance was thus designed to support a strategic bombing campaign, not to assist the tactical commander on the battlefield. By 1935 most aircraft had been placed under the direct control of General Headquarters, Air Corps. Although observation groups were still assigned to Army corps areas, only eight observation squadrons were active, a trend that threatened to deprive Army commanders of adequate air intelligence support.[16]

The "Black Chamber" and the Signal Intelligence Service

Army Intelligence made its greatest advances in the field of cryptology during the years between the wars. Following World War I, MI–8's previously comprehensive responsibilities in this field were realigned. The Signal Corps took over the responsibility for communications security, employing William F. Friedman, a former AEF officer and Riverbank Laboratories cryptanalyst, as a one-man code compilation bureau. The Adjutant General's Office was tasked with printing and distributing the codes. Officially, MI–8's responsibilities were reduced to approving cryptosystems for Army-wide use and establishing regulations for their employment. In reality, however, MID continued to be deeply

---

15 Goddard has provided a useful autobiography in *Overview: A Lifelong Adventure in Aerial Photography* (Garden City, N.Y.: Doubleday, 1969).

16 Robert F. Futrell, *Command of Observation Aviation: A Study in Control of Tactical Airpower* (Maxwell Air Force Base, Ala.: Air University, 1956), p. 2. It should be noted that balloons and dirigibles were in the Army inventory of reconnaissance platforms in the early 1920s. A short but helpful overview of Air Corps support to ground operations between the wars is provided by Weinert, *A History of Aviation, Phase I*, pp. 2–4. In *Army Air Corps Airplanes and Observation, 1935–1941* (St. Louis: U.S. Army Aviation Systems Command, 1990), Howard Butler offers an alternative view to the standard interpretation of Air Corps history, arguing that the Air Corps remained firmly under the thumb of a ground Army–dominated General Staff during this period.

involved in cryptanalysis. In the fall of 1919 retired Maj. Herbert O. Yardley, wartime chief of MI–8, set up a clandestine government cryptanalytic unit in a brownstone house in New York City. Jointly funded by MID and the State Department, Yardley's bureau continued to work on diplomatic code–breaking, a task that MI–8 had initiated in World War I. Using material provided secretly by some of the major U.S. cable companies, Yardley and his small civilian staff achieved several notable successes, the most important of which was breaking the Japanese diplomatic code in time to give American diplomats a key negotiating edge during the Washington Peace Conference of 1921–1922.[17]

Despite the success of Yardley's bureau in producing hard diplomatic intelligence, it still ran into difficulties. Peacetime economies sharply reduced its funding. By 1929 the organization consisted of Yardley himself and a handful of assistants, and its functions seemed increasingly less relevant to both its sponsors. The United States had just signed the Kellogg-Briand Pact purportedly outlawing war, the international order seemed stable, and the State Department saw little need for secret intelligence in a world without enemies. On the other hand, the Army had no direct peacetime interest in the diplomatic cryptosystems Yardley's group exploited, while the clandestine and civilian nature of his bureau prevented its serving as a training vehicle for Army Intelligence reservists. By the spring of 1929 there was already a move to centralize all Army cryptologic functions under the Signal Corps, using Friedman's office as a nucleus. When Henry L. Stimson, a rather excessively upright statesman of the old school, became secretary of state that year, Yardley's fate was sealed. Discovering that the State Department had obtained access to decoded diplomatic messages, Stimson withdrew funding from Yardley's bureau. His attitude was later described: "Gentlemen do not read each other's mail."[18]

Loss of funding led to the termination of Yardley's organization. Yardley and his colleagues were offered employment in the new Signal Corps cryptologic agency, but they declined. The Civil Service pay scale could not match salaries subsidized by MID confidential funds. Instead, Yardley attempted to recoup his fortunes by writing *The American Black Chamber*, which publicly exposed America's code-breaking activities for the first time. The work was a best-seller, but proved to be a major diplomatic embarrassment for the United States and only further damaged American intelligence efforts. Yardley would later work as a cryptanalyst for Chiang Kai-shek in China and for the Canadian government, but he would never again be allowed to hold a position in any U.S. cryptologic organization.

---

17 Yardley recounted—some say embellished—his accomplishments in his book, *The American Black Chamber* (New York: Bobbs-Merrill, 1931). A brief biography can be found in David Kahn, *Kahn on Codes; Secrets of the New Cryptology* (New York: MacMillan Co., 1983), pp. 62–71.

18 Kahn, The *Codebreakers*, p. 360. A detailed study of the rise and fall of the Yardley organization is contained in SRH 29, A Brief History of the Signal Intelligence Service, pp. 3–12.

Upon the demise of Yardley's bureau, Army cryptanalysis and Army cryptography were both integrated into a new Signal Corps element, the Signal Intelligence Service (SIS), which also assumed responsibility for secret inks. The new unit was set up within the Signal Corps rather than the Military Intelligence Division to reduce its visibility and better meet the technical requirements of signals intelligence. After 1934, when it took over the printing and distribution of codes from the Adjutant General's Office, the SIS became the focal point for all Army cryptologic activity.

Friedman, who headed the Signal Intelligence Service until an Army officer became director in 1935, quickly recruited a small but talented staff. The four principal members of his initial group—mathematicians Solomon Kullback, Frank Rowlett, and Abraham Sinkov and Japanese linguist John Hurt—would all become prominent figures in U.S. Army cryptology in World War II. At first the thrust of the work was oriented towards theory, training, and the development of advanced cryptographic systems. The Army had fought World War I using codes. In 1922 the Army adopted a simple cylindrical cipher device, the M94, for tactical operations.[19] Friedman introduced a more secure but cumbersome strip cipher device, the M138. More importantly, he began developmental work on machine ciphers. The SIS provided the Army with the M134 and M134A "converters" to protect top-level communications. These were electromechanical cipher machines of great sophistication and security.[20] Meanwhile, in 1936 Friedman and Rowlett hit upon the cryptographic principles of an even more advanced machine cipher device. Unfortunately, funding was not immediately available to put the prototype into production.

The Signal Intelligence Service also began to set up an intercept organization, which Yardley's bureau, with its dependence on cooperative cable companies, had never attempted. A Provisional Radio Intelligence Detachment was organized at Fort Monmouth, New Jersey, in 1933. We may discern something of the flavor of the times from the fact that its first commander found none of the twelve men in his unit present for duty when he assumed command—all had been detailed to President Franklin D. Roosevelt's Civilian Conservation Corps. This detachment was later expanded to become a provisional company, and the 1st Radio Intelligence Company was formally activated at Fort Monmouth in 1938. Meanwhile, in September 1936 the Signal Intelligence Service had set up a chain of numbered monitoring stations in the overseas departments and in the Eighth and Ninth Corps Areas, creating SIS

---

19 The M94 was the brainchild of Joseph O. Mauborgne, an Army Signal Corps officer who later became a major general and Chief Signal Officer. It was an exact copy of a device invented by Thomas Jefferson.

20 The early history of the Signal Intelligence Service is described in SRH 131, Expansion of the Signal Intelligence Service. For the use of the term "converters," see SRH 349, Achievements of the Signal Security Agency in World War II, pp. 42–43.

detachments in five signal service companies. Since the Federal Communication Act of 1934 had made it illegal to divulge foreign communications, this had to be accomplished under tight security.[21]

These initial arrangements for providing the SIS with an intercept capability were not completely satisfactory. Tasking the 1st Radio Intelligence Company with an operational assignment interfered with the unit's primary mission, training for deployment in the field to support tactical elements. In addition, the intermingling of intercept and regular communications personnel in the existing signal service companies not only posed a security threat, but also worked against effective personnel management. Under Army regulations, trained intercept personnel working abroad were automatically returned to the general Signal Corps pool when they returned to the continental United States and thus were lost to the SIS. To solve these problems, a centralized signals intelligence unit, the 2d Signal Service Company, was set up at Fort Monmouth on 1 January 1939 to control all Signal Corps personnel at the permanent monitoring installations. The result was an efficiently functioning Signal Intelligence Service and an intercept organization that would represent the Army's principal strength in the intelligence field.[22]

The SIS paid less attention to intelligence collection at the tactical level. Under the Army's Protective Mobilization Plan, a World War I–style general headquarters was to be fielded in the event of any crisis demanding troop mobilization, and available troops would be concentrated as needed under one of the four field armies into which the Army had been divided in 1933. The actual field army selected would depend on the direction from which the threat was expected. These plans also specified that the existing 1st (and only) Radio Intelligence Company be placed in support of GHQ. To provide signals intelligence at field army level, the Signal Corps relied on the National Guard to organize two additional radio intelligence companies, one on each coast.[23] These modest preparations would soon be overtaken by the rush of events.

---

[21] The sensitivity of the whole topic of communications intelligence during this period may be inferred from a revealing piece of Signal Corps correspondence on the subject, which ended with the statement "It is suggested that this letter be burned after perusal." Ltr, Lt Col Dawson Olmstead, Executive Officer, Office of the Chief Signal Officer, to Col Joseph O. Mauborgne, 28 Jun 36, sub: Comment on Lieut. Corderman's Report, Army Cryptologic Records.

[22] G. R. Thompson and Dixie R. Harris, *The Signal Corps: The Outcome*, United States Army in World War II (Washington, D.C.: U.S. Army Center of Military History, 1966), pp. 333–35.

[23] Ltr, Maj Gen Joseph Mauborgne, Chief Signal Officer, to Chief, National Guard Bureau, 13 Sep 38, sub: Organization of National Guard Radio Intelligence Companies, Army Cryptologic Records.

4

Military Intelligence in Crisis

Ominous developments in the latter part of the 1930s finally woke the Army out of its long torpor. The Great Depression, which had ravaged the economy of the United States and focused the interests of the American people on domestic problems, had also profoundly rearranged the international order and set the stage for the rise of totalitarianism and the advance of aggression. Adolf Hitler was sworn in as chancellor of Germany in January 1933. He quickly turned his country into a one-party dictatorship. Under Nazi rule, Germany rapidly rearmed and entered into alliance with Fascist Italy and militarist Japan. International crises developed with monotonous regularity. Germany occupied the Rhineland in 1936, swallowed Austria in the spring of 1938, and humiliated Czechoslovakia with the disastrous settlement at Munich in the fall of that year. Meanwhile, its junior partners were also active. The Italian dictator Benito Mussolini invaded Ethiopia in 1935, and Japan, having seized Manchuria in 1931, went to war against all of China in 1937.

Britain and France responded with massive rearmament programs, but in the short run they relied on a general policy of appeasement to avert a European war, while ignoring Soviet attempts to resurrect their old World War I alliance with Russia. The American reaction was guarded. At President Franklin D. Roosevelt's direction, the Federal Bureau of Investigation (FBI) began investigating Nazi and Communist subversion in 1936, and Congress authorized modest steps to rebuild the nation's neglected defenses.[1] The size of the Army was increased, and the Military Intelligence Division was allowed to enlarge its attache system. Slowly, it also edged back into the counterintelligence arena, setting up a small Counterintelligence Branch in April 1939. That summer, concern about foreign espionage caused the Army to issue its first regulation dealing with the security of military information.[2] At the same time, the Army and

---

[1] Richard G. Powers, *Secrecy and Power: The Life of J. Edgar Hoover* (New York: Free Press, 1987), p. 229.
[2] The Army Regulation, AR 380–5, much revised, is still in effect.

the Navy formed the Interdepartmental Intelligence Committee with the FBI to coordinate the handling of espionage cases. However, the real threat to America's national interests would not be from within, but from without.

On 1 September 1939, the armed forces of Nazi Germany invaded Poland. Two days later, in response to previous treaty commitments, Britain and France declared war on Germany. World War II had begun. President Roosevelt proclaimed American neutrality but indicated that he did not expect American citizens to be neutral in their thoughts. On 8 September he declared a state of limited national emergency.

The U.S. Army of 1939 was unprepared for conventional warfare. As Army Chief of Staff General George C. Marshall later confessed, "We had no field Army. There were bare skeletons of three and one-half divisions scattered in small pieces over the entire United States."[3] Army troop strength was a little less than 174,000 men, and much of the equipment was still of World War I vintage. Although the Army Air Corps had received the lion's share of Army appropriations and attention, the planes of its sixty-two squadrons were obsolete by the standards of European combat. The restrictions imposed by the National Defense Act of 1920 on the size of the War Department General Staff were still in force.

The structure of the Army's intelligence element reflected the weakness of the whole. The Military Intelligence Division's small staff, still headed by a colonel, consisted of 20 officers, 3 enlisted men, and 46 civilians. Its elements were dispersed among four office buildings in the Washington, D.C., area. Intelligence collection was limited largely to what could be derived from the attache system. Although this system belatedly had been expanded, the representational nature of the attaches' mission necessarily limited the intelligence value of the product. Worse, only 16 Corps of Intelligence Police agents were available to provide counterintelligence support to the entire Army. The Signal Corps' Signal Intelligence Service had just 14 civilians and 1 Army officer on its Washington staff when Europe went to war, and they were not yet in a position to generate substantive intelligence. Efforts to rectify this situation were slow. In October 1939 a new intercept station was set up at Fort Hunt, Virginia. In November the Army authorized 26 additional civilians for the SIS. The headquarters of the 2d Signal Service Company moved to Washington, D.C., that same month, allowing it closer proximity to the Signal Intelligence Service which it supported.

In the spring of 1940 the deceptive tranquility of the "phony war" in Europe ended. In April Germany invaded Denmark and Norway, and in May Hitler launched his main offensive in the West. When it was over, a little more than a month later, France lay prostrate, Germany controlled Western Europe, and only a beleaguered Great Britain and the broad reaches of the Atlantic

---

3 General George C. Marshall, *Biennial Report of the Chief of Staff of the United States Army, July 1, 1943, to June 30, 1945, to the Secretary of War* (Washington, D.C.: Government Printing Office, 1945), p. 117.

Ocean stood between the United States and the triumphant forces of totalitarianism. Meanwhile, in the East, Japan threatened to take advantage of the situation by incorporating the orphaned colonies of the beaten Western democracies into her "Greater East Asia Co-Prosperity Sphere." The world had been turned upside down.

At this point the United States at last began to look to its defenses. The Regular Army was now rapidly increased in size, Congress passing no less than three Supplemental Appropriations Bills for 1941, funding an Army of one million men. The legislation instituted a one-year draft, federalized eighteen National Guard divisions, and placed Reserve officers on active duty, while the Army organized a wartime General Headquarters. By the fall of 1940 the United States had negotiated a Destroyers-for-Bases deal with Great Britain, securing strategic military bases in British possessions in the Atlantic and Caribbean in exchange for fifty over-age destroyers. More important, during the second half of 1940 and throughout 1941, the Roosevelt administration labored strenuously to clear away or bypass neutrality legislation that impeded American support to Great Britain. This process slowly paved the way for American entrance into the war well before the Japanese attack on Pearl Harbor.

All these events had a great effect on Military Intelligence. Brig. Gen. Sherman Miles, the former military attache to Great Britain, took over the Military Intelligence Division, and the organization began to grow rapidly. As always, however, its initial priority was domestic, and its planners fretted tirelessly about German espionage and sabotage on the home front. In June 1940 MID, the Office of Naval Intelligence, and the FBI signed a formal delimitations agreement. Under its provisions, the FBI would take the lead in domestic intelligence; there would be no repetition of the World War I scenario in which Military Intelligence had assumed responsibility for surveilling American civil society. The agreement did give the Army responsibility for conducting investigations of those civilians employed or controlled by the military in the continental United States and of all civilians in the Canal Zone and the Philippines. That same month, the Military Intelligence Division sent out confidential instructions to intelligence officers, ordering them to set up a countersubversive program that would bring potential hostile agents on military installations to its attention. To handle these efforts, the Corps of Intelligence Police was expanded to an authorized strength of 42 agents in July and 188 in November.

MID planners were also concerned about the possibilities of German penetration into Latin America, where there were large ethnic German communities and important German business interests. Although the delimitations agreement had given intelligence responsibilities in this region to the FBI, the Army's Military Intelligence Division, with its existing attache system and military missions in Latin America, would not be denied a role. Thus, in July 1940 it moved to strengthen its capabilities for collecting foreign intelligence on Latin America by setting up a branch office in New York City. It seemed that the location

would provide both better access to reference material and improved relationships with American corporations doing business south of the border. About the
same time MID was relieved of its responsibilities for supervising Army public
relations, a function that would have diverted it even further from its primary
missions, had it not been moved elsewhere.

While the Military Intelligence Division worried about domestic subversion
and Fascist infiltration of Latin America, the more prosaic and demanding intelligence tasks were performed elsewhere. The Army Air Corps wanted an independent role in the field of intelligence, even though Air Corps officers were
serving on the MID staff. Largely as a result of Air Corps initiatives, in
September 1940 all the Army's technical services were directed to form their
own intelligence staffs to collect information on foreign equipment and techniques, areas in which MID appeared to have little interest.[4] In addition, intelligence staffs were created for GHQ, for the new defense commands that sprang
into existence, for the Army Air Forces when they gained autonomy in July
1941, and for subordinate tactical formations. The Engineer Reproduction Plant
of the Corps of Engineers was transformed into the Army Map Service, laying a
foundation that ultimately would provide indispensable cartographic intelligence for the American military.[5]

Even before it was assigned responsibility for technical intelligence, the
Signal Corps was deeply involved in intelligence- and security-related activities. Its major contribution was in cryptanalysis. In August 1940, after twenty
months of effort, a team of SIS civilians succeeded in breaking the Japanese
diplomatic machine cipher. The unraveling of the riddle of the so-called
Purple machine was accomplished by purely cryptologic means, without any
access to the machine itself. The Purple analog built by SIS experts allowed
the United States to read Japanese diplomatic messages as fast as their intended recipients. The strains of this intellectual accomplishment ultimately sent
William Friedman, the senior cryptanalyst, into the hospital with a nervous
breakdown. However, the feat allowed the United States to follow the tortu-
ous workings of Japanese diplomacy starting in the fall of 1940.[6] Within a
short time, the Army shared intercept and exploitation of the Purple material
with the Navy on a daily rotating basis. The resulting decrypts of Japanese
diplomatic communications were assigned the code name MAGIC, and their
contents were closely controlled. At times, however, the arrangement led the

---

[4] Bidwell, *History of the Military Intelligence Division*, p. 305.

[5] Blanche D. Coll, Jean E. Keith, and Herbert Rosenthal, *The Corps of Engineers: Troops and Equipment*, United States Army in World War II (Washington, D.C.: U.S. Army Center of Military History, 1958), pp. 441–42.

[6] Ronald William Clark, *The Man Who Broke PURPLE: A Life of the World's Greatest Cryptographer, Colonel William F. Friedman* (Boston: Little Brown, 1977), is the only full length biography of Friedman. Its worth can perhaps be gauged by the fact that there are two errors in the title: Friedman was a cryptologist, not just a cryptographer, and his highest rank in the Army Reserve was lieutenant colonel.

services to become rivals in rushing juicy tidbits produced by cryptanalysis to the attention of high officials.

The success of the SIS against Purple facilitated its expansion, and another hundred persons were added to its headquarters. Additional personnel were needed not only to perform cryptanalysis and translation, but also to meet the cryptographic needs of a much larger Army, especially since the SIS was now introducing important technical innovations in this area. The organization procured two new devices to improve the security of Army communications at both the tactical and strategic levels. For the first purpose, it acquired the rights to a small compact machine cipher designed by Swedish inventor Boris Hagelin. Under the designation M209, this became the mainstay of Army tactical communications. For high-level communications, SIS adopted the M134C electro-mechanical cipher machine from the Navy, assigning to it the short title SIGABA. Friedman and Rowlett had originally designed this machine, but prewar budgetary constraints had made it a Navy project. The SIGABA used rotors instead of one-time tapes for enciphering, and this gave communications arrangements much greater flexibility.[7]

The Signal Intelligence Service was not the only Signal Corps element involved in intelligence-related activities. The Signal Corps also had responsibility for radar. By May 1940 the corps had successfully developed fixed and mobile early-warning radar sets. The first radar-equipped aircraft warning company began operations in Panama a month later. This would have a substantial long-term effect on the evolution of Army Intelligence. Some Army officers defined radar itself as "another highly specialized type of signal intelligence."[8] But radar would also become an intelligence target, and its widespread use by all major powers would ultimately lead to the development of what is sometimes called the electronic battlefield.

1941: MID on the Brink

During 1941 the Military Intelligence Division grew to a strength of 200 officers, supported by 848 civilians. In addition to its New York branch, the organization now maintained regional offices in New Orleans and San Francisco to collect foreign intelligence. The changing nature of the international situation had finally refocused collection activities on Germany and Japan, as well as Latin America. However, MID's traditional primary information source, the attache system, had only limited capabilities against wartime Axis powers, even though it had grown to encompass 136 attaches on duty in 50 countries. In February 1941 Brig. Gen. Sherman Miles, the assistant chief of staff, G–2,

---

7 SRH 349, pp. 43–44, 46–47.

8 Memo, Air Communications Division, Signal Corps, 26 Nov 41, sub: Recommendations on Signal Intelligence Manual MID SR 30–60, Army Cryptologic Records.

concluded that it was "imperative that the Army develop an efficient espionage service that can function independently of any nation," but nothing was
done to implement this concept.9

The perceived inadequacies of American Military Intelligence in a situation of growing crisis caused deep concern. In April Miles fretted that "this
Division has expanded considerably since last May, but always in a piecemeal
manner," and admitted that "the work being done by the division is still far
below what should be expected of the military intelligence of a great power in
our present situation."10 Others agreed, notably the president of the United
States. In June 1941 Roosevelt appointed prominent lawyer and World War I
hero William J. Donovan as coordinator of information, with a large mandate
to establish an organization to collect intelligence and conduct radio propa-
ganda.11 But such an edifice could not be constructed overnight and its early
efforts were, not surprisingly, somewhat amateurish. An agent dispatched to
the Pacific, for example, reported that there would be no war that year, while
Donovan's central staff estimated the combat strength of the German *Luftwaffe*
at 29,000 war planes when in fact it was only 3,100.12 Given the lack of
urgency that characterized MID's own approach to collecting foreign intelligence on America's most probable enemies, Donovan's organization filled a
vital need. But this did not preserve it from the enmity of MID, which resent-
ed the intrusion of a civilian organization with powerful political backing into
what it regarded as its own preserve.

The clash between the two organizations was exacerbated by MID's having
acquired an interest of its own in the area of propaganda in 1941. Unfounded
credit had been given to German proficiency in manipulating public opinion
and the subsequent role of propaganda in bringing about the defeat of France.
Moreover, since the United States was not yet a belligerent, a radio war was
about the only one in which it could participate actively. In July 1941, therefore, MID set up a special study group on "psychological warfare" under conditions of strict secrecy. Rivalry between MID and Donovan's office in this area
thus began almost immediately and continued unabated even after America
entered the shooting war and it became clear that it would take more than
slogans to defeat the enemy.

---

9 History of the Counter Intelligence Corps, vol. 4, U.S. Army Intelligence Center, 1960, p.
125.

10 Memo, Brig Gen Sherman Miles for Chief of Staff, 12 Apr 41, sub: Project for the
Expansion of the Military Intelligence Division, MID Documents.

11 Troy, *Donovan and the CIA*, pp. 63, 74.

12 To be sure, the Army's estimates of *Luftwaffe* strength were almost equally exaggerated.
See David Kahn, "U.S. Views of Germany and Japan," *Knowing One's Enemies: Intelligence
Assessment Before the Two Wars*, ed. Ernest May (Princeton: Princeton University Press, 1984), pp.
492–93.

Counterintelligence Concerns

Although MID's role in foreign intelligence and propaganda provided a matter for dispute, coexistence with the FBI in the field of domestic intelligence was less of a problem, as the delimitations agreement gave the Army its own secure sphere of activities. However, Army Intelligence developed growing pains as it sought to fulfill its responsibilities. The Corps of Intelligence Police had expanded elevenfold by the beginning of 1941, and this expansion changed the nature of the force. Until then the appointment of CIP personnel had been centralized at the War Department level, but in January of that year appointment authority for agents was decentralized to the corps area and overseas department level in an attempt to gain more manpower. At the same time, MID authorized the creation of the Office of Chief, Corps of Intelligence Police, and the establishment of a CIP training school. The Army also approved the detail of officers to the Corps of Intelligence Police. In addition, to conduct specialized investigations, the Army attempted to recruit African-American and Asian-American agents for the first time in the organization's history.

The Corps of Intelligence Police continued to expand during the course of 1941. In April it was authorized a strength of 288 enlisted men, and this figure was raised to 513 in May. The growth was accompanied by renewed disputes over the degree to which the recruitment, assignment, and promotion of CIP agents should be centralized and who should supervise investigations. Traditionally, the G–2s of the various corps areas and departments had carried out the latter function. But the reserve officer who became the first head of the Corps of Intelligence Police, Maj. Garland Williams, wanted a centralized organization structured along the lines of the FBI, with its chief responsible to the secretary of war for "detecting and investigating" all matters pertaining to espionage, sabotage, and subversion.[13] He also believed that the decentralized personnel arrangements impaired the quality of his manpower. However, all proposals to strengthen the powers of the chief, Corps of Intelligence Police, were vigorously rebutted by the commanders in the field, and these arrangements remained unchanged. Williams protested in vain that this meant he would have to deal with "14 different policies, 14 different practices, 14 different methods of work, and, in general, 14 separate and distinct units."[14] The unhappy officer was soon reassigned to the Infantry School.

Lack of adequate central control over operations in the field thus presented a serious problem for the entire investigative effort. Agents too often were misused by commanders unfamiliar with counterintelligence work. On the other hand, the investigative work load in some commands resulted in agents' being pressed into service without ever undergoing basic training. And as the Army

---

[13] History of the Counter Intelligence Corps, vol. 4, p. 123.
[14] Ibid., p. 122.

adjutant general later explained to one of the corps area commanders, delegation of personnel procurement authority to the field had resulted in the recruitment of "a larger percentage of agents whose character, education, adaptability,
and experience in no way qualified them for the duties they would be called
upon to perform."15

Another type of problem presented itself when a rival organization emerged
in the counterintelligence field. In September 1941 the newly created Provost
Marshal General's Office took over the function of conducting all personnel
background investigations of civilians applying for military or defense-related
employment. Ninety CIP agents were transferred to the new organization, further intensifying both the shortage of manpower and the lack of centralized
direction. For a time, the demands of the work load forced the Army to hire
civilian investigators to supplement its force of CIP agents.

The Road to Pearl Harbor

Manpower problems were not restricted to the Corps of Intelligence Police,
but were pervasive throughout the Army Intelligence community in 1941. The
vast expansion of the nation's intelligence apparatus threatened to outstrip the
supply of qualified people in all services. Although the Army reservists of the
prewar Military Intelligence Officers Reserve Corps had been called up, only
573 existed, many of whom were actually public relations specialists rather than
trained intelligence officers. Reserve intelligence training had not been an Army
priority. Although the Corps of Intelligence Police and the Signal Intelligence
Service now had specialized schools, located respectively at Chicago, Illinois,
and Fort Monmouth, New Jersey, there was no institute to train intelligence personnel in other disciplines. The Operations and Training Division stubbornly
refused to give the Military Intelligence Division any authority over intelligence
training in general. Only in the area of language instruction was there some
progress: a handful of officers were enrolled in language programs overseas, and
the Fourth Army established a language school at the Presidio of San Francisco
in the fall of 1941. By the end of the year, ninety students were learning the
Japanese language.

But even if trained intelligence personnel had been available, there would
have been little for them to do besides manning the traditional tactical intelligence staffs. The need for communications intelligence personnel and cryptanalysts was serious but limited, and there was no organization for gathering
human intelligence or for acquiring information on a large scale. At the initiative
of the State Department, both the Army and the Navy had briefly posted a
handful of undercover agents in French North Africa in 1941, but these men
were transferred to the control of Donovan's new agency soon after it came into

---

15 Ibid., p. 110.

existence in the summer of that year.16 The entire intelligence apparatus thus seemed too disparate and too disorganized to pull itself together for the great contest ahead.

On the positive side, Army Intelligence could draw on the resources of an experienced ally for the first time since World War I. In 1941 secret staff talks between the top military leaders of the United States and Great Britain were accompanied by an intelligence liaison between the two countries. In February 1941 a party from the Signal Intelligence Service visited Great Britain and established a limited collaboration in the field of cryptology. The Americans brought with them a Purple analog for the British Government Code and Cypher School, the British cryptanalytic organization, thus furnishing the British with the solution for a cryptanalytic problem that had baffled their best efforts. This marked the beginning of a cooperation that would bring the United States unparalleled benefits. In the summer of 1941 a permanent British liaison officer was assigned to SIS. The British also helped out in other intelligence-related areas. In September 1941, for example, the Army dispatched an Electronic Training Group of 300 second lieutenants to England to study British developments in radar.

By the end of 1941 the Army had also put together a tactical signals intelligence organization. Seven signal radio intelligence companies numbered in the 100 series were now active, including the original 1st Radio Intelligence Company, now redesignated the 121st Signal Radio Intelligence Company. Additionally, there was a signal radio intelligence company, aviation, designed to provide communications intelligence to the Army Air Forces.17

However, there were still grave deficiencies in battlefield intelligence capabilities. Apart from the success of the Signal Intelligence Service in decoding Japanese diplomatic communications, the Army had only limited sources of intelligence collection and no way of moving intelligence down to commanders in the field, who still tended to rely on their own resources, much as they had done in the nineteenth century. The use of MAGIC, the Army's most valuable intelligence source, highlighted the problem. The cryptologic success of the SIS was simply not matched by intelligence exploitation of the product. Because the decrypts were so sensitive, they were closely held—only a few individuals within MID and the highest military and political figures in the administration were aware of their existence, and intelligence analysts were kept out of the picture for security reasons. As a result, although policy makers were exposed to individual messages, there was never an attempt to put the flow of the material into an ordered framework. As Friedman later put it, "each message represented only

---

16 Ray S. Cline, *The CIA Under Reagan, Bush, and Casey* (Washington, D.C.: Acropolis Press, 1981), pp. 64–66.

17 War Department, Adjutant General's Office, *Directory of the Army of the United States and War Department Activities, July 1941* (Washington, D.C.: War Department, 1941), p. 32, and August 1941, p. 33.

a single frame, so to speak, in a long motion picture film"; unfortunately, nobody was in a position to see the whole movie.[18] The same security considerations denied key Army and Navy field commanders any knowledge of the existence of the material.

And so, in the end not even MAGIC could save the United States from military surprise at Pearl Harbor, when the Japanese attacked at dawn on 7 December 1941. High-level Japanese diplomatic messages had simply not contained any mention of Japanese military plans; consular messages had contained clues, but resources had not been available for the timely exploitation of low-level traffic. The Japanese Navy codes were still unbroken, and the Japanese fleet that struck Pearl Harbor had approached its target under strict radio silence. Although radar manned by the Signal Corps' Air Warning Service Company, Hawaii, had detected the Japanese attack formation 130 miles away, the reports were misconstrued at the operations center and no alert had been given. Pearl Harbor was both a military disaster and an intelligence failure.[19] Confronted by attack in the Pacific and a German declaration of war, Army Intelligence prepared to set matters right and bring victory out of defeat.

---

[18] SRH 125, Certain Aspects of "Magic" in the Cryptologic Background of the Various Official Investigations into the Pearl Harbor Attack, p. 63.

[19] The best study of the intelligence failure at Pearl Harbor remains Roberta Wohlstetter, *Pearl Harbor: Warning and Decision* (Stanford: Stanford University Press, 1962).

Nineteenth-century intelligence collectors: scouts and guides of the Union Army in the Civil War.

In 1908 the War Department's intelligence organization moved to new quarters at the Army War College on the grounds of present-day Fort McNair in Washington, D.C., and soon lost its separate identity.

Pioneers of Military Intelligence.
Clockwise, Col. Ralph M. Van Deman,
who reestablished the General Staff's
Military Intelligence organization in
World War I; Col. (later Brig. Gen.)
Dennis Nolan, G–2 of the American
Expeditionary Forces (AEF) in France;
Brig. Gen. Marlborough Churchill,
first chief of the restored Military
Intelligence Division. (*NARA*)

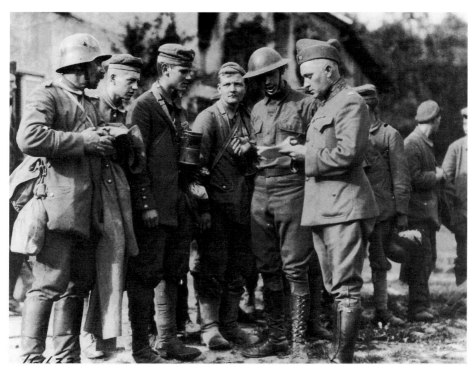

Intelligence in World War I: AEF interrogators question German prisoners of war. (*NARA*)

Technology at the service of intelligence: an Army aerial photographer. (*NARA*)

Herbert O. Yardley, intelligence hero and villain. In the 1920s his clandestine "Black Chamber," jointly funded by the War and State Departments, broke the Japanese diplomatic code; then he wrote a book about his accomplishments. (*National Security Agency*)

After 1929 the Army's tiny but supremely effective Signal Intelligence Service (SIS), headed by William F. Friedman, took over the dual mission of code-breaking and code making. The Army's peacetime cryptologic successes would be repeated in World War II. (*U.S. Army Intelligence and Security Command* [*INSCOM*])

In 1942 the SIS relocated to Arlington Hall, a former girls' school in Arlington, Virginia. The organization was soon redesignated as the Signal Security Agency (SSA). (*INSCOM*)

SSA personnel decrypt Japanese diplomatic traffic enciphered by the PURPLE machine. (*INSCOM*)

SSA guarded the security of U.S. Army communications, designing and producing electro mechanical cipher machines like the SIGABAs used in this communications center. (*INSCOM*)

Officers of Signal Security Detachment D, the field operating arm
of the Signal Intelligence Service, European Theater of
Operations. (*INSCOM*)

A Counter Intelligence Corps agent of the
94th Infantry Division questions a source
in the European Theater of Operations.
(*NARA*)

Soldiers of the elite Alamo Scouts reconnoitered
Japanese-held islands in support of the Army's campaigns
in the Southwest Pacific Area (SWPA). (*NARA*)

Postwar headquarters of Army Security Agency Europe, in the I. G. Farben building, Frankfurt, Germany. (*INSCOM*)

A Nisei Counter Intelligence Corps agent shows his badge to a sentry of the 23d Infantry Division during the occupation of Japan. (*NARA*)

5

World War II
Military Intelligence at the Center

World War II confronted the U.S. Army with the problems of fighting a global conflict across enormous distances. The beginnings were not easy. During the first six months of fighting in the Pacific, the United States suffered an unprecedented string of military reverses. German U-boats in the Atlantic ravaged the sea lanes until early 1943, creating a serious shortage of shipping that threatened America's capacity to project its power overseas. However, the military problems were manageable. America's vast industrial base allowed the United States to equip a mobilized Army of 8 million men, with 89 divisions and over 1,000 squadrons of aircraft. By the end of 1943 much of this vast force had been deployed overseas. Following preliminary operations in North Africa and the Mediterranean, the invasion of Normandy in June 1944 allowed the U.S. Army to bring its main forces to bear against Germany on the decisive battlefield of continental Europe. In the Pacific, the secondary theater of war, America eventually launched a two-pronged attack on the Japanese Empire from bases in Australia and Hawaii. By August 1945 the war had been brought to a triumphant close.

The history of Military Intelligence in the war was paradoxical. Largely because of the success of British and American cryptanalysts in exploiting enemy communications, the Army ultimately was provided with better intelligence than it had ever enjoyed in its history. Yet all during the war, there was a constant drumfire of criticism directed against Military Intelligence. In late 1943 Secretary of War Henry L. Stimson agreed with his colleague, Secretary of the Navy Frank Knox, that "our two intelligence services are pretty bum."[1] The same year Admiral Ernest King complained of "overlaps and wasted effort in the various activities" of Army and Navy Intelligence.[2] In retrospect, the Army's World War II deputy chief of staff, Lt. Gen. Joseph McNarney, stated that Army G–2 "was always a headache for the War Department and was reorganized con-

---

[1] Troy, *Donovan and the CIA*, p. 317.
[2] Ibid., p. 316.

tinuously and unsuccessfully throughout the war."3 Although the intelligence end product was superb, the machinery that produced it was beset by disorder. The situation was not improved by a high rate of turnover in MID's leadership: between 1941 and 1944, the Army had four different assistant chiefs of staff, G–2.

The onset of the war led inevitably to major changes in Army Intelligence. Pearl Harbor provided an obvious spur to greater efforts at interservice coordination on intelligence matters. A Joint Intelligence Committee (JIC) that brought together working-level representatives of MID and the Office of Naval Intelligence had a belated first meeting on 11 December, a month after it was first authorized. Once the Joint Chiefs of Staff were in place, a new JIC was formed, consisting of the heads of MID and the Office of Naval Intelligence (ONI). Membership in the committee was expanded to include representatives of the Coordinator of Information, the Department of State, and the Board of Economic Warfare. The JIC had the dual mission of providing intelligence advice to the Joint Chiefs of Staff and representing the United States in combined Military Intelligence matters with its British counterparts. The principals on the JIC were supported by a larger working group known as the Joint Intelligence Survey Committee. With the growing independence of the Army Air Forces, the AAF's principal intelligence officer, the assistant chief of air staff, intelligence (A–2), was added to the JIC in May 1943, and the subordinate body became known as the Joint Intelligence Staff.4

This joint structure did accomplish some useful purposes by fostering interservice cooperation. Under its supervision, a joint prisoner-of-war interrogation center was set up at Fort Hunt, Virginia, in May 1942 to process high-ranking German prisoners. A similar facility was organized at Byron Hot Springs, California, in December to handle Japanese prisoners. By the fall of 1942, Joint Army-Navy Intelligence Studies were being published, and small Joint Intelligence Collection Agencies were later fielded in North Africa, the Middle East, India-Burma, and China to acquire nontactical information of potential use to Washington. At the end of 1942 there was even a serious proposal to merge MID with ONI, creating a joint intelligence agency. However, this idea ran into too many practical difficulties, since MID performed broader functions than ONI, and the two organizations were not parallel. MID, for example, was an element of a larger staff but ONI was not, since the Navy had no such body.

The exchange of information between Army and Navy Intelligence was also hampered by tradition. Both service intelligence agencies had long been conditioned to operate independently and departmentally. Communications intelligence was particularly sensitive: until November 1944 the Navy did not share all information derived from this source with the Army, and no joint organiza-

---

3 Ibid., p. 211.

4 For a further discussion of AAF intelligence in World War II, the reader is referred to John F. Kreis, ed., *Piercing the Fog: Intelligence and Army Air Forces Operations in World War II* (Washington, D.C.: Air Force History and Museums Program, 1996).

tion to coordinate activities in this field was put in place until 1945.5 The lack of secure telephone links between MID and ONI, even at the end of the war, reflected the limits on cooperation between the armed services in the intelligence field.

Although MID was willing to work with its Navy counterpart, it regarded cooperation with other players in the intelligence arena with distaste. Both military services distrusted the civilians, especially Donovan's organization. This rivalry did not abate even after the Office of the Coordinator of Information, shorn of its propaganda functions, was placed under the Joint Chiefs of Staff in July 1942, redesignated the Office of Strategic Services (OSS), and given a heavy fill of military personnel, with Donovan himself ultimately receiving general's stars. MID never allowed OSS intelligence analysts any access to high-grade communications intelligence (COMINT).6 One of the motives behind the proposal for creating a joint intelligence agency was to strip OSS of most of its intelligence functions. Moreover, when plans began to be made for Operation TORCH, the invasion of North Africa, the Joint Intelligence Committee was carefully cut out of the picture. Instead, intelligence support to the operation was provided by a Joint Security Control group with its membership restricted to representatives from Army and Navy Intelligence. Later the Joint Chiefs of Staff used this body to coordinate deception operations.

The Reorganization of Military Intelligence

At the same time that Army Intelligence was beginning to embark on intelligence collaboration with other elements, it was also undergoing reorganization. The first change came about as a result of a wholesale shakeup of the Army staff system in March 1942. Army Chief of Staff General George C. Marshall and his top planners decided to sharply cut back the Army staff and to centralize control of operations in a War Department Operations Division, which would become a Washington command post for the chief of staff. Administrative duties previously performed at the staff level were to be delegated to new subordinate commands. The staff would become a body engaged exclusively in planning and supervision.

This change, which divided the Army into the Army Ground Forces, the Army Air Forces, and the Services of Supply (later redesignated as the Army Service Forces), had a major impact on the structure of Military Intelligence.

---

5 Ray Cline notes that "Neither the JIC [Joint Intelligence Committee] Weekly nor any component of the OSS ever used signal intelligence in its reporting. I know from Navy experience that this source was essential for all authoritative all-source intelligence, and it was a serious limitation that OSS had only minimal exposure to intercepts." *The CIA under Reagan, Bush, and Casey*, p. 78.

6 Army-Navy rivalry over communications intelligence was conducted almost at the level of the Cold War. At one point a senior Army Intelligence officer wrote: "It is now apparent that the Navy proposes to do business at arm's length. We should accept that attitude and act accordingly." Memo for General Bissell, sub: Army-Navy Agreement Regarding ULTRA, in *Listening to the Enemy*, ed. Ronald H. Spector (Wilmington: Scholarly Resources, 1988), p. 199.

Each of the components had its own intelligence staff. Initially, Army Ground Forces took over responsibility for combat intelligence training. The intelligence organization of the Army Air Forces (AAF) devoted itself to studying the technical and tactical aspects of the air-related threat, while the War Department G–2, in which AAF personnel were well represented, continued to have responsibility for strategic air intelligence. The Services of Supply, in addition to exercising supervision over counterintelligence operations in the United States, took over responsibility for the intelligence activities of the seven Army technical services: the Chemical Warfare Service, Corps of Engineers, Medical Corps, Ordnance Corps, Quartermaster Corps, Signal Corps, and Transportation Corps. Among other things, this meant that the Services of Supply now had jurisdiction over the Signal Intelligence Service, a step which had important adverse implications, since it placed the Army's most productive intelligence arm under a service organization with no background in intelligence and with low priorities for obtaining personnel and resources in this area.

The organization most affected, however, was the Military Intelligence Division itself. At the time the reorganization went into effect, it was by far the largest single element in the Army Staff, containing 50 percent of all officers on the staff and 60 percent of all other personnel. The March 1942 reorganization reduced the division to just 26 people, 16 of them officers. To carry out all the operating functions—collecting, analyzing, and disseminating intelligence—the new and theoretically separate Military Intelligence Service (MIS) was set up. Initially, MIS included an Administrative Group, an Intelligence Group, a Counterintelligence Group, and an Operations Group. By April 1942 the new organization already consisted of 342 officers and 1,000 enlisted men and civilians, and it continued to expand.

On paper, the separation of the Military Intelligence Division from its operating arm, the Military Intelligence Service, was a drastic change. In practice, it proved otherwise. The head of MID at the time was the rather imperious Maj. Gen. George V. Strong. Although charged with responsibility for carrying out the plan, Strong emphatically did not believe in it and effectively frustrated its implementation. He justified this bit of institutional sabotage on the grounds that he was still responsible for providing intelligence advice to the chief of staff and needed to retain command and administrative control over the assets required to accomplish his mission. As a result, until the general departed in early 1944, the separation between MID and MIS remained essentially a paper arrangement. By the end of Strong's tenure as assistant chief of staff, G–2, there were two organization charts for the Military Intelligence Service, one drawn to please the reformers on the General Staff, and the other reflecting actual command arrangements.

Although Army planners had an impact on Military Intelligence organization at the War Department level, the imperatives of the war itself were greater. At the time of Pearl Harbor, MID's production unit, the Intelligence Branch, was internally divided into traditional geographic sections, and the organization still derived the bulk of its intelligence, apart from MAGIC, from the attache system. The involvement of the United States in actual overseas combat changed both the sources of intelligence and the information-gathering process. Intelligence production was now assigned to the Military Intelligence Service. MID's former Intelligence Branch became the Intelligence Group of the MIS and was reorganized to reflect the various theaters of war. In addition, new functional elements sprang up beside the area elements as the needs of wartime expanded the scope of MIS's interests.[7]

Perhaps the most important organizational change within the MID/MIS organization was the development of an element charged with exploiting sensitive communications intelligence. This occurred as a result of the weaknesses in handling such sources at Pearl Harbor. The restrictions on dissemination that had been placed on the MAGIC intercepts had left Army Intelligence oblivious to the Japanese threat. Immediately after the Pearl Harbor attack, Secretary of War Stimson called upon a prominent Chicago lawyer, Alfred McCormack, to examine the implications of the problem. McCormack recommended the creation of a branch within the Military Intelligence Service to deal with the processing of communications intelligence. The Special Branch was established in May 1942 with Col. Carter W. Clarke as its head and with McCormack, now commissioned as a colonel, as his deputy. To acquire the necessary high-caliber personnel to staff the new organization, McCormack drew heavily on lawyers from elite firms, who were given reserve commissions.[8]

The Special Branch was an important step in the rationalization of the Army's handling of communications intelligence. For the first time, analysts in sufficient numbers would have access to the material in ways that would allow them to exploit it properly for evaluation. MAGIC could now be viewed in its entirety and used to build up an intelligence picture. However, although the Special Branch was a step in the right direction, it was not the final answer. The rest of the Military Intelligence Service, cut off from compartmentalized intelligence, was forced to operate in a vacuum. Additionally, even though the branch received its intelligence from the Signal Intelligence Service, it did not control the operations of the SIS, which still remained under the direction of the Chief Signal Officer.

---

[7] Among the diverse elements of the Military Intelligence Service were MIS–Y, which ran an interrogation center for high-level German officers, and MIS–X, which was involved in making arrangements for procuring intelligence from captured Army Air Forces flight crews, as well as for implementing escape and evasion measures. Both organizations operated from a secret headquarters at Fort Hunt, Virginia. See Lloyd R. Shoemaker, *The Escape Factory* (New York: St. Martin's Press, 1990). Maj. Gen. Otto L. Nelson later commented, "Organizationally, G–2 was a mongrel, with many uncertain strains mixed in and not always recognizable." *National Security and the General Staff* (Washington, D.C.: Infantry Journal Press, 1946), p. 526.

[8] A detailed history of the organization is contained in "History of the Special Branch, MIS, War Department, 1942–1944," *Listening to the Enemy*, pp. 171–94.

The Special Branch was not the only organizational innovation introduced into the MIS. The Military Intelligence Service had inherited from MID small branches located in New York City, San Francisco, and New Orleans. In April 1942 a new branch was established in Miami, Florida, to counter the threat of Axis penetration and subversion in Latin America. In August the entire Latin American Section of the Military Intelligence Service moved to Miami. Successively redesignated the American Hemisphere Intelligence Command, the American Intelligence Command, and the American Intelligence Service, the unit became what one historian described as a "huge, semi-independent military intelligence agency."9 It engaged in both counterintelligence activities and positive collection, controlling subordinate field offices in the Canal Zone and in Brazil, and operating its own intercept system to locate possible agent transmitters throughout Latin America. Additionally, MIS expanded its overseas operations further, setting up a small secret intelligence service in 1942 and a Military Intelligence Research Section, with offices in London and Washington, D.C., for exploitation of captured documents in January 1943.10

The Military Intelligence Division also ventured into areas rather far afield from pure intelligence work. For a brief time, one was psychological warfare. The Special Studies Group that had previously dealt with the subject became the Psychological Warfare Branch of MID shortly after the declaration of war. However, one year later the Joint Chiefs of Staff assigned the Office of Strategic Services responsibility for conducting all activities in this field, and the Army's Psychological Warfare Branch was discontinued. Nevertheless, MID eventually reassumed responsibility for the Army's remaining efforts in this area, setting up the Propaganda Branch in 1943. In a move that took the Military Intelligence Division even further afield from purely intelligence-related concerns, in April 1943 the organization was given responsibility for conducting the Army's World War II historical program.11

A function more pertinent to intelligence was that of training intelligence personnel. The Army had decided rather belatedly that intelligence training was an intelligence responsibility. The Army Air Forces had led the way in this area, opening up an AAF Intelligence School for their own personnel in February 1942. Classes were held at the University of Maryland until April, when the Army Air Forces acquired a more permanent facility at Harrisburg, Pennsylvania. In June 1942 the Military Intelligence Service activated its own

9 Bruce W. Bidwell, History of the Military Intelligence Division, Department of the Army, vol. 5, unpublished Ms, U.S. Army Center of Military History, 1963, pp. 52–53.

10 On the War Department's World War II secret intelligence service, see National Security Act of 1947. Hearing Before the Committee on Expenditures in the Executive Departments, 80th Cong., 1st sess. (Washington, D.C.: Government Printing Office, 1982), pp. 7–8, 53–54. Further references to this organization can be found in the footnotes to Christopher Felix (pseud.), A Short Course in the Secret War (New York: Dell Publishing, 1988), pp. 168–69.

11 Stetson Conn, Historical Work in the United States Army, 1862–1954 (Washington, D.C.: U.S. Army Center of Military History, 1980), pp. 83–114.

Military Intelligence Training Center (MITC) at Camp Ritchie, Maryland, a former National Guard installation.

The Camp Ritchie center trained order of battle specialists, photo interpreters, some linguists, and general intelligence personnel. After August 1944 the center also offered counterintelligence training. Intelligence personnel proceeded from Camp Ritchie to a staging area at Camp Sharpe, Pennsylvania, where they received additional combat training, were formed into teams, and assigned directly to theater control. Over 19,000 students passed though Camp Ritchie's gates during the course of World War II. The training offered at Ritchie may not have been perfect—officers in the European theater would later complain that members of their military intelligence specialist teams showed "a lack of basic military training and a certain ineptness about caring for themselves"— but it was a more extensive effort than the Army had ever before undertaken in this arena.[12]

To meet the special needs of the Army in the Pacific, the Military Intelligence Service also took over the direction of a separate school for Japanese linguists, with a student body composed primarily of second generation Japanese Americans known as Nisei. This school had been established originally at the Presidio of San Francisco, under Fourth Army control in the days before Pearl Harbor. In May 1942 it became the Military Intelligence Service Language School, moved to Camp Savage, Minnesota, and was greatly expanded. To acquire better facilities, the school moved once more to Fort Snelling, Minnesota, in August 1944. By the end of the war, it had graduated over 4,800 Japanese-language specialists, most of whom served in the Pacific theater as members of interpreter-interrogator-translator teams.[13] The Army also sponsored instruction for smaller numbers of Japanese, Chinese, and Russian linguists at selected universities, and the MIS itself trained 1,750 Army censorship personnel at Fort Washington, Maryland, until February 1944, when the Army Service Forces assumed the function. Army counterintelligence personnel assigned to MIS had their own separate school in Chicago until 1944.

Not all intelligence training was directly under the auspices of the Military Intelligence Service. The Signal Security Agency (SSA), SIS's wartime successor, provided cryptologic and language training for military and civilian personnel at Arlington Hall Station, Virginia, and maintained a school for officers and enlisted personnel at Vint Hill Farms Station, Virginia. Intelligence personnel for the Army Air Forces continued to attend the AAF facility in Harrisburg, Pennsylvania, until this school was relocated to Orlando, Florida, in the spring

---

12 Rpt of the General Board, U.S. Forces, European Theater, Study no. 12, The Military Intelligence Service in the European Theater of Operations, p. 8, copy in CMH files.

13 An account of Nisei accomplishments in intelligence is provided by Joseph D. Harrington, *Yankee Samurai: The Secret Role of Nisei in America's Pacific Victory* (Detroit: Pettigrew Enterprises, 1979). For a firsthand account of one individual's experience, see Interv, author with Mr. Harry Fukuhara, pt. 1, 5 Jun 90, INSCOM History Office files.

of 1944. Finally, the responsibilities for training soldiers assigned to tactical signals intelligence units were peculiarly fragmented. Units were organized and trained both by the Army Ground Forces and the Army Air Forces, while advanced training was administered under SSA supervision at its own facilities and at Signal Corps installations at Fort Monmouth, New Jersey, and Camp Crowder, Missouri.[14]

The ULTRA Breakthrough

Events of the spring of 1943 would reshape the entire structure of Military Intelligence. In April Army cryptanalysts scored their first success against Japanese military codes. A month later, a party of officers from MIS and from the Signal Security Agency visited the British Government Code and Cypher School at Bletchley Park. For the first time, American Military Intelligence became aware of the dimensions of the British success against high-level German communications. British efforts in breaking the German Enigma and other ciphers used on command links had laid bare many of the most important secrets of the Nazi high command. The intelligence derived from this source, known as ULTRA, was disseminated by the British under rigidly controlled conditions. Although such intelligence had been provided to Eisenhower during the invasion of North Africa, U.S. Army Intelligence had not been fully aware of its origins. Now the British agreed to share this intelligence with the U.S. Army on an unrestricted basis, in exchange for reciprocal access to American communications intelligence on the Japanese.

These twin developments confronted Army Intelligence for the first time with the problem of disseminating communications intelligence to the field. The previous American success against the Purple machine, although providing valuable background information to Washington during the course of the war, had not had tactical implications. In contrast, ULTRA could be of immediate operational value. The problem was now to transmit this extremely sensitive combat intelligence from central processing centers in the United States and Great Britain to theater commanders thousands of miles away in a fashion that would avoid any compromise of the source of intelligence.

In response, the Special Branch adopted the existing British system of handling communications intelligence. New security classifications were introduced. At first, high-level communications intelligence was termed ULTRA DEXTER, lower-level material designated DEXTER. Later, ULTRA was reserved for the results of high-level cryptanalysis, while intelligence derived from breaking simpler systems was

---

14 These intercept units, an officer of the Signal Security Agency commented, were "organized and trained by the ground forces in a rather 'hit-or-miss' manner without any particular reference to their ultimate employment." SRH 169, Centralized Control of U.S. Army Signal Intelligence Activities, p. 14.

termed CIRO PEARL or PEARL, and information produced from radio-direction finding was labeled THUMB. Ultimately, in order to mesh Army and Navy practice, PEARL and THUMB were merged into a single category, PINUP. Meanwhile, in April 1944 the U.S. Army at last adopted a "top secret" classification to provide a satisfactory equivalent to the British "most secret."

Terminology was only one aspect of the new procedures. The actual dissemination of ULTRA in the field was handled by special security officers (SSOs) selected and trained by the MIS Special Branch and operating under its direct command using special cipher systems. This was both faster and more secure than the usual practice of sending intelligence through successive layers of command channels. Again, this followed British practice. The first three American SSOs went out to commands in the Pacific in the fall of 1943. The British agreement that ULTRA supplied to American commanders in the European theater would henceforth be disseminated through American channels led to the procurement of eighty additional special security officers in December 1943.

At first, the SSOs were attached only to the highest level of commands. They had the dual mission of securing the vital ULTRA material and of explaining its significance to commanders and intelligence officers unfamiliar with the uses and limitations of high-grade communications intelligence. However, by July 1944 the decision had been made to disseminate ULTRA directly to field armies and equivalent AAF commands and even down to independently operating Army corps. This necessitated recruiting 172 more SSOs in August 1944. In addition, 65 enlisted men were brought into the system to operate communications, thus relieving SSOs from the necessity of deciphering their own messages. By the end of the war, the elaborate dissemination system was headed in each theater by a senior special security representative.[15]

The Army's own increasing successes in communications intelligence, combined with the new availability of the British COMINT product, helped bring about a general reorganization of the Military Intelligence Service. Because of the growth of its responsibilities, the Special Branch expanded to the point where it constituted the largest component of the MIS Intelligence Group. This created a situation in which much of the analysis performed at the War Department level was undertaken by individuals without access to the single most important intelligence source exploited in the war. Only a "very select few" top production officials had been granted access to the whole picture.[16]

General Strong's departure in February 1944 paved the way for an institutional readjustment. In April a committee headed by Assistant Secretary of War

---

15 See "History of the Operations of Special Security Officers Attached to Field Commands, 1943–1945," *Listening to the Enemy*, pp. 199–204.

16 Bidwell, History of the Military Intelligence Division, vol. 5, p. 221. Bidwell's treatment of the full implications of the reorganization is necessarily unsatisfactory, since he wrote before the ULTRA secret—and the exact duties of Special Branch—had been decompartmented and released.

John J. McCloy recommended that "extreme compartmentation" be eliminated.[17] As a result, the War Department completely reorganized its Military Intelligence organization. The Special Branch was abolished as a totally separate compartmented entity, although a new Special Branch was formed to handle dissemination of ULTRA to the field. A Military Intelligence Service separate from MID was reestablished and its internal structure realigned, with the organization ultimately reaching a peak worldwide strength of 1,500 officers, 2,000 enlisted men, and 1,100 civilians in October 1944.

The timing of the reorganization, however, demonstrated all too clearly that the nation's strategic decision makers still looked upon Army Intelligence as "a kind of reference service for data rather than for professional judgments."[18] The new arrangements went into effect in early June 1944. As distinguished historian and intelligence analyst Ray Cline later described the situation, the "G–2 [staff] was so little geared into high-level strategic decisions that it was engaged in a colossal struggle for office space when D-Day for the Normandy invasion came along: all of G–2's files were locked up sitting in safes in the halls waiting for moving crews when frantic requests for data on the landing zone situations began to descend on the hapless Army intelligence officers, who hardly knew each others' phone numbers, let alone what was in the files."[19]

The new-model Military Intelligence Service differed substantially from its predecessor. Internally, it was organized into three directorates: Administration; Intelligence; and Information, which supervised collection and dissemination. It now functioned independently of MID and was freed from some of the excessive compartmentation that had hobbled previous operations. Moreover, at last it could concentrate almost exclusively on the production of foreign intelligence. As a result of decisions made earlier in 1944, responsibility for counterintelligence and censorship had been allotted to the Army Service Forces, a move which rather explicitly downgraded the importance of these functions in the Army, and the MIS Counterintelligence Group that had previously exercised staff supervision over this area was thus abolished.

In addition, certain activities previously carried out at dispersed locations in the United States were now centralized in Washington, D.C. The American Intelligence Service operating from Miami, Florida, had been terminated in January 1944. Now that the war had been carried to the shores of Europe, America was no longer worried about Axis subversion in Latin America. Similarly, the branches previously established in San Francisco, New Orleans, and New York City had lost most of their usefulness as the war progressed and other sources of intelligence became available. By June 1944 the first two

---

[17] Ibid., p. 19.
[18] Cline, *The CIA under Reagan, Bush, and Casey*, p. 81.
[19] Ibid., p. 111.
[20] Nelson, *National Security and the General Staff*, p. 526.

of these branches had been shut down, and the New York branch would cease operations that December. However, it should be noted that the Corps of Engineers, which had its own intelligence office in New York City, continued to find the data bases available there to be essential in producing strategic Engineer Intelligence.

Unfortunately, while the new MIS was a changed organization, not everyone agreed that the changes had been for the better. The new Intelligence Directorate at the heart of MIS was organized on lines that soon proved to be confusing, with a layer of geographic "specialists" superimposed upon branches organized along functional lines.[20] It seems to have been envisaged that the specialists, who had no operating responsibilities, would act as a group of "wise men," producing a unified intelligence picture from the myriad details coming from the functional operating echelons. However, the geographical specialists questioned how they could produce cohesive results without controlling any assets, and the chief of the Military Intelligence Service felt they should be on MID's organization chart, not his own. In practice, functional areas of responsibility proved to be overlapping, the new arrangements separated the researchers from the report writers, and MIS found itself organized on different lines from any other intelligence organization with which it dealt.

Two months after the new reforms had been implemented, the chief of the MIS declared the new system "slow and cumbersome."[21] Col. Alfred McCormack, now director of Intelligence, was equally unhappy: the Special Branch he had painstakingly assembled was now dispersed throughout "53 separate branches, sections, and subsections," and he felt MIS was now under "about as impracticable a scheme of organization as could be devised."[22] Additional tinkering with the system went on until the close of the war, but a postwar study of intelligence organization at the General Staff level concluded that from the point of view of producing timely intelligence, the 1944 reorganization was "a total failure."[23]

Whatever its continuing internal weaknesses, MIS took a major institutional step forward. Since 1943 communications intelligence, MIS's main source of intelligence, had been under the control of the chief signal officer or of theater commanders.[24] In December 1944 MIS at last secured operational control over the Signal Security Agency, and was able to give direction to the Army's most important COMINT asset. This step also positioned MIS to take over this whole field of intelligence when the war came to a close.

---

21 Bidwell, History of the Military Intelligence Division, vol. 5, p. 20.
22 SRH 185, War Experiences of Alfred McCormack, pp. 29–30.
23 Bidwell, History of the Military Intelligence Division, vol. 5, p. 21.
24 SRH 141, Papers from the Personal Files of Alfred McCormack, pt. 2, pp. 316–17.

The Counter Intelligence Corps

The Military Intelligence Service was not composed solely of collectors and analysts. For most of World War II, it also included personnel of the Army Counter Intelligence Corps (CIC), formed on 1 January 1942 as the successor to the Corps of Intelligence Police. The new organization had both a more appropriate name and initially a more centralized organization than its predecessor. In January the War Department took over control of all background investigations of prospective counterintelligence agents and in April centralized the issue of credentials. The CIC would be an elite force, picking its enlisted personnel from the cream of Selective Service inductees. As Maj. Gen. George V. Strong, the assistant chief of staff, G–2, put it, "the personnel of this Corps is of officer caliber."[25]

The question of overall control was not resolved finally, however. The service commands, as the corps areas were redesignated in March 1942, were the primary users of CIC agents in the first part of the war, and local commanders naturally wanted the convenience and flexibility of procuring their own counterintelligence personnel. For example, the commanding general of the New York Port of Embarkation began to recruit his own agents for the Transportation Corps in March 1942 and, although these individuals were issued Military Intelligence Division credentials, it was not until early 1943 that part of the contingent was assimilated into the Counter Intelligence Corps.

The scope of the CIC's responsibilities was vastly increased in March 1942, when the Army expanded its existing countersubversive program and gave it new guidelines, modeling it after the similar Army program of World War I. The new countersubversive operation latticed the nation's military establishment with "an elaborate and fine network of secret agents."[26] Intelligence officers secretly recruited informants within each unit, on an average ratio of one informant to every thirty men, resulting in a program of enormous proportions. By the summer of 1943 there were 53,000 operatives in just one of the nine service commands in the continental United States and over 150,000 such reports were being filed monthly once the system became fully operational. Although the countersubversive program was administered by unit and installation commanders, not by the Counter Intelligence Corps, CIC agents were assigned to follow up reports of subversive activity. At the War Department level, the process was monitored and coordinated by the Counterintelligence Group of the Military Intelligence Service, which exiled those suspected of sedition to special holding units in the remoter parts of the country.

Inevitably, the new work load led to the expansion and restructuring of the Counter Intelligence Corps. Expansion itself generated an additional work load,

---

25 U.S. Army Intelligence Center, History of the Counter Intelligence Corps, vol. 5, unpublished Ms, 1960, p. 39.
    26 Ibid., p. 127.

since the official CIC history later estimated that the Counter Intelligence Corps in the continental United States allotted half its man-hours to investigate its own applicants. By July 1943 the Corps was authorized a strength of 543 officers and 4,431 enlisted personnel. Officers previously detailed to the organization were now formally transferred and additional officers allotted from officer candidate schools. In the past, all CIC enlisted men had held the rank of sergeant; now corporals and privates were added to the corps. This permitted functional differentiation. Sergeants served as special agents with full investigative powers, and corporals and privates held subordinate positions as agents and counterintelligence clerks. The new arrangements allowed some relaxation in the Counter Intelligence Corps' appointment standards. For a period in late 1942 and early 1943, service commands once more were allowed to procure and transfer agents and clerks, while Washington retained full control over special agents and officers. In line with the renewed authority given to the field, the Counter Intelligence Corps School in Chicago, previously responsible for training all CIC personnel, now confined its activities to providing advanced courses, allowing the service commands to provide introductory counterintelligence training.

Meanwhile, the Counter Intelligence Corps was forced to relocate its headquarters. At the end of 1942 the War Department, concerned that too many fit young officers were serving in staff assignments in Washington, stipulated that no more than one-third of the officers assigned to any element in Washington, D.C., could be below thirty-five years of age. This "Child Labor Law" literally drove the CIC out of town. In January 1943 the chief of the Counter Intelligence Corps and his staff moved to a dormitory of Goucher College, a fashionable girls' school in Baltimore, Maryland, that had been taken over by the government for the duration of the war.

While these developments were taking place, the Counter Intelligence Corps was beginning to find a new role with the fighting forces. Heretofore, almost all its duties had been concerned with security in the service commands or in base areas overseas. Special agents in civilian clothes had operated from offices, essentially working in much the same fashion as their civilian counterparts in the FBI. In some cases, CIC agents had been recruited and assigned without completing basic military training. However, when plans were drawn up for the American invasion of North Africa in the fall of 1942, it was decided that CIC personnel would be attached to tactical units in the field. The initial CIC experience with field service was not completely happy. The commander of the training camp to which the first group was assigned labeled them "a citizen army of misfits."[27] Nevertheless, the CIC personnel attached to the North African task force ultimately demonstrated their value in a tactical support role.[28]

---

[27] U.S. Army Intelligence Center, History of the Counter Intelligence Corps, vol. 11, unpublished Ms, 1960, p. 8.

[28] Powe and Wilson, *The Evolution of Military Intelligence*, p. 53.

Tactical employment gave the Counter Intelligence Corps a whole new raison d'etre. By the middle of 1943 the Army at last began to deploy a sizable portion of its strength overseas. The CIC was affected by this shift. With deployment of tactical CIC detachments to combat situations imminent, the CIC School in Chicago put its students in uniform and placed a new emphasis on counterintelligence operations under battle conditions. The same concern for making counterintelligence personnel ready for combat led to the creation of a Counter Intelligence Corps Staging Area in the summer of 1943 to better prepare units about to go overseas. The staging area, initially located at Logan Field in Baltimore, Maryland, soon moved to nearby Camp Holabird, beginning a long association between Military Intelligence and what would become known as "The Bird."

By the fall of 1943 the Counter Intelligence Corps appeared to have solved its initial problems and to have become an established part of the Army. Its organization manual finally had been approved, and the new tactical emphasis placed it in step with the rest of the Army. Agents increasingly served in uniform with the troops rather than working as anonymous "spooks" on the fringes of the military establishment. Finally, the War Department transferred control of CIC personnel from the Military Intelligence Service to the using agencies, again bringing the Counter Intelligence Corps into conformity with the rest of the military establishment.

However, the activities of the Counter Intelligence Corps still managed to generate criticism from both within and outside the Army, placing the corps in a bureaucratically vulnerable position. From the viewpoint of the wartime military, the CIC absorbed a disproportionate percentage of high-quality personnel and used them to accomplish what many regarded as a marginal mission. Tradition-minded Army officers disliked the whole business of counterintelligence operations, especially when they involved enlisted personnel investigating officers. The CIC's investigations of leftist individuals and groups were not universally popular with politicians, particularly since the War Department's Counterintelligence Group had used the results to exclude some well-connected young men from Officers' Candidate School. Moreover, some investigations were conducted with more zeal than prudence. In early 1943, for example, the White House discovered that CIC agents had installed listening devices in the hotel suite of the president's wife in an attempt to monitor the activities of individuals suspected of Communist leanings.[29]

Accumulated resentments eventually found official expression, leading to the temporary eclipse of the Counter Intelligence Corps. In July 1943 Lt. Gen. James J. McNarney, the Army deputy chief of staff, directed the Army inspector general to launch an investigation of the CIC. On 5 November 1943, all CIC agents were ordered out of Washington, D.C., and a day later the inspector gen-

---

[29] Joseph P. Lash, *Love, Eleanor: Eleanor Roosevelt and Her Friends* (Garden City, N.Y.: Doubleday and Co., Inc., 1982), p. 492.

eral submitted a devastating critique of the corps' operations and organization. Charging that many CIC investigations were "superficial, and unproductive of positive results except in rare instances," the inspector general found that the only thorough investigations were those made of applicants for CIC or of military and civilian personnel suspected of subversion. However, these categories were overly thorough, since they dragged on after all immediate allegations had been resolved. Moreover, when officers were investigated, CIC procedures resulted in the indiscriminate dissemination of reports containing unverified derogatory information "based on hearsay, gossip, and innuendo," all of which was "directly contrary to the inherent right of a commissioned officer of the U.S. Army to be advised of imputations and allegations as to his character." In any case, the countersubversive program that had generated much of the work load was nearly worthless, since the million reports submitted in the first part of 1943 had identified only 600 suspects, and it was possible that many reports had been made on the same individual.[30]

The inspector general's report equally criticized the organizational concepts that underpinned Counter Intelligence Corps operations in the continental United States. In the security field, he found, the activities of the Counter Intelligence Corps at least partially duplicated what was being done by the investigators assigned to the Provost Marshal General's Office. In addition, the existing counterintelligence system undermined the concept of command responsibility, since the G–2s in the service commands had to answer both to their commanding generals and to the Counterintelligence Group of the Military Intelligence Service.

The inspector general's report led to the immediate unraveling of the Counter Intelligence Corps. The countersubversive program was terminated, and most CIC agents in the continental United States were merged with the criminal investigators of the Provost Marshal's Office to form a new Security Intelligence Corps that operated under the control of the service commands. Although CIC detachments continued to serve with the Army Air Forces, the Manhattan Project, and tactical units, the presence of the Counter Intelligence Corps on the home front was effectively eliminated. The CIC School was transferred to the provost marshal general, its staging area closed, and the position of chief, Counter Intelligence Corps, abolished. The outgoing chief, Col. Harold R. Kibler, blamed the fall of his command on the enmity of the White House, specifically "Harry Hopkins and the Secret Service."[31] A little later the Counterintelligence Group of the Military Intelligence Service was also eliminated. For the moment, the Army had decided to practically abandon the field of domestic counterintelligence, limiting the CIC to a tactical support role overseas.

---

30 History of the Counter Intelligence Corps, vol. 5, app. 2.

31 FBI memo quoted in Lash, *Love, Eleanor*, p. 492. A more melodramatic but less accurate version of the imbroglio can be found in Richard G. Powers, *Secrecy and Power: The Life of J. Edgar Hoover* (New York: Free Press, 1987), pp. 265–66. "Supposedly, the President had been so furi-

This role, however, proved substantial. CIC detachments rolled up nets of enemy agents in Italy, landed in Normandy with the first wave of paratroopers, screened civilians in France, and arrested Nazi officials as U.S. forces overran Germany. In the Pacific, Counter Intelligence Corps units secured enemy documents on the remote islands of Micronesia and worked with local guerrillas rounding up collaborators in the Philippines. To be sure, some distrust of CIC continued throughout the war. Writing in 1946, two experienced Army intelligence officers noted that "the Counterintelligence [sic] Corps (CIC) in World War II was in many ways a peculiar organization, whose personnel (chosen hurriedly and under pressure for their educational rather than military qualifications) frequently got in everybody's hair."[32] However, counterintelligence support was essential for American units operating in the midst of an alien population, and 241 CIC detachments would serve in overseas theaters during the course of World War II.

In turn, success overseas revitalized the CIC at home. By the summer of 1945 it was clear that the evisceration of the Counter Intelligence Corps had deprived the Army counterintelligence function of essential institutional support just as needs were increasing. The Army's role in the occupation of a defeated Germany had placed new demands on the depleted CIC detachments in the European theater, and the pending expansion of military operations in the Pacific to the Japanese mainland threatened to pose even greater potential counterintelligence problems. But the Army now lacked any effective mechanism either to procure new counterintelligence specialists or to redeploy those it already had. Although the Military Intelligence Training Center at Camp Ritchie had begun training counterintelligence personnel in August 1944, the Camp Ritchie program stressed combat intelligence rather than counterintelligence. Moreover, there was no rotation base for the Army's counterintelligence personnel, since any members of the Counter Intelligence Corps shipped back to the United States were reassigned as individuals to the Army general replacement pool and were lost to their specialty.

These considerations led to the reestablishment of the Counter Intelligence Corps in the continental United States. In July 1945 the Office of Chief, Counter Intelligence Corps, was restored, a new CIC Center and School organized, and both elements placed under the control of the Intelligence Division of the Army Service Forces. Originally located at Fort Meade, the school soon moved to Camp Holabird. In August the Security Intelligence Corps was released from the control of the provost marshal and reassigned to the Intelligence Division, paving the way for its eventual merger into the CIC.

---

ous he had disbanded CIC and ordered its members sent to the South Pacific to 'fight Japs until they were killed.'"

[32] Stedman Chandler and Robert W. Robb, *Front-Line Intelligence* (Washington, D.C.: U.S. Marine Corps, 1986), p. 113.

The Signal Security Agency

The development and expansion of the Army signals intelligence and communications security organization was governed by dynamics quite different from those affecting the structure of Army counterintelligence. Although the growth of the Counter Intelligence Corps was a function of the expansion of the countersubversive program and the need to create new units to give tactical support in the field, the Signal Intelligence Service and its successor organizations evolved largely as a result of increasing success in accomplishing the cryptanalytic mission.

The United States' entry into World War II naturally imposed new demands on the Army's Signal Intelligence Service. Up to this point, the SIS had achieved its main successes against intercepted diplomatic communications provided by its 2d Signal Service Company, which manned seven small fixed sites located at Fort Hancock, New Jersey; Fort Hunt, Virginia; Fort Sam Houston, Texas; the Presidio of San Francisco, California; Corozal, Canal Zone; Fort Shafter, Hawaii; and Fort McKinley, Philippine Islands. At the time of the attack on Pearl Harbor, the Signal Intelligence Service had a strength of 331, almost equally divided between the field sites and its headquarters in the old Munitions Building, a World War I–vintage structure in downtown Washington, D.C.

The shift from peace to war transformed the nature of the Signal Intelligence Service, for it now had to provide military as well as diplomatic intelligence. Initially, the organization concentrated on deciphering Japanese Army cryptosystems, since the Japanese posed the immediate military threat to U.S. forces. To do this, the SIS analysts had to master the elaborate and intricate system of Japanese military codes, which worked on cryptologic principles completely different from those used in the Purple machine of the Japanese Foreign Office. This required not only the expansion of the SIS headquarters, but also the reconfiguration of its intercept network, especially since its most advanced outpost, Fort McKinley, would soon be overrun.[33]

In March 1942 the Military Intelligence Division recommended to the chief signal officer that the SIS move from the Munitions Building into new quarters with greater security. MID also recommended that the Signal Intelligence Service establish two new primary monitoring stations, one on each coast of the United States. Under wartime conditions, these suggestions met a quick response. In June 1942 the Army took possession of Arlington Hall, a former girls' school in Arlington, Virginia, and transformed it into SIS headquarters. That same month, personnel of the 2d Signal Service Battalion, as the 2d Signal

---

[33] The fate of the SIS intercept post at Fort McKinley and of its survivors is detailed in "Reminiscences of Lieutenant Colonel Howard W. Brown," *Listening to the Enemy*, pp. 43–76, and in Michael Maslak, "Signalman's Odyssey," *Military Intelligence: Its Heroes and Legends*, pp. 133–61.

Service Company was now designated, began operations at Vint Hill Farms in Warrenton, Virginia, which had been selected as the site for Monitoring Station No. 1. A second major field station was soon organized at Two Rock Ranch near Petaluma, California.

Paradoxically, as the duties of the Signal Intelligence Service became more important, its relative organizational position within the Signal Corps began to sink steadily lower as the structure of the Signal Corps itself grew more elaborate. By July 1942 the SIS was separated from the Office of the Chief Signal Officer by four organizational layers. As a result the organization was realigned, and since the term "signal intelligence" was thought to be too revealing, it was also redesignated as part of this process, becoming the Signal Security Service in 1942 and the Signal Security Agency (SSA) in 1943. Meanwhile, the positions of chief, Signal Security Service, and commander, 2d Signal Service Battalion, had been merged in 1942, effectively converting the battalion into a personnel center for the enlisted ranks at Arlington Hall and for both officer and enlisted personnel in subordinate detachments manning intercept stations worldwide.[34]

During the first part of the war, the performance of the Army's signals intelligence organization was somewhat disappointing. In July 1942 it received responsibility for all intercept of diplomatic communications, a mission previously shared with the Navy, thus becoming the sole producer of MAGIC. However, despite its continuing successes in the diplomatic field, it found its main task—coping with the mysteries of Japanese military communications— intractable. No cryptologic continuity on Japanese military communications had been built up before Pearl Harbor, principally because of the impossibility of intercepting the existing Japanese military nets either in the home islands or on the mainland of East Asia. It was not until April 1943 that an initial entry was made into one of the principal Japanese Army systems, and General MacArthur's own cryptologic center in Australia made the discovery simultaneously. Even so, Arlington Hall was not able to read enough of the code to produce any intelligence until June of that year.

The summer of 1943, however, proved to be something of a watershed for the Signal Security Agency. Once cryptanalysis of Japanese messages proved to be possible, SSA expanded enormously, recruiting a largely civilian work force. There were 395 persons at agency headquarters at the beginning of 1943 and 3,455 by the end of the year. Although two large temporary buildings had been hastily constructed at Arlington Hall in the winter of 1942 to provide additional office space for this work force, the influx of new personnel still made for cramped quarters. However, in 1943 the War Department gave the British primary operational responsibilities for code breaking in Europe, which freed the SSA to concentrate most of its energies on the Japanese military problem.

---

[34] A conscientious, if pedestrian, account of the unit can be found in SRH 135, History of the 2d Signal Service Battalion.

The year 1944 saw the full maturation of SSA's activities. In January Australian forces captured the codes of the Japanese 20th Division at Sio on New Guinea. The find led to full exploitation of Japanese military communications and triggered another period of growth. By June 1944 over 5,100 civilians, most of them female, were working at Arlington Hall, assisted by 2,000 more military personnel. In the spring of 1944 the intercept facilities of SSA's 2d Signal Service Battalion were also extended when new fixed stations were established at New Delhi, India; Asmara, Eritrea; Fairbanks and Amchitka, Alaska; and Fort Shafter, Hawaii. In the fall the steady advance of American forces in the Pacific allowed another fixed site to be established on the island of Guam. Additionally, the 2d Signal Service Battalion assumed control over former Office of Strategic Services "listening posts" at Bellmore, New York, and Resada, California, converting them into security monitoring stations.[35]

Arlington Hall thus became the center of an enormous web of collection activity. Intercept was provided not only by the fixed stations of the 2d Signal Service Battalion, but also by Signal Corps tactical units under theater control in the field. By the end of the war, 26,000 American soldiers were involved, one way or another, with the intercept and processing of signals intelligence. In addition, U.S. Army collection efforts were supplemented by material forwarded to Arlington Hall by MacArthur's multinational center and by British, Canadian, and Indian sources. To process the material, which came by courier pouch and through forty-six teletype lines at Arlington Hall, the Signal Security Agency's military and civilian work force of 7,000 was supported by a battery of 400 IBM punch-card machines.

All this was conducted under the tightest secrecy, which would be maintained for thirty years. The stringent security measures that cloaked the Army's signals intelligence organization, however, denied it the credit and stature it deserved. That the positions of chief of the Signal Security Agency and commander of the 2d Signal Service Battalion continued to be combined under one colonel throughout most of World War II indicates something of the nature of the problem. Col. Preston W. Corderman, who had commanded the agency since 1943, finally received a brigadier general's star in June 1945.[36]

The assumption of operational control over the Signal Security Agency by MIS in December 1944 made sense for both organizations. By this time, the agency had become the Army's most significant producer of high-grade intelligence. The Military Intelligence Service now had control of targeting and could rearrange operational priorities. In addition, the change benefited the Signal Security Agency. As long as the agency had been simply a part of the Signal

---

35 The OSS had originally used these stations to monitor Axis propaganda and news broadcasts.

36 A short account of the SSA's code-breaking activities in World War II can be found in SRH 349, Achievements of the Signal Security Agency in World War II, pp. 1–38.

Corps, its request for increased personnel allotments had to pass through the chief signal officer and the general commanding the Army Service Forces, neither of whom were indoctrinated for communications intelligence or knew the true importance of the agency's mission. Col. Alfred McCormack of MIS's Special Branch believed that this factor had delayed the breaking of Japanese codes by a year.[37] The new arrangement ended this anomaly. Although the chief signal officer still retained administrative control of the SSA, the action was a significant first step toward the postwar integration of all Army communications intelligence under G–2 control.

A second step soon followed, precipitated by the growing, if belated, collaboration between the Army and the Navy in the communications intelligence field. At one point the Army had maintained closer COMINT working relationships with the British than with the U.S. Navy. In February 1945 Admiral Ernest King, Commander in Chief, United States Fleet, and Chief of Naval Operations, agreed with Army Chief of Staff General George Marshall to create the Army-Navy Communications Intelligence Board (ANCIB) to direct a joint effort in this field. The board would report directly to the two service chiefs, not to the Joint Chiefs of Staff, and would use as its staff support the existing Army-Navy Communications Intelligence Coordinating Committee (ANCICC), a working-level group set up on an informal basis in early 1944 by the Signal Security Agency and its Navy opposite number, OP–20–G. However, the new head of the Military Intelligence Division, Maj. Gen. Clayton Bissell, vetoed the idea on the grounds that "the Army cannot participate on an inter-service project of this sort as long as its own signal intelligence efforts remain as decentralized as they now are."[38] The Navy, Bissell claimed, had a monolithic communications intelligence organization, while MID controlled only the Signal Security Agency.

Bissell's bureaucratic ploy spurred the deputy chief of staff and the all-powerful Operations Division into relooking at the entire structure of Army signals intelligence. In May 1945 the War Department requested that the three senior Army commanders engaged in the war against Japan—Lt. Gen. Albert J. Wedemeyer, commanding general of the China Theater, Lt. Gen. Daniel I. Sultan, commanding general of the Burma-India Theater, and General of the Army Douglas MacArthur, commanding general of Army Forces, Pacific—submit their views regarding the desirability of unifying the whole Army communications intelligence effort under a single War Department agency. Only MacArthur opposed the idea, and even he agreed that he had no objections once the fighting had stopped. The stage thus had been set for a postwar reorganization of signals intelligence.

---

37 SRH 141, pt. 2, pp. 221–22.

38 Memo, Maj Gen Clayton Bissell for Deputy Chief of Staff, 2 Mar 45, sub: Army Navy Communications Intelligence Board—Establishment of, Army Cryptologic Records.

Communications Security

The Signal Security Agency was shield as well as sword in World War II, since the agency had the duty of protecting Army communications in addition to exploiting those of other nations. Here, the agency's performance was smoother since much spade work had been done before Pearl Harbor. Army communications security had already been enhanced by the development of various kinds of cipher machines. The problem of distribution was overcome successfully. By mid-1942 the Army had replaced its older M134s and M134As with the M134C, more commonly known by its short title, SIGABA. Issued down to division level, the SIGABA served as the backbone of the Army's secure high-level communications throughout the war. The handy little M209, designed for use at lower command echelons, was in the hands of American troops before the first American landings in North Africa in November 1942.

Technological advances in this area continued throughout the war, expedited by the streamlining of the developmental process. Until early 1942 responsibilities in the area of communications security had been fragmented. The Signal Intelligence Service had worked out the cryptologic principles for the cipher devices, the Signal Corps Laboratories had prepared the engineering plans, and private firms had done the actual manufacturing. Wartime needs for greater security and compartmentation made this arrangement obsolete, and the Signal Security Agency was assigned all developmental work, introducing numerous innovations in the process. New crypto-communications devices produced by the Signal Security Agency allowed direct on-line encryption of teletype messages as well as speech. By June 1943 the agency had developed a secure telephone apparatus used for transatlantic conversations between Roosevelt and Churchill and later employed to link theater commanders with Washington. The SIGSALY, as it was called, afforded high security, although with the device weighing ninety tons, its use was obviously confined to major headquarters. Smaller voice "scrambler" devices offering less security were made available to lower echelons of command.

In addition to producing and distributing various types of cipher machines, the Signal Security Agency supplied the Army with huge quantities of codes, strip ciphers, and key lists. It also monitored military communications to guard against security violations and disguised major military movements by creating false patterns of message traffic. The multifaceted communications security (COMSEC) operation absorbed the efforts of a sizable portion of agency personnel.[39]

---

[39] SRH 349, Achievements of the Signal Security Agency, pp. 39–50. This document does not mention, however, that the Army suffered one major compromise and one near disaster in its cryptographic program. In early 1942 the Axis Powers read the coded messages of Col. Bonar Fellers, the Army attache assigned to Cairo. This provided them with an inside view of British preparations in North Africa. Kahn, *Kahn on Codes*, p. 105. In 1945 an unguarded truck that contained a SIGABA belonging to the 28th Infantry Division disappeared in France. An investigation disclosed that the farmer responsible for the theft had only been interested in the truck. Thomas M. Johnson, "Search for the Stolen SIGABA," *Army* 12 (February 1962): 50–55.

The Electronic Battlefield

In addition to its traditional cryptologic functions, the Signal Security Agency assumed new responsibilities in the fields of electronic warfare and electronic intelligence. After Pearl Harbor the Signal Corps had transferred its Air Warning Service radar companies to the control of the Army Air Forces, ultimately turning over all responsibilities in radar development to the air arm. However, the Signal Corps continued to exercise staff supervision over Army radio countermeasures and "radio or radar deception" through a newly formed Protective Security Branch, which was reassigned to the Signal Security Service at Arlington Hall in December 1942. The transfer was made for administrative convenience, in an attempt to sidestep the provisions of the same "Child Labor Law" that had forced the move of CIC headquarters to Baltimore. It seemed easier to relocate the unit than to replace its trained and specialized personnel. However, the Protective Security Branch remained semi-autonomous.

Although the initial concern of the Protective Security Branch was to protect the Army's own communications from enemy jamming, it began to consider a more positive role as the balance of the war started to shift. In June 1943 the branch laid down the first guidelines for the use of countermeasures in the field. Only theater commanders could authorize the use of radio or electronic countermeasures, although task force commanders might be delegated this authority when actually engaging the enemy. At the same time, Army Ground Forces fielded two provisional countermeasures detachments to provide support in the 1943 summer maneuvers. In practice, however, American forces did not attempt communications jamming to any extent in World War II, since it would risk interfering with the vital flow of communications intelligence. The Americans made one significant attempt to disrupt enemy communications circuits during the Ardennes campaign, using electronic jamming equipment mounted in aircraft to interfere with the radio transmissions from German tanks.[40]

In other areas, the activities of the Protective Security Branch were more fruitful. The branch supported the Signal Security Agency's communications security program by monitoring traffic patterns on the Army's radio teletype links to ensure that pending military operations would not be compromised by a sudden surge of message traffic between two points. Additionally, the branch played a role in Army radio deception operations, training personnel, procuring equipment, and providing technical data. The 3103d Signal Service Battalion, activated in December 1943 for deployment in the European Theater of Operations (ETO), could simulate the communications nets of large formations. It

---

[40] Alfred H. Price, *The History of U.S. Electronic Warfare*, vol. 1 (Westford, Mass.: Association of Old Crows, 1984), pp. 177–78.

played an important role in diverting the Germans from the real locations of American troop concentrations before the invasion of Normandy. A smaller deception unit, the 3153d Signal Service Company, went to the Pacific in 1944.[41]

The branch's activities in electronic intelligence and electronic countermeasures—jamming enemy radars—were of even greater future significance. The rapid developments of radar technology in World War II and the employment of radar by both Germany and Japan meant that the new device became both an important new intelligence target and an object suitable for electronic countermeasures. In this exotic war, the Protective Security Branch, along with the rest of the Army's ground elements, played only a small role. The civilian Radio Research Laboratory of the National Defense Council conducted the initial research on methods of blinding enemy radar. The Army Air Forces generated the requirements in this field, since the threat posed by the early-warning and gun-laying radars of the day was against aircraft. Similarly, the Army Air Forces initially employed the first radar jammers and engaged in the first electronic intelligence operations from aircraft.

However, there proved to be a role for ground-based electronic countermeasures also. Under the aegis of the Protective Security Branch, a provisional unit, the 1st Signal Service Platoon (Special) was organized at Arlington Hall in July 1943 to find and jam enemy radar and moved almost immediately to Amchitka in the Aleutians. Since the Army could find no Japanese radars in the area, the unit subsequently redeployed to the island of Corsica in the Mediterranean and operated against German targets. Additional specialized companies and detachments were formed later, operating mainly in the Pacific.[42] The Signal Security Agency continued to exercise staff supervision over such units until April 1945, when most of the functions of the Protective Security Branch were transferred to other Signal Corps agencies. It would take another decade for electronic warfare and electronic intelligence to be reintegrated into the Army's communications intelligence organization.

Summation

The institutional evolution of the Military Intelligence structure in the continental United States during the World War II was slow and painful. Many factors hindered this process: the low resource baseline from which it had to begin; misplaced priorities; rivalry between Regular Army officers and the elite group of civilians who eventually received commissions and managed much of the effort; and the historical accident that had placed the Army's most important

---

[41] Deception operations, along with radar countermeasures, are covered in Thompson and Harris, *The Signal Corps: The Outcome*, pp. 315–16.

[42] For a thorough discussion of electronic warfare in World War II, see Price, *The History of U.S. Electronic Warfare*. Operations in the Aleutians are discussed on page 134.

collection arm, the Signal Security Agency, under the control of the Signal Corps rather than the Military Intelligence Division. In retrospect, some of the effort seems to have been misspent. Both the countersubversive program and the early focus on developments in Latin America may have diverted needed assets from more urgent areas. And it is clear that without British help in the way of example and assistance, the system would not have attained whatever efficiency it did. In the estimate of one official historian, the War Department's intelligence apparatus did not become effective until late 1944. Even then, serious defects remained in the internal organization of the Military Intelligence Service and in the degree of interservice cooperation in the communications intelligence field. It was not until May 1945 that the War Department developed a mechanism for setting intelligence priorities. It is perhaps unsurprising that the evolution of Army collection capabilities in the field would reflect the same pattern of awkward and uneven development.

6

World War II
Intelligence in the Field

The Military Intelligence Service, the Signal Security Agency, and, for a time, the Counter Intelligence Corps were centrally directed organizations under the control of headquarters elements in the continental United States. However, the bulk of the Army's intelligence assets were in the field, at the disposal of commanders in the different theaters of operation established during the course of World War II. At the beginning of World War I, Brig. Gen. Joseph E. Kuhn had stated that intelligence was "as essential to modern armies as ammunition," and a second world conflict continued to demonstrate the truth of this dictum.[1] In all the various theaters there were certain uniformities of intelligence organization. Army officers served on combined intelligence staffs with various Allies. The theater signal intelligence service was operated on a compartmented basis separate from other intelligence activities, and assignment of intelligence and counterintelligence specialists to units was normally under centralized theater control. However, there were also differences in intelligence arrangements from theater to theater, depending on local conditions and circumstances.

In its allotment of campaign credits, the U.S. Army recognized the existence of only three great theaters of operation in World War II: the American, the Asiatic-Pacific, and the European–African–Middle Eastern. The actual command structure was more fragmented than this might suggest. During the course of World War II, major Army formations were committed to combat in four geographic areas: the Pacific Ocean Area (POA); the South West Pacific Area (SWPA); the European Theater of Operations (ETO); and the North African Theater of Operations (NATO), later redesignated the Mediterranean Theater of Operations (MTO). Paradoxically, U.S. Army contributions from an intelligence standpoint were greater in the Pacific area, but the European war had a larger impact on the ultimate organization of Army Intelligence. Most of American military resources in the field went into the fight against Germany, including the

---

1 Powe, *The Emergence of the War Department Intelligence Agency*, p. 84.

bulk of Military Intelligence assets. In addition, the nature of the language problem inherent in operations against the Japanese made Pacific requirements more specialized and less universal. The Army's focus on Europe and the relatively shorter distances between Washington and the field in this theater allowed lessons learned to translate rapidly into structural modifications.

Europe

The United States first entered the war in Europe as a junior partner. This was especially true in the field of intelligence, where Great Britain had developed extensive experience in field operations against the Axis, had a long tradition of successful intelligence operations, and had managed to break into the highest level of German communications with the help of its skilled cryptanalysts at Bletchley Park. British predominance in the communications intelligence field in Europe would continue throughout the war. The War Department was not apprised of the full dimensions of British success until mid-1943. The United States played no part in the exploitation of high-level German communications until 1944, when the Signal Intelligence Division of the European Theater of Operations, United States Army (ETOUSA), committed three American detachments in a War Department project to support the efforts of Bletchley Park.[2] Significantly, Eisenhower had a British G–2 in each of the theaters he successively commanded.[3]

From the intelligence perspective, the war in Europe was characterized by the gradual evolution of independent theater-level signal intelligence services, Military Intelligence services, and the institution of centralized control at the theater level over Army counterintelligence specialists. These developments took place at first in the Mediterranean and then in the European Theater of Operations.

When the Army entered World War II, it envisaged only two types of tactical signal intelligence units: radio intelligence platoons organic to the divisional signal companies and signal radio intelligence (SRI) companies assigned to field armies on a basis of one per army. The signal radio intelligence companies were quite sizable units, each with an assigned strength of slightly over 300 officers and men, internally divided into a headquarters platoon, an intercept platoon, a direction-finding platoon, and a wire platoon for communications. Neither of the two types had any analytical personnel. Analysis and translation were to be accomplished centrally by small radio intelligence staff elements at the theater and field army levels, as had been the case in World War I. These elements now reported to the chief signal officer,

---

2 A popular account of this effort is contained in Thomas Parrish, *The Ultra Americans: The U.S. Role in Breaking the Nazi Codes* (New York: Stein and Day, 1986).

3 Unfortunately, the memoirs of Eisenhower's G–2 were written before the release of the ULTRA secret. Maj. Gen. Sir Kenneth Strong, *Intelligence at the Top: Recollections of an Intelligence Officer* (New York: Doubleday, 1969).

not the G–2. The arrangement left the corps level without any dedicated communications intelligence support.[4]

The process of restructuring the Army's intelligence instruments began with the invasion of North Africa in 1942.The operation was launched with good intelligence—the British provided intensive support in this area, including furnishing the American high command with ULTRA-derived material. However, in the crunch of combat, American Intelligence organization was deemed less than adequate. The organization of Army tactical signal intelligence proved to be particularly deficient. The divisional platoons, in exposed locations near the front, were in too great a danger of being overrun to practice their specialty securely; the radio intelligence companies, as organized, were too large and too unwieldy to be used to support the corps, the command level most in need of such intelligence. Central processing proved to be impracticable, and the limited staffs available at the field army level to handle signals intelligence proved to be completely inadequate. At the same time, the communications practices of the European members of the Axis presented large volumes of material sent in clear or low-level codes that were susceptible to timely forward exploitation.[5]

In the initial stages of the North African campaign, the British bolstered the raw and badly organized American signals intelligence units with their own personnel. In early 1943 the U.S. Army deployed a theater signals intelligence service to North Africa. The 849th Signal Intelligence Service—the only such service to receive a numerical designation—was originally intended to function as a staff section, operating under the Signal Intelligence Division of Armed Forces Headquarters. Instead, in a hasty improvisation, it became a field unit. As the historian of the 849th SIS noted, "the unit set up in an isolated ravine in North Africa, without a telephone, a foot of field wire, a radio set, or a power unit, to mention only a few of the more obvious necessities."[6] Even toward the end of the war, the unit was handicapped by the ad hoc nature of its creation. A report deemed "the present organization . . . amorphous and unsatisfactory."[7]

Despite its organizational deficiencies, the 849th Signal Intelligence Service provided tactical signal intelligence units with the necessary analytical support. When the fighting moved to Italy, the problem of signal intelligence was solved by breaking the unwieldy signal radio intelligence companies into detachments and adding a small analytical element from the 849th SIS to each detachment to accomplish processing. Although this arrangement presented certain administrative complexities, since each element had a different parent headquarters, it

4 SRH 391, American Signal Intelligence in North Africa and Western Europe, pp. 6–7.

5 Memo, Col Harold G. Hayes, 1 Dec 43, sub: SIS: Lessons from North Africa, Army Cryptologic Records.

6 SRH 124, Operational History of the 849th Signal Intelligence Service, Mediterranean Theater of Operations, U.S. Army, p. 10.

7 Memo, Lt Col M. E. Rada for Colonel Shukraft, 27 Jan 45, sub: Reorganization of 849th Signal Intelligence Service, Army Cryptologic Records.

served to provide adequate communications intelligence to American ground and air forces. Later in the war, the Army Air Forces' own signals intelligence units took responsibility for the air dimension.

Combat experience in North Africa and the Mediterranean led to an over-haul of the entire structure of Army tactical signals intelligence in Europe. In 1943 the War Department gave the Signal Intelligence Division of ETOUSA operational control of all radio intelligence units in the theater. Further reforms followed. A revision of the divisional tables of organization and equipment (TOEs) in November 1943 eliminated the radio intelligence platoon from the divisional signal company, although it is not clear that this change was always implemented in the field. New tables provided for the incorporation of two radio intelligence platoons into the corps signal battalion.

This organizational concept was not especially happy, since it repeated the mis-take of lumping a small number of communications intelligence personnel with a larger unit performing an unrelated function, with all the security and operational disadvantages this entailed. In the Pacific, when this reorganization went into effect, a knowledgeable intelligence officer would find the corps-level radio intelli-gence platoon he observed "fatally handicapped by lack of information and plan-ning."[8] In the European theater, however, planners found a better solution. They devised a completely new type of communications intelligence unit to support the corps—a small signal service company with an organic cellular detachment of ana-lytical personnel. These companies, numbered in a sequence beginning with 3250, required less than half the personnel spaces allotted to the regular signal radio intelligence companies and were formed from in-theater resources.[9]

Meanwhile, the war's lessons and the Army Air Forces' wishes had led the War Department to authorize similarly self-contained units, designated "radio squadrons, mobile," to meet the special needs of the Army's air arm. These squadrons replaced the mix of signal radio intelligence companies, aviation, and monitoring platoons in signal service companies, aviation, which previously had supported the Army Air Forces. In addition to containing a large analytical sec-tion, the new squadrons could intercept both continuous wave (Morse code) and voice transmissions from dispersed locations.[10]

American forces in Great Britain were finally committed to the cross-Channel attack on 6 June 1944. Once fully deployed, they mustered an impres-

---

8 SRH 32, Reports by U.S. Army Ultra Representatives with Field Commands in the Southwest Pacific, Pacific Ocean, and China Burma India Theaters of Operations, 1944–1945, p. 69.

9 A description of the operations of the corps-level signal service companies can be found in SRH 42, Third Army Radio Intelligence History in Campaign of Western Europe. This develop-ment was alluded to, but not fully explained, in the official World War II Signal Corps history. See Thompson and Harris, The Signal Corps: The Outcome, pp. 22, 347.

10 AAF Manual 100–1, AAF Radio Squadrons Mobile (Washington, D.C.: Headquarters, Army Air Forces, 1944).

sive array of tactical signal intelligence units. Signal Security Detachment "D," a field element of the Signal Intelligence Division, ETOUSA, provided analytical support to the signal radio intelligence companies at the army-group and field-army levels, while AAF radio squadrons furnished signals intelligence to the numbered air forces. The signal service companies with their organic intelligence detachments operated in support of fourteen of the American corps that fought under Eisenhower. A similar type of unit was fielded in the Mediterranean Theater of Operations in 1945.

In theory, the signal radio intelligence companies were designed to fill the Army's communications security needs, as well as to provide signal intelligence. A section within the headquarters platoon of each company was allotted for communications monitoring. In practice, however, this function usually was neglected because of the press of more urgent duties. As a partial solution, the commander of Army forces in the Mediterranean area suggested that the Army develop a TOE for a new type of unit that could carry out a signal information and monitoring (SIAM) mission. Two such units were ultimately formed from Army assets in the Mediterranean: the 3151st Signal Information and Monitoring Company, which was assigned to the U.S. Seventh Army to support the invasion of Southern France, and the 3326th SIAM Company, which operated in support of the U.S. Fifth Army in Italy. These large units, each containing about 500 men, monitored Army communications for the dual purpose of checking for security violations and tracking the positions of the friendly units themselves. Under the fast-moving conditions of mobile warfare in Europe, normal command channels often operated too slowly, making such byproducts a useful tool for the field commander.[11]

Army counterintelligence organization in the field was also shaped by lessons learned in combat in North Africa and the Mediterranean. The first group of counterintelligence agents to be deployed had been a 71-man-strong detachment that accompanied the Western Task Force in the invasion of North Africa. Lacking in combat training, scattered in small sections over wide areas, and confronted by unsympathetic G–2s ignorant of the functions of the Counter Intelligence Corps, this initial element encountered many operational difficulties. However, under combat conditions, Counter Intelligence Corps personnel slowly resolved the initial problems. For example, new agents were trained in field security duties as well as in investigative functions. By mid-1943, with operations on Italian soil about to commence, all CIC agents in the theater were placed under the centralized administrative control of Counter Intelligence Corps, North African Theater of Operations, United States Army (NATOUSA). Also, a theater TOE had been developed, calling for 6-man divisional detachments and 13-man detachments at the corps level. Similar arrangements were introduced in the European Theater of Operations.

---

[11] Thompson and Harris, *The Signal Corps: The Outcome*, pp. 37–38, 65–67.

Some problems remained unsolved. Counter Intelligence Corps personnel were still controlled from Washington as part of the Military Intelligence Service. Although the rationale for this arrangement was Washington's fear that highly specialized counterintelligence assets otherwise might be misused, administration from 3,000 miles away created enormous problems. The arrangement slowed promotion in the field, and the CIC came to be nicknamed the "Corps of Indignant Corporals."[12] The attempt to run the Counter Intelligence Corps from offices in Washington also hampered local efforts to make timely adjustments in organization and doctrine based on field experience. The 6-man divisional detachments authorized in the Mediterranean area were obviously inadequate, since under combat conditions some CIC personnel needed to stay behind to provide continuity of coverage, while others advanced with their units. Moreover, the War Department tables of basic allowances (TBAs), under which detachments functioned, proved to be impracticable. Although CIC units were allotted equipment for performing the most elaborate investigations, they lacked adequate transportation.

Ultimately, these problems also were resolved. Counter Intelligence Corps personnel in the Mediterranean theater passed to local control in November 1943, and their counterparts in the United Kingdom made the same transition in April 1944. In January 1944 a new organizational table restructured Counter Intelligence Corps detachments along cellular lines, allowing units to be tailored to meet the requirements of varying echelons of command. In the ETO this resulted in the creation of a 17-man divisional CIC detachment composed of an administrative team and two operational teams. Larger counterintelligence detachments were attached to higher tactical echelons and to rear area service organizations. Finally, a more realistic allowance of equipment was secured, allocating a jeep to every two counterintelligence agents and giving the CIC the mobility it needed in a combat environment.

The problem of logically identifying CIC detachments was resolved in August 1944, when separate sequences of numbers were allotted to detachments serving with various levels and types of commands. Detachments serving with infantry and airborne divisions were given the numbers of their corresponding divisional organization: the 200 series was reserved for detachments serving with corps, the 300 series for those attached to field armies, the 400 series for CIC units attached to the theaters, the 500 series for detachments serving with armored divisions, and the 600 and 700 series for Counter Intelligence Corps elements attached to major formations of the Army Air Forces.

Intelligence specialists overseas not affiliated with the Counter Intelligence Corps were eventually organized under separate theater-level Military Intelligence services. These organizations evolved gradually. In the case of the

---

12 History of the Counter Intelligence Corps, vol. 2, U.S. Army Intelligence Center, 1959, p. 87.

European Theater of Operations, the first non-CIC intelligence organizations to deploy in England were forward elements of MIS–X and MIS–Y: specialized sections of the War Department's Military Intelligence Service that were tasked respectively with assisting the escape attempts of downed American fliers and interrogating captured enemy personnel in depth. In April 1943 both elements were merged into a Military Intelligence Service detachment under theater control. With the arrival of additional diverse intelligence units, such as Military Intelligence specialist teams, censors, topographic and photographic intelligence personnel, and a training team, all field agencies except counterintelligence detachments were folded into the integrated, theater-level Military Intelligence Service, European Theater of Operations, in August 1943.

Intelligence specialists in the field operated in four types of teams during World War II: interrogation, interpreter, photo interpreter, and order of battle. In the European Theater of Operations, the first three types were allotted two officers and four enlisted men; order of battle teams had a single officer and two enlisted men. The Military Intelligence Service, European Theater of Operations, attached two prisoner interrogation teams and one of each of the other three types to each division, where they operated under the control of the divisional G–2. Larger numbers of teams were allotted to higher formations, and groups of teams at this level were sometimes formed into detachments with attached administrative personnel. Although the individual teams were small, the number of intelligence personnel assigned to them was considerable. The European Theater of Operations had 3,500 officers and men organized into specialist teams, not counting Military Intelligence personnel assigned to headquarters elements and to censorship duties.[13]

The collection of technical intelligence was not the responsibility of the theater-level Military Intelligence Service, but of "enemy equipment intelligence services" directed by the individual technical services. Technical intelligence personnel operated in teams at the field army level. Teams varied in size—the Signal Corps collection unit, for example, consisted of five officers and six enlisted men.[14] The efforts of the individual technical services in the field were supplemented by those of other organizations. The Army was represented on the Combined Intelligence Objectives Subcommittee, an element under the control of the Combined Chiefs of Staff which fielded joint United States–British, military-civilian teams to investigate scientific targets. The Army also played a leading role in the specialized mission, code named ALSOS, set up

---

13 The activities of Military Intelligence Service specialist teams in Europe are discussed in detail in U.S. Forces, European Theater, *Report of the General Board*, Study no. 12, *The Military Intelligence Service in the European Theater of Operations* (U.S. Forces, European Theater, 1946). Brig. Gen. Oscar Koch, Patton's G–2, recalled that "each division had at least fifty auxiliary intelligence specialist personnel attached in the form of teams." Koch, *G–2, Intelligence for Patton* (Philadelphia: Whitmore, 1971), p. 131.

14 Thompson and Harris, *The Signal Corps: The Outcome*, pp 165–66, 521.

at the instigation of the director of the Manhattan Project to look for evidence of German atomic research.15

In the war against Germany, technical intelligence teams often combined with other intelligence and counterintelligence personnel in ad hoc task forces to exploit newly liberated areas of intelligence interest. In Italy, "S Force" gave coverage to liberated Rome; "T Force" performed similar operations in France and Germany. These elements reached formidable size: the "T Force" that entered Paris contained representatives from seventeen different Allied intelligence elements and had a strength of 1,800, although most were administrative and security personnel.

Topographic intelligence was another specialized case. During World War I, the American Expeditionary Forces in France had placed this function within the G–2 section. In World War II theaters of operation, the function reverted to the Chief of Engineers, who maintained an Engineer Intelligence office. Mobile Engineer topographic battalions, relying on aerial photography, prepared maps. Field armies usually had a topographic engineering battalion, and a topographic Engineer company was assigned to each corps.16

For positive collection operations in the MTO and ETO, the Army relied on the Office of Strategic Services (OSS), the independent intelligence and special operations organization under the direct control of the Joint Chiefs of Staff. Although at the departmental level considerable rivalry existed between the OSS and the MID, Army commanders in Europe found the OSS a useful organization. In fact, Army personnel provided the bulk of OSS strength. In May 1944 friction in the European Theater of Operations was further eased when OSS and its British counterparts were directly subordinated to the theater commander under the newly created Headquarters, Special Troops, Supreme Headquarters, Allied Expeditionary Force. Members of OSS field units engaged both in collection and in special operations. Support was provided to Army units down to the division level. In addition, the X–2 Branch of OSS deployed small counterintelligence detachments. These detachments, which had access to selected ULTRA information, did not engage in active field operations, but provided CIC detachments information on enemy agents obtained at Bletchley Park.17

During World War I, the AEF's G–2 had been responsible for both propaganda operations and deception. This arrangement was not repeated in World War II. Eisenhower ran limited psychological warfare operations using pam-

---

15 The leader of this mission, Boris Pash, has provided a detailed account of the quest for a nonexistent Aryan atom bomb in *The Alsos Mission* (New York: Award House, 1969).

16 For engineer intelligence at the theater level, see *Engineers of the Southwest Pacific*, vol. 3, *Engineer Intelligence* (Washington, D.C.: Government Printing Office, 1950), p. 6.

17 OSS support for Army operations in World War II is described in Bradley F. Smith, *The Shadow Warriors: OSS and the Origins of the CIA* (New York: Basic Books, 1973), p. 203, and in Rhodre Jeffreys-Jones, *The CIA and American Democracy* (New Haven: Yale University Press, 1989), p. 307.

phlets and loudspeaker units through a special staff section, not through his intelligence staff. Planning the extensive deception operations that shrouded the time and place of the Allied landings was a British monopoly, carried out by the London Controlling Section. However, the U.S. Army deployed specialized units to support such operations in Europe, including Signal Corps elements and the 23d Headquarters, Special Troops, a composite unit that used rubber tanks, noise-making equipment, and dummy communications nets to simulate an armored division.

The Pacific

In the Pacific, Army Intelligence was structured a little differently. In the Pacific Ocean Area—the vast oceanic operational theater commanded by Admiral Chester W. Nimitz—the Army served as an adjunct to the Navy and the Marine Corps, and intelligence work was largely a naval preserve. However, an Army officer eventually did serve as J–2 controlling the Joint Intelligence Center, Pacific Ocean Area (JICPOA); Army topographic engineer companies provided JICPOA with mapping support; and two SRI companies were ultimately deployed.[18] In addition, toward the end of the war, a joint Army-Navy COMINT exploitation center, RAGFOR—for Radio Group, Forward—was set up on recaptured Guam to attack Japanese Army and Navy air-ground traffic, using the Army Air Forces' 8th Radio Squadron, Mobile, as its intercept arm.[19] This unit included Nisei interpreters. Military Intelligence interpreter, interrogator, and translator teams attached to Army divisions in the Pacific seem to have consisted of four, rather than six, persons.[20]

The major Army presence in the war against Japan was located in the South West Pacific Area, a theater that opened up when General Douglas MacArthur regrouped his forces in Australia following the American defeat in the Philippines. Here, organizational arrangements differed strikingly from those prevailing in the trans-Atlantic theaters. The creation of the SWPA committed the United States to the defense of beleaguered Australia. Significantly, the theater was directly subordinated to the U.S. Joint Chiefs of Staff, not to the Anglo-American Combined Chiefs of Staff. The objective situation, coupled with

---

[18] Capt. Jasper W. Holmes served as chief of JICPOA and describes the organization in *Double-Edged Secrets: U.S. Naval Intelligence Operations in the Pacific During World War II* (Annapolis, Md.: Naval Institute Press, 1979).

[19] SRH 133, Report of Mission to Hawaii and Marianas to Study Security of 21st Bomber Command Communications, MIS, WDGS, March 1945, pp. 23–25.

[20] Chandler and Robb, *Front-Line Intelligence*, p. 157. In September 1944 the TOEs for such linguist units were revised to call for four-man, rather than six-man, teams. War Department, Military Intelligence Service, History of Military Intelligence Training at Camp Ritchie, Maryland, 19 June 1942–1 January 1945, pp. 65–66, copy in INSCOM History Office files. However, the change was not implemented in the European theater. The Military Intelligence Language School at Camp Savage, not Camp Ritchie, provided linguist teams in the Pacific.

MacArthur's autocratic proclivities, allowed him to set up a U.S. Army staff to direct theater operations. At the same time, only limited American military assets were available initially. These considerations exerted strong pressure on the organization of intelligence in the theater. In contrast to the situation in Europe, U.S. Army Intelligence personnel in the SWPA were integrated into combined organizations under the direction of an American G–2, Brig. Gen. Charles Willoughby.21

In the spring of 1942 MacArthur set up a centralized cryptologic agency, Central Bureau, Brisbane (CBB). Headed by MacArthur's chief signal officer, Brig. Gen. Spencer Akin, a former chief of the Signal Intelligence Service, CBB was jointly manned by personnel of the U.S. Army and the Royal Australian Army and Air Force. The American component consisted at first of two officers and a few intercept operators drawn from a detachment of the 2d Signal Service Company on Corregidor, later reinforced by a signal service detachment furnished by Arlington Hall. The latter detachment included Col. Abraham Sinkov, one of the four men Friedman had initially recruited for the Signal Intelligence Service.

Thus, from the beginning Army Intelligence personnel in the Pacific were part of a high-level processing center that eventually broke Japanese military codes and thus generated ULTRA. Despite its name, CBB was not a static organization; an advance echelon of the Central Bureau accompanied MacArthur's GHQ in successive forward deployments, and by July 1945 almost the whole organization had been moved to San Miguel on the Philippine island of Luzon. By the end of the war, the Central Bureau had 1,500 personnel, more than half of them American, had acquired batteries of IBM machines, and was directing the collection efforts of four American signal radio intelligence companies and some ten equivalent British Commonwealth units.22 In addition to this theater-level communications intelligence effort, an Army Air Forces radio squadron, mobile, operated in support of each of the two separate numbered American air forces assigned to the theater, and at least some tactical elements appear to have had their own radio intelligence platoons.

At the tactical level, communications intelligence was carried out in the South West Pacific Area under field conditions that differed significantly from those in Europe. Although the signal radio intelligence companies frequently operated in detachments, there was less requirement for analytical personnel to

---

21 The achievements of MacArthur's intelligence organization are documented (and glorified) in *Operations of the Military Intelligence Section, GHQ, SWPA/FEC/SCAP*, 10 vols. (Far East Command, 1948).

22 Discussion of Central Bureau Brisbane was inhibited for many years by the fact that the organization's host government preferred not to have the subject discussed. However, a photographic history of the American contribution was published shortly after the war. Curiously, the organization even was named somewhat inaccurately. It was hardly central—the naval communications intelligence effort was run on a completely separate basis—and it soon left Brisbane. One of the few open-source publications to mention it is D. M. Horner, *High Command: Australia and Allied Strategy, 1939–1945* (Sydney: George Allen and Unwin, 1982), pp. 224–46.

be decentralized at unit level in the Pacific, since Japanese low-grade systems "were practically nonexistent."23 Furthermore, because of the vast distances in the Pacific, field sections were seldom close enough to the enemy to pick up low-powered tactical circuits.

The Central Bureau, Brisbane, was a purely cryptologic organization. A separate multinational organization, esoterically designated Section 22, General Headquarters, SWPA, was set up under Akin in 1943 to collect electronic intelligence on the rapidly increasing number of Japanese radar sets deployed in the theater. Section 22 differed from CBB in that it included representatives of the Navy and Marine Corps, as well as Signal Corps, Army Air Forces, and foreign personnel.

Other intelligence activities in the Pacific were also conducted on a multinational basis. The Allied Geographic Service provided topographic information on this little-mapped theater, while the Allied Translator and Interpreter Service (ATIS) blended Australian and American intelligence personnel into an integrated structure. Here, the nature of the target played a large part in the selection of personnel and in the approach to intelligence collection. Most of the 2,000 Americans who served in ATIS were Nisei, second-generation Japanese Americans. Because few soldiers of the Imperial Army surrendered, the emphasis was mostly on translation of documents written in the complex and polyalphabetic Japanese language. In Europe, three times as many interrogators as translators were needed. In the Far East, the ratio was reversed.24

Human intelligence collection operations in the SWPA came under the direction of the Allied Intelligence Bureau (AIB), because MacArthur barred the Office of Strategic Services from the theater. In addition to employing a network of stay-behind Australian coast-watchers to monitor Japanese shipping, the Allied Intelligence Bureau engaged in extensive penetration operations.25 U.S. Army efforts in this field focused on the Philippine Islands where guerrillas already engaged in resisting the Japanese provided useful intelligence assets. To better exploit this resource, MacArthur fielded a special reconnaissance element largely manned by Filipinos recruited in the United States. This unit, the 1st Reconnaissance Battalion (Special), and its attached 978th Signal Service Company inserted radio-equipped teams by submarine into the islands to link with the guerrillas and collect intelligence.

Not all Army Intelligence assets in the Southwest Pacific Area, however, were integrated into combined operations. The U.S. Army ran its own counterintelligence operations, which were controlled by the G–2 of U.S. Army Forces, Far East

---

23 SRH 169, p. 47.

24 Col. Sidney F. Mashbir headed the Allied Translator and Interpreter Service. An account of its operations can be found in Mashbir's rather melodramatically entitled book, *I Was an American Spy* (New York: Vantage, 1953).

25 Col. Allison Ind, who headed the bureau, also wrote a book, *Allied Intelligence Bureau: Our Secret Weapon in the War Against Japan* (New York: McKay, 1958).

(USAFFE), the base command responsible for the administration and supply of Army elements in the SWPA. Due to difficulties in securing counterintelligence agents from the United States, because of the enormous distances that separated Australia from the North American continent, a CIC school under theater control was set up to procure and train counterintelligence personnel. After August 1944 Brig. Gen. Elliot Thorpe, the G–2, U.S. Army Forces, Far East, exercised control over thirty-nine CIC detachments scattered around the Pacific through the theater-level 441st Counter Intelligence Corps Detachment. Divisional detachments in the Southwest Pacific Area were smaller than in the European Theater of Operations, but were augmented by Filipino linguists once the fighting reached the Philippine Islands. Although counterintelligence was clearly a national responsibility—the Counter Intelligence Corps in Europe reported to G–2, European Theater of Operations, U.S. Army, not to G–2, Supreme Headquarters, Allied Expeditionary Force—the fact that Willoughby lacked control over counterintelligence produced much bureaucratic friction.[26] Interestingly enough, when all Army troops in the Pacific were placed under MacArthur's control through the creation of U.S. Army Forces, Pacific (AFPAC), in April 1945, counterintelligence operations were again allotted to a special staff section, not to G–2.

U.S. Army tactical elements in the theater operated under separate American command after the end of 1942 and were supported by their own intelligence structure. However, interrogators and document translators were provided by advance echelons of ATIS. Optimally, two officers and ten men would be assigned to a division. In April 1945 separate language detachments, numbered in the 100 series, were activated from ATIS assets. In August the system was bolstered by fifteen headquarters elements dispatched from the Military Intelligence Training Center at Fort Ritchie. These received designations as numbered intelligence service organizations.[27]

Army Intelligence assets in the South West Pacific Area also included an elite reconnaissance force, the ALAMO Scouts. This provisional unit was used to conduct the type of long-range operations that the OSS conducted in Europe. Small parties of scouts were landed by submarine and flying boat on remote

---

26 The antagonism between the SWPA G–2, Maj. Gen. Charles Willoughby, and the USAFFE G–2, Brig. Gen. Elliott Thorpe, continued to be nourished after the war ended. The Willoughby-sponsored official intelligence history of Far East Command claimed that counterintelligence arrangements were "contrary to staff manuals and ultimately led to friction, overlap, duplication, and general inefficiency." *Operations of the Military Intelligence Section, GHQ, SWPA/FEC/SCAP*, vol. 3, *Intelligence Series* (I) (Far East Command, General Headquarters [GHQ], Military Intelligence Service, General Staff, 1948), p. 14. Thorpe, in his own book, *East Wind, Rain: The Intimate Account of an Intelligence Officer in the Pacific* (Boston: Gambit, 1969), is more reticent. One CIC agent assigned to SWPA has written personal reminiscences. See William A. Owens, *Eye-Deep in Hell: A Memoir of the Liberation of the Philippines, 1944–1945* (Dallas: Southern Methodist University Press, 1990).

27 *Operations of the Allied Translator and Interpreter Section, GHQ, SWPA*, vol. 5, *Intelligence Series* (Far East Command, GHQ, Military Intelligence Service, General Staff, 1948), pp. 27–28.

islands, both to gather intelligence and to engage in special operations. The unit derived its name from ALAMO Force, which controlled all American tactical units in the SWPA until September 1944, when it was replaced by the Sixth Army.28 Technical intelligence for the Army was collected by the 5250th Technical Intelligence Composite Company (Provisional), a unique unit commanded by a colonel and formed from intelligence personnel of six Army technical services in the South West Pacific Area.29

Common Collectors

In all of the worldwide theaters, Army tactical units also played a role in the Military Intelligence process. The S–2 of each maneuver battalion had an intelligence section of 1 sergeant and 6 other soldiers, while the staff of the division G–2 was comprised of 2 officer assistants and 9 enlisted personnel. For reconnaissance purposes, each infantry and armored regiment had an intelligence and reconnaissance platoon. At the division level, a reconnaissance troop was organic to each infantry division, and each armored division had its own reconnaissance squadron.30 Groups of mechanized cavalry were available to higher echelons of command; however, in practice these units were usually employed as combat elements in a screening role, rather than as intelligence collectors. At the corps level, the field artillery observation battalion also provided some incidental intelligence input.

Ground reconnaissance assets were not the only collection elements available. One major source of intelligence was provided by the L–4 "Grasshopper" light aircraft, organic to all divisions and artillery groups. These planes were first introduced in 1942, when it became clear that the semi-autonomous Army Air Forces, which had prime responsibility for both photographic and visual observation, intended to implement its mission in ways that scanted the priorities of the ground forces. The ten light aircraft assigned to each infantry division were used primarily for artillery spotting, but, at least in the European theater, they flew 30 percent of their missions for general intelligence support.31

---

28 An excellent article on the Alamo Scouts is Les Hughes, "The Alamo Scouts," *Trading Post* 45 (April–June 1986): 2–16.

29 Marc B. Powe and Edward E. Wilson, *The Evolution of American Military Intelligence* (Fort Huachuca, Ariz.: U.S. Army Intelligence Center and School, 1973), p. 76.

30 Chandler and Robb, *Front-Line Intelligence*, pp. 35, 83, 87. The reconnaissance troops were sometimes known as "tincan cavalry," and were often diverted to nonintelligence functions.

31 *Report of the General Board*, Study no. 20, *Liaison Aircraft with Ground Forces Units* (U.S. Forces, European Theater, 1946). The Army Air Forces observation squadrons and groups previously assigned to Army tactical units were resubordinated to AAF Air-Ground Support Commands in 1941; concurrently, it became all too apparent from the experience of the other warring air forces that existing observation aircraft could not survive in a combat environment. Ultimately, the "observation" mission was subsumed into reconnaissance, and carried out by stripped-down converted fighters and bombers assigned to the AAF's tactical air commands. Futrell, *Command of Observation Aviation*, pp. 6–29.

Conclusion

Several points in the field organization of Army Intelligence during World War II are notable. At the tactical support level, the Army organized Intelligence into a multitude of single-discipline teams and detachments. Intelligence work was still largely thought of as a staff function, not a line function, and intelligence specialist teams were attached to tactical formations to assist the G–2 staff.[32] This approach was reflected in unit structure. Signals intelligence, a specialized case, was carried out by company-size Signal Corps units and by the Signal Security Agency's single oversized battalion. In the other intelligence disciplines, there were no units larger than detachments or teams, apart from the provisional technical intelligence company that operated in the South West Pacific Area and a one-of-a-kind provisional 1st Combat Intelligence Platoon at Fort Richardson, Alaska.

As the war went on, the Army made some attempts to introduce higher-level organizational structures. To improve command and control of intelligence work in the field, by 1945 the Military Intelligence Training Center had activated twenty-six three-man military intelligence headquarters detachments, each capable of coordinating the efforts of several intelligence specialist teams. The compartmented work and reporting channels of signals intelligence also produced a more hierarchical form of organization. Such measures were, however, exceptional.

During the war, some commanders questioned the prevailing organizational concepts. Lt. Col. H. Gordon Sheen, who had served as the first chief of the CIC, proposed that intelligence battalions be formed from Army-level troops and attached down to corps level as needed. He envisioned an integrated multi-discipline battalion, consisting of a headquarters and headquarters company, a counterintelligence company, an engineer topographic company, a prisoner-of-war interrogation company, and a radio intelligence company.[33] However, Sheen was ahead of his time. It would take a dozen more years to integrate even counterintelligence and positive collection functions into a single unit, and much longer before signals intelligence could be brought under the same umbrella as the other intelligence disciplines.

Whatever deficiencies existed in the organization of Army Intelligence, it had at least performed well enough to help bring about victory in World War II. On 9 May 1945, Nazi Germany unconditionally surrendered to Allied forces. Japan followed suit on 14 August. The United States had fully achieved all its military objectives. However, victory did not bring security. As an

---

32 "It may be said that the general organizational plan of intelligence forces in the Army is designed to locate the G–2 section or its counterpart, as a 'staff' unit rather than a 'line' unit." History of Military Intelligence Training at Camp Ritchie, p. 15.

33 History of the Counterintelligence Corps, vol. 11, U.S. Army Intelligence Center, 1959, p. 62.

inevitable result of the destruction of German power in Central Europe, the forces of the Soviet Union had extended their influence deep into Europe. And the USSR, a totalitarian society committed to a messianic ideology, would prove to be as great a danger to the stability of the world order as had the Axis. The war had produced a quantum advance in technical progress, but the most ingenious of the new devices—the atomic bomb which the United States had invented and employed—in the long run threatened civilization itself. It was now the task of the U.S. Army and its Intelligence component to help keep the uncertain peace.

7

The Cold War and Korea

Euphoria over the American victory in World War II was short lived. It became apparent that the destruction of the Axis Powers had only created a power vacuum into which another totalitarian state, the Soviet Union, steadily and inexorably moved. The United Nations, created to guide a lasting peace, soon appeared to be a hollow shell, its Security Council paralyzed by Russian vetoes. Confronted by Soviet repression in Eastern Europe and Communist subversion in the West, the United States slowly moved to meet the new challenge. In this Cold War between East and West, at first the weapons were economic and diplomatic. The United States succored hard-pressed Greece and Turkey with military and economic aid in 1947, then moved to restore the destroyed economy of Western Europe with the Marshall Plan in 1948. A Soviet blockade of the Western zones in Berlin was countered by a massive airlift. Finally, the United States abandoned two centuries of tradition and joined in a peacetime military alliance with the European democracies when it became a member of the North Atlantic Treaty Organization (NATO) in 1949.

However, the threatening international scene was not reflected in America's military posture. The vast armies fielded in World War II had been demobilized quickly. Once the draft came to an end in 1947, the Army shrank to a strength of 550,000. Much of this force was tied down in occupation duty, with four skeleton divisions in Japan, two for a time in Korea, and another in Germany. In the summer of 1948 Congress renewed Selective Service, spurring recruitment and allowing a slight buildup of Army strength to about 600,000. Many Americans hoped that the American monopoly of the atomic bomb would preserve the peace. But the Soviets demolished this assumption in 1949 by exploding a nuclear device of their own. Meanwhile, stability in the Far East was deteriorating. By 1949 Communist Chinese armies had brought all of mainland China under the red flag. The United States had withdrawn its occupation troops from South Korea, and a Communist government in the North now stared balefully across the 38th Parallel at its democratic neighbor to the South. In June 1950 it marched across the border. In response, an unready America was drawn into a new war.

The shock of the Korean War—and the subsequent Chinese Communist intervention—transformed American national security policy. The Army grew to 1.5 million men, organized into twenty active divisions. Large forces were deployed not only on the Korean peninsula, but also on the continent of Europe. At the time, American leaders feared that the Korean attack might be an attempt to divert the West from a possible Soviet onslaught against the West European democracies. Originally, NATO had been a paper alliance; now it was backed up by American steel.[1] For a whole generation, American soldiers would man many of the lines first established in both Asia and Europe during the early 1950s. And Army Intelligence, initially reeling from two major surprises (the initial Korean attack and the later Chinese offensive) was ultimately revitalized.

Restructuring Military Intelligence

In the aftermath of World War II, Army Intelligence was affected not only by the massive postwar contraction of military strength, but by sustained organizational turbulence. This was brought about by two conflicting types of pressure. Some policy makers simply wanted to return to prewar conditions, dismissing wartime expedients as aberrations caused by a never-to-be-repeated crisis. Others attempted to make use of the lessons learned in World War II to create a better structure. As a result, much of the Military Intelligence architecture with which the country had fought World War II was dismantled and intelligence assets placed in new configurations.

During World War II, control of communications intelligence collection assets had been split between the Signal Security Agency and the theater commanders. This arrangement had created significant problems, since it was impossible to neatly separate the tactical aspects of communications intelligence from the strategic ones.[2] Even before the fighting had ended, the Army had decided to entrust exploitation of the electronic communications spectrum to a single agency. On 15 September 1945, the Signal Security Agency was separated from the Signal Corps and became the Army Security Agency (ASA), assuming command of "all signals intelligence and security establishments, units, and personnel" of the Army.[3] The new agency, which continued to function under direct control by the Army G–2 in Washington, inherited the mission, functions, and assets of its wartime predecessor and took over the communications intelligence and communications security resources previously at the disposal of theater and Air Force commanders. In addition to unifying the Army's cryptologic structure, the formation of the Army Security Agency also marked a brief

---

[1] A broad overview of U.S. defense policy during this period is provided in Doris M. Condit, *History of the Office of the Secretary of Defense, Volume II: The Test of War, 1950–1953* (Washington, D.C.: Historical Office of the Secretary of Defense, 1988).

[2] SRH 169, p. 59.

[3] Ibid., p. 85.

reversal in the tendency towards increased autonomy for the Army Air Forces in this field, since the AAF's radio squadrons, mobile, and other cryptologic assets were resubordinated to the agency.

Army counterintelligence organization also underwent a substantial restructuring. By the time World War II ended, the Counter Intelligence Corps and the Security Intelligence Corps formed in 1944 had both been placed under the Army Service Forces' director of Intelligence. Agents of both organizations now received the same training and operated under the same regulations. Under these new conditions it was obviously pointless to maintain two parallel counterintelligence elements. Accordingly, in April 1946 the Security Intelligence Corps was merged with the Counter Intelligence Corps. In May numbered CIC detachments were constituted to operate in support of each of the nine service commands and the separate Military District of Washington (MDW). These detachments were assigned numbers in a sequence running from 107 to 116.

President Harry S. Truman presented a different kind of organizational challenge to the Army when he abolished the wartime Office of Strategic Services on 1 October 1945. The assets of the OSS were divided: analytic personnel were shipped off to the State Department, but the bulk of the organization, consisting of military personnel trained in clandestine collection, counterintelligence, covert action, and black propaganda, combined into the new Strategic Services Unit under the War Department. However, the organization was not assigned to G–2, but to the Office of the Assistant Secretary of War, which created an anomalous situation.

The existence of the Strategic Services Unit forced a reexamination of the entire national intelligence structure, a task which the Lovett Board assumed at the end of 1945. An executive order early in 1946 established a new Central Intelligence Group, a rudimentary national-level intelligence agency. This prototype central intelligence agency was at first merely a cooperative interdepartmental activity that depended on the armed services and the State Department for its staff, budget, and facilities. However, it did serve as a holding area to dispose of what remained of the Strategic Services Unit, most of whose members were slated for demobilization with the rest of the Army.[4] Nevertheless, in 1946 a vestigial undercover capability still remained at the disposal of the U.S. intelligence community.

A further step in the immediate postwar reorganization of U.S. Army Intelligence came about in May 1946 when the Army did away with its wartime structure. Not unexpectedly, the reorganization gave greater power to the traditional Army Staff and to the heads of the old-line technical services. One important result of the post–World War II Army reorganization was that MID, now redesignated the Intelligence Division, was restored to its prewar status as one of five equal functional divisions on the War Department General Staff. Now

---

[4] Bradley F. Smith doubts that the SSU ever exceeded 750 people. *The Shadow Warriors,* p. 408.

headed by a director of Intelligence, the division was specifically intended to serve as an operating agency as well as an element engaged in intelligence planning and staff supervision. Fortunately for all parties involved, the Intelligence Division had already relinquished the task of preparing the Army's official histories, which it had taken on in World War II. The Intelligence Division's resumption of operating functions led to the abolition of the separate Military Intelligence Service.[5] In addition, the discontinuance of the Army Service Forces at this time resulted in the Counter Intelligence Corps' once more falling under the control of the War Department's Intelligence Division.

The Intelligence Division now set intelligence requirements for the Army, supervised collection, conducted evaluation, produced finished intelligence, and disseminated this information throughout the Army. Compartmented intelligence continued to be channeled through the Special Security System created in World War II. In November 1946 two separate detachments, both sharing a common commander, were set up within the division to manage the various Special Security Offices (SSOs). Detachment F supervised those at three locations in the continental United States; Detachment M directed a more extensive network overseas.

The Intelligence Division focused on the global requirements imposed by the rapidly deepening Cold War between the West and the Soviet Union. It had not only Army-wide intelligence taskings, but was responsible as well for satisfying national needs for political and economic intelligence. The 1946 reorganization placed the Intelligence Division and its director at an apogee of institutional power. The director of Intelligence had sole authority over the Army assets he needed to discharge his responsibilities. In addition to the internal resources which he controlled directly, he wielded influence in the management oversight of the Central Intelligence Group through his membership on the National Intelligence Board. The director also served on the board that governed national signals intelligence policy.

Almost immediately, however, the scope and autonomy of the Intelligence Division and its director came under attack. There were already conflicts in jurisdiction between the Intelligence Division and the intelligence arm of the now practically autonomous Army Air Forces. It was obvious that the pending creation of a separate Air Force, a process well under way by 1946, would result in the transfer of the air-oriented portions of Army Intelligence to the new service. There were other kinds of pressures at work. Many believed that lack of coordination between Army and Navy Intelligence had helped to bring about the disaster of Pearl Harbor. With tensions between the United States and Russia growing visibly, there was a demand to create a national-level intelligence

---

5 James A. Hewes, *From Root to McNamara: Army Organization and Administration, 1900–1963* (Washington, D.C.: U.S. Army Center of Military History, 1975), p. 160, mistakenly indicates that MIS was redesignated as the Army Security Agency.

body with greater powers than the Central Intelligence Group to coordinate the activities of the service intelligence components and to specialize in gathering political and economic intelligence.[6]

Both of these pressures came to a head in June 1947, when Congress passed the National Security Act. The bill created an independent Air Force and simultaneously unified all armed services under the secretary of defense. These actions significantly affected the structure of Army Intelligence. The Air Force developed a separate intelligence organization of its own. Air attaches took their places beside military attaches; counterintelligence assets already serving with Air Force units were withdrawn from the Counter Intelligence Corps; the Army Security Agency gave up control of its three radio squadrons, mobile, and one radio security detachment to the new service.[7] Finally, in 1950 the Air Force established its own special security officer system.

The most important impact of the 1947 act, however, came with the establishment of the Central Intelligence Agency (CIA). This new national-level intelligence authority reported to the freshly created National Security Council (NSC). Unlike its predecessor, the CIA was not subordinate to the services, but had its own budget and personnel and a large mandate to independently gather and produce intelligence at its own discretion. The formation of the CIA did not directly interfere with the independence of Army Intelligence, but the role of the Army's director of Intelligence in influencing national intelligence decisions was decidedly curbed, although not eliminated, and the new agency assumed control over large areas of political and economic intelligence for which the Army had been responsible.

Postwar Operations: Human Intelligence and Counterintelligence

Under peacetime conditions, the Intelligence Division in the post–World War II period had at its disposal three major institutional elements: the Army attache system, the Counter Intelligence Corps, and the Army Security Agency. The oldest and most traditional of these, the attache system still provided the Army with 80 percent of its uncompartmented intelligence. The attache network was large—before the final separation of the Air Force and later

---

6 Considering the substantial American Intelligence successes in World War II, one is surprised at some of the sentiments expressed during the congressional hearings that led up to the establishment of the Central Intelligence Agency. Army Air Forces' General Hoyt Vandenberg expressed the opinion that the United States was "400 years behind" in the intelligence field, which he appeared to equate with clandestine human intelligence collection. *National Security Act of 1947: Hearing Before the Committee on Expenditures in the Executive Departments, H.R. 2319*, 80th Cong., 1st sess., 27 June 1947, p. 10.

7 ASA units transferred to AFSS were the 1st, 2d, and 8th Radio Squadrons, Mobile, and the 136th Radio Security Squadron. Frank M. Whitacre, *A Pictorial Review of USAFSS, 1948–1973: 25 Years of Vigilance* (San Antonio: U.S. Air Force Security Service, 1973).

economies by the Truman administration 285 officers were serving in seventy stations—and increasingly professional. As early as October 1945 the Intelligence Division had begun offering training courses to officers selected for attache duty, and by 1946 this effort was being directed by a Strategic Intelligence School. Although the work of its graduates was increasingly hampered by tight security measures in Communist countries, they continued to provide valuable military information from their far-flung assignments.

For a short period, the Intelligence Division also operated the Gehlen Organization, an intelligence apparatus inherited from the German Army of World War II. Maj. Gen. Reinhardt Gehlen, former head of German intelligence on the Eastern Front, thoughtfully had brought his complete files with him when he surrendered to the American Army. Gehlen, his documents, and his personnel were moved to the United States for a time and placed under Intelligence Division control.[8] Ultimately, the organization returned to Germany, passed under CIA direction, and finally became the nucleus of the present West German *Bundesnachrichtendienst*.

For counterintelligence, the Intelligence Division relied on the reestablished Army Counter Intelligence Corps, responsible for the procurement, training, and administration of all counterintelligence personnel. In the continental United States, six numbered Zone of Interior armies had taken over the functions of the nine former service commands following the dissolution of the Army Service Forces, and this brought about a realignment of existing CIC elements. Three CIC detachments were inactivated, and the 108th, 109th, 111th, 112th, 113th, and 115th Counter Intelligence Corps Detachments were subordinated respectively to the First, Second, Third, Fourth, Fifth, and Sixth Armies, while the 116th CIC Detachment continued to support the Military District of Washington. These geographic arrangements would remain unchanged for twenty years. Other counterintelligence units were attached to divisions based in the United States: to the Armed Forces Special Weapons Project that dealt with the military applications of atomic energy, to overseas commanders, and to the Intelligence Division itself. Usually, investigations continued to be supervised by the local G–2s, although the most sensitive cases were controlled by the director of Intelligence.

When the Counter Intelligence Corps first came under the command of the Intelligence Division, it was supervised directly by the division's counterintelligence staff element. However, it proved impracticable to exercise detailed control over a Camp Holabird–based organization from the Pentagon, so the position of chief, Counter Intelligence Corps, and commanding general, Counter Intelligence Corps Center, was authorized in April 1947. In short, the Counter Intelligence Corps had reverted to the institutional status it had originally held during the first part of World War II.

---

8 Gehlen's defection and early connection with Army Intelligence are described in E. H. Cookridge, *Gehlen, Spy of the Century* (New York: Random House, 1971), pp. 115–54.

Holabird, redesignated a fort in 1950, soon became an important center of intelligence activities. In addition to housing the CIC's administrative headquarters and the Counter Intelligence Corps School, it was the seat of the Counter Intelligence Corps Board, which directed research and development and handled personnel matters. The fort also began housing certain field activities of the Intelligence Division of the General Staff. In 1950 the Central Personality Index, the name file which the Intelligence Division had set up the year before, was moved on post, and in 1951 Holabird became the home of the Army's Central Records Facility, which served as a centralized repository for the records of all the Army's personnel security investigations in the continental United States and contained microfilmed copies of the files of overseas CIC detachments.

In the aftermath of World War I, the Army had allowed its counterintelligence function to atrophy. This course was not paralleled after World War II. The Army was first confronted with the necessity of providing large occupation forces abroad with counterintelligence support and then by the security demands of the Cold War. As a result, while total Army strength melted away in the course of postwar demobilization, the number of CIC personnel declined only modestly, falling from a high point of 5,000 in World War II to 3,800. However, there was a worrisome decline in quality. Rapid demobilization of veterans and the termination of the draft eliminated the reservoir of skilled and highly educated personnel upon which the Counter Intelligence Corps had been able to draw. In World War II, two-thirds of all enlisted agents had been college graduates; half had possessed law degrees or the equivalent. Now, overseas commanders were soon reporting that only 10 percent of Counter Intelligence Corps School–trained personnel had completed a college education. The Army partially solved the problem by increasing the proportion of officers in the force and authorizing the recruitment of warrant officers. Moreover, not all trends were negative. In 1946 members of the Women's Army Corps (WAC) were admitted to the CIC School, and in 1950 CIC personnel were first trained to make use of a new and promising investigative technique, the polygraph.[9]

The years following the war saw the Counter Intelligence Corps come out on the losing side in several jurisdictional disputes. In 1949 the corps lost responsibility for the Army's industrial security program to the Provost Marshal General's Office. It also clashed with the Federal Bureau of Investigation (FBI). In 1947 President Truman issued Executive Order 9835 instituting a Federal Loyalty Program, which directed that all investigations of civilians be performed by the FBI. This contradicted the existing Delimitations Agreement between the armed services and the FBI, in existence since before World War II. Ultimately, the Army signed a new agreement with the FBI in 1949, allowing the FBI to investigate Army civilians in the Western Hemisphere, while the Army handled

[9] CIC activities in the postwar period are covered in History of the Counter Intelligence Corps, vol. 24, U.S. Army Intelligence Center, 1959.

investigations overseas. However, areas of friction between the two organizations continued to exist.

One problem, as the G–2, Sixth Army, pointed out perceptively, was "a basic
difference in concept of subversive intelligence." The FBI's responsibility was
"primarily for accumulation of admissible evidence to provide the basis for legal
action against individuals or organizations, usually for acts which are already
completed." Army Intelligence, on the other hand, functioned "primarily to
forestall acts of violence or to prevent the spread of disorder; anticipatory planning is essential; and advance information on trends and developments must be
continuously available."[10] As it turned out, these differences in concept would
prove even more troubling twenty years later.

Much of the work of the Counter Intelligence Corps was performed abroad,
as American occupation forces in Europe and the Far East first attempted to root
out the remaining vestiges of Nazism and militarism and then faced the task of
countering Communist subversion.[11] In Germany, all Army counterintelligence
assets were consolidated into a single large unit, the 1,400-man-strong 970th
Counter Intelligence Corps Detachment, which blanketed the American Zone of
Germany with a network of regional and field offices. In 1948 this was converted into the 7970th Counter Intelligence Corps Detachment, organized under a
table of distribution (TD) as a one-of-a-kind unit to perform a specific mission.
The change brought about difficulties in obtaining personnel, however, and as a
result the 7970th was superseded by a new TOE outfit, the 66th Counter
Intelligence Corps Detachment, in 1949.[12]

The 441st Counter Intelligence Corps Detachment, at one point almost as
large as its European counterpart, played a similar role in supporting the occupation of Japan. Counterintelligence in Japan was facilitated by the activation of
a unique unit, the 319th Military Intelligence Company, formed in 1946 of
Nisei interpreters from MacArthur's Allied Translator and Interpreter Section.[13]
Although the Counter Intelligence Corps and its predecessor organization had
accepted Japanese-American personnel since 1940, there were too few of them
in Japan to meet the needs of the occupation. To remedy this situation, the men

---

10 Bidwell, History of the Military Intelligence Division, vol. 6, pp. 649–50.

11 Sometimes the Nazis were used against the Communists, as demonstrated in Allan A.
Ryan, Jr., *Klaus Barbie and the United States Government: A Report, with Documentry Appendix, to the
Attorney General of the United States* (Frederick, Md.: University Publications of America, 1984).

12 For Army lineage purposes, the distinction between TOE and TD units lies in the fact that
TOE units are permanently placed on Army rolls and are activated and inactivated as needed,
whereas TD units are organized on a one-time basis for a particular mission and are not perpetuated after discontinuance. A typical example of a TOE unit would be an infantry battalion, while a
typical TD unit would be an Army garrison. Because of the peculiar demands of intelligence work,
many intelligence personnel have historically served in TD (later TDA, or table of distribution and
allowances) units.

13 However, the Translator and Interpreter Service—in April 1946 it lost its allied status and
title—continued an independent existence under G–2 control.

of the 319th Military Intelligence Company were given theater counterintelligence credentials to make use of their invaluable language capabilities in assisting investigations.

Counter Intelligence Corps operations overseas faced their own special problems. Some higher commanders abroad objected to the idea of CIC agents living in civilian clothes apart from the structure of the Army as a whole and sought to remilitarize the operations. At one point, all counterintelligence personnel in Germany were put back into uniform and ordered into Army billets with considerable loss of operational effectiveness. Another problem was that some CIC personnel acclimatized themselves to life overseas all too well and had married foreign wives. In June 1950 the CIC chief issued an order that any CIC member marrying a foreign national without grant of a waiver would be terminated. Finally, operational necessity drew the corps into unfamiliar activities. In Germany, for example, CIC agents helped crack down on the black market. In most overseas commands, Cold War needs forced Counter Intelligence Corps units to engage in positive collection of intelligence. With no mechanism for gathering human intelligence at its disposal outside of the attache system, the Army was forced to misapply its counterintelligence assets to fill the void.

The Army Security Agency

The Intelligence Division's most important asset was provided by the newly formed Army Security Agency (ASA). In many ways the Army Security Agency was unique; its official historian later wrote that it was "within, but not part of, the overall military establishment."[14] A large portion of the headquarters continued to be staffed by civilian experts, and the agency's organizational pattern had no parallel in the rest of the Army. The Army Security Agency was put together on the "stovepipe" principle, and Arlington Hall controlled the activities of all units through a separate ASA chain of command. This distinctive vertical command structure, which provided centralized control over all Army signals intelligence and communications security assets, set ASA apart, as did the high walls of compartmented secrecy surrounding its sensitive operations. All that most members of the Army knew about the Army Security Agency was that they were not supposed to know anything about it.

As a separate entity within the Army, the agency was almost completely self-sufficient. In addition to conducting its own operational missions, ASA administered its own personnel system, ran its own school, arranged for its own supplies, and conducted its own research and development. The agency's cryptologic activities continued to be indispensable to the nation's security. The postwar drawdown of strength affected the ASA just as it did the rest of the armed forces, and the

---

14 Army Security Agency, History of the Army Security Agency and Subordinate Units, FY 1951, vol. 1, p. 5.

organization had to be realigned to meet new national priorities. But the competence which had marked the activities of its predecessors was still there.

In the field, ASA's principal assets were seven large fixed field stations, most of them left over from World War II, at Vint Hill Farms, Virginia; Two Rock Ranch, California; Helemano, Hawaii; Clark Field, the Philippines; Fairbanks, Alaska; Herzo Base, Germany; and Asmara, Ethiopia. Although the headquarters of the 2d Signal Service Battalion was disbanded in 1946, having become redundant when the Army Security Agency established its own personnel system, the stations continued to be manned by lettered detachments of the battalion until May 1950, when all of ASA's TDA elements were redesignated as numbered Army Area Units in the 8600 series. Field stations were supplemented by tactical units—signal service companies and detachments—operating from semifixed positions. The ASA exercised command and control of overseas elements through its regional headquarters in Europe and the Pacific, and later through smaller headquarters elements in Hawaii, Alaska, and the Caribbean. Overall direction of the Army's cryptologic effort and necessary analysis and production work were centralized at ASA's Arlington Hall headquarters.

Since the Army Security Agency's mission had a national impact, it had to be responsive to requirements generated by agencies outside the Army. Initially, ASA operated under the umbrella of the Army-Navy Communications Intelligence Board established during World War II. Other players soon became involved in the results of ASA's work, however, and membership on the board was expanded. At first it became the State-Army-Navy Communications Intelligence Board, evolving a little later into the United States Communications Intelligence Board (USCIB), an element which included FBI and CIA participation.

As part of its mission, the agency supervised all Army communications security, produced and distributed all cryptomaterial, and served as the ultimate maintenance point for cryptomachinery. It also had responsibility for strategic communications cover and deception. All this entailed a substantial commitment of resources. The Army Security Agency's major effort in the communications security field after World War II was the replacement of the super-secure SIGABA with a cryptomachine that operated on less sensitive design principles, the SIGROD, later redesignated as ASAM–5. The idea was to place SIGABA in a reserve status for possible wartime demands, and to use SIGROD, the compromise of which would be less damaging.

ASA's initial organization proved short lived. Ever since World War II, the demand for the centralization of all cryptologic activities under the control of a single body had been increasing. By 1946 the Army had realized that both Army and Navy cryptologic organizations should be placed under the direction of a common agency to ensure a proper coordination of effort. The creation of an independent Air Force, with its own Air Force Security Service, seemed to threaten the field with greater fragmentation than ever before. In response, during 1949 the Armed Forces Security Agency was established under the Joint Chiefs of Staff.

The Armed Forces Security Agency, commanded by officers from the various services on a rotating basis, brought together at a high level all U.S. cryptologic operations and relieved the individual services of their direction and production functions in this field. In practice, the design concept behind this new agency proved flawed. The Armed Forces Security Agency was responsive only to the needs of the armed forces, leaving wider national concerns unmet. Moreover, the planned musical chairs rotation scheme for providing the agency's leadership destroyed administrative continuity.[15] In 1952 the National Security Agency (NSA), a civilian agency under the Department of Defense, replaced the Armed Forces Security Agency.

In 1949, however, it seemed that the formation of the Armed Forces Security Agency would gut ASA, reducing it to the role of a residual Army cryptologic agency with a function limited to ensuring Army communications security. In addition to giving up a major portion of its original mission, the ASA transferred most of its civilian staff to the new national-level agency, including William Friedman and almost the whole group of Signal Intelligence Service pioneers. A long Army tradition that stretched back to the days of the World War I Cipher Bureau thus passed to a joint service organization. The Army Security Agency met the organizational challenge by restructuring itself to meet Army-specific needs. After 1949 the agency turned its attention to developing mobile field units to support tactical commanders at every level, a task accelerated by the outbreak of the Korean War in June 1950.

Postwar Military Intelligence: Deficiencies

There were definite weaknesses in the structure of post–World War II Military Intelligence. Army Intelligence as yet had not become truly professional. Officers served in intelligence assignments on the basis of detail; their commissions, and in many cases, their career interests, lay with their basic branches.[16] Continuity in the more specialized areas of intelligence, such as counterintelligence and signals intelligence, rested in the pool of reserve officers who had continued in active service after World War II. Their numbers, however, inevitably diminished. To remedy this situation, in 1946 a panel of intelligence officers, the Forney Board, had recommended that a Military Intelligence Corps be established, consisting of both detailed and permanently assigned members. But other elements of the Army Staff had vigorously rejected the recommendation, on the usual grounds that any officer should be capable of performing intelligence duties.

---

15 SRH 123, The Brownell Report, pp. 47–52.

16 This tendency was reflected even at the top. In 1949 the Hoover Commission reported that "four of the last seven G–2's were without any intelligence experience whatsoever." Henry Howe Ransom, *The Intelligence Establishment* (Cambridge: Harvard University Press, 1970), pp. 109–10.

Training presented another problem. Under the new Army organization adopted in 1946, the director of Intelligence had limited responsibilities in the training field. The Strategic Intelligence School, the attache training facility under the direct control of the Intelligence Division, was an exception. So was the area of language training. In 1946 the Military Intelligence Service Language School organized in World War II was redesignated the Army Language School and moved to the Presidio of Monterey in California. There, it continued to function under Intelligence Division control until it was resubordinated to Sixth Army headquarters in 1950.[17] The Intelligence Division also maintained lettered language detachments in Germany, Japan, and (briefly) China for advanced individual instruction. The Army Security Agency had a training school for its own personnel. Originally located at Vint Hill Farms, near Warrenton, Virginia, the school relocated to Carlisle Barracks, Pennsylvania, in 1949 and found a more permanent home at Fort Devens, Massachusetts, in 1951. The Counter Intelligence Corps maintained an equivalent institution at Fort Holabird.

Linguists, signals intelligence personnel, and counterintelligence specialists were all needed in peacetime. However, there was no similar demand for photo interpreters and order of battle specialists. As a result, the combat intelligence specialties were allowed to atrophy. The Military Intelligence Training Center at Camp Ritchie, Maryland, which had trained combat intelligence specialists during World War II, was closed shortly after the war came to an end. The Army General School at Fort Riley, Kansas, offered some intelligence courses, but the Army Ground Forces, not the director of Intelligence, had jurisdiction over its offerings.

Lack of trained personnel, along with lack of money, meant that the TOE for a Military Intelligence Service Organization issued in 1948 could not be implemented. On paper, the Military Intelligence Service Organization was a model plan, calling for intelligence organizations made up of cellular teams tailored to meet the intelligence requirements of each level of command. The concept called for administrative, linguist, and nonlinguist teams, each made up of one officer and two enlisted personnel. A Military Intelligence Service platoon made up of appropriate teams would support each division, while MIS companies and battalions would perform similar functions at corps and army level, respectively. Overall control would be vested in a group commander at theater level. Subordinate commanders would perform administrative and housekeeping duties only.[18] However, none of the larger units envisaged by the arrangement was ever organized in peacetime. Apart from ASA units and the CIC's oversized detachments, by 1949 the only intelligence unit in the U.S. Army larger than a platoon was the Nisei-manned 319th Military Intelligence Company in Japan.

---

[17] One of the first heads of the Army Language School was Brig. Gen. Elliott Thorpe, MacArthur's former counterintelligence chief.

[18] TO&E 30–600, M.I.S. Organization: A Pictorial Presentation . . . . (January 1952) (Fort Riley, Kans.: Army General School, 1952).

The same problems of inadequate resources also plagued the intelligence elements in the Army's reserve components. The situation here was considerably better than it had been after World War I, since there were many more intelligence-trained officer and enlisted personnel, and various types of intelligence units had been formed, including new strategic intelligence detachments and signals intelligence units. The Army's Reserve Officer Training Corps (ROTC) had also instituted programs for training both Military Intelligence and Army Security Agency officers. However, reserve unit training was weak, with equipment lacking, and the Military Intelligence Reserve's officer component was imbalanced. Of the over 10,000 Military Intelligence Reserve officers, there were too many field grade and too few company grade personnel to meet mobilization needs.

At the level of tactical collection, although technological advances afforded some improvements, this was counterbalanced by the shrinking of collection assets within the skeleton Army. Although additional aircraft were assigned to the division, and a new type of light plane, the L–19 (later the O–l "Bird-dog"), specifically designed to meet Army observation requirements, entered the inventory in 1950, there were not very many divisions left to support. Similarly, the flash- and sound-ranging capabilities of the field artillery observation battalion were now supplemented by radar, but by 1950 there was only one observation battalion left.

Finally, there were gaps in the intelligence architecture. What little electronic warfare and electronic intelligence capacity remained in the Army was controlled by the chief signal officer and operated without reference to the Army Security Agency, even though it was already all too clear that jamming would certainly have a great effect on the collection of signals intelligence in any wartime situation. Except for the attache system, the Army still lacked any dedicated capabilities for collecting human intelligence in peacetime, although Counter Intelligence Corps units overseas did provide some incidental positive intelligence. It would take the impact of another crisis to force the Army to reevaluate its intelligence structure and to make the necessary improvements. In June 1950 the crisis arrived.

Korea

The war in Korea confronted the U.S. Army with two major intelligence failures within the space of six months. The initial North Korean invasion came as a surprise, as did the later Chinese intervention. In each case Army Intelligence had been aware of hostile capabilities and had misinterpreted intentions. The reasons, apart from normal human fallibility, were unsurprising. Peacetime budgetary constraints had depleted Army Intelligence assets, and what remained had been targeted against Soviet Russia and the European threat. The Korean peninsula had been declared beyond America's defense perimeter and therefore outside the jurisdiction of the major theater commander in the Far East. The hard fact was that before June 1950 Korea was not high on the list of intelligence priorities for either the CIA or the Army. Once the conflict began, political and diplomatic constraints limited the ability of American collection assets to provide a definite early warning of the thirty-division Chinese attack that ultimately materialized.

Army Intelligence initially responded to the outbreak of hostilities in Korea through desperate improvisation. There were only two Korean linguists on the staff of MacArthur's G–2. The Technical Intelligence Section of the Far East Command had been disbanded in 1949. The four occupation divisions in Japan had been stripped of their tactical Counter Intelligence Corps detachments, and when they deployed to Korea provisional CIC detachments had to be cobbled together from the assets of the 441st Counter Intelligence Corps Detachment in Japan. The three Army Security Agency units in the Far East were manning semifixed installations and were unable to take the field. Not until October did the first sizable ASA unit, the 60th Signal Service Company, reach the Korean peninsula, and the company had to be transported from Fort Lewis, Washington. In the meantime, the Eighth Army depended for cryptologic support upon a small unit organized by making use of locally available resources. Communications security was lax, both among Republic of Korea (ROK) troops and the Eighth Army. The Eighth Army had come from restful occupation duty in Japan, and the chief of the Army Security Agency put it, with some exaggeration, "They receive about 400 violations a minute over there."[19] Communications security was threatened further by the initially fluid tactical situation; several high-level machine cipher devices had to be destroyed to prevent their capture in the early stages of the fighting.

Chinese intervention created another set of problems. The security-conscious Chinese initially approached the battlefront completely undetected, even though MacArthur personally conducted a visual reconnaissance mission over North Korea.[20] Even after the Chinese engaged, ground patrols repeatedly lost contact with the enemy. In a desperate attempt to find out more about the Chinese advance, Korean nationals equipped with smoke grenades were air-dropped into the intelligence vacuum to signal the presence of the enemy. General Matthew Ridgway assumed command of the Eighth Army in late December 1950 at the height of the crisis. He found himself confronted with an intelligence map showing only "a big red goose egg . . . with '174,000' scrawled in the middle of it" north of his lines, all that Army Intelligence knew then

---

[19] Army Security Agency Staff Meeting Notes, 14 Nov 50, Army Cryptologic Records.

[20] D. Clayton James, *The Years of MacArthur*, vol. 3, *Triumph and Disaster, 1945–1964* (Boston: Houghton Mifflin, 1985), p. 216. Intelligence problems presented by the Chinese intervention are discussed at length (insofar as security considerations allowed) in Roy H. Appleman, *South to the Naktong, North to the Yalu, June–November 1950*, U.S. Army in the Korean War (Washington, D.C.: U.S. Army Center of Military History, 1961), pp. 757–65, 769–70. Some additional insights are contained in Eliot A. Cohen and John Gooch, *Military Misfortunes: The Anatomy of Failure in War* (New York: Free Press, 1990), pp. 175–82.

about the strength and disposition of the enemy. The following month, he too undertook a personal aerial reconnaissance behind enemy lines.[21]

The inadequacy of the Army's tactical intelligence capabilities on the Korean peninsula took many months to rectify. As late as 1951 a survey revealed that only 7 percent of Eighth Army personnel holding intelligence positions had either previous training or prior experience in intelligence, which spurred the creation of a Far East Command intelligence school at Camp Drake, Japan. Intelligence exploitation was handicapped also by the Army's limited supply of Mandarin linguists. Even toward the end of the war, deficiencies abounded. Ridgway's successor with the Eighth Army, General James Van Fleet, commented that there were still serious problems in aerial photography, aerial visual reconnaissance, covert collection, ground reconnaissance, and communications reconnaissance. He went on to observe: "During the two years that the U.S. Army has been fighting in Korea . . . it has become apparent that during the between-war interim we have lost, through neglect, disinterest, and possible jealousy, much of the effectiveness in intelligence work that we acquired so painfully in World War II. Today, our intelligence operations in Korea have not yet approached the standards that we reached in the final year of the last war."[22]

Nonetheless, the shock of the Korean conflict did give a new impetus to the development of Army Intelligence, causing a rapid growth both in personnel and in organizational structure. The strength of the Office of the Assistant Chief of Staff, G–2, as the Intelligence Division was called after April 1950, grew to exceed 1,000 men. The SSO system managed by G–2 was expanded to service the three corps which the United States committed to Korea. In addition, the role of the SSO became significantly enhanced. In 1949 these officers had begun to provide an "eyes only" system of private communications to commanders. After the Korean War, special security officers became deeply involved in the production of finished intelligence for the commands they supported.

Changes were not confined to the Army Staff level. The Counter Intelligence Corps more than doubled; the position of chief of the Counter Intelligence Corps was elevated to a major general's slot. The largest CIC unit, the 66th Counter Intelligence Corps Detachment that supported USAREUR, was raised to group status in 1952. At the outset of the Korean War, a counterintelligence detachment was organized to protect the Pentagon, and subse-

---

21 General Matthew B. Ridgway, *Soldier: The Memoirs of Matthew B. Ridgway*, as told to Harold H. Martin (Westport: Greenwood Press, 1974), pp. 205, 216. Another senior commander was even more personally involved in reconnaissance activities in this war. In January 1951 the Air Force chief of staff, General Hoyt S. Vandenberg (a former Army assistant chief of staff, G–2), joined a ground patrol twelve miles in front of the main U.N. lines while on an inspection trip to Korea. James F. Schnabel, *Policy and Direction: The First Year*, U.S. Army in the Korean War (Washington, D.C.: U.S. Army Center of Military History, 1990), p. 327.

22 Bidwell, History of the Military Intelligence Division, vol. 7, p. 1080.

quently was incorporated as a subelement into the newly activated 902d Counter Intelligence Corps Detachment. This unit, operating under the direct control of the assistant chief of staff, G–2, was tasked with conducting exceptionally sensitive worldwide missions in support of Department of the Army requirements. Another development in the counterintelligence field that took place during the Korean War was the creation of Technical Service Countermeasures teams to ferret out possible listening devices, an initiative prompted by the 1952 discovery that the Great Seal of the U.S. Embassy in Moscow had been "bugged" by the Soviet Intelligence Service.

In the field, large intelligence organizations were developed to meet the needs of the combat forces. The Military Intelligence Service Organization concept at last became a reality, and tactical groups, battalions, and companies of intelligence specialists were formed to support the Army around the globe. The first Military Intelligence service group, the 525th, was organized in December 1950; its commander, Col. Garland Williams, had been the first Chief of the Corps of Intelligence Police before Pearl Harbor.23 Two additional groups were activated before the Korean War came to an end—the 500th Military Intelligence Service Group in Japan, which absorbed the personnel and mission of the old Translator and Interpreter Service, and the 513th Military Intelligence Service Group in Germany. Five Military Intelligence Service battalions were also activated, along with numerous numbered companies and platoons. Additionally, four Military Intelligence Service groups and ten Military Intelligence Service battalions, all in the 300 series, were activated in the Organized Reserve Corps, redesignated the Army Reserve in 1952.

Korea was a limited war: at first the conflict was described not as a war at all, but as a United Nations "police action."24 This had limited the scope of certain kinds of intelligence activities. The intelligence community made no attempt to revive the World War II Counter Subversive program which had laced the Army's ranks with informers. Censorship activities were limited, and the press was allowed to operate under a "voluntary" self-censorship until the spring of 1951. The assistant chief of staff, G–2, did set up an Army Security Center in Washington, D.C., to handle high-level prisoner interrogation and document exploitation, but this turned out to be less important than its World War II predecessors, since enemy prisoners of war were retained in Korea, and few high-ranking prisoners were captured. However, some World War II precedents were found useful. In Operation INDIANHEAD, a multidiscipline intelligence task force—a World War II "T" Force in miniature—was dispatched to sift through the rubble of Pyongyang after that

---

23 During World War II, Williams had also been in charge of supply and procurement for the OSS.

24 T. R. Fehrenbach, *This Kind of War: A Study in Unpreparedness* (New York: MacMillan Co., 1963), p. 90.

North Korean capital was overrun by United Nations troops.25 And the various collection techniques perfected in World War II proved useful in the new conflict.26

The Korean War revitalized the Army Security Agency, which found a new role in providing support to tactical operations. During the course of the war, the agency reorganized and redesignated its existing signal service companies as communication reconnaissance companies and activated new communication reconnaissance companies, battalions, and groups to support tactical commanders at every level.27 The new concept placed a communication reconnaissance group in support of the field army. The group would command subordinate ASA units and had the mission of dispatching liaison teams to the combat divisions. At the corps level, flexibly organized communication reconnaissance battalions directed the activities of separate numbered companies.

By the end of the Korean War, the Army Security Agency's 501st Communication Reconnaissance Group was supervising the operations of three attached battalions and five companies in support of the Eighth Army. Another major ASA tactical element, the 502d Communication Reconnaissance Group, commanded subordinate units giving support to the expanded Army presence in Europe. The 503d Communication Reconnaissance Group served as a command and control element for various ASA units in the continental United States. Additionally, new field stations had been established in Europe and the Far East. After 1951 the position of chief of the Army Security Agency was usually filled by a major general.28

Finally, the Army at last took steps to enhance its human intelligence collection capabilities. Confronted by an almost complete intelligence void in the early stages of the Korean War, it expanded an existing small intelligence element set up by the Far East Command following the withdrawal of American occupation troops in 1949 into a full-fledged collection organization. Initially, a provisional

---

25 Memo, GHQ, FEC, Military Intelligence Section, 6 Feb 51, sub: After Action Report, Task Force INDIANHEAD, INSCOM History Office.

26 In *The Korean War* (New York: Simon and Shuster, 1987), p. 244, Max Hastings states that "throughout the war United Nations intelligence about Chinese and North Korean strategic intentions remained very poor." It should be pointed out, however, that not all material bearing on the subject has been released yet.

27 The buildup of the Army Security Agency that took place during the Korean War was facilitated, in part, by the deployment of the two ASA companies in the National Guard and two other ASA companies in the Organized Reserve Corps.

28 However, none of the three general officers who headed up the Army Security Agency during the period of the Korean conflict possessed any background in Military Intelligence. ASA chief Brig. Gen. William Gillmore admitted, "I have had no experience in this line of work. I am going to depend on you people for guidance and support all the way through." ASA Staff Meeting Notes, 15 Aug 50, Army Cryptologic Records. In contrast, the first three chiefs of the Army Security Agency—Brig. Gen. Preston W. Corderman, Col. Harold G. Hayes, and Brig. Gen. Carter W. Clarke—had all served in communications intelligence during World War II.

CIC unit, the 442d Counter Intelligence Corps Detachment, used tactical liaison office teams assigned to each division to dispatch locally recruited line-crossers. These generally unskilled and untrained Korean agents were told to gather whatever low-level intelligence they could.29

Following the Chinese intervention, this approach expanded greatly. The provisional status of the 442d Counter Intelligence Corps Detachment was dropped. The divisional teams continued to function, but, in addition, the Army undertook more ambitious collection projects. By the summer of 1951 the Army was devoting increasing resources to the effort. Since the mission was not really appropriate for the Counter Intelligence Corps, the 442d was inactivated and its functions assumed by the 8240th Army Unit, a TD-based organization with elements in both Japan and Korea. The Counter Intelligence Corps personnel initially transferred to the 8240th Army Unit were replaced gradually by specialists from other intelligence disciplines.

In late 1951 the scope of the unit's mandate widened to include special operations. This came about when the Eighth Army unit supporting Korean guerrillas on the offshore islands was integrated into the 8240th Army Unit in accordance with doctrine that such activities belonged at the theater level. At the same time, the 8240th Army Unit itself became the Army element of Combined Command Reconnaissance Activities, Korea, a theater-level joint-service agency created to coordinate intelligence and special operations activities in the war zone.

By the time the Korean armistice was signed in the summer of 1953, the 8240th Army Unit had 450 military personnel assigned and had evolved into an Army simulacrum of the World War II OSS. It not only provided the Far Eastern Command with information, but also ran a 20,000-man private army of Korean guerrillas, the United Nations Partisan Forces in Korea. With five infantry and one airborne regiment, the Partisan Forces harassed the enemy from bases on islands off the shores of both coasts of the Korean peninsula. As if all this were not enough, the 8240th also engaged in an extensive program of "black propaganda."30

Summation

The Korean War was another major milestone in the development of Army Intelligence. It revived intelligence capabilities which had grown moribund in the post–World War II retrenchment. It also witnessed the development of large-scale intelligence formations in the field. For the first time, Army Intelligence personnel were organized into groups and battalions. However,

---

29 S. L. A. Marshall mentions such collection activities in his book, *The River and the Gauntlet: Defeat of the Eighth Army by the Chinese Communist Forces, November 1950, in the Battle of the Chonchon River, Korea* (New York: Morrow, 1953), pp. 3–4.

30 Alfred H. Paddock, Jr., *U.S. Army Special Warfare: Its Origins* (Washington, D.C.: National Defense University Press, 1982), pp. 100–108.

although the Army Security Agency imposed these arrangements on its reserve components in the aftermath of the war, the Army decided that large reserve units were not needed in the other intelligence disciplines, and by mid-1953 all the Military Intelligence Service groups and battalions in the Army Reserve had been inactivated.[31] For the next few years, the Military Intelligence presence in the Army Reserve would be confined largely to numerous small counterintelligence, censorship, or strategic research and analysis detachments.

In addition, the war can be seen as a milestone in the development of intelligence technologies. The war itself was fought mostly with World War II equipment. The venerable M209 still provided communications security for tactical units. The light planes organic to the divisions were only slightly improved versions of the Piper Cubs that had given the Army reconnaissance support in the previous conflict. ASA's radios as well as its trucks represented war surplus. Yet this was beginning to change. A new family of cipher machines began to enter the Army inventory at this time. Scientists started to find ways in which new and evolving technologies could be applied to the Military Intelligence field. In 1953 the Army became involved in Project MICHIGAN, a research and development effort in which civilian scientific personnel explored the possibilities of using various types of manned aircraft, drones, balloons, and missiles carrying television and other sensors to allow surveillance and target location up to 200 miles behind enemy lines.[32] The new technologies under development would have profound consequences for the structure of Army Intelligence in the years that followed.

---

31 For reasons which have escaped documentation, all reserve component ASA units after the Korean War were in the Army Reserve, not the National Guard.

32 Bidwell, History of the Military Intelligence Division, vol. 7, pp. 1102–03.

8

From Korea to Vietnam

During the twelve years that elapsed between the signing of the Korean armistice in 1953 and the first commitment of American combat troops to defend South Vietnam in 1965, the Army was affected by the fluctuations of U.S. national security policies and defense management structures. Responding to American dissatisfaction with the bloody and ultimately indecisive fighting in Korea, the Eisenhower administration that took office in 1953 adopted a "New Look" in defense policies. America, it declared, would no longer be bogged down in ground warfare at a time and place of the adversary's choosing. Instead, the United States would meet aggression with the "massive retaliation" of strategic atomic weapons.

This policy called for a reduction of land forces. The Army was drastically retrenched. Policy makers' belief that increasingly available tactical nuclear weapons would be decisive in any future conflict led to the revamping of the basic force structure in 1957. New "pentomic" divisions supposedly capable of operating in a nuclear environment were organized, and the Army regiment was abolished as a tactical entity in favor of smaller and more flexible battle groups. However, massive retaliation was never invoked. The Soviet threat continued after the death of Stalin, but its initiatives evolved in ways that could not be countered suitably by American preponderance in the nuclear weapons arena. The French defeat at Dien Bien Phu in 1954 led to the creation of a new Communist state in North Vietnam. Soviet power, hitherto confined to the Eurasian land mass, catapulted across the oceans. Soviet arms and influence appeared in Egypt, and a pro-Communist regime came to power in Cuba. Simultaneously, the Soviets startled the Americans with their success in the area of guided missiles; "Sputnik," the first orbiting satellite, was launched in 1957.

Taking advantage of a belief that the United States was not coping adequately with these new Soviet challenges, Democratic presidential candidate John F. Kennedy's campaign of 1960 focused on the need to meet the broad Communist challenge. Upon election, Kennedy and his secretary of defense, Robert S. McNamara, scrapped the strategy of massive retaliation in favor of a new doctrine, "flexible response," in which America would meet any military challenges with the gradually increasing employment of deterrent force.1 Coupled with a fresh crisis regarding the status of Berlin, the new emphasis on conventional forces powered the expansion of the Army, which soon rose to a strength of 1.2 million. New Army leaders found the pentomic division organization unsatisfactory for protracted fighting in a nonnuclear environment, and introduced a new divisional structure, the so-called Reorganization Objective Army Division (ROAD). Finally, McNamara's zeal for cost effectiveness led to a substantial restructuring of the whole Defense Department and of the individual services. As usual, Army Intelligence was affected by the currents of the times.

Military Intelligence at the Center: The 1950s

At the Army General Staff level, intelligence benefited from an expansion of its sources and technological capabilities during the post–Korean War era. Previously, the foreign intelligence collection resources of the Army Intelligence staff during peacetime had been confined to overt human intelligence provided by the attache system and signals intelligence collection. Now the Army augmented these sources with other types of intelligence collection. Its capabilities for collecting both human and electronic intelligence became increasingly significant. In addition, photographic intelligence became a viable peacetime source for the first time. After 1956 imagery from national-level sources became available to the Army. To take better advantage of this, the Army's existing Photo Interpretation Center at Fort Holabird established a special exploitation unit in the Washington, D.C., area.

Other developments at the Army Staff level under the Eisenhower administration were also significant. On the domestic front, the assistant chief of staff, G–2, regained control of the Industrial Security Program from the Provost Marshal General's Office in 1953, a reorganization that gave it custody of the extensive investigative data base compiled on Army contractor employees. Exploitation of growing masses of intelligence data was enhanced also by G–2's use of automatic data processing techniques. In 1957 the Radio Corporation of America began work on Project ACSI-MATIC, an intelligence data system that became operational in 1960.

However, intelligence was still something of a second-class citizen in the Army. In 1955 the Army's deputy assistant chief of staff, G–2, confessed that he viewed his appointment "almost as the kiss of death."2 And in two important respects, the Army Intelligence staff lost ground during the Eisenhower years—

---

1 A useful overview of defense and intelligence-related developments during the Eisenhower and Kennedy administrations can be found in Alan R. Millett and Peter Maslowski, *For the Common Defense; A Military History of the United States of America* (New York: Free Press, 1984), pp. 508–41.

2 Ransom, *The Intelligence Establishment*, p. 116.

it declined both in status and in budget. In 1955 the assistant chief of staff, G–2, lost command of the Army Security Agency. In 1956, during the course of another Army-wide reorganization, his office lost both its name and its equality with other major staff elements. Under the terms of the reorganization, the three other principal staff functions—personnel, operations, and supply—were assigned to deputy chiefs of staff. But Army Intelligence, now headed by the assistant chief of staff for intelligence (ACSI), remained at the assistant chief level.[3] The implicit downgrade preceded budget cuts and pressure on the Office of the Assistant Chief of Staff for Intelligence (OACSI) to move operational personnel out of its official table of distribution and to reduce personnel occupying headquarters slots. Ever since the late 1940s the intelligence section of the General Staff had maintained smaller operating elements in the field. After 1956, however, ACSI was forced to shift as many operational functions as possible from headquarters to field agencies.

The first step in this process began in 1956, when the ACSI staff element assigned to manage the industrial security program was reorganized as the Industrial and Personnel Security Group and transferred to Fort Holabird. In 1960 the new Technical Intelligence Field Agency assumed the mission and functions of ACSI's technical intelligence branch. The agency soon moved to Arlington Hall Station, where it was collocated with the intelligence elements of five of the seven Army technical services. Similarly, the OACSI component of the National Indications Center, a joint-service element designed to provide warnings of impending hostile attack, became a separate field detachment, as did the topographic collectors incorporated into the U.S. Army Geographic Specialist Detachment in early 1961.

Pressures on the existing structure of the Army's Intelligence staff came from outside as well as from within the Army. In 1958 the Department of Defense was reorganized. The old organizational concept, under which one service had served as executive agent for the Joint Chiefs of Staff (JCS) in war (as the Army had done in the Korean conflict) was abolished, and the armed forces of the country were placed in a system of unified and specified commands under JCS control.[4] The U.S. Communications Intelligence Board and the Intelligence Advisory Committee were concurrently abolished and their consolidated functions transferred to the new U.S. Intelligence Board (USIB). This reorganization reduced the role of the individual services to procuring, training, and fielding forces that would then pass under a JCS-directed command structure. Although the new arrangement did not immediately affect the Army's departmental intelligence agency, its implications for the future of Army Intelligence would soon become apparent.

---

[3] Hewes, *From Root to McNamara*, p. 239.
[4] Ibid., pp. 297–98.

Reshaping the Tools

One of the most significant developments within Army Intelligence during the 1950s was the conversion and expansion of the existing Counter Intelligence Corps Center at Fort Holabird into an Army Intelligence Center. This came about as an indirect byproduct of two separate initiatives. One of them was a movement begun during the Korean War to make intelligence more professional. Knowledgeable intelligence officers had become concerned about the difficulties of retaining a cadre of trained intelligence personnel in peacetime. Intelligence was not a basic branch of the Army, and most intelligence officers were reservists on detail. In 1950 a legislative oversight had even temporarily eliminated the Military Intelligence Reserve first created in 1921. This had been corrected in 1952 with the creation of two separate reserve branches, Military Intelligence (redesignated Army Intelligence in 1958) and Army Security. But since only reserve component officers could be commissioned in these branches, the active Army lacked any focus for intelligence career professionals.

The massive opposition of Army traditionalists to the establishment of an Intelligence Branch in the Regular Army led the assistant chief of staff, G–2, to advocate a more modest reform. In early 1952 he put forward a proposal to create the new Corps of Reconnaissance, U.S. Army. This corps would have incorporated all intelligence assets at the division level and above, including the units of the Army Security Agency. The plan would have provided Army Intelligence with a centralized institutional framework, but still would have allowed commanders their traditional prerogative of selecting their own intelligence staffs regardless of the branch to which they belonged. Even though this concept posed less threat to vested interests than a new separate branch, it never won acceptance.

As a fallback position, in June 1953 the assistant chief of staff, G–2, came up with a new program. He recommended that an intelligence board be established and collocated with a single intelligence school, a field intelligence center, and the intelligence units in the Army's central reserve in the continental United States. Fort Holabird, with its existing Counter Intelligence Corps School and Center and its counterintelligence records facility, would be the most logical site for the new arrangement.

The second factor leading to the expansion of Holabird's role was the Army's decision to make its collection of human intelligence more professional. The experience of the Korean War, when the Army had to improvise a collection apparatus, had caused the Army see that such work was a permanent peacetime requirement. At the end of 1952 General Matthew Ridgway, then Supreme Allied Commander, Europe, specially recommended that the Army organize its own institutionalized human intelligence collection element. Such a force would meet Army needs and at the same time prevent any future diversion of Counter Intelligence Corps assets from their assigned functions. Ridgway's recommendations were accepted and endorsed by the chief of staff in early 1953. In

November 1953 the Army issued a regulation that set standards for procurement of personnel to carry out this new function.

These twin developments resulted in a steady expansion of the scope and
nature of the responsibilities assigned to the chief, Counter Intelligence Corps.
In April 1954 the Department of Field Operations Intelligence was added to the
existing training facility at Fort Holabird. As a result, collection personnel began
to train side by side with CIC agents. This was just the beginning of a snow-
balling accretion of new activities that fell under the control of the CIC chief. In
August 1954 he assumed command of the former G–2 Records Facility at
Holabird, which contained the Army's counterintelligence files. At this point,
the Counter Intelligence Corps Center was redesignated the Army Intelligence
Center, and the chief, Counter Intelligence Corps, assumed a new title as the
center's commanding general. In March 1955 an Army Photo Interpretation
Center was established at Fort Holabird. Finally, during the same month,
responsibility for conducting training in combat intelligence transferred from
the Army General School at Fort Riley to the new U.S. Army Intelligence Center
and School at Holabird.[5] The arrangement centralized almost all intelligence
training at one post. Only the G–2's Strategic Intelligence School in Washington,
D.C., and the Army Security Agency facility at Fort Devens, Massachusetts,
remained outside the complex.

In practice, the original concept of an all-embracing Army Intelligence cen-
ter was never quite realized. It seems to have been the intention of Maj. Gen.
Arthur C. Trudeau, the assistant chief of staff, G–2, that Holabird would become
the directing hub for Army Intelligence. Under the original plan, the chief,
Counter Intelligence Corps, in his capacity as commanding general of the U.S.
Army Intelligence Center, would not only assume responsibility for training all
Army Intelligence personnel, but would also take over responsibility for their
administrative supervision. This arrangement would have extended the benefits
of the CIC personnel structure to the rest of the Army Intelligence community.
Although the concept was approved by the Army chief of staff, it was not completely implemented, and the center never achieved the position of importance
originally envisioned for it. However, it did serve as a basis for more modest
reforms and initiatives.

The year 1955 also witnessed the inception of an intelligence civilian career
program within the Army. This step, first advocated by the second Hoover
Commission on governmental reform, would augment nontactical Military
Intelligence units with trained civilian specialists who would provide continuity
to operations. Three hundred such positions were authorized originally. Actual
implementation began in 1957, overseen by an Administrative Survey
Detachment organized within the Army Intelligence Center. However, the Army
soon began to have second thoughts about the program. Civilians were limited

---

[5] General Order (GO) 20, Headquarters, Department of the Army (HQDA), 11 Mar 55.

to working a forty-hour week and were not under court-martial jurisdiction. Moreover, Army leaders believed it was counterproductive to keep civilians on indefinite assignments in any one single geographic area. As a result, they limited the effort to employ more civilians.

Meanwhile, the Army Intelligence Center became involved in an attempt to remedy some of the perceived deficiencies in field intelligence programs. Initially, the commanding general, Army Intelligence Center, was responsible for training new field operations intelligence specialists, but had no authority over their assignments in the field. Some human intelligence collectors were in units under theater control, organized years before the field operations intelligence program, as such, had come into existence; others served in a detachment under direct ACSI control. The field operations intelligence program thus operated under a separate and less rigid personnel system than the Counter Intelligence Corps. Its military occupational specialty (MOS) could be awarded by ACSI and by theater commanders as well as by the Army Intelligence Center, and the Army could recruit individuals whose foreign connections would have barred them from enlisting in the Counter Intelligence Corps.

The differences between these two intelligence elements soon led to an unhealthy rivalry. As one report pointed out, "there is too much bickering and snideness at the [Intelligence] Center regarding these two fields."[6] The situation was made worse by the fact that intelligence officers on the Army Staff and in Europe considered field operations intelligence personnel better qualified to handle especially sensitive counterespionage operations than CIC agents. But Counter Intelligence Corps members saw any such transfer of functions as "an emasculation of CIC."[7] Another problem area arose when field operations intelligence personnel, because of the nature of their mission requirements, lacked an adequate rotation base in the continental United States. Although a majority of CIC billets were in the United States, four-fifths of those billets in the field operations intelligence program were overseas.

Eventually, the ACSI decided that it would be more economical and efficient to merge all field operations intelligence assets with the Counter Intelligence Corps and cross-train personnel to serve both as counterintelligence agents and as human intelligence collectors. Accordingly, a consolidated Intelligence Corps, commanded by the former CIC chief and operating under tight centralized control, was created on 1 January 1961. The new organization incorporated slightly over 5,000 personnel, about 85 percent of whom came from CIC. Entrance requirements for the Intelligence Corps were less restrictive than they had been for the old Counter Intelligence Corps.

---

6 Memo, Maj C. A. Lynch for G–3, U.S. Army Intelligence Command (USAINTC), 11 Nov 58, sub: Proposed Advisory Committee for USAINTC, RG 319, NARA.

7 Memo for Commanding General, 10 Dec 58, sub: Long Range Policy and Planning Committee for USAINTC, RG 319, NARA.

Attempts to bring the new organization even closer to the Army mainstream soon followed. During the 1950s the Counter Intelligence Corps had embodied the "best and the brightest." Ever since the Korean War, the draft had furnished it with a steady stream of college-trained applicants attracted to the idea of fulfilling their service obligation by working in civilian clothes in a glamorous and exotic field, and the CIC had been able to choose among them. Unfortunately, most of these individuals did not show any propensity for making intelligence work a career. The retention rate was abysmal—7 percent for lieutenants and just 3 percent for enlisted personnel. Accordingly, the Army decided that "selection of applicants must be made with consideration for those offering the best career potential and not necessarily the bright college student."[8] The Intelligence Corps would accept only applicants who volunteered for a three-year enlistment. At the same time, the age limit for enlisting in the corps was lowered and brought into line with the rest of the Army; eighteen-year-old personnel now became eligible for entry-level positions involving clerical rather than investigative duties. Finally, in 1965 the minimum Army General Test score for joining the Intelligence Corps was lowered from 110, the same requirement imposed on officer candidates Army-wide, to 100, which more closely approximated the Army average.

The Army Security Agency

If Fort Holabird was one pole of Army Intelligence in the 1950s, Arlington Hall Station was the other. Arlington Hall continued to serve as headquarters for the ASA, the largest single intelligence and security element in the Army, and it also came to house intelligence elements of five of the Army's technical services after the consolidation of NSA headquarters at Fort Meade in 1957 made office space available. During the Eisenhower administration, Arlington Hall's main Army tenant, the Army Security Agency, grew steadily. Personnel strength rose from 11,500 in 1952 to 18,300 by 1957; new field stations and tactical units appeared; and a substantial restructuring of the agency's mission took place.

By 1954 the Army Signal Corps was fielding a number of units to collect electronic intelligence and continued to be responsible for the conduct of electronic warfare. In April 1954 the Department of the Army analyzed the feasibility of combining all these capabilities into a single agency. As a result of this study, the Army Security Agency took over responsibility for electronic intelligence and communications-related electronic countermeasures (ECM) from the Signal Corps in 1955, assuming control of a number of dispersed units and a battalion and four companies stationed at Fort Huachuca, Arizona. In return, the agency surrendered its responsibilities for Army cryptologistics and cryptomaintenance, along with associated personnel, to the Signal Corps.

---

8 Min, Intelligence Corps Commanders' Conference, 1961, sec. 10, p. 7, RG 319, NARA.

In budgetary terms, the reorganization was significant: the Army was introducing a new generation of machine cipher devices to replace the venerable M209, and purchase of the new machines had consumed 60 percent of the Army Security Agency's fiscal year 1953 budget. However, the change had the important benefits of eliminating duplication of facilities and allowing for proper integration of signals intelligence with electronic intelligence. The term signals intelligence (SIGINT) was now redefined and used to refer to both of these functions. Actual implementation of this mission transfer was delayed for a short time until the Signal Corps personnel transferred to the Army Security Agency had their clearance levels upgraded.

The new arrangements meant that the Army Security Agency was no longer exclusively an intelligence organization. By acquiring responsibility for electronic warfare, the agency now managed a weapons system, even though the weapon was invisible. In recognition of this change, the Army Security Agency became a Department of the Army field operating agency on 23 June 1955.[9] It now reported directly to the Army chief of staff, not to the assistant chief of staff, G–2. However, the agency continued to focus primarily on the cryptologic mission, and electronic warfare in practice did not receive much emphasis.

Having acquired responsibility for electronic intelligence and electronic warfare, the Army Security Agency made further attempts to enlarge the scope of its mission. In September 1955 the chief, Army Security Agency, recommended to the Army chief of staff that his organization be given the responsibility for dissemination and protection of sensitive compartmented information Army-wide, thus eliminating the special security officer system maintained by the assistant chief of staff, G–2, which had just been consolidated into a single element, Detachment M. The rationale for this proposal was economy. However, both the Army's Intelligence staff and commanders in the field vigorously resisted it. Intelligence personnel claimed that the Army Security Agency was not qualified to produce the all-source intelligence which special security officers provided to their supported G–2s. Field commanders unanimously endorsed the existing arrangement, pointing out that ASA units were not conveniently located in or near the major Army headquarters and that eliminating the special security officers would deprive them of their secure "back-channel" communications. The Army chief of staff tabled the proposal, but the Army Security Agency refused to drop the issue. The bureaucratic struggle over the matter would go on for the next two decades, at times fought with considerable acrimony.

The Army Security Agency pursued other initiatives with greater success. In 1956 the agency became aware for the first time of the possibility that emissions radiating from electronic data processing equipment might compromise security and initiated a program, nicknamed TEMPEST, to counter the threat. In 1957 the U.S. Army Security Agency Board was created to provide long-range planning,

---

9 AR 10–122, *Organization and Functions, Army Security Agency,* 23 Jun 55.

and in 1960 its functions were expanded to include combat development. At the same time, the Army Intelligence Board at Fort Holabird acquired parallel responsibilities for overseeing combat developments in the field of human intelligence. Meanwhile, the ASA and its field stations underwent redesignation. As a result of an Army-wide change, the agency became the U.S. Army Security Agency (USASA) on 1 January 1957. Concurrently, its fixed field stations, which previously had been known as numbered Army administrative units in the 8600 series, acquired new designations as numbered USASA field stations.[10]

The agency's tactical elements underwent a more significant restructuring during this period. During the Korean War, the Army Security Agency had operated with flexible battalion headquarters overseeing the operations of independent security and collection companies. In 1955 fixed battalions with organic companies combining both functions were created, and in 1956 all communication reconnaissance units were redesignated as Army Security Agency units. However, in 1957 the secretary of defense's decision to cut the Army's strength by a total of 50,000 threw the force structure of the agency into disarray. The decrement left the ASA without sufficient personnel to fill its existing tactical TOE units, which at the time accounted for about a quarter of its total strength. In response, the Army Security Agency inactivated all its TOE units and replaced them with mission-tailored units based on individual tables of distribution. The new TD units included the 507th and 508th U.S. Army Security Agency Groups, located respectively in Germany and Korea, and six U.S. Army Security Agency battalions numbered from 316 to 321. These units were given the designator U.S. Army Security Agency to distinguish them from Army Security Agency TOE units. The battalions retained the fixed structure of their TOE predecessors.

Originally, the Army intended this as a temporary measure, to remain in force only until new organizational tables could be drawn up. In practice, however, the ASA continued to operate exclusively with TD units until 1962, when tactical TOE units were formed in the continental United States to support the Army's new strategic reserve for contingency operations. Later, additional TOE elements were activated to serve in Vietnam. Some of the mission-tailored TD units soon acquired new and exotic designations as special operations units and special operations commands.

The U.S. Army Security Agency was the principal tenant at Arlington Hall after 1957, but not the only one. Intelligence elements of five technical services ultimately located there. Only the Corps of Engineers, the intelligence arm of which was concentrated in the Army Map Service, and the Quartermaster Corps held back, although the Ordnance Corps also maintained a separate missile intelligence center at Redstone Arsenal. Although most of these technical service intelligence units engaged in analysis and production, the Signal Corps contin-

10 GO 58, *Army Security Agency*, 13 Dec 56.

ued to engage in some specialized collection activities even after it had surrendered its electronic intelligence and communications-related electronic warfare functions to the Army Security Agency.

Military Intelligence in the Field

Until the late 1950s the tactical formations of the Army received their intelligence support from Military Intelligence specialist units put together on the cellular principle. Combat intelligence units were organically separate from counterintelligence units under this arrangement, and the G–2s of the supported units had to coordinate the efforts of the two diverse elements themselves.

At the end of 1957 the Army introduced a new category of intelligence units organized under a concept plan entitled the Military Intelligence Organization. Under this plan interrogators, photo interpreters, order of battle specialists, and other combat intelligence personnel were integrated into single units with counterintelligence and collection elements. These new units operated under a fixed table of organization and were designed to be administratively self-sufficient.

Under the Military Intelligence Organization concept, the basic building block was the Military Intelligence battalion supporting a field army. This unit had its own specialized organic companies: a headquarters and headquarters company containing photo interpreters, order of battle and technical intelligence specialists, and censorship personnel; and lettered linguist, security, and collection companies. In addition, the battalion furnished tactical units down to the division level with attached multidiscipline intelligence detachments.[11] The creation of the Military Intelligence Organization was one of the first steps in bringing truly multidiscipline intelligence support to the field. Only ASA units remained outside the new organizational structure because of the Army Security Agency's vertical, or "stovepipe," command structure and its tight centralization and compartmentation.

In practice, implementation of the new force structure was limited. Under the Military Intelligence Organization concept, four Military Intelligence Battalions eventually were reorganized: the 319th and 519th in the continental United States; the 532d in Germany; and the 502d in Korea. However, only the headquarters and headquarters companies and linguist companies were initially activated in the two battalions in the United States.[12] Meanwhile, the bulk of Army

---

[11] A major factor behind the Military Intelligence Organization concept was the belief that under the new arrangement, "personnel losses resulting from decentralized administration or misassignment are less likely to occur." Folder, Military Intelligence Support in the Field Army, 1960, Background of MI Branch/Corps file, INSCOM History Office, Fort Belvoir, Va. A more detailed description of the organization can be found in Irving Heymont, *Combat Intelligence in Modern Warfare* (Harrisburg: Stackpole Co., 1960), pp. 124–29.

[12] The 519th Military Intelligence Battalion eventually received active Companies B and C in 1962.

counterintelligence and field operations intelligence personnel continued to serve in single-discipline cellular units supporting the theaters and the Zone of Interior armies until 1961, when consolidated Intelligence Corps groups and detachments were formed.

Not all intelligence disciplines were well served by this new arrangement. In the continental United States, linguists had to be concentrated at battalion level, rather than spread among the detachments that were attached to divisions and other tactical units, as the Military Intelligence Organization concept dictated. Each detachment might be involved in several contingency plans, and each plan often required expertise in a different language. There was simply no way to assign the appropriate linguists to a Military Intelligence detachment until actual implementation of a specific plan or major field exercise began.

Photo interpreters also fit rather uneasily into the new structure. At the tactical level such personnel lacked access to the imagery that national-level reconnaissance elements began to generate in the late 1950s, and thus felt that their skills were not being adequately used. Units based in the United States had no operational mission, and photo interpreters found themselves all too often assigned to housekeeping and administrative positions unrelated to their specialty. Detailed to kitchen police and other "rock-painting" chores, many felt slighted and complained of "harassment."[13]

To remedy the situation, in 1963 the Army Intelligence Center proposed that all photo interpreters in the United States be placed under centralized control in the same fashion as the Army's linguists. They could find more useful employment either at the Army Photo Interpretation Center or with the Army's lone specialized tactical photo unit in the United States. However, field commanders strongly resisted the proposal on the grounds that stripping Military Intelligence detachments of their photo interpreters would deprive G–2s of access to this intelligence field and would result in equipment maintenance problems. The status quo thus continued.

Finally, the Army continued to neglect tactical-level technical intelligence. There were no provisions for a technical intelligence company in the initial TOEs for the Military Intelligence battalion (field army), and it would take ten years for the Army to remedy this discrepancy. By that time, the Vietnam conflict would be in full swing, creating an insatiable demand for personnel resources, and only one field army–level battalion would ever receive its technical intelligence company.

At the tactical level, intelligence organization was also influenced by the Army's increasing reliance on aircraft. By 1960 there were 5,000 aircraft in the Army inventory. Many of them were helicopters, items that had first seen extensive use in medical evacuation during the Korean War. It soon became apparent

---

13 Memo, 8 Feb 63, sub: Centralization of Image Interpreters under USAPIC, RG 319, NARA.

that improved versions of rotary-wing aircraft could serve as useful reconnaissance assets. During the course of the 1950s the Korean-vintage L–19 that had served as the all-purpose workhorse within the division was phased out in favor of the helicopter, and aircraft within the division were concentrated in larger formations. Under the structure of the pentomic division fielded in 1957, Army aviation within the divisions was consolidated into company-size units. The ROAD division of 1962 included a complete aviation battalion, one company of which was equipped with scout helicopters. In addition, observation helicopters were assigned to divisional artillery, and a helicopter-borne aerial cavalry troop formed part of the divisional reconnaissance battalion.[14]

Along with its helicopters, the Army also developed more sophisticated fixed-wing aircraft for reconnaissance. In 1962 it acquired the AO–1 Mohawk. This twin-engine craft came in three configurations: one equipped with a high-performance camera; one with newly developed infrared night vision equipment; and the third with the equally new side-looking airborne radar device. Mohawks were employed both in divisional aerial surveillance and targeting platoons, as well as in aerial surveillance companies that operated at corps level.[15]

In addition to developing its own aerial assets, the Army took steps to improve its interaction with Air Force tactical reconnaissance. To better exploit aerial photography produced by Air Force reconnaissance squadrons, the Army fielded the 1st Air Reconnaissance Support Battalion in 1959. The unit consisted of a headquarters and headquarters detachment, a signal air photo reproduction and delivery company, and a photo interpretation company. A similar unit, the 24th Air Reconnaissance Support Battalion, was activated in the Army Reserve the same year, thus becoming the first non-ASA intelligence battalion active in the reserve components since the Korean War. In 1961 the Army activated another Regular Army air reconnaissance support battalion to support the Seventh Army in Germany, and in 1962 these units were reorganized and redesignated as Military Intelligence battalions (air reconnaissance support), or "Mibars." Two years later it devised a new TOE for this type of unit that provided for a headquarters and headquarters company and four lettered imagery interpretation detachments.[16] The diverse nature of the products which photo interpreters now had to manage—infrared and radar imagery, as well as conventional photography—led to the Army's redesignating photographic intelligence as imagery intelligence in 1964.

There were also new developments in the Army's arrangements for ground reconnaissance. From 1957 on, each combat division had its own reconnaissance battalion. The successive restructurings of the division in 1957 and 1962

---

14 John J. Tolson, *Airmobility, 1961–1971*, Vietnam Studies (Washington, D.C.: Department of the Army, 1973), p. 10.

15 Ibid., p. 12.

16 373 Card, 1st Military Intelligence Bn, Unit Data Branch, U.S. Army Center of Military History.

meant that reconnaissance assets previously held at the regimental level were moved down, first to battle group, and then to battalion. An armored cavalry platoon and a ground surveillance section equipped with mobile radar sets became part of the headquarters company of each infantry battalion.

Intelligence Support to the Theaters

By the late 1950s the deployment of the Army overseas had become fixed in a pattern that would remain largely unchanged for the duration of the Cold War.[17] The completion of the European buildup, the drawdown of forces in Korea, and the signing of a peace treaty with Japan resulted in a force structure that gave the Army five divisions in Europe and two in Korea, commanded respectively by the Seventh and Eighth Armies. The diversity of the theaters, the disparate numbers of the supported forces in each one, and the differing nature of intelligence requirements in Europe and in the Pacific dictated that arrangements for intelligence support would not be uniform. Moreover, even if the positioning of troops on the ground remained relatively static, theater command relationships did not, and these shifts also impacted on the theater intelligence structure.

In Europe a continuing flood of refugees from behind the Iron Curtain provided American forces with ample opportunities for intelligence exploitation. From 1951 to 1962 collection of intelligence from border crossers was carried out by the Seventh Army's 532d Military Intelligence Battalion, a field-army type of unit organized under the Military Intelligence Organization concept and headquartered in Stuttgart-Vaihingen, Federal Republic of Germany. During an average year, the battalion screened between 20,000 and 30,000 refugees.

At the theater level, counterintelligence support for U.S. Army, Europe (USAREUR), was provided by the 66th Counter Intelligence Corps Group. This unit, with headquarters in Stuttgart, provided counterintelligence coverage through a network of regional and field offices that not only extended over West Germany but also reached occupied Berlin and the USAREUR Communications Zone in France. The 513th Military Intelligence Service Group, activated at Oberursel, Federal Republic of Germany, in 1953 to take over operations previously performed by the 7077th USAREUR Intelligence Center, soon was redesignated the 513th Military Intelligence Group and then expanded its scope of activities to include active collection. With the inception of an Army civilian intelligence career program in the 1950s, both units received large TD augmentations of civilian specialists.

In 1959 USAREUR experimented with organizing intelligence work on an area rather than on a functional basis. Consequently the 513th Military

---

[17] Strategist Edward M. Luttwalk noted in 1984, "Our deployment overseas resembles geological layers, each the enduring residue of some past crisis or war, now hardened into a 'commitment.'" *The Pentagon and the Art of War* (New York: Simon and Shuster, 1984), p. 73.

Intelligence Group was given northern Germany as its area of responsibility, and the 66th Counter Intelligence Corps Group (later successively redesignated as the 66th Military Intelligence Group and the 66th Intelligence Corps Group) was allotted the south, where the preponderance of American forces was stationed. This arrangement caused more problems than solutions and was later abandoned.

Meanwhile, opportunities for exploitation of sources began to diminish. In 1961 the construction of the Berlin Wall and the simultaneous imposition of tighter border controls by East Germany effectively shut off the refugee flow. This development reduced the need to have three large intelligence units with partially overlapping responsibilities in Europe. As a result, in 1962 there was a major realignment of intelligence resources. The 513th Intelligence Corps Group, as it was now designated, assumed complete responsibility for active intelligence and certain sensitive counterespionage missions for USAREUR, while the 66th Intelligence Corps Group was reassigned to Seventh Army and assumed the mission of the inactivated 532d Military Intelligence Battalion. During this process, the group lost its regional form of organization and emerged as the command headquarters for various numbered Army Intelligence units, including the tactical intelligence elements attached to the Seventh Army's corps and divisions.[18]

Cryptologic support in the theater was provided by an entirely separate organizational structure, in conformity with Army practice. The U.S. Army Security Agency maintained a theater headquarters in Frankfurt that exercised command and control over various field stations in Europe and over a group headquarters with three subordinate battalions and some other units operating in support of the Seventh Army.

In the Pacific, following the conclusion of the armistice in Korea, the Army broke up its elaborate intelligence and special operations organization, the 8240th Army Unit. Under conditions of relative peace, the Korean partisan forces it had mustered were transferred to the control of the South Korean government, the least productive of its operations terminated, and its mission restricted to intelligence collection. The unit's Korean-based element, the Army Collection Detachment, continued to report to a theater-level Army command reconnaissance activity until 1961, when a number of Army Intelligence assets in Korea combined to form the 502d Military Intelligence Battalion. The other elements used to form the battalion came from the 308th Counter Intelligence Corps Detachment and the Eighth Army's 528th Military Intelligence Company, which were concurrently inactivated.

At the theater level, U.S. Army Forces, Far East (USAFFE), served as the Army's principal headquarters element in the Pacific until 1957. It was supported

---

18 It should be pointed out that in addition to the units which supported USAREUR and Seventh Army during this period, the 450th Counter Intelligence Corps Detachment provided security to Supreme Headquarters, Allied Powers in Europe, from 1951 on. The unit was redesignated the 650th Military Intelligence Detachment in 1966 and upgraded to group status in 1970.

by an elaborate intelligence architecture directed by the USAFFE G–2 in Tokyo, Japan. The organization's principal human intelligence collection arm was the U.S. Army Command Reconnaissance Activity, Far East. The other major field elements were the 500th Military Intelligence Group, an interpreter unit, and the 441st Counter Intelligence Corps Group. These three units reported to the U.S. Army Intelligence Support Center, Japan, under command of a brigadier general.

The Eisenhower-Kishii agreement of 1957 led to a drawdown of American troop strength from Japan and relocation of the Army's main Pacific headquarters from Tokyo to Hawaii. The discontinuance of USAFFE and the establishment of United States Army, Pacific (USARPAC), led to a rapid decrement in Japan-based Military Intelligence assets. The 500th Military Intelligence Group was inactivated, the Intelligence Support Center discontinued, and the functions of both organizations absorbed by the successor of the U.S. Army Command Reconnaissance Activity, Far East, the U.S. Army Command Reconnaissance Activity, Pacific. Following the departure of most American troops from Japan in 1959, the 441st Counter Intelligence Corps Detachment, as it was now known, was in turn inactivated. In 1961 the U.S. Army Command Reconnaissance Activity, Pacific, was discontinued and the 500th Military Intelligence Group once more reactivated to carry out all aspects of the human intelligence mission. This group redeployed to Hawaii in 1965, a move dictated by the U.S. government's attempts at that time to reduce the outflow of gold reserves overseas.

U.S. Army Security Agency operations in the Far East were under the direction of a regional headquarters located in Tokyo until 1958. This was consolidated briefly with ASA headquarters elements in Hawaii from 1958 to 1960 to become the U.S. Army Security Agency, Pacific. In 1960 it returned to Tokyo, where it remained until it again relocated to Hawaii in 1965. The withdrawal of the agency's Pacific headquarters back to American soil also came about because of the government's concern over the balance of payments.

After 1957 the Eighth Army in Korea received its cryptologic support from the 508th U.S. Army Security Group (a TD unit) and the 321st U.S. Army Security Agency Battalion, another TD unit. The battalion was discontinued in 1964—another casualty of the government's worries about the gold flow.

One unique feature of the Pacific theater was the existence of the U.S. Army Intelligence School, Pacific. Unlike other Army Intelligence training facilities overseas, the Pacific intelligence school, set up on Okinawa in 1958, trained foreigners, not Americans. The students from seven different countries bordering the Pacific basin took courses in combat intelligence and counterintelligence techniques until the reversion of Okinawa to Japanese sovereignty brought operations to a halt in 1975.[19]

---

[19] History of the U.S. Army Intelligence School Pacific, U.S. Army Intelligence School Pacific, 1971, copy in INSCOM History Office files.

The McNamara Revolution

The outcome of the presidential election of 1960 led to major changes in the structure of the Army and the Army's intelligence components. President John F. Kennedy rejected the strategic assumptions of the previous administration, believing that any military challenge had to be met through graduated deterrence. This approach placed a new emphasis on the importance of the nation's conventional forces, including the Army. Kennedy selected Secretary of Defense Robert S. McNamara to implement the new strategy. In carrying out his assignment, McNamara, a former Ford Motors executive with a background in systems analysis, proved to be the very model of a rationalizing, centralizing bureaucrat. Making the most of the powers of his office, McNamara introduced a series of reforms that altered the way the American military machine was constructed and had a profound effect on the Army Intelligence community.[20]

Since 1958 there had been discussions at the national level concerning the advisability of setting up some kind of intelligence agency at the Department of Defense (DOD) level to better coordinate the intelligence elements of the armed services. In 1960 a Joint Study Group had criticized the existing arrangements within the Military Intelligence community. Three separate and uncoordinated service intelligence agencies, each with its own parochial bias, could not provide DOD with the integrated intelligence it needed to formulate a coherent national strategy. Air Force Intelligence in particular had embarrassed policy makers, since its estimates of alleged "bomber gaps" and "missile gaps" between the United States and the Soviet Union were widely disseminated and later demonstrated to be incorrect.[21]

Once in office, McNamara became a vigorous proponent of centralization, especially with respect to Military Intelligence operations under DOD. As a result, the Defense Intelligence Agency (DIA) began operations on 1 October 1961. The new organization would impose the same kind of centralized direction and control on the general Military Intelligence program as NSA was already providing to signals intelligence. Its creation meant that Army Intelligence would become a distinctly subordinate element within a wider Military Intelligence structure and marked a further cutback in ACSI's powers and responsibilities. However, this did not happen immediately. At its inception, DIA consisted of a cadre of twenty-five people housed in 2,000 square feet of borrowed office space in the Pentagon. The new agency pulled together rather slowly at first, initially taking on only the estimative, current intelligence, and requirements missions from the service intelligence agencies.

---

20 One standard biography of the secretary of defense, Henry L. Truehitt's *McNamara* (New York: Harper and Rowe, 1971), has little to say about his role in Army reorganization.

21 The role of Air Force Intelligence as a "loose cannon" and how this helped bring about the formation of DIA is documented in John Prados, *The Soviet Estimate: U.S. Intelligence Analysis and Soviet Military Strength* (Princeton: Princeton University Press, 1986), pp. 43–44, 93, 115–16, 124.

Meanwhile, McNamara was reorganizing the Army itself in ways that had a substantial effect on the Army's intelligence architecture. In 1962 the secretary of defense implemented Project 80, which involved the wholesale restructuring of the Army into functional, centralized commands. In the process, ACSI lost control over intelligence training, research and development, and doctrinal matters. Five of the Army's technical services were abolished, with only the Corps of Engineers and the Office of the Surgeon General remaining in place, and their intelligence personnel were split up among a number of different elements.[22]

A few order of battle specialists from the dissolved technical services joined the ACSI staff. A larger group engaged in scientific and technical intelligence became part of a new Foreign Science and Technology Center or stayed in place at the Army Missile Intelligence Agency which the Ordnance Department maintained at Redstone Arsenal. Both of these centers were assigned to the Army Materiel Command, which McNamara had just created. The largest group, consisting of 700 persons engaged in area analysis, was absorbed into the Area Analysis Intelligence Agency established at the direction of the chief of Engineers.

The Area Analysis Intelligence Agency was intended to be only a temporary holding area. When DIA assumed production responsibilities in 1963, the organization was discontinued, and its personnel, together with part of the OACSI staff, transferred to DIA. All in all, the Army contributed 1,000 spaces and its ACSI-MATIC computer system to the new DIA Production Center. In the process, OACSI lost 235 spaces, one-third of its strength, to the new agency. The centerpiece of OACSI had been its Directorate of Foreign Intelligence, the intelligence production unit. This was reduced to a shell, retaining only a residual responsibility for analyzing and interpreting national agency production in support of the Army and in maintaining liaison with DIA. As a result of this devolution of responsibilities, the center of gravity of Army Intelligence would move from the staff in Washington, D.C., to the units in the field.

However, even after the reorganization of 1963 DIA did not hold a complete monopoly over the production of intelligence for the Army. Subordinate elements within the Army continued to conduct production activities. These included the Army Materiel Command, with its two scientific and technical intelligence centers; the Office of the Chief of Engineers, which administered the Army Map Service; and the Office of the Surgeon General, which still had the responsibility of meeting some of the Army's medical intelligence requirements. In addition, a new production element was formed at Fort Bragg, North Carolina, to support the mobile reserve forces assigned to the Continental Army Command (CONARC).

Other intelligence-related functions previously performed by the Army were also centralized. In 1963 the Army's Strategic Intelligence School was merged with its Navy counterpart to form a new Defense Intelligence School, which

---

22 Hewes, *From Root to McNamara*, p. 364.

began to provide training for attaches from all the military services. The process was carried through to its logical conclusion in 1965, when DIA assumed control over the military attache system that had served as an Army information source since 1889. All service attaches were integrated into the new Defense Attache System. Meanwhile, the Defense Language Institute had replaced the separate language schools previously maintained by the services.

Although DIA acquired production and collection assets from Army Intelligence, another new McNamara creation (the Defense Supply Agency) asserted itself on the counterintelligence front. In March 1965 this agency took over the whole field of industrial security, absorbing all the related spaces from ACSI's Industrial and Personnel Security Group. Ever since World War II, the function had rebounded between G–2 and the Provost Marshal General's Office. The new arrangement seemed to mark a definitive end to this particular jurisdictional dispute within the Army.

OACSI responded to these institutional challenges in much the same way as ASA had met the threat of the Armed Forces Security Agency: it found a new role in devoting itself to Army-specific needs. Shorn of many of its operational functions, OACSI reoriented itself and began providing intensified staff supervision to intelligence areas of growing interest to the Army. In the summer of 1963 the Directorate of Surveillance and Reconnaissance was added to the Army's Intelligence staff to develop the doctrine and hardware that would allow the Army to glean information from the battlefield through innovative technologies. Additional new Directorates of Security and Combat Intelligence were formed in 1964 to supervise functional areas of primary interest to the Army. The Combat Intelligence Directorate included a section responsible for overseeing developments in the fields of special warfare and foreign assistance. Finally, OACSI found ways to edge back into fields of activity theoretically preempted by DIA. In 1963 it set up a Special Research Detachment as a liaison element at NSA, soon expanding it into an all-source production element. The same year the Special Security Detachment formed an Intelligence Support Branch to provide the Army Staff with current intelligence.

The U.S. Army Intelligence Command and the U.S. Army Security Agency

The McNamara-directed reorganization of the Army had significant consequences for the Army Intelligence Center at Fort Holabird, Maryland. The center, commanded by the chief of the Intelligence Corps, had functioned as a field operating agency under direct ACSI control. Two of its main assets were the Army Intelligence School and the Army Intelligence Board, charged with framing doctrine and developing specialized equipment. The McNamara restructuring intruded on both of these arrangements. The Intelligence School was resubordinated to CONARC and the functions of the Intelligence Board split between the Army Materiel Command and another McNamara creation, the Combat Developments Command.

As a result, ACSI created a new administrative entity, the U.S. Army Intelligence Corps Activity, which took over the remnant of the former Intelligence Center's assets and residual functions. The organization served as a vehicle through which the chief of the Intelligence Corps could exercise control over those elements the McNamara restructuring had left under ACSI jurisdiction. These consisted of the Army's counterintelligence records facility, a new Intelligence Corps Supply Activity, the Strategic Intelligence School (until its transfer to DIA), the Army Photo Interpretation Center, and the Administrative Survey Detachment that supported the Intelligence Civilian Career Program which ACSI had started in the 1950s. However, the establishment of the Army Intelligence Corps Activity did nothing to alleviate the confusion in the intelligence command chain resulting from the reorganizations. Since the chief of the Intelligence Corps continued to act as commandant of the Army Intelligence School and commander of Fort Holabird, he now reported simultaneously to three different superiors. As commanding general of the U.S. Army Intelligence Corps Activity and chief of the Intelligence Corps he was responsible to ACSI, but he was under the jurisdiction of CONARC in his capacity as school commandant and subordinate to the U.S. Second Army in his role of post commander. This Rube Goldberg–like arrangement offered no promise of stability.

These changes represented only the beginning of the restructuring of Army counterintelligence organization. In 1963 and 1964 the Army undertook a major study of its personnel security system, an effort spurred by the discovery that an Army sergeant in a sensitive position at the National Security Agency had been passing information to the Soviets for years without being detected.[23] The study, Project SECURITY SHIELD, found serious weaknesses both in the traditional decentralized approach to counterintelligence operations and in the coordination that existed between Army counterintelligence and the criminal investigators of the Provost Marshal General's Office. SECURITY SHIELD led to yet another wholesale reorganization of Army counterintelligence.

On 1 January 1965, the Army created the U.S. Army Intelligence Corps Command as a Department of the Army major field command. Operating under a new design concept, the command took over centralized direction over all counterintelligence operations in the continental United States. The Intelligence Corps Command assumed authority over the seven Intelligence Corps groups that had previously operated under six armies and the Military District of Washington. (The large CIC detachments in the United States had been redesig-

---

23 The errant sergeant was Sfc. Jack Edward Dunlap. The story of the case can be found in James Bamford's popular but highly unauthorized book, *The Puzzle Palace: A Report on NSA, America's Most Secret Agency* (Boston: Houghton Mifflin, 1982), pp. 150–53.

nated as "groups" between 1956 and 1959.) At the same time, the Army ordered the field offices of the Intelligence Corps Command and the provost marshal's Criminal Investigation Division (CID) to be brought together wherever possible, and the records of the CID repository removed from Fort Gordon, Georgia, and collocated with the counterintelligence records at Fort Holabird.

The creation of the Intelligence Corps Command gave its commander, the chief of the Intelligence Corps, operational responsibilities for the first time in the history of Army counterintelligence. At the same time, he lost certain assets. Not all the elements of the former Army Intelligence Corps Activity were transferred to the new command. Since the Intelligence Corps Command was intended to be purely a counterintelligence organization, the Army Imagery Interpretation Center, as the Photo Interpretation Center had been redesignated, reverted back to the direct control of the ACSI.

There were still certain anomalies in the new pattern of organization. Despite its title, the Intelligence Corps Command controlled only about half of all Intelligence Corps personnel in the continental United States. The rest were on school or organizational staffs, with the TOE organizations supporting tactical elements in the field, or in the "pipeline." Intelligence Corps personnel deployed outside the continental United States were not a part of the new command. The Intelligence Corps Command's commander, in his other capacity as chief of the Intelligence Corps, thus had substantial administrative responsibilities extending beyond his own command; and the Intelligence Corps he headed was engaged in active intelligence collection as well as in counterintelligence. The creation of the new headquarters also had left the chain of command more tangled than ever. Its commander now wore four hats. As head of a major field command, he now reported directly to the Army chief of staff, in addition to reporting to ACSI, the commander of CONARC, and the commander of the U.S. Second Army in his other various roles.[24]

In one sense, this arrangement conformed to the civilian theories of matrix management popular in the 1960s. Matrix management held that someone marketing refrigerators to Latin America should report to a vice president for marketing, a vice president for refrigerators, and a vice president for Latin America. But the scheme did not accord with normal Army command procedures and was in practice unworkable. Not surprisingly, reorganization plans were begun as soon as the new command had been assembled. The U.S. Army Intelligence Corps Command lasted just six months.

There seemed to be only two possible solutions to the organizational tangle created by the existence of the Intelligence Corps Command. One duplicated

24 As the U.S. Army Intelligence Corps Command's own fact sheet noted at the time, "USAINTCC is only one facet of the intelligence complex located at Fort Holabird. The integrated staff serves four masters." Fact Sheet, U.S. Army Intelligence Corps Command, p. 2. U.S. Army Intelligence Command file, INSCOM History Office.

the Army Security Agency's centralized, vertical command structure, creating a self-sufficient organization. However, because of its mission, that agency was a special case, and its organization had no parallel in the rest of the Army. The other solution, the one adopted, decentralized the structure of the Intelligence Corps Command.

The U.S. Army Intelligence Command (USAINTC) was created on 1 July 1965 to conduct counterintelligence operations within the continental United States.[25] The combined headquarters organization of the former Intelligence Corps Command was broken up, and the Army Intelligence School and Fort Holabird placed under separate commanders. Functions previously performed by the Intelligence Corps Command that were unrelated to counterintelligence—administering the intelligence civilian career program and procuring intelligence-related supply items—reverted to ACSI, resulting in the establishment of the Administrative Survey Detachment and the Intelligence Materiel Development Support Office as separate field operating activities. Finally, the Intelligence Corps itself was discontinued in March 1966, and its personnel functions shifted to the Department of Army level. This ended the Army's attempts to integrate human intelligence and counterintelligence personnel under a single organizational structure. Discontinuance of the Intelligence Corps also resulted in the redesignation of all Intelligence Corps units as Military Intelligence units.[26]

The creation of the U.S. Army Intelligence Command meant that the Army counterintelligence organization had been turned inside out. The old Counter Intelligence Corps had selected, trained, and administered Army counterintelligence personnel, but counterintelligence operations themselves had been decentralized under the control of local Army commanders. The new major Army field command was a centralized operational organization without any personnel or training functions. The demise of the Intelligence Corps ended a special tradition that went back to the Corps of Intelligence Police in World War I, but the new arrangements meant that Army counterintelligence was now aligned with the rest of the Army.

If McNamara's organizational innovations destroyed the Intelligence Corps, they left the Army Security Agency substantially untouched. Because of its specialized mission and compartmented operations, the agency escaped the loss of its training and research and development functions. Instead, it expanded physically, geographically, and functionally. An ASA element, with the in-country designation of the 3d Radio Research Unit, deployed to Vietnam to support the ongoing advisory effort as early as 1961.[27] The agency also acquired an impor-

---

[25] GO 23, HQDA, 1 Jul 65.

[26] Intelligence Corps groups were redesignated Military Intelligence groups on 16 October 1966.

[27] One member of the 3d Radio Research Unit was Sp4c. James T. Davis, who was killed in action on 22 December 1961, and whom President Lyndon Johnson later described as the first fatality of the Vietnam War.

tant new acoustical intelligence mission in 1962, following the abolition of the Signal Corps as an Army technical service. A year later, the Army Security Agency achieved a monopoly of Army electronic warfare functions when it took over control of the noncommunications-jamming function and associated units from the Signal Corps. In 1964 it set up its third field station in the continental United States at Homestead, Florida, to better meet new mission requirements which had evolved in the early 1960s. Finally, the agency's independence and unique position within the Army was ratified on 14 April 1964, when it achieved the status of a major Army field command.[28]

The Army Intelligence and Security Branch

The changes within the Army Intelligence community during the 1960s were not confined to shifts in function and in command relationships. Army Intelligence took a giant step in the direction of full professionalism in 1962, when the Army Intelligence and Security Branch was set up as a basic branch of the Regular Army. This development was long overdue. Since World War II, intelligence professionals had argued that the very existence of intelligence units created the need for a separate intelligence branch. The logic of this argument was increasingly reinforced by practical necessities. The pool of reserve officers capable of filling intelligence slots was becoming exhausted. Without a reform in the Army personnel system, analysts projected that half the Army's intelligence officer positions would be without qualified occupants by 1965. The incumbent ACSI, Maj. Gen. Alva R. Fitch, pushed vigorously for the creation of a new branch to remedy the situation. Yet even the Army Intelligence community was divided on the issue. The ASA chief protested that the proposed integration of signals intelligence officers with other intelligence personnel would be like putting infantry and artillery into one branch. But Fitch won his case. The new branch came into existence formally on 1 July 1962.[29]

The Army Intelligence and Security Branch embraced about 5 percent of officers in the active Army. The initial group joining the branch consisted of 283 Regular Army and 3,652 reserve officers who had a background in intelligence or were assigned to intelligence positions. A quarter of the group consisted of cryptologic specialists; the remainder broke down about evenly into combat intelligence personnel and members of the Intelligence Corps. The formation of the new branch significantly enhanced the Army's capacity to promote and retain qualified intelligence officers.

---

28 GO 14, HQDA, 14 Apr 64. As a result of this upgrade in status, the chief, Army Security Agency, assumed the new title of commanding general, Army Security Agency.

29 Marc B. Powe and Edward E. Wilson, *The Evolution of American Military Intelligence* (Fort Huachuca, Ariz.: U.S. Army Intelligence Center and School, 1973), p. 105.

However, the new branch had problems initially. It contained only a small number of Regular Army officers, and many of the reserve officers brought into the Army Intelligence and Security Branch lacked higher education or prospects for career advancement. The branch was designated as one that performed a combat service support function, not the most prestigious role in the Army. Finally, it was the only branch in the Army without a common basic course. Although most Intelligence officers attended Fort Holabird for training, Army Security Agency officers still trained separately at the U.S. Army Security Agency Training Center and School (USASATC&S) at Fort Devens, Massachusetts. Nevertheless, within the space of four years, much of Army Intelligence had been reconfigured. The new structure would meet its first test in the foreign and domestic challenges during the war in Vietnam.

Antenna array of the 326th Communication Reconnaissance Company during the Korean War. (*INSCOM*)

Photointerpreters of the 45th ("Thunderbird") Infantry Division examine imagery of the Korean countryside. (*NARA*)

The sphinx—historically identified with Military Intelligence—stands in front of the headquarters of Fort Holabird, Maryland, home of the Army Intelligence School from 1954–1971. (*INSCOM*)

Antenna array of the 276th Army Security Agency Company at an overseas site. (*INSCOM*)

The durable OV–1 "Mohawk" served as the Army's main aerial reconnaissance platform for a generation. (*DA Photograph*)

Assistant Chief of Staff for Intelligence Maj. Gen. Alva Fitch was instrumental in establishing the Intelligence and Security Branch (later Military Intelligence Branch) in the Regular Army in 1962. (*Courtesy of Maj. Gen. Joseph A. MaChristian, U.S. Army [Ret.]*)

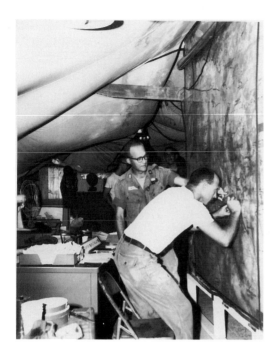

Members of the 25th MI Detachment plot suspected enemy positions on a map at the Cu Chi base camp during the Vietnam conflict. (*NARA*)

An intelligence officer interrogates a suspected member of the Viet Cong. (*NARA*)

A Special Forces team operates an AN/PRD–1 radio direction finder. (*INSCOM*)

Operations room at the head-quarters of the U.S. Army Intelligence Command, which directed Army counterintelligence activities in the continental United States during the troubled Vietnam era. (*NARA*)

As a result of the Intelligence Organization and Stationing Study, the Army formed new Combat Electronic Warfare and Intelligence (CEWI) units to support its tactical formations. A soldier of the 519th Military Intelligence Battalion demonstrates a PRD–11 radio direction finder. (*519th MI Battalion Photograph*)

New systems such as the Guardrail Common Sensor mounted aboard the RC–12 platform enhanced the Army's electronic warfare and intelligence capabilities. (*DA Photograph*)

Organization Day ceremonies for the Military Intelligence Corps at Fort Huachuca, Arizona, in 1987. The Army had relocated its Military Intelligence schoolhouse to the post in 1971. (*U.S. Army Intelligence Center and Fort Huachuca*)

The Army Intelligence and Security Command, organized in 1977 to conduct multidiscipline intelligence and electronic warfare operations at the echelon above corps, finally moved into this new headquarters building at Fort Belvoir, Virginia, in 1989. (*INSCOM*)

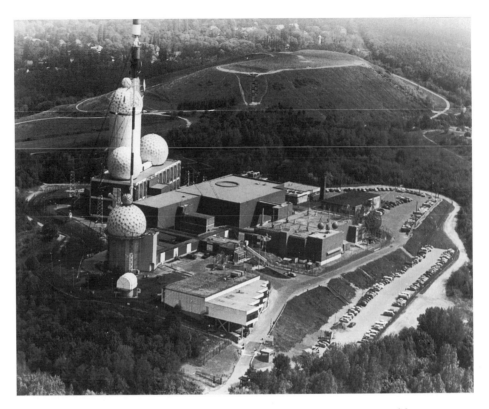

A Disneyland castle perched atop an artificial hill, U.S. Army Field Station Berlin served as INSCOM's forward outpost behind the Iron Curtain until termination of the Cold War brought about its closure in 1992. (*INSCOM*)

A soldier of INSCOM's 704th MI Brigade. Increased use of sophisticated automation and communications systems would help pave the way for Army Intelligence to carry out its diverse and demanding missions following the end of the Cold War. (*704th MI Brigade Photograph*)

9

Vietnam and Beyond

The 1960s began with brave promises; however, events soon began to go awry. Although successive crises with the Soviet Union over Berlin and the Soviet deployment of missiles to Cuba were resolved peaceably, the Viet Cong insurgency in South Vietnam continued to fester, despite the involvement of an increasing number of American military advisers. In early November 1963 a beleaguered President Ngo Dinh Diem of South Vietnam was assassinated during a coup by his own Army. Intended to stabilize the deteriorating security situation in South Vietnam by removing an unpopular leader, the coup had the opposite effect. As a revolving-door series of ephemeral governments came and went in Saigon, Communists gained an increasing foothold in the countryside. Meanwhile, President John F. Kennedy had been assasinated in Dallas; his successor, Lyndon B. Johnson, had a wealth of experience in domestic politics but no substantive understanding of foreign affairs. Johnson won election in 1964 on a platform of peace and social reform, but soon found that developments in Vietnam would imperil both goals. By early 1965 a Viet Cong victory seemed imminent.

America responded initially with limited air raids against the Viet Cong's sponsor, North Vietnam. When this action proved unproductive, ground troops were committed to the South under the direction of the Military Assistance Command, Vietnam (MACV), a joint, Army-dominated "sub-theater" headquarters. The North Vietnamese countered by steadily increasing their war buildup, sending in their own regular forces to supplement the activities of the guerrillas. Thus the United States lurched into an undeclared war.[1] On the American side, this remained a limited effort. The president's main focus was on constructing a "Great Society" at home, and he regarded the war in Southeast Asia as an unpleasant distraction. As a matter of deliberate management, the conflict was fought without passion, without censorship, without mobilization, and without raising taxes. Increasingly, it was fought without

---

[1] For a caustic evaluation of the Johnson administration's conduct of the war, see David Halberstam's *The Best and the Brightest* (New York: Random House, 1972).

popular enthusiasm. On the other hand, for the North Vietnamese and their Viet Cong proxies, the war was total.

By the end of 1967 an American Army of 485,000 soldiers and marines, backed up by an enormous logistical system, had deployed in country; and officials talked brightly that there was now "light at the end of the tunnel."[2] The Tet offensive at the beginning of 1968 dispelled this dream, however. It broke the will of an administration and shattered the confidence of the American people. After Tet, all roads ran downhill. The Johnson administration decided to stop reinforcing the war effort; its successor chose to withdraw gradually from the war and return the tar baby to the luckless South Vietnamese. In the meantime, the United States was unraveling on the domestic front. Racial unrest resulted in rioting on a massive scale, while an increasingly violent antiwar movement grew in strength on the nation's campuses.

What ensued was an almost complete debacle. A cease-fire in place in Vietnam at last was signed in Paris in 1973. A similar agreement, signed in Korea twenty years before, had endured. However, the government of South Korea had been in full control of its own territory, and American military might had backed up the agreement. Neither of these conditions proved true in Southeast Asia. Hundreds of thousands of North Vietnamese troops remained in place in the South, and a peaceful end to the conflict seemed remote. American ground forces were completely withdrawn from Vietnam, and any chance that the peace settlement would stand was undermined by the disintegration of the Nixon administration amid the toils of the Watergate scandal. Confronted by a North Vietnamese blitzkrieg and abandoned by its American allies, in 1975 the South Vietnamese government collapsed.[3]

All of these events had a massive impact on Military Intelligence. Some structural changes that took place during this period were driven by new developments in technology. Most, however, were brought about by the military commitment to Southeast Asia and its manifold repercussions. The Vietnam conflict, its domestic side effects, and the economic and psychological constraints produced by the outcome of the venture all worked to reshape the organization of Army Intelligence.

Vietnam: Buildup and Deployment

The Vietnam conflict proved a formidable challenge to Army Intelligence, as well as to the rest of the American defense establishment. The Army was forced to function in an unfamiliar environment and deal with an unfamiliar language, under rules of engagement giving the enemy a chance to accept or decline battle

---

2 Kathleen J. Turner, *Lyndon Johnson's Dual War: Vietnam and the Press* (Chicago: University of Chicago Press, 1985), p. 211.

3 It should be noted that the official Army photo history of the Vietnam War, which begins its coverage in 1945, tactfully chooses to end its account in 1973.

at will. The detailed, quantified information which the decision makers of the day demanded was not easy to develop when the enemy was a guerrilla under jungle canopy, and when the exact state of the "hearts and minds" of an indigenous population involved in a civil war was so hard to assess. Under such conditions it is not surprising that the performance of Army Intelligence engendered controversies that lived on long after American troops had left Southeast Asia.[4]

Previous conflicts had witnessed a vast expansion of the Army's departmental-level intelligence staff. However, these conflicts had been fought before the subordination of Army Intelligence to unified intelligence agencies. In Southeast Asia, the Defense Intelligence Agency would be responsible for the analytical effort. As a result, the OACSI staff actually contracted over the course of the war, and its internal organization was shaped as much by factors such as the increased availability of computer support, the need to manage new technologies, and the necessity for coping with counterintelligence problems on the domestic front as it was by the war in Southeast Asia itself. The real growth of the Army's intelligence and security organization was in the field. The Army Security Agency built up to a strength of 30,000, one-fifth of which was deployed in Vietnam at any one time, and other components grew correspondingly.

As long as the American military presence in South Vietnam had been confined to an advisory role, the demands on the Army's intelligence resources had not been excessive. In early 1965 the MACV was receiving intelligence support from a collection detachment subordinate to the Japan-based 500th Intelligence Corps Group, a counterintelligence detachment, and some two hundred intelligence officers serving as advisers with South Vietnamese troops. In-country cryptologic work was handled by the Army Security Agency's 3d Radio Research Unit (RRU), which comprised aerial as well as ground-based elements.[5]

The influx of American troops in large numbers changed all this. In response to the requests of Maj. Gen. Joseph A. McChristian, MACV assistant chief of staff for intelligence, or J–2, in 1965 the 525th Military Intelligence Group was deployed in packets from Fort Bragg, North Carolina, to serve as command and control headquarters for the intelligence effort.[6] It was joined by the 1st Military Intelligence Battalion (Aerial Reconnaissance Support) and the 519th Military Intelligence Battalion (Field Army). Soon afterward, two additional Military Intelligence groups were introduced, built up from cellular teams dispatched from the United States. These were the 135th Military Intelligence

---

4 Some of the controversies are explored in T. L. Cubbage II, "Westmoreland vs. CBS: Was Intelligence Corrupted by Policy Demands," *Intelligence and National Security* 3 (July 1988): 118–80.

5 Operations of this little-known unit are mentioned in Neil Sheehan's *A Bright Shining Lie: John Paul Vann and America in Vietnam* (New York: Random House, 1988), p. 203, and in Robert F. Futrell's *The Advisory Years to 1965*, The United States Air Force in Southeast Asia (Washington, D.C.: Office of Air Force History, 1981), p. 244.

6 Lt. Col. Arthur D. McQueen, "The Lion Goes to War," *Military Intelligence* (April/June 1977): 28–36.

Group, a counterintelligence unit, and the 149th Military Intelligence Group, with a collection mission.[7] The groups absorbed the personnel and functions of the 519th Military Intelligence Battalion's counterintelligence and collection companies. Meanwhile, the 519th was itself greatly expanded to support four combined United States–Vietnamese processing and production centers. The unit included a large technical intelligence detachment augmented by detachments from the Army technical branches.

In the fall of 1967, following the departure of General McChristian, there was another substantial reorganization of intelligence units within South Vietnam. The 525th Military Intelligence Group restructured its subordinate units into six provisional battalions, respectively located at Da Nang, Nha Trang, Bien Hoa, Can Tho, Saigon, and (for a time) Tan Son Nhut Air Base; the 135th and 149th Military Intelligence Groups subsequently were inactivated.[8] This effort was supplemented by the activities of over six hundred intelligence advisers serving with the Vietnamese; by intelligence detachments attached to all independent brigades and higher formations; and by aerial surveillance companies that operated in support of the "field forces," Army corps-level headquarters organizations with additional advisory functions. Army Special Forces and the Vietnamese Montagnards under their control also played a significant role in furnishing combat intelligence.

Army Security Agency support in country expanded as well. At the height of the war effort, the agency's 509th Radio Research Group, which had replaced the 3d Radio Research Unit, commanded a fixed field station at Phu Bai; the 224th Aviation Battalion (Radio Research); the 303d and 313th Radio Research Battalions, each attached to an Army field force; a communications security company; and some twenty direct support units (DSUs) attached to divisions and brigades.[9] Other ASA assets positioned in Thailand and the Philippines also supported the cryptologic effort.

As it evolved, the Army Intelligence effort in Vietnam became heavily committed to collaboration with the South Vietnamese, who knew the language and terrain and already possessed a useful, if fragmented, data base. General McChristian organized a Combined Intelligence Center at Tan Son Nhut Air Base near Saigon, manned by U.S. and South Vietnamese personnel and under the joint control of MACV and the South Vietnamese high command. Similar combined centers handled prisoner-of-war interrogation, document exploitation, and analysis of captured materiel.[10] In a kind of reverse advisory role,

---

7 The reorganization of Army Intelligence in the Republic of Vietnam between 1965 and 1967 is described in General Joseph A. McChristian, *The Role of Military Intelligence, 1965–1967* (Washington, D.C.: Department of the Army, 1974), pp. 3–20.

8 Shelby Stanton, *Vietnam Order of Battle* (Washington, D.C.: U.S. News Books, 1981), pp. 235–36.

9 Ibid., pp. 233–34.

10 McChristian, *The Role of Military Intelligence*, pp. 21–78. A description of the Combined

South Vietnamese Military Intelligence detachments worked directly with American formations at the level of independent brigade and above.

Vietnamese assistance was necessary because of some American deficiencies. Vietnamese linguists were in especially short supply, which made close cooperation with the South Vietnamese essential. And although there had been an American advisory presence in the country since the 1950s, America went into the war without benefit of an adequate intelligence data base. At the time DIA was formed, ACSI had delegated the task of compiling order of battle data for Southeast Asia to the U.S. Army, Pacific, while USARPAC in turn had assumed that the Military Assistance Advisory Group, Vietnam, was carrying out this responsibility. In reality, no one had done the job, and American combat forces deploying into Southeast Asia had been confronted with an intelligence vacuum.[11]

Moreover, although the McNamara regime had strengthened the previously neglected conventional forces, the Army still lacked enough trained intelligence professionals to meet its needs in Vietnam. It took a long time for the Army's intelligence training establishment to retool to meet the needs of the conflict. The Army Intelligence School did not begin to offer a Vietnam-oriented short course until 1968, and training for intelligence officers serving as advisers at the district and province level in Vietnam was not provided until 1970. Moreover, in this conflict, the reserve components could not compensate for the deficiencies of the Regular Army. There was a substantial Military Intelligence presence in the reserves, but linguistic skills were lacking, and in any case the administration had declined to deploy them. This may have been a blessing in disguise, since unit readiness in many cases was low. Maj. Gen. Charles Denholm, commanding general, U.S. Army Security Agency, deemed the ASA reserve units "almost useless."[12]

As in previous wars, communications security in the field continued to be a major problem for the Army. This was aggravated by the compartmentalized nature of the war, the extensive use of aircraft, and above all by the ubiquitousness of the radio-telephone. A Vietnam-era division, for example, had 3,000 of

---

Intelligence Center, Vietnam (and much else), is contained in Bruce E. Jones, *War Without Windows: A True Account of a Young Army Officer Trapped in an Intelligence Cover-Up in Vietnam* (New York: Vanguard Press, 1987). See also Col. Huang Ngoc Lung, *Intelligence*, Indochina Monographs (Washington, D.C.: U.S. Army Center of Military History, 1982), pp. 82–83. Lung feels that the relationship between U.S. and Vietnamese intelligence did not become "really close and effective" until 1969.

[11] General Bruce Palmer, Jr., *The 25-Year War: America's Military Role in Vietnam* (New York: Simon and Shuster, 1984), pp. 39–40.

[12] The Secretary of the Army's Program for Command Supervision of Readiness: Command Presentation by U.S. Army Security Agency, 10 Sep 68, p. 19, Army Cryptologic Records. During the Berlin Crisis of 1961 the deployment of two ASA battalions had ended in a fiasco; the units were so ill trained that that they never got beyond the gates of the ASA Training Center and School at Fort Devens, Massachusetts. Eventually, the 241st and 277th Military Intelligence Detachments were called into federal service in the token reserve mobilization following the Tet offensive, but they never went overseas.

these transmitters, compared to 225 in a representative World War II division. Proper communications security often required units to shift radio frequencies and call signs. But the crowded electromagnetic environment presented by a communications-rich war meant there were not enough available frequencies, while helicopter companies that operated over hundreds of miles in support of units drawn from a number of nations found that any change in call signs produced paralyzing confusion. The Army's manpack speech security devices were too heavy and cumbersome to be lugged through the jungle easily, and troops resorted to the use of homemade radio-telephone codes that became transparent all too easily. Many commanders preferred to ignore the whole problem, choosing to sacrifice security considerations to speed and availability of communications.[13]

There were other shortfalls. At first, lower-echelon commanders complained that they were deprived of vital timely intelligence, either because of compartmentation considerations or because scarce intelligence assets were being held under close control at higher levels. Ultimately, however, Army Intelligence constructed a serviceable organization in Vietnam, even though some of its problems were never solved. Units down to the maneuver battalion learned to coordinate intelligence with operations by establishing joint tactical operations centers. Commanders improvised special companies with the capacity to conduct long-range reconnaissance patrols; in 1969 the Army formally made these units elements of the 75th Infantry and designated them as "Rangers."[14] The Army also met the expanding intelligence and security needs of the combat divisions committed to Vietnam by expanding their intelligence detachments to full companies and providing the divisions with TOE ASA companies in direct support. In addition, Special Security Offices in each division disseminated the most sensitive intelligence derived from national-level acquisition systems. Intelligence sources available only to high-level commanders for strategic applications during World War II now could be put to tactical use. As the war progressed, the number of individuals indoctrinated for compartmented intelligence in combat divisions tripled.

Additional ground intelligence was provided by the teams of the 5th Special Forces Group, 1st Special Forces, in Vietnam and the Vietnamese Civilian Irregular Defense Groups they advised. The Special Forces camps, scattered along the thinly populated interior spine of South Vietnam, served as an outpost screen to detect the movement of infiltrating enemy columns. Besides engaging in ground reconnaissance, the Special Forces conducted intelligence and counterintelligence operations through their contacts with the local Montagnard tribesmen. Members of the Special Forces also served as the Army component of the MACV Studies and Observation Group, a joint service element under JCS

---

13 John D. Bergen, *Military Communications: A Test for Technology*, United States Army in Vietnam (Washington, D.C.: U.S. Army Center of Military History, 1987), pp. 396–401.

14 Powe and Wilson, *The Evolution of American Military Intelligence*, p. 115.

supervision that collected intelligence and carried out special operations in denied areas in conjunction with its Vietnamese counterpart organization.[15]

American advisers also contributed to the intelligence effort. Working hand in hand with their Vietnamese counterparts at the province and district levels, they became increasingly involved in an attempt to identify and neutralize the Viet Cong infrastructure that supported the insurgency through a network of district intelligence and operations coordinating centers established throughout South Vietnam. The centers had "a dual mission to produce and exploit *both* VC infrastructure and tactical Military Intelligence." Originally begun as a unilateral American effort to upgrade the effectiveness of Republic of Vietnam security organizations, the program was formally embraced by the South Vietnamese government in 1968 and assigned the dual code name PHOENIX/PHUONG TRANG.[16]

Better cryptologic support to the field came about when the Army Security Agency established management centers to service each Army field force and introduced tactical direct support units down to the level of the individual combat brigades. In the process, the agency moved into the front lines. ASA special operations personnel worked with the patrols of the Special Forces, and an ASA element mounted in armored personnel carriers was organized to provide support to the 11th Armored Cavalry Regiment.[17] The guerrilla nature of the war meant that Army Security Agency personnel usually working in safe rear areas were exposed to hazard. The large fixed field station at Phu Bai was maintained as a fortified camp, bristling with minefields, concertina wire, pillboxes, sandbagged bunkers, watchtowers, trenches, and mortar positions. ASA casualties during the Vietnam conflict were many times greater than during the Korean War.[18]

---

[15] Shelby Stanton, *Green Berets at War: U.S. Army Special Forces in Southeast Asia, 1956–1975* (Novato, Calif.: Presidio Press, 1985). See also the same author's *Vietnam Order of Battle*, pp. 239–53.

[16] ICEX Newsletter 67–4, 4 Dec 67, p. 6. By 1969, however, the Army command in Vietnam had become disenchanted by the program because of the perceived excesses of the Provincial Reconnaissance Units that served as executive agents in "neutralizing" Viet Cong cadre. Jeffrey J. Clarke, *Advice and Support: The Final Years*, United States Army in Vietnam (Washington, D.C.: U.S. Army Center of Military History, 1988), pp. 379–80. Perhaps participants took too literally the injunction to take "a 'rifle shot' approach" in dealing with the infrastructure problem. ICEX Briefing Paper, 30 Aug 67, p. 1. A recent detailed examination of PHOENIX is Dale Andrade, *Ashes to Ashes: The Phoenix Program and the Vietnam War* (Lexington, Ky.: D.C. Heath, 1990). For the personal account of an Army participant in this much maligned and misunderstood program, see Stuart H. Herrington, *Silence Was a Weapon: The War for the Vietnam Villages, A Personal Perspective* (Novato, Calif.: Presidio Press, 1982).

[17] Some of these ASA activities are captured in photographs in John P. Finnegan, *Military Intelligence: A Picture History* (Washington, D.C.: Government Printing Office, 1985), pp. 167–68.

[18] Casualties among Military Intelligence personnel were not restricted to members of the Army Security Agency. During the Tet offensive, the Hue detachment of the 525th MI Group was overrun and its members killed or captured. The first Medal of Honor ever granted to a Military Intelligence officer was awarded posthumously to 1st Lt. George Sisler, assistant intelligence officer of a Special Forces team.

In the area of communications security, the Army Security Agency sought to bring about improvement by changing its approach. During the first stages of the war, tactical units in the field received communications security support from their attached ASA companies and detachments. At that time, communications security was conceived of as essentially a police-type function of monitoring friendly communications and warning of possible compromises. This arrangement proved to be ineffective, producing conflicts with supported commanders. As a remedy, the agency evolved a new concept of "before the fact" assistance, having its personnel serve as advisers rather than as policemen.[19] Under this doctrine, communications security personnel assisted in planning operational communications procedures and instructed troops on the necessity of communications security. To implement this better, in 1969 the agency's in-country communications security assets were withdrawn from the direct support units and concentrated in the 101st Radio Research Company. A similar centralized ASA security company was also formed in Europe. The new, non-punitive approach was facilitated by the simultaneous fielding of the Nestor family of speech security devices, which eliminated much of the security problem at the source.[20]

Organizational innovations in the intelligence and security field were supplemented by the introduction of new technologies. Airborne electronic support, first pioneered in Vietnam and conducted from fixed-wing aircraft and later from helicopters, was one.[21] Other elements of Army Intelligence were able to make productive use of gadgets such as unattended ground sensors and "people-sniffers." Infrared and side-looking airborne radar sensors supplemented the traditional visual and optical techniques of aerial observation, while the pairing of observation and armed helicopters into "pink teams" with the dual missions of finding and fighting gave another dimension to traditional aerial reconnaissance. At the top, MACV's J–2 staff slowly automated its intelligence data base and collection management procedures.

In the end, of course, it was not enough. Although Army Intelligence could provide the higher commanders with significant forewarnings of the 1968 Tet offensive, the intensity of the enemy attack was underestimated. But the fact remains that Army Intelligence could provide the kind of warning before Tet in 1968 that it had been unable to furnish before the Battle of the Bulge in 1944. However, despite the similar military outcomes of the Tet and Ardennes counteroffensives—in each case, the enemy scored some disconcerting gains, but paid for them with disproportionate losses—Tet did something that the German

---

19 USASA Commanders Conference, 5–12 May 69, Staff Presentation Roundtable Discussions, Army Cryptologic Records.

20 Bergen, *Military Communications*, pp. 407–08.

21 The 224th Aviation Battalion (Radio Research) managed the fixed-wing assets, flying 100 aircraft at the height of the conflict. Included in its inventory was a handful of four-motored reconverted patrol bombers acquired from the Navy.

Ardennes offensive had not done: it convinced the home front that the war could not be won. The fighting went on, but negotiations and a program of Vietnamization became the order of the day. As the American military presence in South Vietnam shrank, so did the presence of Army Intelligence. The last Army Intelligence elements left South Vietnam in 1973, following the signing of the Paris Peace Accords.[22]

The Vietnam conflict had furnished Army Intelligence with a short list of lessons learned and a long list of casualties. The war's effects on the structure of Army Intelligence were not confined to Vietnam. The rapid turnover of personnel engendered by the policy of troop rotation adversely impacted the cohesion and professional capacity of units far removed from the war zone, as had the diversion of equipment and spare parts to the fighting front. On the home front, the war and the opposition it provoked led Army Intelligence into a situation that compromised its image. Finally, the antimilitary and anti-intelligence reaction that prevailed in America as the Vietnam conflict came to a close posed deep threats to the whole Army Intelligence organization.

The U.S. Army Intelligence Command and the Home Front

Even while the fighting went on in Vietnam, Army Intelligence was actively engaged in operations in another area, the American home front. The principal Army player here was the U.S. Army Intelligence Command (USAINTC), the Army counterintelligence element formed in 1965 to conduct operations in the continental United States. The command had been allotted substantial personnel to carry out its mission. Its seven Military Intelligence groups controlled a network of 300 field and resident offices across the nation. The merger of Army counterintelligence and criminal investigative records into the Investigative Records Repository (IRR) gave the command a massive data base, which was supplemented in 1966 when USAINTC became the DOD agent administering the newly created Defense Central Index of Investigations, a master file of all counterintelligence and criminal investigations performed by the armed services, and the National Agency Check Center, which performed records searches on files maintained by non-DOD agencies such as the Federal Bureau of Investigation (FBI) and local police departments. By 1967 the command had extended its responsibilities beyond its original jurisdiction, assuming the case control function for routine background investigations requested by the major commands overseas.

Centralizing counterintelligence operations in the United States under a single Army command produced the desired effects in terms of speed and efficiency. The new organization not only had a greater capacity to coordinate and conduct counterespionage investigations against military suspects but also was bet-

---

22 Individual Army Intelligence personnel did remain behind as members of the Defense Attache's Office.

ter able to conduct background investigations. Under the old decentralized system, it had taken an average of ninety-seven days to process a standard background investigation. By 1967 USAINTC completed these investigations in an average time of thirty-one days. However, centralization would prove to have less desirable effects. It gave Army counterintelligence a high profile, and gave civilian policy makers an organization to task for domestic intelligence collection in what was rapidly becoming a time of trouble. The end result for Army Intelligence was less than satisfactory.

Under delimitations agreements dating back to the 1940s, the FBI had primary responsibility for counterintelligence investigations of civilians in the continental United States. Army counterintelligence confined its attention to the military and to those civilians who applied for security-sensitive civilian and military positions with the Army. Most of the Army's counterintelligence effort and resources were devoted to background investigations of the latter. However, the events of the 1960s conspired to break down the neat demarcation line between military and civilian counterintelligence jurisdiction in the United States and to draw Army Intelligence deeply into civilian affairs. Federal troops were frequently alerted and occasionally deployed to restore order when local authorities were unable to maintain control in the numerous crises of the period. Commanders needed intelligence support, and it quickly became apparent that it was too late to attempt to gather intelligence once an actual troop deployment had begun. It also became apparent that the existing civilian intelligence agencies were fragmented and often ineffectual.

The FBI may have had theoretical responsibility for civilian counterintelligence, but its director, J. Edgar Hoover, was aging and increasingly uncooperative. The bureau itself, although having a good track record in apprehending interstate car thieves, kidnappers, and the occasional spy, was primarily a crime-fighting agency with neither the capacity nor the inclination to produce finished domestic intelligence. Moreover, the overwhelming majority of FBI agents were middle-aged white males, limiting the bureau's capability to conduct effective undercover work against the radical black and student groups that seemed to pose the greatest threat to national security. As conditions of disorder became progressively worse, the Army moved to fill an intelligence void.

Local commanders had first begun to request counterintelligence support from the assets they controlled during the civil rights disturbances in the South in the first part of the decade. USAINTC became involved in giving crisis support soon after it had been set up, as a result of Army involvement in the Watts rioting in August 1965. The command formulated its first contingency plan for collecting domestic intelligence in early 1966. STEEP HILL, as the plan was code named, was designed to be implemented only after there had been an actual deployment of federal troops.

The command soon realized that STEEP HILL, redesignated GARDEN PLOT in 1967, was inadequate. For USAINTC to be of any help to Army commanders in a civil disturbance situation, it would have to begin collection as soon as there was any likelihood of a deployment of federal troops. To meet the requirement, the command devised a new collection plan, ROSE HILL, later redesignated PUNCH BLOCK and LANTERN SPIKE, successively. Unrest in America's cities caused PUNCH BLOCK to go into effect eight times during the summer of 1966. By this time, in the words of the USAINTC official history, civil disturbance collection had become a "minimal, but increasing" part of the command's work load.23

The troubled summer of 1967 brought matters to a head. The LANTERN SPIKE civil disturbance collection plan was implemented four times, and federal troops were actually committed to deal with a major riot in Detroit. As a result of the Detroit disturbances, Deputy Secretary of Defense Cyrus Vance, who had served as the agent of the Executive Branch in handling the federal intervention, tasked the Army with "reconnoitering the major cities" to gain information on critical elements of topography and vulnerability before troops were sent in again. He also suggested that "the assembly and analysis of data with respect to activity patterns is also needed."24 This put the Army into the domestic intelligence business on a greatly enlarged scale.

After the Detroit riots, the priorities of the U.S. Army Intelligence Command changed perceptibly. The Army now began to collect intelligence data that would not only allow it to intervene effectively in urban riots, but would also help it to cope with the threat of the increasingly violent antiwar movement. By 1967 the popular consensus in support of American commitment to Vietnam was beginning to waver. An uncensored media had brought the horrors of war to American living rooms, and the Johnson strategy of fighting a painless war by allowing generous exemptions for college students while tripling the draft call had made a time bomb out of the nation's campuses. Radical students and others had started to challenge not only the war, but the whole American system allegedly responsible for it. The Army now felt it had to defend its personnel and installations from possible subversion, sabotage, and even guerrilla warfare. In response to these perceived menaces, USAINTC steadily widened its collection activities, and the files of the Intelligence Records Repository began to bulge with the names of individuals and groups with no connection to the Department of Defense except their reputed opposition to it.

---

23 U.S. Army Intelligence Command Annual Report of Major Activities, FY 1971, p. 40, copy in INSCOM History Office files.

24 Ibid., p. 41. Vance was not the only high government official interested in Army collection capabilities against civil disorders. In late 1967 Attorney General Ramsey Clark established the Inter-Divisional Information Unit in the Justice Department "to make full use of available intelligence." For the first two years of its existence, the unit drew heavily on Army counterintelligence for its data. Paul Cowan, Nick Eggleson, and Nat Hentoff, *State Secrets: Police Surveillance in America* (New York: Holt, Rinehart, and Winston, 1974), pp. 14–15.

The rioting that devastated the nation's capital following the assassination of Dr. Martin Luther King, Jr., was the final straw. In response, OACSI set up civil disturbance units in its Counterintelligence and Counterintelligence Analysis Branches in 1968, and the Department of the Army issued a classified Civil Disturbance Collection Plan levying intelligence requirements upon USAINTC that were so sweeping that they could not be filled by the traditional methods of overt collection or liaison with FBI and local law enforcement officials.

To accomplish the tasking, the command had to initiate an extensive collection program against domestic targets. And by now, Army Intelligence elements other than USAINTC were also involved in the domestic intelligence field. In an independent effort, CONARC and several Zone of the Interior armies had deployed counterintelligence personnel from their tactical units to engage in domestic collection operations and had compiled computer data bases on suspected potential troublemakers. The Army Security Agency had used its own assets on several occasions in 1967 and 1968 to monitor the demonstrators' citizen-band radios.

Even at the height of this type of activity, the bulk of USAINTC's resources remained committed to the traditional role of conducting background investigations. But the amount of activity devoted to domestic intelligence had a significance beyond its limited size. The perceived domestic crisis, coupled with Johnson administration demands for more and more information, led Army Intelligence into dangerous waters. Its activities crossed the traditional dividing line between the civilian and military in American life and overstepped the law, since neither the collection activities nor the civilian intelligence data bank of USAINTC had been authorized by statute.[25]

As early as 1969, after a change of administrations, Robert F. Froehlke, assistant secretary of defense for administration, expressed doubts about the wisdom of the whole operation. The Army went beyond its own requirements to involve itself in civilian concerns to such a degree, and the assistant secretary was concerned that the Army might be diffusing its limited intelligence assets, trying to collect intelligence on too large a portion of American society. As Froehlke ruefully admitted, the demands made upon USAINTC for domestic intelligence had gone "substantially beyond the capability for Military Intelligence units to collect. They reflected the all encompassing and uninhibited demand for information directed at the Department of the Army."[26]

What ended the Army's domestic intelligence program, however, was not doubts, but public exposure. In early 1970 the American Civil Liberties Union sued the Army and the U.S. Army Intelligence Command for "spying on civil-

---

[25] Christopher H. Pyle, *Army Surveillance of Civilian Politics, 1967–1970* (New York: Garland Publishers, 1970), is a scholarly account of the Army's domestic intelligence activities by a participant-observer and whistle-blower.

[26] U.S. Army Intelligence Command Report of Major Activities, FY 1971, p. 48.

ians."27 The subsequent publicity, accompanied by recriminations from politicians and journalists, led not only to the end of this particular program, but ultimately to the end of USAINTC itself. The whole Army Intelligence community had suffered a major setback.

Beyond the Battle: Intelligence Trends in the 1960s

The Vietnam War and the domestic crisis within the United States were not the only forces exerting pressure on the structure of Army Intelligence during the 1960s. Increasing technology also shaped its development. This was especially important for the Army Security Agency. Personnel and financial constraints also impinged upon the structure of Army Intelligence during this period. The Army was engaged in fighting a large-scale war in Southeast Asia for which the country had never been properly mobilized. The short tours of duty in Vietnam caused constant personnel turbulence. The demands of the war gutted units outside the combat zone of equipment as well as people; ASA, with its dependence on high technology, was particularly affected. By the end of 1968 those ASA tactical units not actually committed to Vietnam, having been stripped of equipment and spare parts, delivered only 50 percent of their support requirements.

The financial problem was compounded in that the United States had an unfavorable balance of trade, and policy makers at the national level were constantly concerned with the bleeding away of America's gold reserves. Economic as well as technological considerations prompted the drive to consolidate many of ASA's European operations at a major new facility in Augsburg. Financial pressures were also partially responsible for the consolidation of the two Military Intelligence groups in Europe into a single unit in 1969. The headquarters of both the 513th and 66th Military Intelligence Groups moved to Munich, Germany, where the 66th absorbed the personnel and functions of the former.

Although Army Intelligence had its problems during this era, it improved its institutional position in a number of ways. One of the most significant advances was in professional development. As a result of a study undertaken by the Norris Board, the Army Intelligence and Security Branch was redesignated the Military Intelligence (MI) Branch on 1 July 1967. The new title symbolized the unity of the intelligence field rather than its diversity. More important, the Army assigned the renovated branch an official combat support function, whereas the old branch had been designated as a combat service support organization only.

---

27 Palmer, *The 25–Year War*, p. 83. A surprisingly measured evaluation of what all this amounted to can be found in Cowan et al., *State Secrets*, p. 13. "The overall picture is of a moderately large bureaucratic apparatus built to conduct formal interviews for background checks and trying to do the impossible job of predicting major social disorders. It sponged off the FBI for most of its information and used plainclothes operatives for the rest. The information filled numerous computerized files, caused irrelevant briefings, and did little else—within the army."

The upgrade presented the prospect of attracting better officers to intelligence careers and providing members of the branch with greater access to the system of Army higher education that had become professionally indispensable for military career advancement.

As a step toward providing further integration of the various intelligence disciplines within the Military Intelligence Branch, in 1968 the U.S. Army Intelligence School began to offer an MI Officers Advanced Course intended for Army Security Agency officers, as well as for other Military Intelligence professionals. This step was taken in accordance with the recommendations of the Haines Board, another Army study group that had concentrated on deficiencies in intelligence training.[28] The new advanced course did not completely solve all the problems associated with the area, since the Haines Board's proposal to consolidate the Army Security Agency Training Center and School with the Army Intelligence School was not accepted, but the branch course represented a major step in breaking down the wall of isolation between signals intelligence officers and those with other intelligence specialties.

There were also new organizational developments. The Army Intelligence staff moved back into the field of intelligence production, as the Army soon discovered it had needs in this area that DIA could not fulfill. By 1966 OACSI's Special Research Detachment, originally set up as a liaison group with NSA, had become a full-fledged production center. The same year, OACSI created a threat analysis element to produce Army-specific studies. By 1967 even DIA had to admit that the task of conducting all Military Intelligence production simply was too great for one organization and agreed that the Army and the other services should provide "special finished intelligence" directly related to departmental missions.[29] Two years later, USAREUR organized its own production element, the U.S. Army Intelligence Center, Europe.

The Army's mechanism for disseminating its most secret intelligence also was expanded significantly. In 1965 ACSI had decided to attach special security offices to each Army division by fiscal year 1968. Although every Army division assigned to Vietnam had such support, the constraints on resources imposed by the fighting in Southeast Asia prevented implementation of the plan worldwide. However, the system expanded into other areas, as Army requirements for access to sensitive compartmented intelligence grew. In addition to servicing military and diplomatic needs, the Special Security Detachment increasingly became involved in providing private contractors with the highly classified information they needed to do research and development for the government. In 1967 the steady growth of these tasks led the Norris Board to recommend that the Army establish four geographic Special Security regions to act as subor-

---

28 Powe and Wilson, *The Evolution of American Military Intelligence*, p. 105.
29 Intelligence Organization and Stationing Study (IOSS), Aug 75, Exec Sum, p. 29, copy in INSCOM History Office files.

dinate headquarters for the Special Security Detachment's fifty-five field offices. The recommendations were accepted, and shortly afterward the status of the detachment was upgraded to that of a "group" headquarters.

The Army Security Agency was substantially restructured during the course of the 1960s. TOE units were reintroduced to the United States and Vietnam, and in 1966 all the agency's battalions were converted from a fixed to a flexible structure. There were also more cosmetic changes. At the end of 1967 the Department of the Army decided that TDA units would no longer bear numerical designations. As a result, on 15 December 1967, the Army Security Agency's numbered field stations, special operations commands, and special operations units received new geographic designators. Finally, the Army undertook some qualitative initiatives in the human intelligence field, even though resources and personnel allocated to this area declined steeply after 1963. In 1969 ACSI organized a field operating agency to direct certain programs in this area.

Westmoreland, McChristian, and Military Intelligence

In mid-1968 the former MACV commander, General William Westmoreland, became the Army chief of staff and subsequently supervised three major organizational changes within Army Intelligence. The first came about in 1969, when Westmoreland reviewed the organization of the Army Staff and decided that the number of field operating agencies under ACSI's direct supervision was not compatible with the proper organization of a DA staff element. ACSI's job, in Westmoreland's estimation, entailed staff supervision and program management, not operations. As a result, OACSI underwent a sweeping reorganization. Six major elements were spun off and resubordinated to USAINTC. These included the 902d Military Intelligence Group, which had previously performed high-level counterintelligence operations under direct ACSI control; the Administrative Survey Detachment, which ran Army Intelligence personnel programs; the Personnel Security Group, which adjudicated loyalty and suitability cases for the Army; the Army Imagery Interpretation Center; the Intelligence Materiels Supply Office; and the newly created field operating agency for human intelligence.[30]

In certain ways, the new reorganization amounted to another reinvention of the wheel. At the Army Staff level, it meant returning to the organizational principles originally adopted during World War II. The U.S. Army Intelligence Command was transformed from the continental United States–focused counterintelligence organization originally planned into a simulacrum of the earlier U.S. Army Intelligence Corps Activity. In addition, however, the command assumed control of sensitive operations heretofore controlled only at the DA

---

[30] *Department of the Army Historical Summary, Fiscal Year 1970* (Washington, D.C.: U.S. Army Center of Military History, 1973), p. 82.

level, a trend strengthened in 1972 when OACSI transferred its Special Research
Detachment to the command.

A second change that came about at this time was an enlargement of
OACSI's area of functional responsibilities. Army Intelligence had delegated
oversight of the Army's mapping work to the chief of Engineers since World
War II. In 1969 Westmoreland directed ACSI to assume staff supervision of certain Army topographic activities, and the Engineer Topographic Command was
created to carry out the map-making function by consolidating the Army Map
Service with other Engineer elements involved in topography. ACSI also took
over staff supervision of Army weather intelligence at this time.

The last organizational innovation of the Westmoreland years initially
promised to be the most sweeping. Early in 1969 the ACSI, Maj. Gen. Joseph A.
McChristian, who had served as Westmoreland's J–2 in Vietnam, concluded that
the Army's fragmented intelligence assets in the continental United States were
too physically dispersed to provide the Army with enough support. Reviving the
old proposal of the 1950s, he recommended concentrating them in a single
intelligence center. The proposal did not, however, touch upon the operations
of the Army Security Agency.

McChristian initially had an ambitious concept for the center. It would concentrate in one location an operational intelligence headquarters much like the
one McChristian had set up in Vietnam, a counterintelligence center (essentially
USAINTC), the U.S. Army Intelligence School, support troops, and tactical
units. This would give many elements of the Army Intelligence community a
home for the first time. The tactical units and aircraft would be necessary
because McChristian felt that one of the center's main purposes would be to give
the troops realistic intelligence training in the field. The first plans called for the
center to have a troop base of 21,000.

The existing Army Intelligence center at Fort Holabird, Maryland, was obviously unsuited for such an expanded role. The post was small, and the training
requirements imposed by the Vietnam War had greatly overcrowded it. The post
was hemmed in by an industrial area that precluded expansion. Although the
streets of Baltimore were as good a place for counterintelligence agents to practice surveillance techniques as anywhere, Holabird offered no room for field
maneuvers. In addition to all these liabilities, the air space in the area was overcrowded, and the electromagnetic environment was cluttered. In a search for an
alternative, the initial survey team narrowed the choice to Fort Riley, Kansas,
and Fort Huachuca, Arizona, and selected the latter.

At this point, the plan for a new Army Intelligence center began to narrow
sharply in scope. Planners soon realized that although Fort Huachuca offered
space, it had little water. McChristian then suggested that Fort Lewis,
Washington, might be developed as an alternative site, but the post would have
needed extensive rehabilitation, and this would take too much time and money.
Because of these constraints, the proposed composition of the center shrank,

and then shrank again. It turned out that Fort Huachuca could not comfortably accommodate even a brigade of supporting troops. Originally, planners had thought that the U.S. Army Intelligence Command would move bodily to the new center, leaving behind a kind of USAINTC rear, consisting of a Directorate of Investigative Records to administer the command's bulky and hard-to-move data base. This idea was scrapped also. Since most of USAINTC's activities were in support of the Department of the Army and other national-level agencies, the command could not practicably move beyond the Washington-Baltimore corridor.

Ultimately, the composition of the new Army Intelligence center was scaled down drastically. The final version of the center included the Army Intelligence School and the U.S. Army Combat Development Command Intelligence Agency, together with Army combat surveillance and electronic warfare activities already in place at Fort Huachuca, all of this supported by a bare minimum of tactical units. As part of the process, the Army Intelligence School was redesignated and given the more prestigious title of the U.S. Army Intelligence Center and School. The school moved to its new desert home at Huachuca in phases during the first part of 1971.[31] By this time, events were in process that would be much more damaging to Army Intelligence than the reduced plans for its new center.

Lean Years

The early 1970s saw the U.S. Army in decline. The decision to stage a phased withdrawal from Vietnam led to a drastic cut in troop strength, and between 1969 and 1973 the Army shrank in size by almost half, from a force of 1.5 million to one of 800,000. More important, its ranks were plagued with incidents of drug abuse, racial turmoil, and lack of discipline. The final elimination of the draft in 1973 deprived the Army of its reservoir of college-trained enlisted men and confronted it with daunting recruitment problems. Operating in an environment of constraints, the Army would have to rely increasingly on reserve forces to meet any future combat contingencies. The STEADFAST reorganization of 1973 made this dependence on the reserve components explicit, in addition to retrenching the Army Staff and realigning much of the Army's command structure.[32] If the Army as a whole struggled during this period, Army Intelligence was particularly hard hit. It fell victim not only to popular disillusionment with the results of the war, but also to public indignation against alleged counterintelligence abuses.

The unraveling of the Army's domestic counterintelligence program began in the first months of 1970, when the American Civil Liberties Union initiated a lawsuit against the Department of the Army and the U.S. Army Intelligence

---

[31] Dr. Bruce Saunders, "U.S. Army Intelligence Center and School," *Military Intelligence* 10 (April–June 1984): 61.

[32] *Department of the Army Historical Summary, Fiscal Year 1973* (Washington, D.C.: U.S. Army Center of Military History, 1977), pp. 45–46.

Command on the grounds that they were involved in illegal surveillance of civilians. The initial suit was followed by a fire storm of adverse media publicity, all of which culminated in a congressional investigation in early 1971. The controversy had immediate effects on USAINTC. On 19 February 1970, all civil disturbance and civilian biographic data stored in the Investigative Records Repository were ordered destroyed. A similar purge was ordered of the independent domestic intelligence data bases maintained by CONARC and several of the field armies in the continental United States. The ambitious Civil Disturbance Information Collection Plan was formally rescinded in June. The U.S. Army Intelligence Command went into a 180-degree reversal, of course. As the command's official historian stated, "instead of collect, process, and store, the order of the day was research, screen, and destroy."[33] The effect of the "spying on civilians" charges was to degrade the whole counterintelligence mission. By the end of February 1971 the Army had suspended all USAINTC countersubversive and offensive counterespionage activities.

These new developments soon affected the organizational structure of Army counterintelligence. On 1 March 1970, the Defense Investigative Review Council was set up under the assistant secretary of defense for administration to exercise general supervision over the counterintelligence activities of all the armed services and to curb any possible abuses. After some deliberation, the council decided to centralize all service-connected background investigations under a new civilian body, the Defense Investigative Service, which was established at the end of 1971 and became operational in October 1972.[34] Meanwhile, contrary opinions had been voiced. In June 1970 presidential assistant Frederick Huston, unnerved by the depth of dissent over the recent American incursion into Cambodia, suggested that all government intelligence agencies conduct their operations without regard to legal or Constitutional niceties. His views did not prevail.[35]

The formation of the Defense Investigative Service was the beginning of the end for the U.S. Army Intelligence Command as a major Army headquarters. Conducting standard personnel background investigations had been the command's bread and butter, constituting 90 percent of its work load. USAINTC had to give up 1,400 personnel spaces to the new agency. Three of its Military Intelligence groups were inactivated, and the number of field offices was reduced from 303 to 50. The command turned over control of the Defense Central Index of Investigations and the National Agency Check Center to the Defense Investigative Service. USAINTC retained custody of Army counterintelligence files, but the criminal investigation records held by the Intelligence

---

33 U.S. Army Intelligence Command Report of Major Activities, FY 1971, p. 219.

34 *Department of the Army Historical Summary, Fiscal Year 1973*, pp. 53–54.

35 Theodore H. White, *Breach of Faith: The Fall of Richard Nixon* (New York: Dell Publishing, 1976), pp. 174–77.

Records Repository were removed from its control and assigned to a new U.S. Army Criminal Investigation Command. Since 1949 a major general had controlled Army counterintelligence activities. By 1972 the U.S. Army Intelligence Command was under the command of a colonel.

After the Army Intelligence School moved to Fort Huachuca, Fort Holabird became superfluous to Army Intelligence. In the interests of economy, USAINTC relocated in the summer of 1973 to Fort George G. Meade, Maryland, a large, multipurpose post. However, since the records of the Army Criminal Investigation Command remained behind at Holabird, the move was a further blow to the concepts behind the SECURITY SHIELD study of 1964. By 1974, USAINTC had lost most of its mission responsibilities and numbered less than 2,000 persons. In addition, the Office of the Secretary of Defense criticized that the Army's counterintelligence structure was top heavy in management and not cost effective.

USAINTC's remaining activities hardly seemed significant enough to warrant its retention as a major command, especially at a time when the Army was under heavy pressure to reduce its headquarters establishments. The command was particularly vulnerable to charges of managerial layering—it shared Fort Meade with the headquarters of a major subordinate unit, the 109th Military Intelligence Group. Another major element, the 902d Military Intelligence Group, had been programmed to move to Fort Meade in the summer of 1974. As a result, the Army discontinued the command on 30 June 1974.[36] On the same day, the Army also inactivated USAINTC's three remaining Military Intelligence groups with area responsibilities for the continental United States and reassigned the Army Imagery Interpretation Center and Special Research Detachment to ACSI's direct control.

USAINTC was replaced by the U.S. Army Intelligence Agency, a field operating agency directly subordinated to ACSI with an initial force structure of just two CONUS counterintelligence groups: the 902d Military Intelligence Group, which lost its traditional high-level mission and became responsible for the geographic area east of the Mississippi, and the 525th Military Intelligence Group, of Vietnam fame, which was reactivated to perform a parallel mission in the western part of the United States. The agency inherited (sometimes in rearranged form) some smaller miscellaneous elements from USAINTC: a technical service activity providing polygraph, technical service countermeasures, and computer security assistance; the U.S. Army Counterintelligence Support Activity, comprising the Investigative Records Repository and the Personnel Security Group; and the Administrative Survey Detachment.

USAINTC was not the only part of the Army Intelligence community affected by the currents of the times. Centralization and economy were the watch-

---

[36] *Department of the Army Historical Summary, Fiscal Year 1974* (Washington, D.C.: U.S. Army Center of Military History, 1977), p. 42.

words of the day. In 1970 a blue ribbon panel appointed by President Nixon had called for much greater integration of service intelligence activities at the DOD level. The Defense Investigative Service was just one of three new Department of Defense agencies that the Nixon administration created to assume intelligence functions which the uniformed services previously had performed. In 1972 the Army topographic assets that ACSI had supervised since 1969 were integrated into the new Defense Mapping Agency.[37] During the same year, an attempt was made to integrate all service cryptologic elements into a Central Security Service that would act as the military arm of the National Security Agency. This threatened to strip the Army of much of its remaining role as a manager in the cryptologic field. In practice, however, the Central Security Service did not live up to its initial expectations, and the reorganization did not bring about any substantial change in the relationship between the Army Security Agency and the National Security Agency.

The Army Security Agency, although still the largest single intelligence element in the Army, shared the problems of the greater Army during this period. It had to deal with strength ceilings, recruiting problems, and diminished funding. Additionally, it suffered from the problems caused by a large shortfall of equipment and spare parts in the field. As a result of the demands of the war in Vietnam, much of the remaining equipment was obsolete and ill suited to the demands of a high-intensity conflict.

The retrenchment of the agency began in 1970, when it turned over its acoustical intelligence mission to the U.S. Air Force. In 1971 the Army discontinued the 507th and 508th U.S. Army Security Agency Groups, located respectively in Europe and in Korea, and replaced them with smaller elements: the 502d Army Security Agency Group, a TOE unit, in Europe and an unnumbered field station in Korea.[38] The reduction continued inexorably as the agency stood down from Vietnam and closed long-established field stations. Of the 99 separate units which ASA fielded in 1970, only 73 still existed in 1972. For reasons of economy, ASA's traditional regional headquarters in Europe and the Pacific were discontinued in 1972.

Meanwhile, the approaching end of the draft made questionable whether the Army Security Agency could enlist enough men to meet mission requirements. As a result, for the first time in its history the agency began recruiting women for cryptologic specialties. Although WACs had served with the SSA's 2d Signal Service Battalion in the continental United States during World War II, the WAC detachment stationed at Arlington Hall at the time of the Korean con-

---

[37] *Department of the Army Historical Summary, Fiscal Year 1972* (Washington, D.C.: U.S. Army Center of Military History, 1974), p. 44.

[38] The discontinuance of the 508th USASA Group in Korea in 1971 took place in the context of a major reduction in troop strength there. This drawdown was part of the implementation of the "Nixon Doctrine," which sought to shift the main burden of providing ground forces for defense to our allies.

flict had performed largely administrative functions. By 1976, however, one-tenth of ASA's uniformed personnel worldwide were female.

Although the Army Security Agency was deeply affected by developments in the cryptologic field, it survived the STEADFAST reforms intact. STEADFAST had resubordinated almost all Army training centers, including the U.S. Army Intelligence Center and School, to the newly created Training and Doctrine Command (TRADOC), but ASA's vertical command structure allowed it to retain its own training base. However, the 1973 reorganization of the Department of the Army did have its effect on Army Intelligence at the staff level. In line with the thrust of STEADFAST, the staff of the Office of the Assistant Chief of Staff for Intelligence was reduced by one-third between 1973 and 1974.[39] Production and support functions previously carried out within OACSI were transferred to separate detachments with their own TDAs in 1973, and responsibility for administering attache personnel was transferred to the Administrative Survey Detachment in 1974.

A Time of Transition

After the setbacks of the early 1970s, Army Intelligence began to regroup. Even though it operated under continuing personnel and fiscal restraints, the Army Intelligence community undertook a series of initiatives that would put it in a better position to respond to future challenges.

The U.S. Army Intelligence Agency (USAINTA), established in mid-1974, was originally intended as a low-profile organization with the narrowly limited mission of conducting the Army's residual counterintelligence operations in the continental United States. The assets initially assigned to the new agency were modest. Moreover, its mission was constrained and its activities hampered by congressional legislation, congressional investigations, and executive orders that cumulatively had a chilling effect on counterintelligence operations.[40] By early 1975 the agency's Investigative Records Repository was required to establish a Freedom of Information Act Office to respond to queries from the public about the contents of the Army's files. However, the agency came into existence just at the time that the disestablishment of U.S. Army, Pacific, made it necessary to resubordinate USARPAC's 500th Military Intelligence Group, primarily a collection element. For want of any more plausible arrangement, the Army gave the U.S. Army Intelligence Agency command of the orphaned group, thus acquiring an area of overseas intelligence responsibility that had been denied its predecessor, USAINTC. Since

---

39 *Department of the Army Historical Summary, Fiscal Year 1974*, p. 38.

40 A telling indication of the disfavor into which any type of military counterintelligence operation had fallen at this time was Congress' decision in 1974 to discontinue all military censorship units in the reserve components.

the 500th Military Intelligence Group no longer had the mission of supporting a major Army headquarters in Hawaii, it redeployed to Japan in the summer of 1976.

The Army's desire to realign its counterintelligence command and control
system to better satisfy the civilian leadership also contributed to the expansion
of the U.S. Army Intelligence Agency's geographical area of responsibility. The
Defense Investigative Review Council established guidelines that prohibited
Army investigations of non–DOD-affiliated civilians within the fifty states and
the Panama Canal Zone, but less stringent prohibitions were in effect overseas.
To ensure uniform adherence to these policies, it seemed wise to bring all counterintelligence operations within the council's jurisdiction under the control of a
single agency. This again resulted in USAINTA's assuming responsibilities that
USAINTC had never exercised. The U.S. Army Intelligence Agency gained control of counterintelligence investigations in the Canal Zone and Hawaii and was
assigned command of the 901st MI Detachment, which previously had reported
directly to the Defense Nuclear Agency. Moreover, the command began to diver-
sify the scope of its activities, upgrading and redesignating its technical services
element as the Operational Security Group and embarking on initiatives in collecting human intelligence.

ACSI's Special Security Group also expanded its activities. With the fighting
in Vietnam over, the group could at last find enough resources to implement its
long-delayed plan to provide each Army division with a special security office.
Experience gained in Vietnam had demonstrated this to be a necessity under
conditions of modern warfare.

The Army Security Agency also began to evolve in fresh directions. The first
step was to give ASA's signal security activities in the Western Hemisphere an
organizational base that would conform to the new doctrine that stressed providing advice and support to commanders on signal security issues, rather than
monitoring communications to detect violations. This concept emphasized the
positive aspects of security rather than the negative, and it allowed ASA to deal
with the possibility that improperly secured electronic equipment could now
pose as much of a security hazard as badly trained communications personnel.
To facilitate this approach, the agency organized the Signal Security Activity at
Vint Hill Farms Station in June 1975.

The Signal Security Activity took over a support function that previously
had been fragmented among eleven separate units in the continental United
States, Alaska, and the Canal Zone. Four subordinate field detachments, each
with a TEMPEST capability, monitored the possibility of information compromise
from electronic emanations. At the same time, the Army shifted general staff
supervision over the communications security/signal security area from ACSI to
the assistant chief of staff for communications and electronics. Among its other
advantages, the transfer distanced the Army Security Agency from any further
charges of "spying on civilians."

Even more important for the Army Security Agency was the growing importance of electronic warfare, part of the agency's mission since 1955. In 1969 the Joint Chiefs of Staff expanded the definition of electronic warfare beyond the accepted "jamming" and "antijamming" roles to encompass the new concept of electronic support measures, which embraced threat detection and avoidance, targeting, and homing. Because of the nature of the combat situation in Vietnam, electronic warfare had played almost no role in that conflict. However, the rapid development of electronic warfare technology and the emphasis given to "radioelectronic combat" in the fighting doctrine of what was then the Army's most probable future adversary made it clear that things would be very different in any potential high-intensity war.[41]

Unfortunately, the agency's traditional emphasis on its cryptologic mission and the damage the Vietnam conflict had caused, both to equipment readiness and to research and development, had left it poorly positioned to meet the electronic warfare threat. In 1972 the Army's Scientific Advisory Board estimated that less than 10 percent of Army Security Agency resources were devoted to electronic warfare and pointed out that much of the available equipment was obsolete.

In response, the agency began to restructure itself to give greater electronic warfare and signals intelligence support on the tactical level. Aerial platforms were fielded in Europe and Korea, and the agency began to develop new types of units that could integrate signals intelligence with electronic warfare. These units were to coordinate with the tactical formations they supported through ASA-manned elements within unit tactical operations centers responsive to the needs of both the intelligence and operations staff officers. The events of the Arab-Israeli War of 1973 gave a striking demonstration of the importance of electronic warfare even in a mid-intensity conflict. In the aftermath of this conflict, Maj. Gen. George Godding, commanding general, U.S. Army Security Agency, proposed that his organization be redesignated the U.S. Army Electronic Warfare Command. Although the proposal was not accepted, it showed that ASA was now prepared to redefine its traditional mission.

By the end of 1974 the structure of Army Intelligence was in flux. It was still adjusting to painful shortages of money and personnel, while at the same time major components of the Army Intelligence community were moving in new directions. However, changes were being made on a piecemeal basis, without any overall plan or centralized guidance. The Army secured a chance to impose a new coherence on its intelligence structure on 31 December 1974, when the chief of staff directed the implementation of a comprehensive study he hoped would impose some cohesion on the many significant changes in process.

---

41 Don E. Gordon, *Electronic Warfare: Element of Strategy and Multiplier of Combat Power* (New York: Pergamon Press, 1981), p. 153.

10

Reorganization and Renewal

The year 1975 marked a low point for both America's influence on the international scene and the institutional position of the Army. The growing power of the Organization of Petroleum Exporting Countries (OPEC), first manifested at the time of the Yom Kippur War, seemed to threaten the economies of the Western industrialized world in an unprecedented way. The Watergate scandal and the subsequent resignation of President Richard Nixon under threat of impeachment had damaged the confidence of the nation in its government and had effectively undercut the foreign policy strategies with which President Nixon had been identified. Southeast Asia fell to Communist armies in 1975, and Soviet-backed regimes came to power in Angola and Mozambique. The Army, underfunded and unpopular, was hard pressed to fill its ranks with quality personnel without the stimulus of the draft. It was under these unpromising circumstances that the Army drew up a new charter for intelligence, which emerged as a result of the Intelligence Organization and Stationing Study (IOSS).

The disillusionment resulting from the nation's long involvement in Southeast Asia was slow to dissipate. Nevertheless, the Iranian hostage crisis, the Soviet invasion of Afghanistan, and continued instability in Central America gradually fostered a renewed interest in American security. Although the nation attempted to put the Vietnam experience behind it, there was no return to isolationism. From 1979 on, the country began to accelerate the buildup its defenses. By the mid-1980s the Army's morale and strength had been restored, a new generation of weapons for ground combat fielded, and the force structure increased. During this period the IOSS reforms, conceived in an environment of tight resources, continued to provide a viable architecture for Army Intelligence in a plentiful time for the Army and for intelligence operations in general.

Remaking Military Intelligence

The Intelligence Organization and Stationing Study originated in a 1974 memorandum from Secretary of the Army Howard Callaway to Army Chief of

Staff General Frederick Weyand. "We maintain considerable information which is of questionable value and seldom used," Callaway noted, and that "really makes me wonder about how much money we are wasting and raises serious questions as to the cost-effectiveness of our intelligence system."[1]

In addition, broader considerations made an overall assessment of Army Intelligence appropriate. Army Intelligence resources for the 1974–1978 time frame had already been reduced significantly by a program-budget decision of the secretary of defense in 1973. The Army inspector general had recently found grave deficiencies in the operations of the Army Security Agency. The dismantling of the U.S. Army Intelligence Command, which had just occurred, meant that the Army counterintelligence and human intelligence organization was in the process of evolution. At the tactical level, the STEADFAST reorganization had abolished the field army command, leaving without a mission the MI tactical units designed to support it. Finally, the Army in general realized that an overall appraisal of the intelligence structure was long overdue. Too many intelligence elements within the Army had been allowed to evolve apart from the development of the Army as a whole. It now seemed time to align Army Intelligence with the rest of the Army. The chief of staff entrusted the initial steps to a panel headed by Maj. Gen. Joseph J. Ursano.

After an exhaustive study of the structure and organization of Army Intelligence, the panel submitted its findings and recommendations in August 1975. The IOSS report was critical. It pointed out that the organization of the ACSI staff did not facilitate effective supervision of the Army's most crucial intelligence resources. The Directorate of Foreign Intelligence, ACSI's major contact point with the rest of the Army Staff and the other functional major Army commands (MACOMs), had only half the resources allotted to the staff elements supervising intelligence collection. Priorities within collection itself were even more skewed. Staff supervision of human intelligence took up a disproportionate amount of effort. The vital signals intelligence function was isolated and neglected.

The panel found intelligence production fragmented. Various aspects of production were being carried on by several ACSI elements as well as the Forces Command; other production elements operated under the Army Materiel Command and the Office of the Surgeon General. The disparate system fully satisfied only a portion of the Army's intelligence needs. Only a unified production center would, in the panel's judgment, alleviate the situation. Specific collection efforts also came under criticism.

The Ursano panel estimated that in the security field some 80 percent of the Army effort went into operations designed to counter the threat from foreign human intelligence organizations, and the remaining 20 percent was devoted to signal security. These were old and familiar functions, carried out respectively

---

[1] IOSS, Aug 75, Exec Sum, p. 6.

by the U.S. Army Intelligence Agency and the Army Security Agency. But there was no effort directed against hostile imagery intelligence and no organization handling the total security picture and providing support to operations security (OPSEC). The panel concluded that as a result the allocation of security resources was wildly disproportionate to the existing threat.

The panel reserved some of its most stinging criticism for the Army Security Agency. The establishment of the National Security Agency/Central Security Service organization, it found, had essentially reduced ASA headquarters to just another bureaucratic layer. Lacking any operational responsibilities or a core of technical cryptologic experts, it was saddled with an immense span of control because of the closing of the various ASA theater headquarters. The Ursano board noted that field commanders could readily assume ASA's remaining support functions. Moreover, despite its best efforts, the agency was not meeting the Army's tactical requirements, since it could not field enough units to support the planned sixteen-division Active Army.

A succession of previous Army reviews—in all, eleven had been made since World War II—had upheld the validity of the Army Security Agency's traditional vertical command structure. The Ursano panel dissented vigorously. In the panel's opinion, the ASA pattern of organization had actually impeded the development of an efficient mechanism for carrying out intelligence and electronic warfare. The monopoly of signals intelligence and electronic warfare by an organization operating under compartmented secrecy had artificially kept signals intelligence out of the general intelligence flow and had largely excluded the rest of the Army from involvement in the vital electronic warfare field. At the same time, ASA's preoccupation with the cryptologic aspects of its mission had prevented it from keeping up with new trends in electronic warfare, despite the emphasis which the Army now had given to the latter function.

In the field, the IOSS report charged, the Army Security Agency's organizational and functional independence worked against the effective integration of all-source intelligence that was now necessary. It also imposed substantial administrative costs, since unit G–2s at tactical operations centers had to coordinate the intelligence flow produced by three separate elements: ASA, regular Military Intelligence units, and the special security officer dissemination system. Each of these elements had its own separate communications system and its own separate support system.

The Intelligence Organization and Stationing Study: Solutions

The Ursano panel recommended radical surgery to correct the perceived deficiencies of the Army Intelligence structure. Its complex prescription called for both centralization and decentralization. The heart of the suggested program, however, was dismantling the Army Security Agency. ASA's tactical units should be resubordinated to field commanders and its training and research and development functions assigned to other major commands in conformity with the pattern which the McNamara reforms and the STEADFAST reorganization of 1973 established for the rest of the Army. The IOSS report offered three alternatives for realigning Army strategic and theater support intelligence assets. Under the proposal finally adopted, the Army Security Agency's headquarters and fixed field stations would become the core of a new major command. By adding the U.S. Army Intelligence Agency, those Military Intelligence groups engaged in a theater support role, and the various intelligence production elements to this base, the Army would create, for the first time, an integrated intelligence, security, and electronic warfare organization capable of fulfilling its national requirements.

At the tactical level, the proposals called for organizational decentralization and functional integration. With the dissolution of ASA's vertical command structure, ASA and MI field units could merge into a single system of unified intelligence and electronic warfare forces. In the committee's view, tactical Special Security Offices could become part of the units they supported. Army tactical commanders at the corps level and below would thus for the first time have substantially the same control over their intelligence assets as they did over the rest of the forces assigned to them. Signals intelligence would be merged into the all-source intelligence needed to meet tactical requirements.[2]

The recommendations raised a number of questions, one of which involved the issue of acceptability. The commanding general of the Army Security Agency, Maj. Gen. George Godding, rather predictably did not concur, not only because of the impending dismemberment and transformation of his organization, but also because of the proposed reorganization's possible effect on cryptology. On the whole, however, the Army's response was very positive. The new arrangements seemed to be designed to give the commander in the field what he wanted. The response from USAREUR, for instance, not only expressed support for the concept, but also demonstrated Army reservations about some of the features previously associated with intelligence work: "MI is fighting its way back to acceptance by the Army community. Stovepiping and restoring the 'spook' image must be avoided."[3] Under the IOSS concept, Army Intelligence would march in step with the rest of the Army, a prospect that pleased many.

One question which the Intelligence Organization and Stationing Study left unresolved was that of command. The ACSI suggested that control of the proposed new intelligence and security command be vested in himself. This arrangement would have given Army Intelligence an institutional structure strongly resembling that of World War II, when the G–2 had controlled the

---

2 *Department of the Army Historical Summary, Fiscal Year 1976* (Washington, D.C.: U.S. Army Center of Military History, 1977), pp. 25–26.

3 IOSS, Aug 75, vol. 1, ch. 8, ann. B, p. 2.

Military Intelligence Service and after 1944 the strategic operations of the Army Signal Security Agency.

This proposal was rejected, however, and the new major command was allotted a commander of its own. The ACSI suggestion ran against the doctrine that staff and line functions should be separated, and it posed another problem. After the adverse publicity of the early 1970s, intelligence was still a sensitive field. At the time Army leadership believed that any merger of policy formulation and program management functions with operational capabilities would "deny the CSA [chief of staff of the Army] a check and balance mechanism believed necessary in today's environment of sensitivity to intelligence activities."[4]

Implementation of the IOSS proposals began in 1976. The Army realigned elements within OACSI, initiated staff planning for a new intelligence and security command, and fielded the first experimental intelligence and electronic warfare battalion. The U.S. Army Security Agency Training Center and School at Fort Devens, Massachusetts, was resubordinated to the U.S. Army Intelligence Center and School at Fort Huachuca, along with its two detachments at Goodfellow Air Force Base, Texas, and the Navy facility at Corry Station, Florida. This shift achieved the long-standing Army goal of centralizing all Military Intelligence training and further enhanced the importance of the Army Intelligence Center and School itself. The latter organization already had achieved the status of a general officer command after absorbing the Combat Developments Command Intelligence Agency and the Combat Surveillance and Electronic Warfare School. In 1983 the rank of the Army Intelligence Center and School commander was elevated to two stars after the commander received proponency over the Military Intelligence Branch and assumed the title of chief of Military Intelligence.[5]

In addition, the Special Security Group was radically reorganized, losing its operational role in communications and its tactical elements. By the end of 1976 tactical special security offices came under the control of ASA direct support units. Ironically, the Army Security Agency achieved the control over this organization, which it had sought for twenty years, just before its own demise. Concurrently, the Army restructured what remained of the Special Security Group along functional rather than regional lines through seven special security commands, each of which controlled subordinate offices servicing different major commands.[6] The culmination of the IOSS reorganization came on 1

---

4 IOSS, Aug 75, vol. 1, ch. 8, p. 61.

5 Saunders, "U.S. Army Intelligence Center and School." The transfer of MI Branch proponency to the commandant of the U.S. Army Intelligence Center and School took place as part of an Army-wide shift of this function from the Army Staff to the TRADOC schools. Proponency allowed the chief of Military Intelligence to initiate and coordinate actions in the areas of force structure, unit deployment and sustainment, and personnel acquisition, training, and distribution. It did not, however, give him control over individual career management.

6 History of United States Army Special Security Group, n.d., p. 6, INSCOM History Office files.

January 1977, with the formation of the U.S. Army Intelligence and Security Command (INSCOM) at Arlington Hall Station, Virginia.

New Directions for Military Intelligence: INSCOM

The Army formed the new major command, INSCOM, by redesignating the U.S. Army Security Agency as the U.S. Army Intelligence and Security Command and reassigning the U.S. Army Intelligence Agency, as well as ACSI's and FORSCOM'S intelligence production units, to the new command.7 At the same time, control of ASA's tactical units reverted to the supported commanders. The training, personnel, research and development, and materiel acquisition and administration functions which the Army Security Agency had carried out were assumed by other major commands and by elements of the Army Staff. INSCOM also assumed command of three Military Intelligence Groups located overseas: the 66th in Germany, the 470th in Panama, and the 500th in Japan. Previously, these units had been assigned respectively to USAREUR and Seventh Army, FORSCOM, and the U.S. Army Intelligence Agency. Despite the similarity of their designations, these groups varied widely in size and mission; moreover, theater commanders continued to exercise operational control over the units. On 1 October 1977, the former U.S. Army Intelligence Agency headquarters became part of INSCOM, and the command established a unified intelligence production element, the Intelligence and Threat Analysis Center, on 1 January 1978.

INSCOM provided the Army with a single instrument to conduct multidiscipline intelligence and security operations and electronic warfare at the level above corps and to produce finished intelligence tailored to the Army's needs. The new major command merged divergent intelligence disciplines and traditions in a novel way. Its creation marked the most radical realignment of Army Intelligence assets in a generation. Without fully realizing it, the Army had achieved not a "multidiscipline" organization, but an interdisciplinary approach to intelligence collection. The new command provided Army Intelligence with a framework within which the individual intelligence disciplines could cross-cue one another; the results of this collective effort would be greater than the sum of its parts.

Traditionally, the Army Security Agency had been the centerpiece of the Army Intelligence community in terms of personnel and resources. When the agency melded into INSCOM under the new realignment, it lost its vertical command structure, many of its functions, and thirty of its tactical units. As a result, Brig. Gen. (later Maj. Gen.) William I. Rolya, the former ASA commanding general who became INSCOM's first head, found himself heading an organization considerably smaller than its predecessor, although it had gained the U.S. Army Intelligence Agency, the theater Military Intelligence groups, and produc-

---

7 *Department of the Army Historical Summary, Fiscal Year 1977* (Washington, D.C.: U.S. Army Center of Military History, 1979), pp. 30–31.

tion elements. However, the U.S. Army Intelligence and Security Command had at its disposal a wide array of diverse assets. Initially, these included eight fixed field stations inherited from ASA—three of them in the Far East, two in the continental United States, two in Germany, and one in Turkey. There were also the three intelligence groups overseas, transformed into multidisciplinary units by incorporating former ASA assets into the previously existing elements. A fourth, the 501st Military Intelligence Group, was soon organized in Korea. Because of Eighth Army's special requirements, the unit not only carried out a theater support mission, but also performed functions executed elsewhere by the Army's corps-level intelligence organizations.

In the continental United States, INSCOM received command over various single-discipline elements: the Intelligence and Threat Analysis Center; the CONUS MI Group, which furnished cryptologic personnel to the National Security Agency and controlled the two field stations in the United States; an expanded 902d Military Intelligence Group, which was assigned a combined counterintelligence and signal security support mission throughout the continental United States; the Central Security Facility, which maintained the counterintelligence records in the Intelligence Records Repository; and a number of other specialized subordinate units. Significantly, one function which the Central Security Facility previously performed—the adjudication of Military Intelligence–related and other sensitive clearances within the Army—shifted in October 1977 to a new Central Clearance Facility administered by the Military Personnel Center. This was done partially to further standardize the clearance process throughout the Army, secondarily to remove the process from Army Intelligence control, on the grounds that the investigative function should not be combined with the judicial.

With the U.S. Army Intelligence and Security Command in place, ACSI found it expedient to surrender control of most of the remaining operating functions to the new organization. Ever since the 1950s, the ACSI's operating responsibilities had waxed and waned cyclically as various incumbents transferred control of field operating agencies back and forth between OACSI and Fort Holabird. Now came another turn of the wheel. In 1978 INSCOM took over the Army's Russian Institute in Germany and in 1980 assumed command of the Special Security Group. A year later, OACSI discontinued its Inspector General's Office, since substantially all of its field activities had gone to INSCOM, and there was little in the field to inspect.

The U.S. Army Intelligence and Security Command faced certain problems when it started out. At first it was hampered by a shortage of resources. By the end of fiscal year 1978 only 10,400 people were assigned to the new command, debilitating shortages in key Military Intelligence specialties existed, and the command found itself unable to completely meet all the national collection requirements with which it had been tasked. However, the readiness situation improved steadily, as a new national consensus regarding the importance of intelligence brought a greater infusion of resources. By 1985, 15,000 persons were assigned to INSCOM.[8]

The command's institutional and structural problems took longer to solve. INSCOM was designed to perform intelligence and security operations at the echelon above corps, but the precise structure of this echelon continued to be a matter of doctrinal dispute within the Army. The Army's traditional echelon above corps, the field army, had been discontinued in 1973 and replaced with a joint command system. INSCOM's broad responsibilities and the diverse nature of the units it commanded posed another problem. Proposals were made to simplify the command structure by creating additional subordinate headquarters overseas, as the Army Security Agency had done originally, but overseas headquarters elements proved expensive, and INSCOM finally abandoned this approach. Additionally, the command's exact role in electronic warfare remained undefined. Although INSCOM was the main proponent, its units were limited in this area.

The field of intelligence production also continued to present difficulties. The IOSS panel had originally recommended that all Army Intelligence production resources be brought together in a single location. However, Army leaders decided that the Army's scientific, technical, and medical intelligence production responsibilities would continue to be dispersed among three separate centers under the Army Materiel Command and the Office of the Surgeon General. It even proved impossible for INSCOM to collocate all elements of its own production center, the Intelligence and Threat Analysis Center. Although most of the center's resources were at Arlington Hall Station, it proved physically impracticable to move some of its major production functions from either the Washington Navy Yard or Fort Bragg, North Carolina.

How to impose a satisfactory organization on all Army intelligence production elements was resolved temporarily in 1985 by a more or less Solomonic decision. The Intelligence and Threat Analysis Center was removed from INSCOM and resubordinated to a new Army Intelligence Agency, a field operating agency of ACSI with headquarters in Northern Virginia. At the same time, the new agency was given command of the Army Missile and Space Intelligence Center and the Foreign Science and Technology Center. The Surgeon General's Medical Intelligence and Information Agency had become a joint service organization. Army intelligence production still remained geographically dispersed, but the situation was improved when elements of the Intelligence and Threat Analysis Center moved to the Washington Navy Yard. The new arrangement again made ACSI a major player in the field of intelligence operations, for the Army Intelligence Agency, with a personnel strength of 1,500, was as large as the Army's intelligence production organization before the creation of DIA.

---

8 One of the few mentions of INSCOM in open sources can be found in Jeffrey Richelson, *The U.S. Intelligence Community* (Cambridge, Mass.: Ballinger Publishing Co., 1985), pp. 66–68.

Finally, INSCOM operations were impeded by physical limitations that split its headquarters elements between two Army posts forty miles apart. The physical facilities which INSCOM inherited from its predecessor organizations, ASA and USAINTA, simply were too limited. Attempts to find a suitable central headquarters location either at Fort Meade, Maryland, or at Vint Hill Farms, Virginia, repeatedly fell to political and fiscal constraints. However, the withdrawal of the large DIA presence from Arlington Hall in 1985 at last made it possible for planners to order that all headquarters elements be consolidated at that site during the following year. Nevertheless, a number of subordinate units at Fort Meade, including the Central Security Facility, remained behind, and Arlington Hall proved only a way station. In 1985 the Army finally decided that INSCOM's permanent headquarters would eventually be located at Fort Belvoir, Virginia. The command finally relocated in the summer of 1989.

Despite its initial growing pains, INSCOM provided a useful base on which the Army could build an expanded intelligence program once the long slide in defense spending was arrested. Human intelligence received fresh emphasis, as did the expansion of the command's cryptologic activities. In 1980 INSCOM established an Army presence at a joint service field station in Kunia, Hawaii. This was the first new Army field station set up outside the continental United States since the Vietnam War. Two years later, it organized another new field station in Panama from resources already in place. Later, the command fielded Army technical control and analysis elements to provide better cryptologic support to tactical Military Intelligence units.

A major new Military Intelligence unit based in the United States, the 513th Military Intelligence Group, was activated in 1982. The group would support possible operations of the Army component of Central Command (CENTCOM), the unified command created that year to deal with contingency situations in Southwest Asia. As initially configured, the group exercised command and control over three flexibly organized battalions: the 201st, 202d, and 203d Military Intelligence Battalions. Later, the 513th organized a TDA Military Intelligence battalion to deal with low-intensity conflict situations.

The group's 203d Military Intelligence Battalion at first was organized as a technical intelligence unit, indicating the Army's renewed interest in this sometimes neglected area. The battalion's main operating unit was the 11th Military Intelligence Company, the latest in a succession of company-size units that had stayed at Aberdeen Proving Ground, Maryland, since the 1960s. In 1978 this company had acquired the important additional mission of supporting the Army's Opposing Forces (OPFOR) training program. However, conflict soon developed between the technical intelligence battalion's mission of deploying overseas with its parent group in a contingency situation and its tasking to support the OPFOR program in the United States. A subsequent reorganization reassigned the technical intelligence function to the Foreign Materiel Intelligence Group, a TDA unit directly subordinate to INSCOM headquarters, but the 513th regained the mission in 1989.9

By 1985 the U.S. Army Intelligence and Security Command was redefining its structure and practices along a variety of fronts. The resubordination of its production element to the Army Intelligence Agency allowed the command to focus most of its energies on its principal mission—managing the Army's strategic and theater-level collection resources. However, a reexamination of INSCOM's organization revealed that it was still carrying out functions of combat development and materiel development that in theory were supposed to have been transferred to TRADOC and the Army Materiel Command. Although INSCOM attempted to step out of these fields, the command's nucleus of resident experts made it difficult to abandon all its developmental efforts, since no other organization was prepared to address such requirements.

More definite resolutions were found in other areas, one of which was counterintelligence. As revelations of successful penetrations of America's most sensitive agencies by hostile intelligence services mounted, 1985 became the "Year of the Spy."10 The Intelligence and Security Command moved to reconfigure its limited counterintelligence assets into more productive arrangements to meet the Army's needs. In the process, the command moved away from a concept of providing general operational security support to all Army elements in favor of a narrower focus on priority objectives, such as expanding polygraph examinations and technical services countermeasures and providing counterintelligence support to the Army's growing number of Special Access Programs (SAPs)—highly sensitive projects that required exceptional security measures.

In turn, this concern led to a reorganization of the command's main counterintelligence unit in the United States, the 902d Military Intelligence Group. Originally organized on geographic lines into three TDA battalions, the group's subordinate elements were restructured on a functional, rather than geographic, basis in 1985. At the same time, the group was given greater responsibility for handling counterespionage operations in the continental United States.

Change continued in 1986. Beginning that year, INSCOM's five multidiscipline intelligence groups were redesignated as brigades. This transition was intended to be more than cosmetic; the units would now be organized for possible warfighting, rather than having structures geared to national collection requirements in time of peace. A basic brigade was designed to consist of a headquarters and headquarters company, a numbered echelon above corps

---

9 The Foreign Materiel Intelligence Group was redesignated the Foreign Materiel Intelligence Battalion and resubordinated to the 513th Military Intelligence Brigade on 16 October 1989. In 1996 this TDA battalion was discontinued and the mission assumed by the provisional 203d MI Battalion.

10 Thomas B. Allen and Norman Polgar, *Merchants of Treason: America's Secrets for Sale* (New York: Delacorte Press, 1988), p. 2.

intelligence center for intelligence production, a signals intelligence battalion, an imagery analysis battalion, a counterintelligence battalion, an interrogation and exploitation battalion, and a collection element. Because of the diversity of intelligence requirements in the several theaters, however, the actual units allotted to each INSCOM brigade would differ. In the event of mobilization, INSCOM leaders planned to call up reserve component units as needed to bring the brigades to full strength. Additionally, the U.S. Army Intelligence Center and School drew up new TOEs that mandated the conversion of the command's flexible battalions into fixed elements.

Finally, INSCOM took action to redesignate some of its TDA units as numbered Military Intelligence brigades, battalions, and companies in the 700 series. Units redesignated included the Continental United States Military Intelligence Group and a number of field stations. This would provide units with designations more intelligible to the rest of the Army, and it would enhance the pride and esprit of their assigned soldiers. As a result of this step, existing command assets combined into three new Military Intelligence Brigades (the 701st, 703d, and 704th) and a number of new battalions in 1987.

The Combat Electronic Warfare and Intelligence Concept

The U.S. Army Intelligence and Security Command was only part of the new organizational design which the Intelligence Organization and Stationing Study imposed upon Army Intelligence. The IOSS also had brought about a major realignment of the Army's tactical intelligence assets in the field. These reforms drastically reshuffled the old command channels in the tactical arena. With the dissolution of the Army Security Agency's vertical command structure, all former ASA tactical elements were now under the command of the units they supported. At the same time, the Army formed new integrated combat electronic warfare and intelligence (CEWI) units to carry out functions previously performed by a variety of different organizations. This new type of Military Intelligence unit joined together Military Intelligence and former Army Security Agency assets.

Two separate institutional thrusts combined to create the ultimate CEWI structure. The first was a growing belief that under conditions of modern warfare it was absolutely essential that a combat division have its own organic intelligence capability. This concept marked a revolution in Army institutional thinking. The Army had reorganized the division force structure twice since the Korean War, creating the pentomic division in 1957 and replacing it with the ROAD division in 1962. Each time, its leaders had explicitly rejected the idea of making an intelligence unit organic to the division, partially because linguistic requirements would vary so greatly under different theater conditions. Until 1969 Army divisions received intelligence support, apart from signals intelligence, from attached Military Intelligence units. Although most of these detachments subsequently had been expanded to full companies, such elements were still only temporary attachments to the division.

In the mid-1970s, after intensive study and testing, the Army reversed its stance and allotted each division an organic intelligence company. Army policy makers had finally concluded that the incorporation of permanent intelligence units into divisions would provide better peacetime training opportunities and would forestall the necessity of hastily assembling the requisite intelligence assets whenever a war broke out. Such units would also furnish a convenient locus from which to manage radar and ground sensor assets previously dispersed throughout the division. One underlying assumption was the growing importance of various technical collection mechanisms in relation to human intelligence sources on the future battlefield. This technology-driven approach complemented the newly developed process the Army termed "the Intelligence Preparation of the Battlefield," in which data on enemy, weather, and terrain would be plotted on map overlays to provide commanders with a graphic intelligence estimate.[11]

The second and more important element leading to the creation of CEWI units was the emphasis of IOSS on the need to integrate diverse intelligence disciplines in the field, both to enhance the support provided commanders and to reduce overhead. The end result of this process came when a TRADOC study group produced the first blueprint for a CEWI type of unit in early 1976. An experimental combat electronic warfare and intelligence battalion, the 522d Military Intelligence Battalion, was fielded later that same year at Fort Hood, Texas, and assigned to the 2d Armored Division. The successful activation of this prototype CEWI battalion meant that the TOE of the divisional intelligence company, which appeared the same year, was already obsolete. The Army's acceptance of the need for battalion-size units to support divisional intelligence requirements demonstrated how far the discipline had come since its World War I beginnings, when divisions had met their intelligence needs with staffs of four officers and a few enlisted men and militarized civilians serving as field clerks.

An agreed-upon TOE for an organic divisional CEWI battalion appeared in 1979. Significantly, the TOE for this new-model Military Intelligence unit was numbered in a different series from previous Military Intelligence and Army Security Agency tables of organization and equipment. The new organizational table provided for a headquarters and headquarters and operations company containing collection management, counterintelligence, and interrogation personnel, and included a platoon of helicopters configured for electronic missions.

---

11 IPB: Intelligence Preparation of the Battlefield (Fort Huachuca, Ariz.: U.S. Army Intelligence Center and School, n.d.). The IPB process was potentially adaptable to automation. This seemed a necessity, since it was estimated in the 1970s that a corps commander in a European war scenario would have to track some 35,000 "movers, shooters, and emitters" in the adversary force. G. Kenneth Allard, *Command, Control, and the Common Defense* (New Haven: Yale University Press, 1990), p. 145.

It also called for three line companies that respectively carried out functional missions of collection and jamming, ground surveillance through radars and sensors, and service support. The new structure thus merged existing intelligence, signals intelligence, and electronic warfare assets available at division level and integrated them with divisional ground sensor and ground surveillance radar elements.[12] Planners also contemplated giving the unit a long-range reconnaissance patrol capability, an addition initially rejected but revived a decade later. Subsequently, the pattern of organization prescribed by the 1979 TOE was modified often in the field, as "company teams" containing elements from all disciplines were organized on an ad hoc basis to support the requirements of each of a division's three brigades.[13]

Although combat divisions continued to have separate reconnaissance battalions and were now allotted target acquisition batteries, the creation of the CEWI unit meant that the division's tactical operations center could draw on the resources of a single element to meet the bulk of its intelligence, security, and electronic warfare needs, rather than having to deal with fragmented elements scattered throughout the divisional structure. The CEWI battalion organization was intended to be strong enough to provide the diverse intelligence disciplines it contained with the necessary support. Since only a quarter of the CEWI battalion's strength consisted of highly trained intelligence specialists, it allowed maximum use of these scarce resources.[14]

The organization of the division-level CEWI battalion was only the beginning of a wholesale restructuring of Army Intelligence at the level of tactical support. Company-size CEWI units were formed to support separate brigades and armored cavalry regiments. The Army also replaced all its active component Military Intelligence battalions, air reconnaissance support, with "military intelligence battalions, aerial exploitation." These new units consisted of a headquarters and headquarters company, an imagery interpretation company, a combat intelligence company (aerial surveillance), and an electronic warfare aviation company (forward). When the battalion operated independently, an electronic warfare aviation company (rear) could be attached. The concept provided a suitable management framework for the Army's own aerial assets and integrated different types of mission aircraft into a single unit.[15]

---

12 Don Gordon, "CEWI Battalion: Intelligence and Electronic Warfare on the Battlefield," *Military Intelligence* 5 (October–December 1979): 22–28.

13 Company Team Commander Responsibilities, 313th MI Bn (CEWI), 82d Airborne Div, Apr 84, copy in INSCOM History Office files.

14 Gordon, "CEWI Battalion," p. 27.

15 This change in force structure was in part dictated by the fact that relying on traditional Air Force photo-reconnaissance platforms in a high-intensity conflict no longer seemed a viable proposition. Army aerial assets could conduct various forms of electronic surveillance while flying in relative safety behind their own front lines. The discontinuance of MIBARS units in the Active Army meant that the Army would henceforth rely on INSCOM IMINT companies and on the reserve components to provide imagery interpreter support for Air Force tactical reconnaissance missions.

Initially the capstone of the new tactical support intelligence structure, the Military Intelligence group functioned at the corps level. The first of these units activated, the 504th Military Intelligence Group, went to support the III Corps at Fort Hood, Texas, in 1978.[16] In 1985, the 201st, 205th, 207th, 504th, and 525th Military Intelligence Groups assigned to support the five corps then operational in the Active Army were all upgraded to brigade status. Each Military Intelligence brigade consisted of a headquarters and headquarters detachment, an operations battalion, an aerial exploitation battalion, and an interrogation and exploitation battalion.

Military Intelligence in the Reserve Components

The integration and reorganization of the Army's intelligence elements were not confined to the Active Army, but also affected the reserve components. The end result of the process was to greatly expand the Military Intelligence presence in these components. While the 24th Military Intelligence Battalion continued as an aerial reconnaissance support unit, the three existing ASA battalions and the single field army type of Military Intelligence battalion in the Army Reserve were all converted to CEWI units, and four additional battalions were activated. Actual implementation of the program took some time. The first Army Reserve CEWI unit, the 138th Military Intelligence Battalion, was not activated until late 1983, and not until 1988 did the last remaining Army Security Agency battalion in the reserve phase out.

Initially, the Army had determined that all combat electronic warfare and intelligence battalions in the reserve structure would belong to the Army Reserve. The National Guard operated under state control in peacetime, and national policy makers had reservations about placing sensitive intelligence assets under state government control. Ultimately, the intelligence community decided that policy considerations did not preclude establishing such units in the National Guard, and the 629th Military Intelligence Battalion was organized in 1988 to service the intelligence and electronic warfare needs of the Maryland-Virginia National Guard's 29th Infantry Division. This issue did not arise in the case of non-CEWI types of National Guard military intelligence units, and aerial exploitation battalions appeared in the Georgia and Oregon National Guards in 1982.

One National Guard unit continued to provide unique support to Army-wide intelligence requirements. In 1980 the 142d Military Intelligence Battalion was organized in the Utah National Guard, replacing a similar company-size unit originally organized in 1960. This TDA battalion, a linguist unit, drew heavily from a pool of expertise provided by members of the Church of Jesus Christ of Latter Day Saints who had previously undergone language training to

---

16 This unit was created by reorganizing and redesignating the 504th Army Security Agency Group, originally activated in 1974 to provide cryptologic support to FORSCOM.

carry out overseas missionary work. Battalion personnel on temporary duty repeatedly assisted the Regular Army in meeting its linguistic needs. The concept was so successful that in 1988 the battalion was converted to a TOE unit; a second similar battalion was organized in the Utah National Guard; and a TDA unit, the 300th Military Intelligence Brigade, was created to provide command and control. Later, the Army approved the organization of Guard linguist battalions in several other states.

Training continued to present difficulties for intelligence units both in the reserve components and in the Regular Army. Many intelligence specialties could not be exercised normally in hometown environments or even under garrison conditions. However, in 1978 the Intelligence and Security Command instituted the Readiness Training Program (REDTRAIN) to expose practitioners of intelligence disciplines throughout the Army to "enrichment" programs. REDTRAIN allowed both reservists and Regular Army soldiers to further their skills by participating in current operations. In practice, this was accomplished either by assigning personnel on temporary duty to units with an operational mission or by bringing the mission to the unit.

Military Intelligence in the 1980s

The 1980s were prosperous years for the Army, especially for its restructured intelligence component. The formation of INSCOM and the implementation of the CEWI concept not only affected intelligence operations throughout the Army, but also drew the Military Intelligence Branch firmly into the mainstream of the service. For the first time, most MI personnel were assigned to TOE units. By 1988 five MI brigades and no less than thirty MI battalions had been formed under the CEWI concept to support tactical units in the field, while another five TOE MI brigades and ten TOE single-function battalions carried out theater- and national-level support missions under INSCOM. Twenty-five thousand Military Intelligence specialists—over 15 percent of them female—were on active duty, backed up by another 8,700 in the reserve components. The active duty Military Intelligence component alone was as large as the entire Regular Army had been in 1885, when the Army first created a permanent intelligence organization. As retired Lt. Gen. James A. Williams, a former director of DIA, pointed out, the Army now had "the equivalent of two combat divisions in collection and analysis."[17]

There were still significant shortfalls in a number of areas. The proliferation of job opportunities presented by an information-based society made recruiting and retaining personnel in a number of intelligence specialties a pressing concern for what continued to be an all-volunteer force. The tactical-level force

---

17 Benjamin F. Schemmer, "Former DIA Director Urges That Four-Star Should Head All Military Intelligence," *Armed Forces Journal International*, Feb 88, p. 24.

structure had grown so large that some Army Intelligence professionals questioned whether it could be maintained indefinitely, given anticipated constraints on Army resources and the competing demands of the Army's echelon above corps intelligence structure. The lightning advance of technology, combined with convoluted contracting and procurement procedures and growing fiscal constraints, had left the Army saddled with equipment that fell far behind the state of the art in many intelligence disciplines. For much of its aerial work, Army Intelligence still depended upon the durable Mohawk, which despite its considerable virtues was now thirty years old. Almost thirty-five years after the inception of Project MICHIGAN, the Army was still struggling to field a satisfactory remotely piloted vehicle—a pilotless reconnaissance aircraft. Army tactical signals intelligence and electronic intelligence resources in the field were mounted on slow and overloaded carriers that could not keep up with the new generation of Army tanks and armored fighting vehicles. Moreover, as 1990 approached there were already signs that the greatest defense buildup since the Korean War was about to end, and this necessitated further changes in the organization of Army Intelligence.

In 1987, however, two significant developments seemed to confirm that the Army had at last accepted its Intelligence arm as an equal member in its family of branches. In May of that year the position of ACSI was upgraded to deputy chief of staff for intelligence (DCSINT), a change that ended the position of perceived organizational inferiority of the Army Intelligence staff post. Lt. Gen. Sidney T. Weinstein became the Army's first DCSINT. That same year, Army Intelligence became part of the regimental system that embodied the heritage of the U.S. Army. On 1 July 1987, the twenty-fifth anniversary of the establishment of intelligence as a Regular Army branch, all Army Intelligence personnel, military and civilian, became part of a single large regiment, the Military Intelligence Corps, headed by the commanding general, U.S. Army Intelligence Center and School. Although symbolic, the measure was significant. Maj. Gen. Julius Parker, the first chief of the Military Intelligence Corps, called the step "a recognition and celebration of our evolution from a plethora of diverse and separate intelligence agencies into the cohesive MI community we enjoy today. In short, it symbolizes the fact that Army Intelligence has truly arrived."[18]

Additional proofs that General Parker's statement was not overly optimistic were soon forthcoming. In 1987 the Army published a detailed Army Intelligence, Electronic Warfare, and Target Acquisition Plan (AIMP). The AIMP conceptualized the future structure of Army Intelligence as a "system of systems" and laid out a detailed and coherent road map of the measures needed to reshape the Army's intelligence organizations and technologies in ways that would satisfy future requirements. In 1989 INSCOM shifted its headquarters

---

[18] Ltr, Chief, Military Intelligence, *Huachuca Scout* (*Military Intelligence Corps Activation Supplement*), 25 Jun 87, p. 2.

from Arlington Hall Station to a site on the north post of Fort Belvoir, Virginia. INSCOM's new headquarters facility, the Nolan Building, was named in honor of Maj. Gen. Dennis E. Nolan, Pershing's G–2 in World War I. This was the first Army Intelligence headquarters ever designed specifically for its purpose. In 1990 the chief of Military Intelligence became commanding general of the U.S. Army Intelligence Center and Fort Huachuca. This step paved the way for the eventual closure of the Intelligence School at Fort Devens, Massachusetts, and the consolidation of almost all Military Intelligence training at Fort Huachuca. Meanwhile, the internal evolution of Military Intelligence within the Army was already being affected by outside events.

11

A Future of Uncertainties

The year 1989 was an "annus mirabilis," a time of wonders, in which the world geopolitical framework in place since the end of World War II was overturned. As military historian Michael Howard commented, "while the nations of Western Europe celebrated the bicentennial of the French Revolution, the nations of Eastern Europe reenacted it."[1] After so many years, the Iron Curtain finally parted, and with it the Berlin Wall and so many of the other symbolic and real barriers that had divided east from west. With tides of democracy sweeping through Eastern Europe, the Warsaw Pact was no longer relevant. The Soviet Union itself appeared in a new light—no longer the Great Bear of international politics, but an ideologically and economically bankrupt society showing ominous signs of fragmentation along ethnic and national lines. For all practical purposes, the looming threat of Soviet power that had gripped the attention of Western policy makers for so many years was suddenly gone.

Since 1989 these developments have dramatically restructured America's defense policy. Ever since the end of the Vietnam War, the U.S. Army had essentially staked its raison d'etre on countering a massive tank-led Warsaw Pact offensive against Western Europe. With this threat no longer viable, the nation's armed forces were slowly downsized and redeployed. The numbers governing the rate, scope, and exact nature of this process shifted with each new indication of communism's decline. In 1990 the Army implemented Project VANGUARD to bring about a controlled reduction of its strength in ways that would leave as much of its fighting forces intact as possible, a task to be accomplished initially through a radical trimming of headquarters elements.

However, just as the Soviet threat receded and pundits began to talk about the pleasant possibilities of a "peace dividend," a new array of international challenges appeared. In December 1989 American forces stormed Panama in Operation JUST CAUSE, overthrowing the regime of its narcotics-linked strong-

---

[1] Michael Howard, "The Springtime of Nations," *Foreign Affairs* 69, no. 1, p. 17.

man, General Manuel Noriega. Eight months later, crisis flared in the Middle East. An Iraqi invasion of the tiny emirate of Kuwait, threatening both the world's oil supply and the stability of a potential new world order, led to a massive American response. The United States deployed over 500,000 men and women to the Persian Gulf region—the largest buildup of troops since Vietnam—and then committed them to battle in Operation DESERT STORM, a lightning air and ground war that resulted in complete victory.

Despite these conflicting crosscurrents of events, planning for retrenchment of the force continued. Nevertheless, it was clear that the post–Cold War world would continue to hold unforeseen and unforeseeable perils. In the unstructured international environment created by the sudden collapse of the bipolar world order imposed by the Cold War, crises could—and did—take place in almost any region of the globe. The prospect of a smaller Army and a more diffused but wider menace would inevitably affect the institutional arrangements of Military Intelligence, since intelligence organizations are necessarily shaped by the threat as well as the force structure in place. In addition to preparing for contingency operations, Army Intelligence now had to monitor arms verification agreements, fight terrorism, maintain a vigilant watch against espionage, and assume a counter-drug mission in support of civilian authorities.

The challenges of JUST CAUSE and DESERT STORM—successive crises occurring half a world apart and in totally unrelated linguistic environments—had already made large demands on Military Intelligence and appeared to serve as a portent for the future. On the whole, the Army had met these demands successfully. INSCOM's 470th Military Intelligence Brigade and its attached 29th Military Intelligence Battalion had been in place in Panama when that crisis broke. INSCOM's 513th Military Intelligence Brigade, with a long-standing contingency mission to support the U.S. Army Central Command, had been at least partially positioned to meet Army intelligence requirements when deployment to the Persian Gulf began. Once brigade elements had moved to Saudi Arabia, the U.S. Army Intelligence and Security Command augmented the unit from its own assets around the globe. As the situation reached its climax, the brigade's echelon-above-corps intelligence center was expanded to a full operations battalion and placed in support of the G–2 of Central Command's Army component. Two corps CEWI brigades, the 504th and 525th MI brigades, and divisional CEWI units supported the intelligence effort in Southwest Asia with their own resources, and reserve component units and individual mobilization augmentees deployed to assist.

In this intelligence campaign, high technology at last came into its own. A variety of ground terminals received information provided by diverse national and theater intelligence systems, unmanned aerial vehicles—the new Army term for remotely controlled pilotless aircraft—were finally fielded to provide collection and targeting data, and the Army engaged in substantive electronic warfare operations for the first time since electronic warfare had become an intelligence responsibility.2

In JUST CAUSE and DESERT STORM, however, the Army had been able to draw on the resources it had built up during the height of the Cold War. The future challenge for Army Intelligence would be to do more with less. Even as DESERT STORM came to an end, it was already evident that the smaller force structure envisaged for the future would necessarily lead to the inactivation of numerous intelligence battalions and brigades, as the divisions and corps to which they were assigned closed down. By 1995 the Army force structure had been reduced from eighteen divisions to just ten. The shrinkage of tactical assets was accompanied by a pullback of much of the Army from its forward-deployed posture. Presumably, this withdrawal would make INSCOM even more central to the Army's intelligence effort, since tactical intelligence units in the continental United States would not have direct access to their intelligence targets, and INSCOM alone had the necessary linkages to national systems to provide the Army with worldwide intelligence support.

However, the elimination of the Soviet threat and the consequent downsizing of the Army meant that INSCOM itself faced the greatest reorganization since its birth with the possibility of not even surviving as a major Army command. Flux was the order of the day. For a brief time, the command regained Army production functions, assuming command of the Army Intelligence Agency in 1991. The following year, however, AIA was disestablished and its subordinate production centers divided up between DIA and INSCOM, with DCSINT retaining operational control of the Intelligence and Threat Analysis Center and the Foreign Science and Technology Center, the two elements that remained with INSCOM. In turn, these two production elements were merged into a single National Ground Intelligence Center. The Special Security Group that had disseminated sensitive compartmented information since World War II was reorganized and most special security officers resubordinated to the major Army commands they supported, thus creating a much smaller Special Security organization to set policy and deal with private contractors. Eventually, the unit's mission was assumed by one of the battalions of the 902d MI Group.

This did not exhaust the list of changes. INSCOM's major field stations in Europe and Panama were discontinued and Army cryptologic organization radically restructured. INSCOM set up a Regional SIGINT Operations Center at Fort Gordon, Georgia, manned by personnel of the newly organized 702d MI Group. Since its 513th MI Brigade concurrently relocated to Fort Gordon, this allowed strategic and tactical assets to be combined. At the same time, the com-

---

2 Details of Army Intelligence operations conducted during the DESERT SHIELD/DESERT STORM mission can be found in Brig. Gen. (P) John F. Stewart, Jr.'s pamphlet, Operation DESERT STORM: The Military Intelligence Story: A View From the G–2, 3d U.S. Army, April 1991.

mand assumed host responsibilities for new sites in Europe that would allow the Army to employ the most advanced communications technologies.

Institutional gains were accompanied by institutional losses. INSCOM's U.S. Army Russian Institute was resubordinated to the European Command. A Foreign Intelligence Command was organized at Fort Meade, Maryland, to provide better support to human intelligence (HUMINT) and counterintelligence units there, but this proved to have the life span of a mayfly: it was discontinued in less than a year as a result of the secretary of defense's decision to incorporate Army human intelligence elements into a Defense HUMINT Service.

As the Army itself restructured and pulled back from Europe and Panama, its leaders planned to merge INSCOM's five existing theater support brigades into two force projection brigades. The new units would operate in a split-based configuration and would have the capability to deploy tactically tailored force packages to meet any level of contingency requirement. Additionally, beginning in 1993 INSCOM provided personnel to augment corps-level production centers and (for a time) joint intelligence centers within the unified commands. INSCOM would no longer simply operate at echelons above corps, but would provide the Army with "seamless connectivity" between national-level agencies and the warfighters on the ground.

Finally, in 1994 the Army set up the Land Information Warfare Activity (LIWA) within INSCOM, operating under the staff supervision of the Department of the Army's deputy chief of staff for operations. This was inspired by the precedent offered by DESERT STORM, in which the centralized Iraqi command structure had been effectively befuddled by deception operations and decapitated by the electronic and physical destruction of its communications system. Still in the formative stage, the LIWA sought to bring together the techniques of electronic warfare, psychological warfare, deception operations, command and control targeting, and operational security to attack the information resources of the enemy while simultaneously defending those of our own armed forces. Once it became fully operational, the LIWA would offer the larger Army a place for "one-stop shopping" in these areas.[3]

Conclusion: The Shaping of Army Intelligence

Although the details of the future necessarily lay hidden, Military Intelligence's current trajectory provides clues as to its future organizational and mission directions.[4] At least five identifiable trends have helped shape the

---

[3] The "information warfare" concept reflected—or at least paralleled—the ideas of the influential futurologists Alvin and Heidi Toffler. See War and Anti-War (Boston: Little Brown, 1994), ch. 10, "The Knowledge Warriors."

[4] Of course, clues can be misleading. Distinguished military historian Russell F. Weigley has commented, "Almost all of the hints of prophecy into which the author was rashly drawn . . . proved wrong." History of the United States Army. Enlarged Edition (Bloomington: Indiana University Press, 1984), pp. 557–58.

post–World War II history of Army Intelligence: a steady devolution of functions to national and joint agencies; a redefinition of the Military Intelligence field to embrace new functions; an enhanced role for technology; a progressive growth both in the number and size of intelligence units and in the diversity of intelligence disciplines they incorporated; and finally, an increasing professionalism.

First of all, continuing pressures for greater service integration has had a major impact on the overall organization of Army Intelligence. As a result of these pressures, and over a period of time, the Army has transferred cryptologic, production, attache collection, and certain counterintelligence and human intelligence functions to national agencies. The creation of the Central Intelligence Agency in 1947 removed the Army from the fields of political and economic intelligence. This preceded the partial breakup of the Army Security Agency in 1949 to form the Armed Forces Security Agency (AFSA), the National Security Agency's predecessor. More reforms followed the revision of the National Defense Act in 1958, which removed the Army as an institution from the chain of national command and turned it into a mechanism for training, administering, and supplying land forces for the unified commands acting under the Joint Chiefs of Staff. The logic of this inevitably dictated the creation of the Defense Intelligence Agency (DIA) in 1961. As DIA grew it took over Army production functions as well as certain training and collection functions.

As the Army drew down during the last stages of the Vietnam conflict, there was another wave of consolidation. The Defense Mapping Agency absorbed Army topographic elements, the Central Security Service took over certain headquarters functions of the Army's cryptologic agency, and the Defense Investigative Service assumed the personnel background investigation function previously performed by Army counterintelligence. The first two integrations were done ostensibly to promote economy and efficiency, while the last eased the Army out of the domestic intelligence field that had left it open to charges of "spying on civilians."

As the Army once more planned to contract in the 1990s, these kinds of pressures on its Military Intelligence organization continued. If anything, the Department of Defense Reorganization Act of 1986 had placed a premium on joint operations. However, despite the steady trend toward integration, Army Intelligence has in fact shown a remarkable resiliency over the years. This is wholly consistent with laws of institutional behavior. Motivated recruits join the Army because they wish to wear green suits, not "purple" ones.[5] The Army most readily surrendered those intelligence functions peripheral to its central mission of warfighting.

---

[5] For an interesting discussion of the differing "personalities," identities, and behaviors of the different armed services, see Carl H. Builder, *The Masks of War: American Military Styles in Strategy and Analysis* (Baltimore: Johns Hopkins University Press, 1989), p. 39. Builder notes that "the unique service identities . . . are likely to persist for a very long time."

Before the creation of the Central Intelligence Agency, the Army had engaged in collection of political and economic intelligence for want of a better alternative. The high-level cryptologic mission turned over to the Armed Forces Security Agency had implications that went beyond the Army. It was also both exotic (most of the personnel who transferred to AFSA were highly specialized civilians) and a mission which naturally lent itself to a joint approach. Moreover, although the impetus behind the creation of AFSA had been to replace three service cryptologic organizations with one, the end result was the creation of four cryptologic organizations. The Army's determination to provide cryptologic support to its own commanders ensured that the Army Security Agency grew larger and more important after 1949 than it had been before. The National Security Agency later attempted unsuccessfully to integrate service management structures into a central security service.

The creation of the Defense Intelligence Agency presented Army Intelligence with a more formidable institutional challenge. Here, the Army and the other services pursued a strategy of more straightforward resistance, refusing to allow their intelligence components to be completely subsumed into the new organization. During the agency's formative period, Army officers posted to DIA found their assignments less than career enhancing. DIA was initially allowed to control only a single collection element, the attache system, and the Army reentered the field of intelligence production almost immediately. Even after thirty years, DIA had not achieved the dominant position in the general intelligence field that NSA had achieved in the cryptologic area.

In 1972 the Army gave up the bulk of its counterintelligence operations in the continental United States to the Defense Intelligence Service, when the latter agency was formed to execute the mission of conducting personnel background investigations for security clearances. This was a forced move, brought about by the fact that the Army had been brought deeply into the field of domestic intelligence during the troubled times of the Vietnam War. However, the transfer of functions, again, did not impact on the Army's wartime mission. Moreover, it could be looked upon as a blessing, since it removed the Army from an area which had been a political land mine since the earliest days of its own counterintelligence operations. The Army had been forcibly extracted from domestic intelligence operations twice before—in 1920, at the end of the Red Scare, and in 1943, following political displeasure at investigations of subversives that had touched upon the president's family. Three experiences of this kind were perhaps enough.

Finally, in 1995 DIA set up the Defense HUMINT Service (DHS), which absorbed all the strategic and theater-level human intelligence collection assets of the armed services. This forced merger was brought about by a post–Cold War drive for economy and efficiency that in many ways paralleled the Department of Defense–level realignments of the Vietnam drawdown. However, once more we could argue that the Army surrendered elements not central to its perceived main mission of warfighting.

A second trend evident during this period was the redefinition and expansion of the intelligence field. Over the years, Military Intelligence organizations absorbed various "special informational services." This process had begun immediately after World War II, when the Military Intelligence Division assumed administrative as well as operational control of the Army Security Agency. In turn, the logic of this realignment eventually made electronic warfare an intelligence responsibility. "Jamming" and collection operations were intimately related, and could not be conducted independently of one another. As a result, the Army Security Agency gained responsibility for communications electronic countermeasures in 1955. Simultaneously, it assumed the electronic intelligence (ELINT) mission from the Signal Corps. This too followed a certain logic: the agency now collected against the whole of the electronic spectrum instead of just a part. Continuing in the same pattern, ASA acquired the noncommunications electronic countermeasures mission from the Signal Corps in 1962.

The formation of combat electronic warfare and intelligence units as a result of the Intelligence Organization and Stationing Study brought additional collection services under the Military Intelligence umbrella. Intelligence units assimilated ground sensors and ground surveillance radars. Meanwhile, Army Intelligence had already taken to the sky. Army aviation had developed specialized reconnaissance aircraft in the late 1950s, and the Army Security Agency had developed its own air arm during the 1960s. In the late 1970s, both types of assets became part of an integrated Military Intelligence battalion, aerial exploitation.

In one area, however, the responsibilities of Military Intelligence contracted after World War II. This was the field of communications security. The Army Security Agency, as first set up, had responsibility for all aspects of military cryptology, including creating and distributing the Army's codes and cipher devices and monitoring the security of Army communications. The 1955 reorganization of the Army Security Agency resulted in the transfer of the first two of these functions to the Signal Corps. As the years went on, a tendency for Army Intelligence to edge away from security monitoring became pronounced; many saw the task as intrusive, unpopular, and not particularly effective. In the long run, as far as the Army was concerned, encryption of all message traffic could render security monitoring obsolete. Meanwhile, some aspects of communications security could now be passed back to the communicators. In 1988 INSCOM, which had inherited from ASA the mission of preparing the Army's Communications-Electronics Operating Instructions, decided that the function would more appropriately belong to the Army's new Directorate of Information Systems for Command, Control, Communications, and Computers. A little later, INSCOM transferred mission responsibility for the inspection of cryptofacilities and the tracking of communications violations to the Army's communicators.

Third, partially as a result of Intelligence's increasing dependence on the technical services, the advance of technology affected almost every intelligence discipline. The combined impact of the communications revolution and the

growth of automation had a profound effect upon intelligence collection, processing, and dissemination. To use only select examples, the development of
infrared and radar imaging techniques revolutionized photographic intelligence
and resulted in that discipline's transformation into imagery intelligence. The
synergistic use of a variety of techniques to measure the distinct profiles displayed by an assortment of target "shooters, movers, and emitters" created the
new intelligence discipline, measurement and signature intelligence (MASINT).
Technology even promised—or threatened—to reverse the nature of the entire
Army Intelligence process. Traditionally, information had passed from lower levels of command, in direct confrontation with the enemy, to higher levels for
evaluation. In the Persian Gulf conflict of 1991, however, Army production elements based in the continental United States had used national intelligence
acquisition systems to generate tactical intelligence that went down to the field.

Counterintelligence was also confronted with fresh challenges as a result of
this trend. The Army faced a wider security threat as technological development
created new vulnerabilities. Not only were the activities of hostile human agents
now supplemented by electronic listening devices, but the radiations emitted by
electronic media were vulnerable to detection, while the computers that supplied the masses of data on which the Army now relied could be infiltrated by
"hackers" and menaced by computer "viruses."

Fourth, intelligence units in the field tended to grow both larger and more
integrated. The Army emerged from World War II with a melange of single-
discipline intelligence elements organized in no common pattern. They
included counterintelligence detachments, ASA's signal service companies and
detachments, and an assortment of teams and detachments that carried out
various combat intelligence functions. Additionally, the Signal Corps had its
own units conducting electronic intelligence and electronic warfare. The
Korean War partially revolutionized this structure, as the Army fielded groups
and battalions to collect combat intelligence and ASA created units of similar
size to carry out military cryptologic functions in support of the tactical Army.
In the latter part of the 1950s, counterintelligence and collection personnel
were integrated into combat intelligence formations under the Military
Intelligence Organization concept, although most counterintelligence personnel continued to serve in separate CIC groups. Roughly around the same time,
various Signal Corps intelligence and electronic warfare units were folded into
the Army Security Agency.

Following the Intelligence Organization and Stationing Study of 1975, the
Army integrated all intelligence disciplines at both the tactical and strategic levels, creating CEWI units and the U.S. Army Intelligence and Security
Command. For the first time, most Army Intelligence assets were contained in
TOE units rather than under tables of distribution and allowances. By 1990
multidiscipline intelligence brigades had been fielded to support both corps and
higher echelons of command.

The development of large intelligence units, combined with institutional pressures to reduce the operational role of the Army's intelligence staff, helped to move the center of gravity of intelligence work in the Army from the staff to the line. It also was one of the factors that helped make Army Intelligence more professional. One could argue logically that just as ordnance officers should command an ordnance unit, intelligence officers should command an intelligence unit. At first the Army Intelligence and Security Branch, as its title indicated, was something of an uneasy compromise, lumping together officers of diverse backgrounds and allegiances. The branch had no common training program, and the Army Security Agency, with its vertical command structure and its roots in the Signal Corps, remained a large, unassimilated segment of the Army Intelligence community. However, the Army made greater steps toward integration in 1967, when the Army Intelligence and Security Branch was redesignated as the Military Intelligence Branch and upgraded in status. The change was more than just a shift in nomenclature, since the common advanced schooling that went into effect at this time imposed a new homogeneity on the Military Intelligence field. Implementation of the IOSS recommendations brought the institutional structure of Army Intelligence into line with the single branch concept.

The professionalization of Army Intelligence, combined with the shift to an All-Volunteer Force in the early 1970s, led in turn to a greater emphasis on military values within the field. As long as intelligence organizations had been dominated by reserve officers, and depended on the stimulus of the draft for their manning, intelligence personnel had tended to identify with their specialties, rather than with the Army as a whole. The fact that so many of them were involved in specialized tasks with no immediate combat relationship only facilitated this ethos. While the mainstream of the peacetime Army focused on a training and readiness mission, Intelligence had (and continues to have) a viable peacetime mission. The bulk of ASA personnel, for example, carried out a strategic cryptologic mission at fixed installations, and most counterintelligence personnel operated in civilian clothes and lived on the civilian economy at a time when the rest of the Army was still in barracks and bachelor officers' quarters. When an applicant for the Counter Intelligence Corps asked his recruiters whether life in the CIC was anything like the Army, they replied, "Not very much." This approach has changed markedly.[6]

In short, we can argue that by 1990 Military Intelligence had become distinctly more military. Intelligence personnel—men and women, officer and enlisted—were soldiers first, specialists second. They trained regularly at Army skills and were held to Army standards of physical fitness. Separate management structures that tended to foster the idea that various groups of intelligence personnel were an elite corps apart from the larger Army had been dissolved:

---

[6] Author's recollection.

the Intelligence Corps was discontinued in 1966, and the Army Security Agency broke up ten years later. The grade structure of intelligence units mirrored that of the rest of the Army, unlike the situation in an earlier period, when 40 percent of a counterintelligence detachment's strength might consist of officers. The danger, of course, was that the process could be carried too far, and that the thrust to make everyone a potential warfighter might unduly divert energies from the proper performance of what remained a demanding real-world mission.[7]

Among other things, the new professionalism meant that Military Intelligence personnel could publicly identify with the traditions of the Army in ways that were not originally thought possible when intelligence work itself was identified, sometimes by its practitioners, as something appropriate only to the shadows. To give only one example, uniformed enlisted personnel assigned to Army Counter Intelligence Corps units during the 1950s wore a simple "U.S." as their collar insignia, officers bore the insignia of their carrier branch, and CIC units in the continental United States presented themselves to the public as "Army Research Groups." During the 1960s, however, Army Intelligence units boasted their own distinguishing unit insignia and their assigned personnel wore Military Intelligence brass. In the 1980s the MI groups of a previous period were redesignated as MI brigades, receiving their own shoulder sleeve insignia. This change would enhance troop esprit and morale by providing the units with more traditional military designations. Certain of INSCOM's TDA field stations and other TDA elements were also given new numerical unit designations. In part, the Army made the change to distinguish troop formations from the geographical locations at which they worked, but it also had the desirable side effect of assigning to these units designations that were more intelligible to the rest of the Army. In short, Military Intelligence identified itself with Army green, abandoning the cloak-and-dagger image of an earlier era. In more ways than one, the motto of the Military Intelligence Corps, "Always Out Front," reflected the new reality.

In 1987 the chief of Military Intelligence declared, "Army Intelligence has truly arrived," and in one sense he was correct. In another sense, however, Military Intelligence was still in transit, progressively redefining itself as the Army, the nation, and the international situation changed. Still, wherever the journey might lead it in the future, clearly Military Intelligence has come a long way from its modest beginning in 1885 as the Division of Military Information.

---

[7] As a visitor to an INSCOM counterintelligence element reported in 1989, "the six military personnel assigned . . . spend an inordinate amount of time detailed away from the office for charge of quarters details, training, physical training, and alerts, none of which is optional." He estimated that "the military personnel spend an average of 67% of their time away from the office." Memo, HQ INSCOM, IAOPS-CI-OC, 10 Oct 89, sub: Summary Report of Temporary Duty Travel to USAREUR.

Bibliography

For a number of reasons, it has seemed inappropriate to provide this volume with a full scholarly apparatus. Security conditions necessarily make the book's coverage of certain aspects of the Military Intelligence story a good deal less than definitive. Moreover, the book does not purport to be a completely original piece of research, since its first portion is based substantially upon material contained in two large previous studies: Bruce W. Bidwell's eight-part survey of the history of the Military Intelligence Division, Department of the Army, prepared for the U.S. Army Center of Military History in the 1950s, and a thirty-volume history of the Army Counter Intelligence Corps which the U.S. Army Intelligence Center compiled in 1959–1960. Initially, both works were fully classified, but now they have been largely declassified. Finally, the latter part of the book draws from a variety of Army files which still remain classified and, in some cases, compartmented; these files will not be accessible to researchers for the foreseeable future. As a result, we decided to provide footnotes only to cite direct quotations, provide additional commentary, and reference open-source publications applying to the subject. For the same reason, this bibliography lists only published, open-source material.

General Works

Bidwell, Bruce W. *History of the Military Intelligence Division, Department of the General Staff, 1775–1941.* Frederick, Md.: University Presses of America, 1986.

Clark, Ronald William. *The Man Who Broke PURPLE: A Life of the World's Greatest Cryptographer, Colonel William F. Friedman.* Boston: Little Brown, 1977.

Clausewitz, Carl Von. *On War.* Ed. and trans. Michael Howard and Peter Paret. Princeton: Princeton University Press, 1984.

Cline, Marjorie W. et al. *Scholar's Guide to Intelligence Literature.* Frederick, Md.: University Publications of America, 1983.

Cohen, Eliot A., and Gooch, John. *Military Misfortunes: The Anatomy of Failure in War.* New York: The Free Press, 1990.

Constantanides, George C. *Intelligence and Espionage: An Analytical Bibliography.* Boulder, Colo.: Westview Press, 1983.

Creveld, Martin Van. *Command in War.* Cambridge: Harvard University Press, 1985.

Crouch, Tom D. *The Eagle Aloft: Two Centuries of the Balloon in America.* Washington, D.C.: Smithsonian Institute Press, 1983.

Dulles, Allen. *The Craft of Intelligence.* New York: Harper and Row, 1963.

Finnegan, John P. *The Military Intelligence Story: A Photo History.* Fort Belvoir, Va.: U.S. Army Intelligence and Security Command, 1994.

———. *Military Intelligence: A Picture History.* 2d ed. Fort Belvoir, Va.: U.S. Army Intelligence and Security Command, 1992.

Hewes, James. *From Root to MacNamara: Army Organization and Administration, 1900–1963.* Washington, D.C.: U.S. Army Center of Military History, 1975.

Ind, Allison. *A Short History of Espionage: From the Trojan Horse to Cuba.* New York: McKay, 1963.

Infield, Glenn B. *Unarmed and Unafraid: The First Complete History of Men, Missions, Training, and Techniques of Aerial Reconnaissance.* New York: MacMillan, 1970.

Gordon, Col. Don E. *Electronic Warfare: Element of Strategy and Multiplier of Combat Power.* New York: Pergamon Press, 1981.

Jefferys-Jones, Rhodri. *American Espionage: From Secret Service to CIA.* New York: Free Press, 1977.

———. *The CIA and American Democracy.* New Haven: Yale University Press, 1989.

Jensen, Joan M. *Military Surveillance of Civilians in America.* Morristown, N.J.: General Learning Press, 1975.

Kahn, David. *The Codebreakers: The History of Secret Writing.* New York: MacMillan, 1967.

Kent, Sherman. *Strategic Intelligence for American World Policy* Princeton: Princeton University Press, 1947.

Knowing One's Enemies: Intelligence Assessment Before the Two Wars. Ed. Ernest May. Princeton: Princeton University Press, 1984.

Levite, Ariel. *Intelligence and Strategic Surprises.* New York: Columbia University Press, 1987.

Lanning, Michael Lee. *Senseless Secrets: The Failures of U.S. Military Intelligence from George Washington to the Present.* New York: Carol Publishing Group, 1996.

Laquer, Walter. *A World of Secrets: The Uses and Limits of Intelligence.* New York: Basic Books, 1985.

Lowenthal, Mark M. *U.S. Intelligence: Evolution and Anatomy.* New York: Praeger, 1984.

Military Intelligence: Its Heroes and Legends, comp. Diane Hamm. Arlington, Va.: U.S. Army Intelligence and Security Command, 1987.

Nelson, Maj. Gen. Otto L. *National Security and the General Staff.* Washington, D.C.: Infantry Journal Press, 1946.

O'Toole, G. J. A. *The Encyclopedia of American Intelligence and Espionage: From the Revolutionary War to the Present.* New York: Facts on File, 1988.

Paddock, Alfred H., Jr. *U.S. Army Special Warfare: Its Origins.* Washington, D.C.: National Defense University Press, 1982.

Petersen, Neal H. *American Intelligence, 1775–1990: A Bibliographical Guide.* Claremont, Calif.: Regina Books, 1992.

Powe, Marc B. and Wilson, Edward E. *The Evolution of American Military Intelligence.* Fort Huachuca, Ariz.: U.S. Army Intelligence Center and School, 1973.

_____. "The History of American Military Intelligence--A Review of Selected Literature." *Military Affairs* 39 (1975): 142–45.

Powers, Richard G. *Secrecy and Power: The Life of J. Edgar Hoover.* New York: Free Press, 1987.

Robertson, K. G., ed. *British and American Approaches to Intelligence.* New York: St. Martin's Press, 1987.

Rowan, Richard W., and Dendofer, Robert G. *Secret Service: 33 Centuries of Espionage.* New York: Hawthorne Books, 1967.

Sayle, Edward F. "Historical Underpinnings of the U.S. Intelligence Community." Reprinted from *International Journal of Intelligence and Counterintelligence* 1 (1986).

Stevens, Philip H. *Search Out the Land: A History of American Military Scouts.* Chicago: Rand McNally, 1969.

Smith, Myron J., Jr. *The Secret Wars: A Guide to Sources in English.* 3 vols. Santa Barbara, Calif.: ABC-Clio, 1980.

Strong, Maj. Gen. Sir Kenneth. *Men of Intelligence.* London: Cassell, 1970.

Vagts, Alfred. *The Military Attache.* Princeton: Princeton University Press, 1967.

Volkman, Ernest. *Warriors of the Night: Spies, Soldiers, and American Intelligence.* New York: William Morrow, 1985.

Weinert, Richard P. *A History of Army Aviation, 1950–1962; Phase I: 1950–1954*, Fort Monroe, Va.: U.S. Continental Army Command, 1971.

West, Nigel. *The Sigint Secrets: The Signals Intelligence War, 1900 to Today.* New York: Morrow, 1988.

Military Intelligence, 1775–1885

Alexander, General E. Porter. *Military Memoirs of a Confederate.* Bloomington: Indiana University Press, 1962.

Bakeless, John. *Turncoats, Traitors, and Heroes.* Philadelphia:J. B. Lippincott Co., 1960.

_____. *Spies of the Confederacy.* Philadelphia: J. B. Lippincott, 1970.

Baker, L. C. *History of the United States Secret Service.* Philadelphia: L. C. Baker, 1867.

Bates, David Homer. *Lincoln in the Telegraph Office: Recollections of the United States Military Telegraph Corps in the Civil War.* New York: The Century Co., 1907.

Brown, J. Willard. *The Signal Corps, U.S.A. in the War of the Rebellion.* New York: Arno Press, 1974.

Bryan, George S. *The Spy in America.* Philadelphia: Lippincott, 1943.

Byrne, Robert. "Combat Intelligence: The Key to Victory at Gettysburg." *Military Intelligence* (1976): 5–9.

The Civil War: Spies, Scouts, and Raiders. Alexandria, Va.: Time-Life Books, 1985.

Fishel, Edwin C. "The Mythology of Civil War Intelligence." *Civil War History* 10 (1964): 344–67.

_____. "Pinkerton and McClellan: Who Deceived Whom?" *Civil War History* 24 (1988): 115–42.

Flexner, James T. *The Traitor and the Spy, Benedict Arnold and John Andre.* New York: Harcourt, Brace, and Co., 1953.

Ford, Corey. *A Peculiar Service.* Boston: Little, Brown, and Co., 1965.

Goetzmann, William H. *Army Exploration in the American West, 1803–1863.* Lincoln: University of Nebraska Press, 1979.

Kane, Harnett T. *Spies for the Blue and Grey.* Garden City, N.Y.: Hanover House, 1954.

McDonald, Archie P., ed. *Make Me a Map of the Valley: The Civil War Journal of Stonewall Jackson's Topographer.* Dallas: Southern Methodist University Press, 1973.

Martin, Steven J. "Custer Didn't Listen." *Military Intelligence* 15 (1989), 15–20.

Miller, Francis T. *Photographic History of The Civil War* (New York: Review of Reviews, 1912.

Pinkerton, Allan. *The Spy of the Rebellion: Being a True History of the Spy System of the United States Army During the Late Rebellion.* New York: G. W. Carleton and Co., 1883.

Schmidt, C. T. "G2, Army of the Potomac." *Military Review* 28 (1948): 45–56.

Sparks, David S. "General Patrick's Progress: Intelligence and Security in the Army of the Potomac." *Civil War History* 10 (1964): 371–84.

Stern, Philip. *Secret Missions of the Civil War*. Chicago: Rand, McNally, 1959.

Swan, Guy C. III et al. "Scott's Engineers." *Military Review* (1983): 61–68.

Tidwell, William A. et al. *Come Retribution: The Confederate Secret Service and the Assassination of Lincoln*. Jackson: University Press of Mississippi, 1988.

Van Doren, Carl. *Secret History of the American Revolution*. New York: Viking Press, 1941.

Military Intelligence, 1885–1941

Bethel, Elizabeth. "The Military Information Division: Origin of the Intelligence Division." *Military Affairs* 11 (1947): 17–24.

Bisher, Jamie. "A Travelling Salesman Fills a Crucial Gap." *Military Intelligence* 15 (1989): 36–37.

Butler, Howard K. *Army Air Corps Airplanes and Observation, 1935–1941*. St. Louis: U.S. Army Aviation Systems Command, 1990.

Coll, Blanche D., Keith, Jean E. and Rosenthal, Herbert. *The Corps of Engineers: Troops and Equipment*. United States Army in World War II. Washington, D.C.: U.S. Army Center of Military History, 1958.

Cutter, C. S. "Intelligence Service in the World War." *Infantry Journal* 20 (1922): 376–83.

Churchill, Marlborough. "The Military Intelligence Division, General Staff." *Journal of the United States Artillery* 52 (1920): 293–315.

Fergusson, Thomas G. *British Military Intelligence, 1870–1914: The Development of a Modern Intelligence Organization*. Frederick, Md.: University Publications of America, 1984.

Finnegan, John P. *Against the Specter of a Dragon: The Campaign for American Military Preparedness, 1914–1917*. Westport, Conn.: Greenwood Press, 1974.

Gilbert, James L. "U.S. Army COMSEC in World War I." *Military Intelligence* 14 (1988): 22–25.

Goddard, George W. *Overview: A Lifelong Adventure in Aerial Photography*. Garden City, N.J.: Doubleday, 1969.

Hitt, Parker. *Manual for the Solution of Military Ciphers*. Fort Leavenworth, Kans.: Press of the Army Service Schools, 1916.

Hubbard, Samuel T. *Memoirs of a Staff Officer, 1917–1919*. Tuckahoe, N.Y.: Cardinal Associates, Inc., 1959.

Johnson, Thomas M. *Without Censor*. Indianapolis: Bobbs-Merrill, 1928.

Linn, Brian McAllister. *The U.S. Army and Counterinsurgency in the Philippine War, 1899–1902*. Chapel Hill: University of North Carolina Press, 1989.

Morgan, William A. "Invasion on the Ether: Radio Intelligence at the Battle of St. Mihiel, September 1918." *Military Affairs* 51 (1987): 57–61.

Parish, John C. "Intelligence Work at First Army Headquarters." *Historical Outlook* 11 (1920): 213–17.

Parson, William Barclay. *The American Engineers in France*. New York: D. Appleton and Company, 1920.

Powe, Mark B. "American Military Intelligence Comes of Age: A Sketch of a Man and His Times." *Military Review* 55 (1975): 17–30.

____. *The Emergence of the War Department Intelligence Agency, 1885–1918*. Manhattan, Kans.: MA/AH Publishing, 1974.

Powell, E. Alexander. *The Army Behind the Army*. New York: Charles Scribner's Sons, 1919.

Scott, Paul R. "The Birth of the 2s: Combat Intelligence in the American Expeditionary Force." *Military Intelligence* 6 (1980): 25–26.

Schwein, Edwin E. *Combat Intelligence: Its Acquisition and Transmission*. Washington, D.C.: Infantry Journal Press, 1936.

Sweeney, Walter C. *Military Intelligence: A New Weapon in War*. New York: Frederick A. Stokes Co., 1924.

Terrett, Dulany. *The Signal Corps: The Emergency*. United States Army in World War II. Washington, D.C.: U.S. Army Center of Military History, 1956.

Thomas, Shipley. *S2 in Action*. Harrisburg: Military Service Publishing Co., 1940.

Trueblood, Edward A. *Observations of an American Soldier During His Service with the AEF in France in the Flash Ranging Service*. Sacramento, Calif.: News Publishing, 1919.

U.S. Army War College, Historical Section. *The United States Army in the World War, 1917–1919*. 14 parts. Washington, D.C.: Department of the Army, 1931.

Van Deman, Ralph H. *The Final Memoranda: Major General Ralph H. Van Deman, USA Ret., 1865–1952: Father of U.S. Military Intelligence*. Ed. Ralph E. Weber. Wilmington, Del.: Scholarly Resources, 1988.

Wagner, Arthur L. *The Service of Security and Information*. Kansas City: Hudson Kimberley Publishing Co., 1893.

War Department. Office of the Chief Signal Officer. *Final Report of the Radio Intelligence Section, General Staff, General Headquarters, American Expeditionary Forces*. Washington, D.C.: Office of the Chief Signal Officer, 1935.

____. *Report of Code Compilation Section, General Headquarters, American Expeditionary Forces, December 1917–November 1918*. Washington, D.C.: Office of the Chief Signal Officer, 1935.

Yardley, Herbert O. *The American Black Chamber*. New York: Bobbs-Merrill, 1931.

World War II Military Intelligence

Alsop, Stewart, and Braden, Thomas. *Sub Rosa: The OSS and American Espionage*. New York: Reynaldo Hancock, 1946.

Ambrose, Stephen E. "Eisenhower, the Intelligence Community, and the D-Day Invasion." *Wisconsin Magazine of History* 64 (1981): 261–77.

Blumenson, Martin. "Will 'Ultra' Rewrite History?" *Army* 28 (1978): 42–49.

Chandler, Stedman, and Robb, Robert W. *Front-Line Intelligence*. Washington, D.C.: Infantry Journal Press, 1946.

Clayton, Aileen. *The Enemy is Listening*. New York: Ballantine Books, 1980.

Cline, Ray S. *The CIA Under Reagan, Bush, and Casey*. Washington, D.C.: Acropolis Press, 1981.

Cochran, Alexander S., Jr. "'Magic,' 'Ultra,' and the Second World War: Literature, Sources, and Outlook." *Military Affairs* 46 (1982): 88–92.

_____. "Protecting the Ultimate Advantage." *Military History* 1 (1985): 42–49.

Conn, Stetson. *Historical Work in the United States Army, 1862–1954*. Washington, D.C.: U.S. Army Center of Military History, 1980.

Davis, Franklin M., Jr. "The Army's Technical Detectives." *Military Review* 28 (1948): 12–18.

Deutsch, Harold C. "Generals and the Use of Intelligence." Intelligence and National Security 3 (1988): 194–260.

_____. "The Historical Impact of Revealing the Ultra Secret." *Parameters* 7 (1977): 16–32.

_____. "The Influence of Ultra on World War II." *Parameters* 8 (1978): 2–15.

Drea, Edward J. "Ultra Intelligence and General Douglas MacArthur's Leap to Hollandia, January–April 1944." *Intelligence and National Security* 5 (1990): 323–49.

Edwards, Duval A. *Spy Catchers of the U.S. Army—In the War with Japan*. Gig Harbor, Washington: Red Apple Publishing, 1994.

Felix, Christopher (James McCarger). *A Short Course in the Secret War*. New York: Dell Publishing, 1988.

Ford, Corey. *Donovan of OSS*. Boston: Little Brown, 1970.

Futrell, Robert F. *Command of Observation Aviation: A Study in Control of Tactical Airpower*. USAF Historical Studies No. 24. Maxwell Air Force Base, Ala.: Air University, 1956.

Gilbert, James L., and Finnegan, John P., eds. *U.S. Army Signals Intelligence in World War II: A Documentary History*. Washington, D.C.: U.S. Army Center of Military History, 1993.

Harrington, Joseph D. *Yankee Samurai: The Secret Role of Nisei in America's Pacific Victory*. Detroit: Pettigrew Enterprises, 1979.

Hinsley, F. H. et al. *British Intelligence in the Second World War: Its Influence on Strategy and Operations*. 3 vols. London: Her Majesty's Stationery Office, 1979–1986.

Hobar, Basil J. "The Ardennes 1944: Intelligence Failure or Deception Success?" *Military Intelligence* 10 (1984): 8–16.

Holmes, Jasper W. *Double-Edged Secrets: U.S. Naval Intelligence Operations in the Pacific During World War II*. Annapolis, Md.: Naval Institute Press, 1979.

Horner, D. M. *High Command: Australia and Allied Strategy, 1939–1945*. Sydney: George Allen and Unwin, 1982.

Hughes, Les. "The Alamo Scouts." *Trading Post* 45 (1986): 216.

Ind, Allison. *Allied Intelligence Bureau: Our Secret Weapon in the War Against Japan*. New York: McKay, 1958.

Johnson, Thomas M. "Search for the Stolen SIGABA." *Army* 12 (1962): 50–55.

Kahn, David. "World War II History: The Biggest Hole." *Military Affairs* 39 (1975): 74–76.

Kirkpatrick, Lyman B., Jr. *The Real CIA*. New York: MacMillan, 1968.

Koch, Oscar W. *G2: Intelligence for Patton*. Philadelphia: Whitmore, 1971.

Lewin, Ronald. *The Other Ultra*. London: Hutchison, 1982.

Mashbir, Sidney F. *I Was an American Spy*. New York: Vantage, 1953.

Mosser, Richard B. "Colonel Attended Crypto School at Vint Hill Farms." *INSCOM Journal* 15 (1992): 4–9.

Owens, William A. *Eye-Deep in Hell: A Memoir of the Liberation of the Philippines, 1944–1945*. Dallas: Southern Methodist University Press, 1990.

Parrish, Thomas. *The Ultra Americans: The U.S. Role in Breaking the Nazi Codes*. New York: Stein and Day, 1986.

Pash, Boris. *The Alsos Mission*. New York: Award House, 1969.

Powys-Lybbe, Ursula. *The Eyes of Intelligence*. London: William Kimber and Co., Ltd., 1983.

Price, Alfred. *The History of U.S. Electronic Warfare*, vol. 1. Westford, Mass.: Association of Old Crows, 1984.

Putney, Diane, ed. *Ultra and the Army Air Forces in World War II. An Interview with Associate Justice of the Supreme Court Louis F. Powell*. Washington, D.C.: Office of the Chief of Air Force History, 1987.

Rosengarten, Adolph G., Jr. "With Ultra from Omaha Beach to Weimar, Germany—A Personal View." *Military Affairs* 42 (1978): 127–32.

Russell, Francis. *The Secret War*. Alexandria, Va.: Time-Life Books, 1981.

Sayer, Ian, and Botling, Douglas. *America's Secret Army: The Untold Story of the Counter Intelligence Corps*. London: Grafton Books, 1989.

Schiffman, Maurice K. "Technical Intelligence in the Pacific in World War II." *Military Review* 31 (1952): 42–48.

Schwarzwalder, John. *We Caught Spies*. New York: Duel, Sloan, and Pierce, 1946.

Smith, Bradley. *The Shadow Warriors: OSS and the Origins of the CIA*. New York: Basic Books, 1983.

Smith, Constance Babbington. *Air Spy: The Story of Photo Intelligence in World War II*. New York: Harper, 1957.

Smith, R. Harris. *OSS, The Secret History of America's First Central Intelligence Agency*. Berkeley: University of California Press, 1972.

Spector, Ronald H., ed. *Listening to the Enemy*. Wilmington: Scholarly Resources, 1988.

Spiller, Roger J. "Assessing Ultra." *Military Review* 49 (1979): 13–23.

Stanley, Col. Roy M., II. *World War II Photo Reconnaissance and Photo*

Interpretation Operations of the Allied and Axis Nations. New York: Charles Scribner's Sons, 1981.

Strong, Maj. Gen. Sir Kenneth. *Intelligence at the Top: Recollections of an Intelligence Officer.* New York: Doubleday, 1969.

Syrett, David. "The Secret Wars and the Historians." *Armed Forces and Society* 9 (1983): 293–328.

Thompson, G. R., and Harris, Dixie R. *The Signal Corps: The Outcome.* United States Army in World War II. Washington, D.C.: U.S. Army Center of Military History, 1966.

Thorpe, Brig. Gen. Elliott R. *East Wind, Rain: The Intimate Account of an Intelligence Officer in the Pacific.* Boston: Gambit, 1969.

Troy, Thomas F. *Donovan and the CIA: A History of the Establishment of the Central Intelligence Agency.* Frederick, Md.: University Publications of America, 1984.

U.S. Far East Command. General Headquarters. *A Brief History of the G2 Section, GHQ, SWPA, and Affiliated Units.* 10 vols. Far East Command, 1948.

U.S. Forces, European Theater. Report of the General Board: Study No. 12, *The Military Intelligence Service in the European Theater of Operations.* U.S. Forces, European Theater, 1946.

———. Report of the General Board: Study No. 13, *Organization and Operation of the Counter Intelligence Corps in the European Theater of Operations.* U.S. Forces, European Theater, 1946.

———. Report of the General Board: Study No. 14, *Organization and Operation of the Theater Intelligence Service, European Theater of Operations.* U.S. Forces, European Theater, 1946.

———. Report of the General Board: Study No. 19, *The Utilization of Tactical Air Force Reconnaissance Units of the Army Air Forces to Secure Information for Ground Forces in the European Theater.* U.S. Forces, European Theater, 1946.

———. Report of the General Board: Study No. 20, *Liaison Aircraft with Ground Forces Units.* U.S. Forces, European Theater, 1946.

Williams, Robert W. "Moving Information: The Third Imperative." *Army* 25 (1975): 17–21.

Wohlstetter, Roberta. *Pearl Harbor: Warning and Decision.* Stanford: Stanford University Press, 1962.

Military Intelligence Since World War II

Allen, Thomas B., and Polgar, Norman. *Merchants of Treason: America's Secrets for Sale.* New York: Delacorte Press, 1982.

Andrade, Dale. *Ashes to Ashes: The Phoenix Program and the Vietnam War.* Lexington, Ky.: D. C. Heath, 1990.

Appleman, Roy H. *South to the Naktong, North to the Yalu.* United States Army in the Korean War. Washington, D.C.: U.S. Army Center of Military History, 1961.

Bamford, James. *The Puzzle Palace: A Report on NSA, America's Most Secret Agency*. Boston: Houghton-Mifflin, 1982.

Bergen, John D. *Military Communications: A Test for Technology*. United States Army in Vietnam. Washington, D.C.: U.S. Army Center of Military History, 1987.

Blair, Clay. *The Forgotten War: America in Korea*. New York: Times Books, 1988.

Clarke, Jeffrey J. *Advice and Support: The Final Years*. United States Army in Vietnam. Washington, D.C.: U.S. Army Center of Military History, 1988.

Cookridge, E. H. Gehlen: *Spy of the Century*. New York: Random House, 1971.

Corson, William R. *The Armies of Ignorance*. New York: Dial Press, 1977.

Cubbage, T. L., II. "Westmoreland vs. CBS: Was Intelligence Corrupted by Policy Demands?" *Intelligence and National Security* 3 (1988): 118–80.

Dabringhaus, Erhard. *Klaus Barbie: The Shocking Story of How the U.S. Used this War Criminal as an Intelligence Agent*. Washington, D.C.: Acropolis Books, 1984.

Davidson, Philip B., and Glass, Robert R. *Intelligence is for Commanders*. Harrisburg: Military Service Publishing, 1948.

DeForest, Orrin, and Chanoff, David. *Slow Burn: The Rise and Bitter Fall of American Intelligence in Vietnam*. New York: Simon and Shuster, 1990.

Emerson, Steven. *Secret Warriors: Inside the Covert Military Operations of the Reagan Era*. New York: Putnam, 1988.

England, James W. *Long-Range Patrol Operations: Reconnaissance, Combat, and Special Operations*. Boulder, Colo.: Paladin Press, 1987.

Fehrenbach, T. R. *This Kind of War: A Study in Unpreparedness*. New York: MacMillan, 1963.

Futrell, Robert F. *The United States Air Force in Southeast Asia: The Advisory Years to 1965*. Washington, D.C.: Office of Air Force History, 1981.

Gordon, Don. "CEWI Battalion: Intelligence and Electronic Warfare on the Battlefield." *Military Intelligence* 5 (1979): 22–28.

_____. *Electronic Warfare: Element of Strategy and Multiplier of Combat Power*. New York: Pergamon Press, 1981.

Harmon, Col. William E. "Some Personal Observations on the CEWI Concept." *Military Intelligence* (1983): 4–6.

Hastings, Max. *The Korean War*. New York: Simon and Shuster, 1987.

Herrington, Stuart A. *Silence Was a Weapon: The Vietnam War in the Villages*. Novato: Presidio Press, 1982.

Heymont, Irving. *Combat Intelligence in Modern Warfare*. Harrisburg: Stackpole, 1960.

Hopple, Gerald W., and Watson, Bruce W., eds. *The Military Intelligence Community*. Westview Special Studies on Military Affairs. Boulder, Colo.: Westview Press, 1984.

Howard, William L. "The Army's Stepchild--Technical Intelligence." *Military Intelligence* 15 (1989): 29–32.

James, D. Clayton. *The Years of MacArthur*, vol. 3, *Triumph and Disaster, 1945–1964*. Boston: Houghton-Mifflin, 1985.

Jones, Bruce E. *War Without Windows: A True Account of a Young Army Officer Trapped in an Intelligence Cover-Up*. New York: Vanguard Press, 1987.

Kennedy, Col. William V. et al. *Intelligence Warfare: Today's Advanced Technology Conflict*. New York: Crescent Books, 1983.

Kirkpatrick, Lyman. *The U.S. Intelligence Community: Foreign Policy and Domestic Activities*. New York: Hill and Wang, 1973.

Lung, Col. Hoang Ngoc. *Intelligence*. Indochina Monographs. Washington, D.C.: U.S. Army Center of Military History, 1982.

Marshall, S. L. A. *The River and the Gauntlet: Defeat of the Eighth Army by the Chinese Communist Forces, November 1950, in the Battle of the Chongchon River, Korea*. New York: Morrow, 1953.

McCauley, Nathan E. "The Military Intelligence Profession in the U.S. Army." *Military Intelligence* 13 (1987): 14–17, 37.

McChristian, Joseph A. *The Role of Military Intelligence, 1965–1967*. Washington, D.C.: Department of the Army, 1974.

McQueen, Lt. Col. Arthur D. "The Lion Goes to War." *Military Intelligence* (1977): 28–36.

Paddock, Alfred H. *U.S. Army Special Warfare: Its Origins*. Washington, D.C.: National Defense University Press, 1982.

Palmer, General Bruce, Jr. *The 25-Year War: America's Military Role in Vietnam*. New York: Simon and Shuster, 1984.

Prados, John. *The Soviet Estimate: U.S. Intelligence Analysis and Soviet Military Strength*. Princeton: Princeton University Press, 1986.

_____. *The Hidden History of the Vietnam* War. Chicago: Ivan R. Dee, 1995.

Pyle, Christopher H. *Military Surveillance of Civilian Politics, 1967–1970*. New York: Garland Publishers, 1986.

Ransom, Harry Howe. *The Intelligence Establishment*. Cambridge, Mass.: Harvard University Press, 1970.

Richelson, Jeffrey. *The U.S. Intelligence Community*. Cambridge, Mass.: Ballinger Publishing Co., 1985.

Ridgway, Matthew B. *Soldier: The Memoirs of Matthew B. Ridgway*, as told to Harold H. Martin. Westport: Greenwood Press, 1974.

Ryan, Allan R., Jr. *Klaus Barbie and the United States Government: The Report, with Documentary Appendix, to the Attorney General of The United States*. Frederick, Md.: University Publications of America, 1984.

Saunders, Bruce. "The U.S. Army Intelligence Center and School." *Military Intelligence* 10 (1984): 61.

Schemmer, Benjamin F. "Former DIA Director Urges That Four-Star Should Head All Military Intelligence." *Armed Forces Journal International* (1988): 24.

Sheehan, Neil. *A Bright Shining Lie: John Paul Vann and America in Vietnam*. New York: Random House, 1988.

Singlaub, John K., with Malcolm McConnell. *Hazardous Duty: An American Soldier in the Twentieth Century*. New York: Summit Books, 1991.

Stewart, Col. John F. et al. "Grenada." 7 parts. *Military Intelligence* 11 (1985): 7–24.

Toffler, Alvin and Heidi. *War and Anti-War*. Boston: Little Brown, 1994.

Tolson, John J. *Airmobility, 1961–1971*. Vietnam Studies. Washington, D.C.: Department of the Army, 1973.

Townsend, Elias C. *Risks: The Key to Combat Intelligence*. Harrisburg: Military Service Publishing Co., 1955.

Watson, Bruce W. et al., eds. *United States Intelligence: An Encyclopedia*. New York: Garland Press, 1990.

Willoughby, Maj. Gen. Charles A., and Chamberlain, John. *MacArthur, 1941–1951*. New York: McGraw Hill, 1954.

Glossary

A–2	Air Forces intelligence
AAF	Army Air Forces
ACSI	Assistant Chief of Staff for Intelligence
AEF	American Expeditionary Forces
AFPAC	U.S. Army Forces, Pacific
AIA	Army Intelligence Agency
AIB	Allied Intelligence Bureau
AIS	Army Intelligence and Security (branch)
ALSOS	secret World War II mission to investigate Nazi atomic research
ANCIB	Army-Navy Communications Intelligence Board
ANCICC	Army-Navy Communications Intelligence Coordinating Committee
ASA	Army Security Agency
ATIS	Allied Translator and Interpreter Service
CBB	Central Bureau, Brisbane
CENTCOM	Central Command
CEWI	combat electronic warfare and intelligence
CIA	Central Intelligence Agency
CIC	Counter Intelligence Corps
CID	Criminal Investigation Division
CIP	Corps of Intelligence Police
COMINT	communications intelligence
COMSEC	communications security
CONARC	Continental Army Command
CSA	Chief of Staff of the Army
CONUS	Continental United States
DCSINT	Deputy Chief of Staff for Intelligence
DIA	Defense Intelligence Agency
DOD	Department of Defense

ECM	electronic countermeasures
ELINT	electronic intelligence
ETO	European Theater of Operations
ETOUSA	European Theater of Operations, U.S. Army (World War II)
FBI	Federal Bureau of Investigation
FORSCOM	Forces Command
G–2	Military Intelligence
G–3	Military Operations
GARDEN PLOT	domestic intelligence collection plan (1960s)
GHQ	General Headquarters
HUMINT	human intelligence
IBM	International Business Machines
INSCOM	United States Army Intelligence and Security Command
IOSS	Intelligence Organization and Stationing Study
IRR	Investigative Records Repository
J–2	joint intelligence officer
JCS	Joint Chiefs of Staff
JIC	Joint Intelligence Committee
JICPOA	Joint Intelligence Center, Pacific Ocean Area
LANTERN SPIKE	domestic intelligence collection plan (1960s)
MACOM	major Army command
MACV	Military Assistance Command, Vietnam
MAGIC	decrypts of Japanese diplomatic messages
MASINT	measurement and signature intelligence
MDW	Military District of Washington
MI	Military Intelligence
MID	Military Intelligence Division
MITC	Military Intelligence Training Center
MIORC	Military Intelligence Officers Reserve Corps
MIS	Military Intelligence Service
MTO	Mediterranean Theater of Operations
NATO	North African Theater of Operations (World War II); North Atlantic Treaty Organization
NATOUSA	North African Theater of Operations, U.S. Army
NSA	National Security Agency
NSC	National Security Council
OACSI	Office of the Assistant Chief of Staff for Intelligence
ONI	Office of Naval Intelligence
OPEC	Organization of Petroleum Exporting Countries
OPFOR	opposing forces
OSS	Office of Strategic Services
PEARL	intelligence derived from low-level enemy encrypted communications (World War II)

PHOENIX	program to target Viet Cong infrastructure
POA	Pacific Ocean Area (World War II)
RAGFOR	Radio Group, Forward
ROAD	Reorganization Objective Army Division
RRU	radio research unit
SECURITY SHIELD	project to improve U.S. counterintelligence
SIAM	signal information and monitoring
SIGABA	World War II high-level cipher machine
SIGINT	signals intelligence
SIGROD	machine cipher device
SIS	Signal Intelligence Service
SSA	Signal Security Agency
SSO	Special Security Officer
STEADFAST	1973 Army reorganization project
SWPA	South West Pacific Area (World War II)
TD	table of distribution
TDA	table of distribution and allowances
TEMPEST	threat from electronic emissions
THUMB	intelligence derived from radio intelligence
TOE	table of organization and equipment
TRADOC	U.S. Army Training and Doctrine Command
ULTRA	high-grade communications intelligence (World War II)
USAFFE	U.S. Army Forces, Far East
USAINTA	U.S. Army Intelligence Agency
USAINTC	U.S. Army Intelligence Command
USAREUR	U.S. Army, Europe
USARPAC	U.S. Army, Pacific
USASA	U.S. Army Security Agency
USASATC&S	U.S. Army Security Agency Training Center and School
USCIB	U.S. Communications Intelligence Board
WAC	Womens' Army Corps
WDGS	War Department General Staff
YMCA	Young Men's Christian Association

Heraldic Items

Heraldic items for Army units include coats of arms, shoulder sleeve insignia, and distinctive unit insignia. Designed on the basis of a unit's official lineage and honors, they reflect each organization's history, traditions, ideals, mission, and accomplishments. Heraldic items also serve as identifying devices and contribute to unit cohesiveness and esprit de corps.

While the custom of bearing various symbols on shields, helmets, and flags existed in antiquity, heraldry was not introduced until the Middle Ages, when the increased use of armor made it difficult to distinguish friend from foe on the battlefield. Heraldic designs included mythological beasts, emblems commemorative of heroic deeds, and other identifying marks to which specific symbolism was ascribed. These heraldic devices were placed on a surcoat worn over the armor, from which the term "coat of arms" was derived. Gradually, a formal system of heraldry evolved, complete with rules for design, use, and display.

At the present time Army regiments and separate battalions are authorized coats of arms. A complete coat of arms consists of a shield, a crest, and a motto. The shield, the most important portion of the coat of arms, contains the field or ground on which the charges or symbols are placed. The crest was originally placed on the top of the helmet of the chief or leader to enable his followers to recognize him during battle. Today the crest is placed upon a wreath of six skeins or twists composed of the principal metal and primary color of the shield, alternately, in the order named. This wreath or torse represents the piece of cloth which the knight twisted around the top of his helmet and by means of which the actual crest was attached. Mottoes have been in use longer than coats of arms. Many of the older ones originated from war cries. Usually of an idealistic nature, they sometimes allude to a well-known event in the history of the unit.

The elements of the coat of arms are embroidered on the organizational flag (color), the central element of which is the American eagle. The shield of the coat of arms is on the eagle's breast, a scroll bearing the motto is held in his beak, and the crest is placed above his head. A crest to the coat of arms is authorized for Regular Army units that have war service or campaign credit.

Army National Guard units display the crest of the state or states in which they are located, and a special crest has been designed for all Army Reserve units.

The currently authorized embroidered shoulder sleeve insignia had their origin during World War I. They serve the same purpose as the corps symbols (badges) used during the Civil War and the War with Spain. Most corps badges were of simple design and could be cut from a single piece of cloth. These emblems, such as a four-leaf clover, a star, or a spearhead, were easily remembered and readily identified. Not only were they worn by soldiers on their headgear, they were also incorporated into the design of unit flags.

The first shoulder sleeve insignia is believed to have been worn by the men of the 81st Division during World War I. On their voyage to France they adopted as their insignia the figure of a wildcat, which they used as a distinctive marking for the division's equipment. Wear of this insignia was officially approved on 19 October 1918 by a telegram from the Adjutant General, American Expeditionary Forces, to the division commander. Insignia for other units of the American Expeditionary Forces were later authorized and designs officially approved. Designs varied greatly. Many had their origin in devices already in use for organizational and equipment markings. Others were based on monograms and geometric figures alluding to a unit's numerical designation. Symbols associated with traditions, geographical locations, and unit mission were also included in some designs.

Since World War I the authorization of shoulder sleeve insignia has expanded. Under the current system, separate brigades and higher echelons are authorized shoulder sleeve insignia for wear by soldiers assigned to the units. The insignia also appear on the organizations' distinguishing flags. Over time, the designs have become more elaborate and complex due to the increased number of authorized insignia and the availability of embroidery machinery for the production of various types of textile insignia. During the Vietnam era the policy governing the wear of subdued insignia on work uniforms was established.

Distinctive unit insignia, manufactured in metal and enamel and worn by all unit personnel, are authorized for separate battalions and higher echelons. The type of distinctive unit insignia currently in use was first authorized during the 1920s for regiments and certain other units. As in the case of shoulder sleeve insignia and coats of arms, authorization expanded as changes in the organization of the Army took place. The designs are based on symbols reflecting each unit's lineage, battle honors, traditions, and mission and usually incorporate the organization's motto. Distinctive unit insignia for most regiments and battalions include the same design elements as their coats of arms.

Today, as in the past, insignia displayed on flags and worn on uniforms are highly visible items of identification. These heraldic items serve to distinguish specific organizations and their members and are significant factors in establishing and maintaining unit esprit de corps.

66th Military Intelligence Brigade

111th Military Intelligence Brigade

112th Military Intelligence Brigade

201st Military Intelligence Brigade

205th Military Intelligence Brigade

207th Military Intelligence Brigade

319th Military Intelligence Brigade

470th Military Intelligence Brigade

500th Military Intelligence Brigade

501st Military Intelligence Brigade

504th Military Intelligence Brigade

513th Military Intelligence Brigade

525th Military Intelligence Brigade

108th Military Intelligence Group

109th Military Intelligence Group

115th Military Intelligence Group

116th Military Intelligence Group

259th Military Intelligence Group

650th Military Intelligence Group

902d Military Intelligence Group

1st Military Intelligence Battalion

2d Military Intelligence Battalion

3d Military Intelligence Battalion

14th Military Intelligence Battalion

15th Military Intelligence Battalion

24th Military Intelligence Battalion

101st Military Intelligence Battalion

102d Military Intelligence Battalion

103d Military Intelligence Battalion

104th Military Intelligence Battalion

105th Military Intelligence Battalion

106th Military Intelligence Battalion

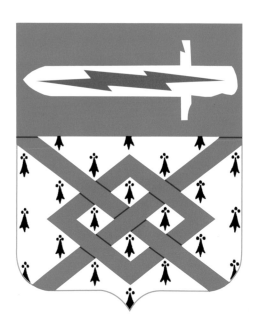

107th Military Intelligence Battalion

108th Military Intelligence Battalion

SEEK AND DISRUPT

109th Military Intelligence Battalion

SENTINELS OF THE SUMMIT

110th Military Intelligence Battalion

124th Military Intelligence Battalion

125th Military Intelligence Battalion

126th Military Intelligence Battalion

128th Military Intelligence Battalion

134th Military Intelligence Battalion

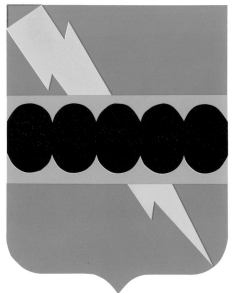

135th Military Intelligence Battalion

138th Military Intelligence Battalion

140th Military Intelligence Battalion

141st Military Intelligence Battalion

142d Military Intelligence Battalion

147th Military Intelligence Battalion

163d Military Intelligence Battalion

165th Military Intelligence Battalion

201st Military Intelligence Battalion

202d Military Intelligence Battalion

203d Military Intelligence Battalion

204th Military Intelligence Battalion

PACIFIC VIGILANCE

205th Military Intelligence Battalion

206th Military Intelligence Battalion

223d Military Intelligence Battalion

224th Military Intelligence Battalion

229th Military Intelligence Battalion

260th Military Intelligence Battalion

297th Military Intelligence Battalion

301st Military Intelligence Battalion

302d Military Intelligence Battalion

303d Military Intelligence Battalion

304th Military Intelligence Battalion

305th Military Intelligence Battalion

306th Military Intelligence Battalion

307th Military Intelligence Battalion

308th Military Intelligence Battalion

309th Military Intelligence Battalion

310th Military Intelligence Battalion

311th Military Intelligence Battalion

312th Military Intelligence Battalion

313th Military Intelligence Battalion

314th Military Intelligence Battalion

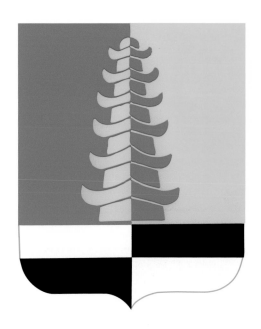

319th Military Intelligence Battalion

326th Military Intelligence Battalion

337th Military Intelligence Battalion

338th Military Intelligence Battalion

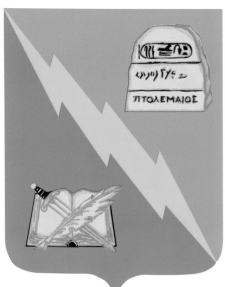

341st Military Intelligence Battalion

344th Military Intelligence Battalion

373d Military Intelligence Battalion

415th Military Intelligence Battalion

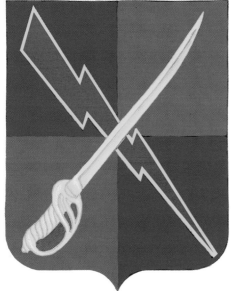

501st Military Intelligence Battalion

502d Military Intelligence Battalion

511th Military Intelligence Battalion

519th Military Intelligence Battalion

522d Military Intelligence Battalion

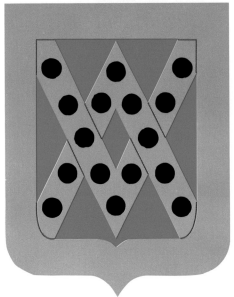

524th Military Intelligence Battalion

527th Military Intelligence Battalion

532d Military Intelligence Battalion

533d Military Intelligence Battalion

542d Military Intelligence Battalion

549th Military Intelligence Battalion

550th Military Intelligence Battalion

629th Military Intelligence Battalion

LINEAGES AND HERALDIC DATA

MILITARY INTELLIGENCE CORPS

Heraldic Items

COAT OF ARMS

Shield: Azure, a key bend sinisterwise in saltire with a lightning flash argent, in fesspoint overall a sphinx or.

Crest: On a wreath of the colors, argent and azure, a torch or enflamed proper in front of two swords in saltire with hilts gold and blades of the first.

Motto: ALWAYS OUT FRONT.

Symbolism: Oriental blue and silver gray are the colors associated with military intelligence. The key, flash, and sphinx symbolize the three basic categories of intelligence: human, signal, and tactical.

The flaming torch between the crossed swords suggests the illumination as provided by intelligence upon the field of battle.

DISTINCTIVE UNIT INSIGNIA

The distinctive unit insignia is the shield and motto of the coat of arms.

HEADQUARTERS AND HEADQUARTERS DETACHMENT 66th MILITARY INTELLIGENCE BRIGADE

HERALDIC ITEMS

SHOULDER SLEEVE INSIGNIA

Description: On a silver gray hexagon, one point up, with an oriental blue border, an oriental blue hexagon bearing a yellow sphinx superimposed by a silver gray dagger hilted black.

Symbolism: Oriental blue and silver gray, representing loyalty and determination, are the colors of the military intelligence branch. Yellow symbolizes excellence. The hexagon borders reflect the numerical designation of the brigade. The sphinx, a traditional military intelligence symbol, indicates observation, wisdom, and discreet silence. The unsheathed dagger reflects aggressive and protective requirements and the element of physical danger inherent in the mission of the unit.

DISTINCTIVE UNIT INSIGNIA

Description: A gold color metal and enamel device consisting of a hexagon composed of a checky of six black and white sections (one angle up), surmounted throughout by a smaller hexagon (flat side up) composed of a checky of nine sections of gold and oriental blue with the center square charged with a gold sphinx head, all above a gold scroll inscribed HONOR VALOR AND SECURITY in oriental blue letters.

Symbolism: The black and white sections symbolize enlightenment and knowledge both day and night around the world. The checky represents the unit's tactical and strategic capabilities in counterintelligence. The sphinx, a traditional intelligence symbol, indicates observation, wisdom, and discreet silence. The hexagon within a hexagon further distinguishes the numerical designation of the organization.

LINEAGE AND HONORS

RA
(inactive)

LINEAGE

Constituted 21 June 1944 in the Army of the United States as the 66th Counter Intelligence Corps Detachment. Activated 1 July 1944 at Camp Rucker, Alabama. Inactivated 12 November 1945 at Camp Kilmer, New Jersey. Activated 10 November 1949 in Germany. Allotted 20 September 1951 to the Regular Army.

Reorganized and redesignated 20 December 1952 as the 66th Counter Intelligence Corps Group. Reorganized and redesignated 1 January 1960 as the 66th Military Intelligence Group. Redesignated 25 July 1961 as the 66th Intelligence Corps Group. Redesignated 15 October 1966 as the 66th Military Intelligence Group.

Reorganized and redesignated 16 October 1986 as Headquarters and Headquarters Company, 66th Military Intelligence Brigade. Reorganized and redesignated 16 October 1992 as Headquarters and Headquarters Detachment, 66th Military Intelligence Brigade. Inactivated 16 July 1995 in Germany.

CAMPAIGN PARTICIPATION CREDIT

World War II
Northern France

DECORATIONS

None.

HEADQUARTERS
111th MILITARY INTELLIGENCE BRIGADE

HERALDIC ITEMS

DISTINCTIVE UNIT INSIGNIA

Description: A gold color metal and enamel device consisting of the major portion of a black and gold heraldic rose above and behind the head and wings of a gold eagle rising out of a gold disc charged throughout with a burst of red flames having eight tongues radiant to base and interspersed with seven five-pointed oriental blue stars, the disc enclosed by an oriental blue scroll inscribed with the words MISSION FIRST in gold.

Symbolism: The heraldic rose, alluding to the insignia of the military intelligence branch, is symbolic of the basic mission (to collect, check, and make available any information about a present or possible enemy), and its position at the top of the design is relative to the unit's motto. The phoenix (eagle) rising out of flames is symbolic of the former location of the unit, Atlanta, Georgia, and the seven states where the unit operated are represented by the ring of oriental blue stars.

FLAG DEVICE

None approved.

LINEAGE AND HONORS

RA
(active)

LINEAGE

Constituted 10 May 1946 in the Army of the United States as the 111th Counter Intelligence Corps Detachment. Activated 22 May 1946 at Atlanta, Georgia. Allotted 6 October 1950 to the Regular Army. Redesignated 1 December 1958 as the 111th Counter Intelligence Corps Group. Redesignated 25 July 1961 as the 111th Intelligence Corps Group. Redesignated 15 October 1966 as the 111th Military Intelligence Group. Inactivated 9 January 1973 at Fort McPherson, Georgia.

Redesignated 13 March 1987 as Headquarters, 111th Military Intelligence Brigade; concurrently transferred to the United States Army Training and Doctrine Command and activated at Fort Huachuca, Arizona.

CAMPAIGN PARTICIPATION CREDIT

None.

DECORATIONS

None.

HEADQUARTERS
112TH MILITARY INTELLIGENCE BRIGADE

HERALDIC ITEMS

DISTINCTIVE UNIT INSIGNIA

Description: A silver color metal and enamel device consisting of a yellow enameled demi-sun emitting five rays surmounted by a silver dagger, point up, beneath an oriental blue chevron bearing five silver stars, all within and below an arc segment of silver oak leaves and a red scroll inscribed with the motto STRENGTH THROUGH SECURITY in silver letters.

Symbolism: Oriental blue and silver gray are the colors traditionally associated with military intelligence. The sunburst further alludes to intelligence and also suggests the former location of the unit, the great Southwest. The yellow sunburst symbolizes the worth of reliable intelligence. The five rays of the sunburst allude to the five former regions of the unit and the chevron, a symbol for support, with the five stars, represents the five states which comprised its former area of operations. The ancient dagger signifies the dangers and silent covert nature of intelligence service. The oak leaves are symbolic of the strong and enduring resolution of the members of the unit, and the motto portrays the goal of a successful intelligence organization.

FLAG DEVICE

None approved.

LINEAGE AND HONORS

RA
(inactive)

LINEAGE

Constituted 10 May 1946 in the Army of the United States as the 112th Counter Intelligence Corps Detachment. Activated 21 May 1946 at Dallas, Texas. Allotted 26 February 1951 to the Regular Army. Redesignated 1 August 1957 as the 112th Counter Intelligence Corps Group. Redesignated 25 July 1961 as the 112th Intelligence Corps Group. Redesignated 15 October 1966 as the 112th Military Intelligence Group. Inactivated 30 June 1974 at Fort Sam Houston, Texas.

Redesignated 1 July 1987 as Headquarters, 112th Military Intelligence Brigade; concurrently transferred to the United States Army Training and Doctrine Command and activated at Fort Devens, Massachusetts. Inactivated 30 January 1993 at Fort Devens, Massachusetts.

CAMPAIGN PARTICIPATION CREDIT

None.

DECORATIONS

None.

HEADQUARTERS AND HEADQUARTERS DETACHMENT 201st MILITARY INTELLIGENCE BRIGADE

HERALDIC ITEMS

SHOULDER SLEEVE INSIGNIA

Description: On a shield divided from upper left to lower right, silver gray above oriental blue with a yellow border, a sword between two flashes all yellow.

Symbolism: Oriental blue and silver gray are the military intelligence branch colors. The two parts symbolize the responsibility for acquisition and processing of tactical and strategic intelligence. The sword symbolizes the aggressiveness and physical danger inherent in military intelligence operations. The lightning bolts refer to the electronic warfare capabilities of the unit and the commander's need for accurate and ready intelligence from all sources.

DISTINCTIVE UNIT INSIGNIA

Description: A silver color metal and enamel device consisting of an oriental blue disc bearing a silver polestar encircled at top and sides by a black scroll inscribed WITH COURAGE AND VISION in silver letters, and in base three alternate wavy bars of oriental blue and silver superimposed by a silver mountain peak supporting a griffin segreant grasping a sword and a lightning flash, all gold.

Symbolism: Oriental blue and silver gray are the colors associated with military intelligence. Black denotes secrecy. The oriental blue disc superimposed by the silver polestar symbolizes the world and the far-reaching capabilities of the unit. The oriental blue and silver wavy bars allude to World War II campaign participation in the Pacific. The mountain peak is representative of Korean War campaigns. The griffin, having the keen eyesight of an eagle and the strength and courage of a lion, indicates the attributes of military intelligence and also alludes to the motto. The lightning flash is indicative of communications, electronic warfare capabilities, and the origin of the brigade as a signal unit. The sword reflects the fighting aspect and suggests the unit's aggressiveness and the physical danger inherent in military intelligence operations.

LINEAGE AND HONORS

LINEAGE

Constituted 23 July 1942 in the Army of the United States as the 323d Signal Company, Wing. Activated 1 September 1942 at Miami, Florida. Inactivated 17 October 1946 at Andrews Field, Maryland. Redesignated 6 September 1950 as the 323d Signal Radio Intelligence Company and allotted to the Organized Reserve Corps. Activated 2 October 1950 at Fort Myer, Virginia.

Converted and redesignated 3 January 1951 as Headquarters and Headquarters Company, 601st Communication Reconnaissance Group. Redesignated 5 February 1951 as Headquarters and Headquarters Company, 503d Communication Reconnaissance Group. Ordered into active military service 1 May 1951 at Fort Myer, Virginia. (Organized Reserve Corps redesignated 9 July 1952 as the Army Reserve.) Released from active military service 16 May 1955 and reverted to reserve status. Inactivated 20 July 1955 at Fort Myer, Virginia. Activated 6 January 1956 at Washington, D.C. Redesignated 3 September 1956 as Headquarters and Headquarters Company, 503d Army Security Agency Group. Inactivated 27 June 1959 at Washington, D.C.

Withdrawn 1 September 1987 from the Army Reserve, allotted to the Regular Army, consolidated with the 201st Military Intelligence Detachment (see ANNEX), and consolidated unit redesignated as Headquarters and Headquarters Detachment, 201st Military Intelligence Brigade; concurrently activated at Fort Lewis, Washington.

ANNEX

Constituted 12 July 1944 in the Army of the United States as the 201st Counter Intelligence Corps Detachment. Activated 20 August 1944 in New Guinea. Inactivated 25 February 1946 in Japan. Activated 6 October 1950 in Korea. Inactivated 21 February 1955 in Korea. Allotted 20 March 1956 to the Regular Army. Activated 12 June 1956 in Korea. Reorganized and redesignated 15 May 1959 as the 201st Military Intelligence Detachment. Inactivated 30 June 1971 in Korea. Activated 1 October 1971 at Fort Hood, Texas. Inactivated 21 June 1975 at Fort Hood, Texas.

CAMPAIGN PARTICIPATION CREDIT
>   *World War II*
>> Antisubmarine
>> New Guinea
>> Western Pacific
>> Luzon
>   *Korean War*
>> UN Offensive
>> CCF Intervention
>> First UN Counteroffensive
>> CCF Spring Offensive
>> UN Summer-Fall Offensive
>> Second Korean Winter
>> Korea, Summer-Fall 1952
>> Third Korean Winter
>> Korea, Summer 1953

DECORATIONS

Meritorious Unit Commendation (Army), Streamer embroidered PACIFIC THEATER (323d Signal Company, Wing, cited; GO 83, Twentieth Air Force, 4 October 1945)

Meritorious Unit Commendation (Army), Streamer embroidered KOREA (201st Counter Intelligence Corps Detachment cited; DA GO 32, 1954)

Philippine Presidential Unit Citation, Streamer embroidered 17 OCTOBER 1944 TO 4 JULY 1945 (201st Counter Intelligence Corps Detachment cited; DA GO 47, 1950)

HEADQUARTERS AND HEADQUARTERS DETACHMENT 205th MILITARY INTELLIGENCE BRIGADE

HERALDIC ITEMS

SHOULDER SLEEVE INSIGNIA

Description: On an oriental blue shield a white fleur-de-lis centered in front of two crossed silver gray lightning bolts.

Symbolism: Oriental blue and silver gray are the colors associated with military intelligence units. The crossed lightning bolts refer to the convergence of all types of intelligence from all sources, enabling commanders to "see the battlefield." The fleur-de-lis alludes to the unit's original activation in France.

DISTINCTIVE UNIT INSIGNIA

Description: A gold color metal and enamel device consisting of an oriental blue fleur-de-lis bearing in gold a dagger, point down, between a lightning flash and a propeller blade all convergent in base on a silver gray background enclosed at the bottom by a gold wreath of rice tied in red and at the top by an oriental blue scroll inscribed VANGUARD OF VIGILANCE in gold letters.

Symbolism: Oriental blue and silver gray are the colors traditionally associated with the military intelligence branch. The oriental blue fleur-de-lis refers to the unit's World War II service in Europe. Campaign participation in Vietnam is symbolized by the gold and red wreath of rice. The lightning flash represents signals intelligence and electronic warfare; the dagger represents human intelligence; the airplane propeller represents airborne imagery intelligence. The slanting of these symbols of the intelligence disciplines employed by the unit toward the fulcrum of the fleur-de-lis represents the convergence of intelligence from all sources to enable commanders to "see the battlefield."

LINEAGE AND HONORS

RA
(active)

LINEAGE

Constituted 12 July 1944 in the Army of the United States as the 205th Counter Intelligence Corps Detachment. Activated 6 August 1944 in France. Allotted 6 October 1950 to the Regular Army. Reorganized and redesignated 25 June 1958 as the 205th Military Intelligence Detachment.

Consolidated 16 October 1983 with the 135th Military Intelligence Group (see ANNEX) and consolidated unit reorganized and redesignated as Headquarters and Headquarters Detachment, 205th Military Intelligence Group. Reorganized and redesignated 16 October 1985 as Headquarters and Headquarters Detachment, 205th Military Intelligence Brigade.

ANNEX

Constituted 19 March 1966 in the Regular Army as the 135th Intelligence Corps Group. Activated 1 June 1966 at Fort Bragg, North Carolina. Redesignated 15 October 1966 as the 135th Military Intelligence Group. Inactivated 25 September 1969 in Vietnam.

CAMPAIGN PARTICIPATION CREDIT

World War II
    Northern France
    Rhineland
    Ardennes-Alsace
    Central Europe
Vietnam
    Counteroffensive, Phase II
    Counteroffensive, Phase III
    Tet Counteroffensive
    Counteroffensive, Phase IV
    Counteroffensive, Phase V
    Counteroffensive, Phase VI
    Tet 69/Counteroffensive
    Summer-Fall 1969

DECORATIONS

None.

HEADQUARTERS AND HEADQUARTERS DETACHMENT 207th MILITARY INTELLIGENCE BRIGADE

HERALDIC ITEMS

SHOULDER SLEEVE INSIGNIA

Description: On an oriental blue disc a silver gray key and lightning bolt crossed slightly above center, with the key's ward at the lower left and the lightning bolt's point to the right, centered below is a dagger, point up, with silver gray blade and black hilt; all within a narrow red outline of a seven-petaled stylized rose.

Symbolism: Oriental blue and silver gray are associated with military intelligence. Red derives from the predominant color of the VII Corps shoulder sleeve insignia and black represents the unknown. The key and lightning bolt represent electronic warfare and security and also signify the numeral two of the unit's designation. The stylized seven-petaled rose has its origin in the more traditional compass, dagger, and rose associated with the military intelligence branch and also represents the numeral seven of the unit's designation as well as the number of the corps it supported. The circular shape of the insignia also refers to the zero of the unit's designation. The dagger denotes the counterintelligence function of the unit.

DISTINCTIVE UNIT INSIGNIA

Description: A gold color metal enamel device consisting of an oriental blue five-petaled heraldic rose and centered vertically thereon a gold lightning bolt surmounted at the bottom by a horizontal gold key, surmounting the lightning bolt at center a white horse's head between two white wings, each with seven feathers. Attached to the bottom of the device a scroll of three parts inscribed with the words SEE STRIKE KNOW in black letters.

Symbolism: Oriental blue is one of the colors associated with the military intelligence branch. The heraldic rose, a part of the military intelligence insignia, indicates the brigade's association with that branch. The winged horse (Pegasus) with seven feathers on each wing signifies aerial vigilance in support of the VII Corps. The key denotes the unlocking of the enemy's secrets.

The lightning bolt represents the unit's electronic warfare capability and its ability to transmit information rapidly.

LINEAGE AND HONORS

RA
(inactive)

LINEAGE

Constituted 10 May 1946 in the Army of the United States as the 113th Counter Intelligence Corps Detachment. Activated 20 May 1946 at Chicago, Illinois. Allotted 6 December 1950 to the Regular Army. Redesignated 1 August 1957 as the 113th Counter Intelligence Corps Group. Redesignated 25 July 1961 as the 113th Intelligence Corps Group. Redesignated 15 October 1966 as the 113th Military Intelligence Group. Inactivated 31 December 1971 at Fort Sheridan, Illinois.

Consolidated 16 October 1983 with the 207th Military Intelligence Detachment (see ANNEX) and consolidated unit reorganized and redesignated as Headquarters and Headquarters Detachment, 207th Military Intelligence Group. Reorganized and redesignated 16 October 1985 as Headquarters and Headquarters Detachment, 207th Military Intelligence Brigade. Inactivated 15 January 1992 in Germany.

ANNEX

Constituted 8 November 1950 in the Regular Army as the 207th Counter Intelligence Corps Detachment. Activated 30 November 1950 at Fort Holabird, Maryland. Reorganized and redesignated 25 June 1958 as the 207th Military Intelligence Detachment.

CAMPAIGN PARTICIPATION CREDIT

> *Southwest Asia*
> > Defense of Saudi Arabia
> > Liberation and Defense of Kuwait
> > Cease-Fire

DECORATIONS

Meritorious Unit Commendation (Army), Streamer embroidered FIFTH ARMY AREA 1946 (113th Counter Intelligence Corps Detachment cited; DA GO 10, 1948)

HEADQUARTERS AND
HEADQUARTERS COMPANY
319th MILITARY INTELLIGENCE BRIGADE

HERALDIC ITEMS

SHOULDER SLEEVE INSIGNIA

Description: On a rectangle arched at top and bottom with a silver gray border, divided beveled from upper right to lower left black above oriental blue, in upper left an oriental blue polestar pierced silver gray.

Symbolism: Oriental blue and silver gray are the colors traditionally associated with military intelligence units. Blue also alludes to the Pacific and the unit's area of operations. Black and blue suggest day and night vigilance. The polestar simulates satellite intelligence collection and communications. The jagged division of the background is reminiscent of a lightning bolt, symbolizing speed, accuracy, and electronic information and systems.

DISTINCTIVE UNIT INSIGNIA

Description: A silver color metal and enamel device consisting of a silver sunburst within an oriental blue oval (with axis vertical) inscribed EYES OF THE PACIFIC in silver letters, overall a diagonal red lightning bolt from lower left to upper right superimposed by a silver knight's helmet crested with a griffin's head in shades of light brown.

Symbolism: Oriental blue and silver gray are the colors traditionally associated with military intelligence units. The griffin, a mythical beast, with keen eyesight and acute hearing, symbolizes constant vigilance. The helmet with the visor closed connotes covert capabilities as well as military preparedness. The sunburst symbolizes knowledge and truth; the lightning bolt underscores electronic communications, speed, and accuracy.

Lineage and Honors

Lineage

Constituted 27 May 1948 in the Organized Reserve Corps as the 319th Headquarters Intelligence Detachment. Activated 15 June 1948 at Springfield, Massachusetts. Inactivated 22 September 1949 at Springfield, Massachusetts. Redesignated 18 August 1950 as Headquarters, 319th Military Intelligence Group. Activated 1 September 1950 at San Francisco, California. (Organized Reserve Corps redesignated 9 July 1952 as the Army Reserve.) Inactivated 1 February 1953 at San Francisco, California.

Redesignated 17 September 1988 as Headquarters and Headquarters Company, 319th Military Intelligence Brigade, and activated at Fort Lewis, Washington.

Campaign Participation Credit

None.

Decorations

None.

HEADQUARTERS AND HEADQUARTERS DETACHMENT 470th MILITARY INTELLIGENCE BRIGADE

HERALDIC ITEMS

SHOULDER SLEEVE INSIGNIA

Description: On a silver gray rectangle arched at top and bottom with a black border, a vertical oriental blue stripe and overall a black griffin's head.

Symbolism: Oriental blue and silver gray are the colors traditionally associated with military intelligence units. The three sections of the background refer to the three types of intelligence: human, signals, imagery. The blue stripe bordered by two gray stripes suggests the Panama Canal and refers to collecting and funneling information. It also alludes to the unit's location. The griffin, a mythological creature of vigilance and strength, a guardian of gold, symbolizes the unit's mission. Black represents the secrecy of the operations.

DISTINCTIVE UNIT INSIGNIA

Description: A silver color metal and enamel device consisting of an erect silver key, double-warded in base, the bow of seven radiating rays and surmounting overall an oriental blue torch with a red flame. Encircling the device in base, the ends terminating at the opposite lower corners of the flame, an oriental blue scroll bearing the inscription TRUTH SECURITY LOYALTY in silver letters.

Symbolism: Oriental blue and silver gray are the colors used for military intelligence. The key, a symbol of authority, secrecy, and wardenship, refers to the basic mission of the organization. The double wards allude to intelligence and counterintelligence and the seven rays of the bow, a reference to the numeral seven, symbolize revealing light, security, and wisdom. The torch represents guidance. Blue represents truth, and red, zeal and valor.

LINEAGE AND HONORS

RA
(active)

LINEAGE

Constituted 12 July 1944 in the Army of the United States as the 470th Counter Intelligence Corps Detachment. Activated 31 July 1944 in the Canal Zone. Allotted 19 October 1951 to the Regular Army. Redesignated 25 July 1961 as the 470th Intelligence Corps Detachment. Reorganized and redesignated 14 September 1964 as the 470th Intelligence Corps Group. Redesignated 15 October 1966 as the 470th Military Intelligence Group.

Reorganized and redesignated 16 October 1987 as Headquarters and Headquarters Company, 470th Military Intelligence Brigade. Reorganized and redesignated 16 October 1991 as Headquarters and Headquarters Detachment, 470th Military Intelligence Brigade.

CAMPAIGN PARTICIPATION CREDIT

World War II
　　American Theater, Streamer without inscription
Armed Forces Expeditions
　　Panama

DECORATIONS

None.

HEADQUARTERS AND HEADQUARTERS DETACHMENT 500th MILITARY INTELLIGENCE BRIGADE
(Pacific Vanguard)

HERALDIC ITEMS

SHOULDER SLEEVE INSIGNIA

Description: An oriental blue rectangle arched at top and bottom with a silver gray border bearing a crossed yellow lightning flash and sword surmounted by an oriental blue globe gridlined and outlined silver gray, and overall a yellow torch with red flame.

Symbolism: Oriental blue and silver gray are traditionally associated with the military intelligence branch. The sword signifies vigilance, the lightning flash alludes to electronic communications and speed, the globe symbolizes worldwide service, and the torch and flame signify knowledge.

DISTINCTIVE UNIT INSIGNIA

Description: A gold color metal and enamel device consisting of an oriental blue conical shape with apex at base bearing a white radiant sun behind a white snowcapped black mountain peak, overall a gold palm tree eradicated, surmounted by a scarlet and ultramarine blue taeguk, and in base a gold Siamese headdress all between two gold bamboo trees with shoots arched, all enclosed at the top with a gold scroll inscribed SCIENTIA POTENTIA EST (KNOWLEDGE IS STRENGTH) in scarlet letters.

Symbolism: Oriental blue is one of the colors used by Army intelligence units. Service in Japan is commemorated by the silhouette of Mount Fuji, while the palm tree denotes service in Hawaii. This unit had intelligence responsibility for several areas: the Republic of Korea, indicated by the red and blue taeguk; Taiwan, represented by the white sun from the Republic of China flag; the Republic of Vietnam, indicated by the bamboo trees; and Thailand, denoted by the Siamese headdress.

LINEAGE AND HONORS

RA

LINEAGE   (active)

Constituted 30 June 1952 in the Regular Army as Headquarters, 500th Military Intelligence Service Group. Activated 1 September 1952 in Japan. Reorganized and redesignated 28 March 1954 as Headquarters, 500th Military Intelligence Group. Reorganized and redesignated 1 July 1955 as Headquarters and Headquarters Company, 500th Military Intelligence Group. Reorganized and redesignated 24 June 1957 as the 500th Military Intelligence Group. Inactivated 25 March 1958 in Japan. Activated 25 March 1961 in Japan. Redesignated 25 July 1961 as the 500th Intelligence Corps Group. Redesignated 15 October 1966 as the 500th Military Intelligence Group.

Reorganized and redesignated 16 October 1987 as Headquarters and Headquarters Company, 500th Military Intelligence Brigade. Reorganized and redesignated 16 October 1992 as Headquarters and Headquarters Detachment, 500th Military Intelligence Brigade.

CAMPAIGN PARTICIPATION CREDIT

None.

DECORATIONS

Meritorious Unit Commendation (Army), Streamer embroidered PACIFIC AREA 1968–1969 (500th Military Intelligence Group cited; DA GO 75, 1969)

Meritorious Unit Commendation (Army), Streamer embroidered PACIFIC AREA 1972–1974 (500th Military Intelligence Group cited; DA GO 13, 1975)

Army Superior Unit Award, Streamer embroidered 1986–1987 (500th Military Intelligence Group cited; DA GO 14, 1989)

HEADQUARTERS AND HEADQUARTERS COMPANY 501st MILITARY INTELLIGENCE BRIGADE

HERALDIC ITEMS

SHOULDER SLEEVE INSIGNIA

Description: On a vertical rectangle arched convexly at top and bottom divided vertically silver gray and oriental blue all within a yellow border, a double-warded inverted yellow key between two yellow lightning flashes issuing from upper left and right corners and conjoining the shaft of the key just above the double ward.

Symbolism: Oriental blue and silver gray are the colors associated with military intelligence and also refer to the constant day and night vigilance mission of the unit. The key is symbolic of authority and control and alludes to security. The lightning flashes are symbolic of worldwide electronic communications and the double-warded key conjoined with the two lightning flashes symbolizes military intelligence and security united.

DISTINCTIVE UNIT INSIGNIA

Description: A silver color metal and enamel device consisting of a silver color rectangle bounded on either side by a vertical white sword at left and a vertical black sword at right, point up, and enclosed at the top and bottom by two arched oriental blue scrolls passing over the ends of the swords and inscribed IN UNITATE (IN UNITY) on the top scroll and ET VIGILIA (AND VILIGANCE) on the bottom scroll in silver letters. On the rectangle a red oriental dragon, his body curved from left to right with tail at top and head below, grasping in his right claw a blue lightning bolt crossed over a blue double-warded key grasped in his left claw.

Symbolism: Oriental blue and silver gray are the branch colors of military intelligence. The red dragon represents the Orient and the lineage of the organization. The lightning bolt signifies worldwide electronic communications and the key symbolizes security and control; crossed in saltire, they represent strength and symbolize Army Security Agency and military intelligence units. The swords are adapted from the military intelligence branch insignia. Their colors, white and black, signify day and night and the continuous mission of the unit.

LINEAGE AND HONORS

RA
LINEAGE   (active)

Constituted 13 October 1950 in the Regular Army as Headquarters and Headquarters Company, 501st Communication Reconnaissance Group. Activated 20 October 1950 at Camp Pickett, Virginia. Redesignated 1 July 1956 as Headquarters and Headquarters Company, 501st Army Security Agency Group. Inactivated 15 October 1957 in Korea.

Redesignated 1 January 1978 as Headquarters and Headquarters Company, 501st Military Intelligence Group, and activated in Korea. Reorganized and redesignated 16 October 1986 as Headquarters and Headquarters Company, 501st Military Intelligence Brigade. Reorganized and redesignated 16 October 1992 as Headquarters and Headquarters Detachment, 501st Military Intelligence Brigade. Reorganized and redesignated 16 November 1995 as Headquarters and Headquarters Company, 501st Military Intelligence Brigade.

CAMPAIGN PARTICIPATION CREDIT

Korean War
    CCF Spring Offensive
    UN Summer-Fall Offensive
    Second Korean Winter
    Korea, Summer-Fall 1952
    Third Korean Winter
    Korea, Summer 1953

DECORATIONS

Meritorious Unit Commendation (Army), Streamer embroidered KOREA (Headquarters and Headquarters Company, 501st Communication Reconnaissance Group, cited; DA GO 22, 1954)

Republic of Korea Presidential Unit Citation, Streamer embroidered KOREA 1951–1953 (Headquarters and Headquarters Company, 501st Communication Reconnaissance Group, cited; DA GO 76, 1953)

HEADQUARTERS AND HEADQUARTERS DETACHMENT 504th MILITARY INTELLIGENCE BRIGADE

HERALDIC ITEMS

SHOULDER SLEEVE INSIGNIA

Description: On an oriental blue shield with a yellow border a silver gray winged lightning flash with wings elevated, the flash topped with a silver gray demi-fleur-de-lis.

Symbolism: Oriental blue and silver gray are the colors associated with the military intelligence branch. The wings suggest loftiness or the advantage obtained from clear observation. The lightning flash alludes to the unit's ability to respond accurately and quickly in support of the commander's needs for intelligence from all sources. The demi-fleur-de-lis is a symbol both of intelligence and of the brigade's roots in the campaigns of Northern France, Rhineland, and Central Europe. Yellow signifies excellence and achievement.

DISTINCTIVE UNIT INSIGNIA

Description: A gold color metal and enamel device consisting of a vertical red enamel winged lightning flash with wings elevated, tipped with a demi-fleur-de-lis, all within a continuous blue scroll arched at top and base and passing behind the wings and demi-fleur-de-lis at the sides and top and inscribed SEMPER PRAEPARATUS (ALWAYS YOU ARE PREPARED) in gold letters and all areas enclosed by the wings and scroll are checky of gold and silver gray.

Symbolism: Oriental blue and silver gray are the colors used for the military intelligence branch. Wings connote loftiness, a vantage point for visual observation. The lightning flash and checky area represent technological capabilities, symbolize vigilant leadership, celerity, and communications, and allude to the unit's concern with control over hostile communications and security of friendly communications. The demi-fleur-de-lis, lightning flash, wings, and checky area also refer to the unit's origin as the 137th Signal Radio Intelligence Company, Aviation. The demi-fleur-de-lis denotes participation in European campaigns during World War II, while the color scarlet alludes to the Meritorious Unit Commendation (Army) Streamer awarded the unit.

LINEAGE AND HONORS

RA
LINEAGE   (active)

Constituted 7 February 1942 in the Army of the United States as the 137th Signal Radio Intelligence Company, Aviation. Activated 20 February 1942 at Mitchel Field, New York. Reorganized and redesignated 25 February 1944 as the 137th Signal Radio Intelligence Company. Inactivated 12 December 1945 at Fort Jackson, South Carolina. Converted and redesignated 15 November 1948 as the 406th Mobile Radio Broadcasting Company and allotted to the Organized Reserve Corps. Activated 23 November 1948 at New York, New York. Inactivated 24 October 1950 at New York, New York.

Redesignated 17 July 1951 as the 504th Communication Reconnaissance Group. (Organized Reserve Corps redesignated 9 July 1952 as the Army Reserve.) Redesignated 21 April 1955 as Headquarters and Headquarters Company, 504th Communication Reconnaissance Group; concurrently withdrawn from the Army Reserve and allotted to the Regular Army. Activated 16 May 1955 at Fort Devens, Massachusetts. Redesignated 1 July 1956 as Headquarters and Headquarters Company, 504th Army Security Agency Group. Inactivated 18 December 1957 at Camp Wolters, Texas. Activated 1 July 1974 at Hunter Army Airfield, Georgia.

Reorganized and redesignated 21 April 1978 as Headquarters and Operations Company, 504th Military Intelligence Group. Reorganized and redesignated 16 April 1982 as Headquarters and Headquarters Detachment, 504th Military Intelligence Group. Reorganized and redesignated 16 September 1985 as Headquarters and Headquarters Detachment, 504th Military Intelligence Brigade.

CAMPAIGN PARTICIPATION CREDIT

World War II
    Northern France
    Rhineland
    Central Europe

DECORATIONS

Meritorious Unit Commendation (Army), Streamer embroidered EUROPEAN THEATER (137th Signal Radio Intelligence Company cited; GO 34, Communications Zone, European Theater of Operations, 17 March 1945)

HEADQUARTERS AND HEADQUARTERS COMPANY 513th MILITARY INTELLIGENCE BRIGADE (Vigilant Knights)

HERALDIC ITEMS

SHOULDER SLEEVE INSIGNIA

Description: On a vertical rectangle arched at the top and bottom, a field divided quarterly silver gray and oriental blue and thereon a yellow lightning bolt issuing from upper left and a white sword point up in saltire surmounted by a white front-facing helmet detailed silver gray; all within a yellow border.

Symbolism: Oriental blue and silver gray are the military intelligence branch colors. The quartered field symbolizes the four primary intelligence functions: collection, analysis, production, and dissemination of intelligence information. The lightning bolt refers to the worldwide capabilities and the electronic warfare functions of the unit. The sword symbolizes the aggressiveness, protection, and physical danger inherent in military intelligence operations. The helmet alludes to the origins of the unit at Camp King in Oberursel, Germany. The helmet's front-facing position suggests alertness and vigilance and the closed faceplate the anonymity and aggressiveness of covert collection.

DISTINCTIVE UNIT INSIGNIA

Description: A gold color metal and enamel device consisting of a gold semicircular scroll bearing the words PER VIGILANTIAM SCIENTIA (KNOWLEDGE THROUGH VIGILANCE) in teal blue letters and containing upright between two green laurel branches a gold helmet facing front with teal blue rivet holes around the neck and a teal blue grill opening, the throat encircled by a collar of checkered white and black edged gold and atop the helmet a gold three-pointed coronet, the center point in teal blue.

Symbolism: The Teutonic helmet with crown is an allusion to Camp King in Oberursel, Germany, and its front-facing position suggests alertness and vigilance. The laurel branches on either side are symbolic of honor and achievement. In the collar the colors black and white denote the two types of intelligence collection provided by the unit and the repetition of the pattern indicates the dissemination of intelligence information.

LINEAGE AND HONORS

RA
(active)

LINEAGE

Constituted 22 October 1952 in the Regular Army as the 513th Military Intelligence Service Group. Activated 15 January 1953 in Germany. Reorganized and redesignated 20 October 1953 as the 513th Military Intelligence Group. Redesignated 25 July 1961 as the 513th Intelligence Corps Group. Redesignated 15 October 1966 as the 513th Military Intelligence Group. Inactivated 25 June 1969 in Germany. Redesignated 2 October 1982 as Headquarters and Headquarters Company, 513th Military Intelligence Group, and activated at Fort Monmouth, New Jersey.

Reorganized and redesignated 16 October 1986 as Headquarters and Headquarters Company, 513th Military Intelligence Brigade. Reorganized and redesignated 16 October 1991 as Headquarters and Headquarters Detachment, 513th Military Intelligence Brigade. Reorganized and redesignated 16 November 1995 as Headquarters and Headquarters Company, 513th Military Intelligence Brigade.

CAMPAIGN PARTICIPATION CREDIT

Southwest Asia
Defense of Saudi Arabia
Liberation and Defense of Kuwait
Cease-Fire

DECORATIONS

None.

HEADQUARTERS AND HEADQUARTERS DETACHMENT 525th MILITARY INTELLIGENCE BRIGADE

HERALDIC ITEMS

SHOULDER SLEEVE INSIGNIA

Description: On a rectangle arched at the bottom with a yellow border, below a yellow and black checkered chief consisting of two rows of five squares each, a field divided from upper left to lower right with silver gray above oriental blue separated by a yellow lightning flash with point at lower right.

Symbolism: Oriental blue and silver gray are the colors traditionally associated with military intelligence. The lightning flash refers to the communication and electronic warfare functions of the unit. The checkered area alludes to the overt and covert aspects of the military intelligence mission, with the black and yellow colors referring to constant vigilance day and night.

TAB

Description: Immediately above and touching the shoulder sleeve insignia, a black arc tab containing the inscription AIRBORNE in yellow letters.

DISTINCTIVE UNIT INSIGNIA.

Description: A gold color metal and enamel device consisting of a black equilateral triangle charged with a gold lion rampant, in base two rows of alternating squares gold and oriental blue all above a voluted gold scroll inscribed FAST FACTUAL FAITHFUL in black letters.

Symbolism: The gold lion rampant on a black background was taken from the coat of arms of Heidelberg in Germany, where the 525th Interrogation Team was activated in 1946. The triangular shape alludes to the deltas in Vietnam and symbolizes the unit's service in that country. The triangle and lion with the checkered rows allude to tenacity, flexibility, and secrecy and represent the combined intelligence programs of the organization.

LINEAGE AND HONORS

LINEAGE   (active)

Constituted 21 June 1944 in the Army of the United States as the 218th Counter Intelligence Corps Detachment. Activated 1 July 1944 at Fort DuPont, Delaware. Inactivated 15 October 1945 at Camp Campbell, Kentucky.

Redesignated 17 September 1947 as the 249th Counter Intelligence Corps Detachment and allotted to the Organized Reserves. Activated 6 October 1947 at New York, New York. (Organized Reserves redesignated 25 March 1948 as the Organized Reserve Corps.) Inactivated 31 December 1950 at New York, New York.

Redesignated 18 April 1952 as the 218th Counter Intelligence Corps Detachment; concurrently withdrawn from the Organized Reserve Corps and allotted to the Regular Army. Activated 30 April 1952 at Fort Holabird, Maryland. Reorganized and redesignated 25 January 1958 as the 218th Military Intelligence Detachment. Inactivated 15 September 1978 at Fort Bragg, North Carolina.

Consolidated 16 June 1979 with the 525th Military Intelligence Group (see ANNEX) and consolidated unit redesignated as Headquarters and Operations Company, 525th Military Intelligence Group; concurrently activated at Fort Bragg, North Carolina. Reorganized and redesignated 16 April 1982 as Headquarters and Headquarters Detachment, 525th Military Intelligence Group. Reorganized and redesignated 16 August 1985 as Headquarters and Headquarters Detachment, 525th Military Intelligence Brigade.

ANNEX

Constituted 18 April 1946 in the Army of the United States as the 525th Interrogation Team. Activated 1 May 1946 in Germany. Inactivated 6 November 1946 in Germany. Redesignated 6 February 1948 as the 525th Headquarters Intelligence Detachment. Activated 21 February 1948 at Fort Bragg, North Carolina. Allotted 5 May 1949 to the Regular Army. Reorganized and redesignated 23 May 1949 as Headquarters, 525th Military Intelligence Platoon. Reorganized and redesignated 4 August 1949 as the 525th Military Intelligence Service Company.

Reorganized and redesignated 1 December 1950 as the 525th Military Intelligence Service Group. Reorganized and redesignated 31 December 1953 as the 525th Military Intelligence Group. Reorganized and redesignated 25 September 1969 as Headquarters and Headquarters Company, 525th Military Intelligence Group. Inactivated 6 March 1973 at Oakland, California. Redesignated 1 July 1974 as the 525th Military Intelligence Group and activated at the Presidio of San Francisco, California. Inactivated 1 January 1978 at the Presidio of San Francisco, California.

Campaign Participation Credit

> *World War II*
>> Rhineland
>> Ardennes-Alsace
>> Central Europe
>
> *Vietnam*
>> Defense
>> Counteroffensive
>> Counteroffensive, Phase II
>> Counteroffensive, Phase III
>> Tet Counteroffensive
>> Counteroffensive, Phase IV
>> Counteroffensive, Phase V
>> Counteroffensive, Phase VI
>> Tet 69/Counteroffensive
>> Summer-Fall 1969
>> Winter-Spring 1970
>> Sanctuary Counteroffensive
>> Counteroffensive, Phase VII
>> Consolidation I
>> Consolidation II
>> Cease-Fire
>
> *Armed Forces Expeditions*
>> Dominican Republic
>> Panama
>
> *Southwest Asia*
>> Defense of Saudi Arabia
>> Liberation and Defense of Kuwait

Decorations

Meritorious Unit Commendation (Army), Streamer embroidered VIETNAM 1967–1968 (525th Military Intelligence Group cited; DA GO 39, 1970)

Meritorious Unit Commendation (Army), Streamer embroidered VIETNAM 1968–1969 (525th Military Intelligence Group cited; DA GO 52, 1974)

Meritorious Unit Commendation (Army), Streamer embroidered VIETNAM 1970 (525th Military Intelligence Group cited; DA GO 52, 1974)

Meritorious Unit Commendation (Army), Streamer embroidered VIETNAM 1971–1973 (525th Military Intelligence Group cited; DA GO 6, 1976)

108th MILITARY INTELLIGENCE GROUP

HERALDIC ITEMS

DISTINCTIVE UNIT INSIGNIA

Description: A gold color metal and enamel device consisting of a white expanded horizontal scroll surmounted vertically by a gold quill in front of a gold demi-sun emitting eight rays; all encircled by an oriental blue scroll with the upper area surmounted by the points of the rays and in base the inscription TRUTH CONQUERS in gold letters.

Symbolism: Oriental blue is one of the colors associated with military intelligence. The quill and scroll allude to the reporting mission of intelligence. The sun, a symbol of enlightenment, with the radiating rays, symbolizes the illumination of dark areas and defense against subversion and espionage. The eight rays further refer to the eight states in the jurisdictional area of the group.

FLAG DEVICE

None approved.

LINEAGE AND HONORS

RA
(inactive)

LINEAGE

Constituted 10 May 1946 in the Army of the United States as the 108th Counter Intelligence Corps Detachment. Activated 10 June 1946 at New York, New York. Allotted 26 February 1951 to the Regular Army. Redesignated 1 March 1957 as the 108th Counter Intelligence Corps Group. Redesignated 25 July 1961 as the 108th Intelligence Corps Group. Redesignated 15 October 1966 as the 108th Military Intelligence Group. Inactivated 31 January 1972 at Fort Devens, Massachusetts.

CAMPAIGN PARTICIPATION CREDIT

None.

DECORATIONS

None.

109th MILITARY INTELLIGENCE GROUP

HERALDIC ITEMS

DISTINCTIVE UNIT INSIGNIA

Description: A gold color metal and enamel device consisting of an ellipse divided quarterly oriental blue and black, overall a vertical gold quillon dagger point up with white blade and six-sectioned red grip extending over the ellipse at the top and base.

Symbolism: Oriental blue is one of the colors associated with military intelligence. Black connotes secrecy and the covert methods sometimes used in accomplishing the unit's mission. The four segments comprising the ellipse refer to the four phases of the intelligence cycle. The dagger signifies the aggressiveness and determination required for successful achievement in performance of intelligence operations. Red denotes martial fortitude and the six sections of the dagger's grip refer to the initials LIDMAC (Loyalty, Integrity, Discretion, Morals, and Character). In addition, the vertical thrust of the dagger, the ellipse, and the nine areas of the weapon (blade, guard, six-sectioned grip, and pommel) allude to the numerical designation of the group.

FLAG DEVICE

None approved.

LINEAGE AND HONORS

RA
(inactive)

LINEAGE

Constituted 10 May 1946 in the Army of the United States as the 109th Counter Intelligence Corps Detachment. Activated 24 May 1946 at Baltimore, Maryland. Allotted 26 February 1951 to the Regular Army. Redesignated 12 September 1956 as the 109th Counter Intelligence Corps Group. Redesignated 25 July 1961 as the 109th Intelligence Corps Group. Redesignated 15 October 1966 as the 109th Military Intelligence Group. Inactivated 30 June 1974 at Fort George G. Meade, Maryland.

CAMPAIGN PARTICIPATION CREDIT

None.

DECORATIONS

None.

115th MILITARY INTELLIGENCE GROUP

HERALDIC ITEMS

DISTINCTIVE UNIT INSIGNIA

Description: A gold color metal and enamel device consisting of three black enamel mountain peaks charged in base with an eight-pointed white enamel star, at top a gold sunburst on an oriental blue enamel background, all enclosed within a convoluted gold scroll in red letters CUSTOS SECRETORUM (CUSTODIAN OF SECRETS).

Symbolism: The sunburst just above the mountain peaks alludes to the sun setting in the west. With the eight-pointed rising star, it signifies the day and night protection given by the group in its eight western state jurisdiction. Oriental blue is one of the colors used by military intelligence.

FLAG DEVICE

None approved.

LINEAGE AND HONORS

RA
(inactive)

LINEAGE

Constituted 10 May 1946 in the Army of the United States as the 115th Counter Intelligence Corps Detachment. Activated 21 May 1946 at Fort Douglas, Utah. Allotted 23 May 1951 to the Regular Army. Redesignated 25 July 1957 as the 115th Counter Intelligence Corps Group. Redesignated 25 July 1961 as the 115th Intelligence Corps Group. Redesignated 15 October 1966 as the 115th Military Intelligence Group. Inactivated 30 June 1974 at the Presidio of San Francisco, California.

CAMPAIGN PARTICIPATION CREDIT

None.

DECORATIONS

None.

116th MILITARY INTELLIGENCE GROUP

HERALDIC ITEMS

DISTINCTIVE UNIT INSIGNIA

Description: A gold color metal and enamel device consisting of an oriental blue disc within a scarlet military belt buckled and edged with gold and inscribed in gold letters VIGIL PROMPTUSQUE (WATCHFUL AND READY); issuing from the inner edge of the belt downward over the oriental blue disc a gold demi-sun emitting rays; surmounted by a representation of the Washington Monument in the District of Columbia, white shaded silver gray, the monument issuing from the lower inner edge of the belt and extending between the two words of the motto beyond the top outer edge.

Symbolism: Oriental blue and silver gray are military intelligence branch colors. The sun and rays are taken from the shoulder sleeve insignia of the former United States Army Intelligence Command. They stand for light and knowledge and indicate that the group served under that organization. The belt refers to the encircling band of security provided by military intelligence and denotes the military nature of the group. The Washington Monument alludes to the District of Columbia, the place where the unit was activated in 1946.

FLAG DEVICE

None approved.

LINEAGE AND HONORS

RA
(inactive)

LINEAGE

Constituted 10 May 1946 in the Army of the United States as the 116th Counter Intelligence Corps Detachment. Activated 31 May 1946 at Washington, D.C. Allotted 5 March 1951 to the Regular Army. Redesignated 26 June 1959 as the 116th Counter Intelligence Corps Group. Redesignated 25 July 1961 as the 116th Intelligence Corps Group. Redesignated 15 October 1966 as the 116th Military Intelligence Group. Inactivated 9 January 1973 at Washington, D.C.

CAMPAIGN PARTICIPATION CREDIT

None.

DECORATIONS

None.

HEADQUARTERS AND HEADQUARTERS DETACHMENT 259th MILITARY INTELLIGENCE GROUP

HERALDIC ITEMS

DISTINCTIVE UNIT INSIGNIA

Description: A silver color metal and enamel device consisting of a silver ring containing a disc divided into quarters alternately from upper left of silver gray and black enamel centered in front of two oriental blue griffins seated back to back all upon a horizontal silver platform, the griffins each holding in a claw at chest level the upper fold of a silver scroll curving downward in three folds, the small fold centered below the platform and the scroll inscribed in black letters with the motto WATCHFUL AND VIGILANT, one word on each fold; the free ends draped below each end of the platform.

Symbolism: Oriental blue and silver gray are the colors used for military intelligence. The griffin, a mythological creature of exceeding alertness and acute hearing, represents qualities necessary to the military intelligence mission. The scroll held up in his claws alludes to the assimilation of military intelligence data and the disc at center, quartered in light and dark colors representing night and day, suggests the importance of constant vigilance. The silver circle refers to the state of Ohio, the unit's original home area.

FLAG DEVICE

None approved.

LINEAGE AND HONORS

LINEAGE

Constituted 24 November 1967 in the Army Reserve as Headquarters, 259th Military Intelligence Group. Activated 22 January 1968 at Sharonville, Ohio. Inactivated 1 March 1972 at Sharonville, Ohio. Redesignated 8 August 1995 as Headquarters and Headquarters Detachment, 259th Military Intelligence Group.

CAMPAIGN PARTICIPATION CREDIT

None.

DECORATIONS

None.

HEADQUARTERS AND HEADQUARTERS DETACHMENT
336th MILITARY INTELLIGENCE GROUP

HERALDIC ITEMS

None approved.

LINEAGE AND HONORS

AR
(inactive)

LINEAGE

Constituted 14 May 1948 in the Organized Reserve Corps as the 336th Headquarters Intelligence Detachment. Activated 2 June 1948 at New York, New York. Reorganized and redesignated 6 July 1950 as Headquarters, 336th Military Intelligence Group. Ordered into active military service 3 September 1950 at New York, New York. Inactivated 1 December 1950 at Fort Bragg, North Carolina. Redesignated 28 March 1996 as Headquarters and Headquarters Detachment, 336th Military Intelligence Group.

CAMPAIGN PARTICIPATION CREDIT

None.

DECORATIONS

None.

HEADQUARTERS AND HEADQUARTERS DETACHMENT 348th MILITARY INTELLIGENCE GROUP

HERALDIC ITEMS

None approved.

LINEAGE AND HONORS

AR
(inactive)

LINEAGE

Constituted 18 April 1967 in the Regular Army as Headquarters and Headquarters Company, 48th Military Intelligence Group. Activated 1 August 1967 at Fort Bragg, North Carolina. Inactivated 26 August 1968 at Fort Bragg, North Carolina.

Redesignated 28 March 1996 as Headquarters and Headquarters Detachment, 348th Military Intelligence Group; concurrently withdrawn from the Regular Army and allotted to the Army Reserve.

CAMPAIGN PARTICIPATION CREDIT

None.

DECORATIONS

None.

HEADQUARTERS AND HEADQUARTERS DETACHMENT 505th MILITARY INTELLIGENCE GROUP

HERALDIC ITEMS

None approved.

LINEAGE AND HONORS

AR
(inactive)

LINEAGE

Constituted 30 January 1951 in the Organized Reserve Corps as Headquarters and Headquarters Company, 505th Communication Reconnaissance Group. Activated 19 February 1951 at Boston, Massachusetts. (Organized Reserve Corps redesignated 9 July 1952 as the Army Reserve.) Redesignated 10 September 1956 as Headquarters and Headquarters Company, 505th Army Security Agency Group. Inactivated 1 July 1959 at Boston, Massachusetts. Activated 15 February 1963 at Boston, Massachusetts. Inactivated 31 January 1968 at Boston, Massachusetts.

Redesignated 1 February 1990 as Headquarters and Headquarters Company, 505th Military Intelligence Group. Redesignated 8 August 1995 as Headquarters and Headquarters Detachment, 505th Military Intelligence Group.

CAMPAIGN PARTICIPATION CREDIT

None.

DECORATIONS

None.

650th MILITARY INTELLIGENCE GROUP

HERALDIC ITEMS

DISTINCTIVE UNIT INSIGNIA

Description: A gold color metal and enamel device consisting of an octagon, issuing from the top a white enamel wedge shape between two black enamel areas each surmounted with a gold sea lion facing outward, and extending in base over an oriental blue enamel area charged in the center with a gold Philippine sunburst, all above a gold scroll of three sections inscribed in sequence SECURITY TRUTH ALLIANCE in scarlet letters.

Symbolism: The sea lions allude to the unit's New Guinea and Luzon campaigns in the Pacific theater during World War II. The Philippine sunburst symbolizes the organization's Philippine Presidential Unit Citation. The octagon refers to the number eight, which in numerology stands for perfect intelligence. The colors black and white symbolize day and night vigilance, while gold, the color of the farseeing sun, which appears bringing light out of an inscrutable darkness only to disappear again into darkness, stands for intuition. Oriental blue is one of the colors used for intelligence and security.

FLAG DEVICE

None approved.

Lineage and Honors

RA

Lineage   (active)

Constituted 12 July 1944 in the Army of the United States as the 450th Counter Intelligence Corps Detachment. Activated 20 August 1944 in New Guinea. Disbanded 22 July 1945 in the Philippine Islands. Reconstituted 25 March 1948 in the Organized Reserve Corps as the 450th Counter Intelligence Corps Detachment. Activated 1 May 1948 in Puerto Rico. Inactivated 4 August 1949 in Puerto Rico. Withdrawn 18 January 1951 from the Organized Reserve Corps and allotted to the Regular Army; concurrently activated at Fort Holabird, Maryland. Redesignated 25 July 1961 as the 450th Intelligence Corps Detachment.

Redesignated 15 October 1966 as the 650th Military Intelligence Detachment. Reorganized and redesignated 20 July 1970 as the 650th Military Intelligence Group.

Campaign Participation Credit

World War II
New Guinea
Luzon

Decorations

Philippine Presidential Unit Citation, Streamer embroidered 17 OCTOBER 1944 TO 4 JULY 1945 (450th Counter Intelligence Corps Detachment cited; DA GO 47, 1950)

HEADQUARTERS AND HEADQUARTERS DETACHMENT 902d MILITARY INTELLIGENCE GROUP
(The Deuce)

HERALDIC ITEMS

DISTINCTIVE UNIT INSIGNIA

Description: A gold color metal and enamel device consisting of three gold sun rays behind an oriental blue enamel disc surmounted at top by a gold chess piece (horse's head) and in base a red enamel and gold chessboard, all above a three-folded gold scroll inscribed in black enamel letters STRENGTH THROUGH VIGILANCE.

Symbolism: The sun rays allude to the Philippine Presidential Unit Citation and to the unit's World War II service in New Guinea and Luzon. The knight, a chess piece shaped like a horse's head, symbolizes the group's ability to make strategic moves while checking any hostile infiltration and advancement. The color red is used to symbolize courage, zeal, and awareness and with the alternating gold squares refers to the unit's counterintelligence mission. Oriental blue is one of the colors used by military intelligence.

FLAG DEVICE

None approved.

Lineage and Honors

RA

Lineage   (active)

Constituted 14 October 1944 in the Army of the United States as the 902d Counter Intelligence Corps Detachment. Activated 23 November 1944 in New Guinea. Disbanded 22 July 1945 in the Philippine Islands. Reconstituted 13 November 1947 in the Organized Reserves as the 902d Counter Intelligence Corps Detachment. Activated 28 November 1947 at Fort Smith, Arkansas. (Organized Reserves redesignated 25 March 1948 as the Organized Reserve Corps.) Inactivated 2 November 1949 at Fort Smith, Arkansas. Withdrawn 3 January 1952 from the Organized Reserve Corps and allotted to the Regular Army. Activated 8 January 1952 at Fort Holabird, Maryland.

Redesignated 15 December 1957 as the 902d Counter Intelligence Corps Group. Redesignated 25 July 1961 as the 902d Intelligence Corps Group. Redesignated 15 October 1966 as the 902d Military Intelligence Group. Reorganized and redesignated 1 January 1978 as Headquarters and Headquarters Company, 902d Military Intelligence Group. Reorganized and redesignated 16 November 1995 as Headquarters and Headquarters Detachment, 902d Military Intelligence Group.

Campaign Participation Credit

World War II
    New Guinea
    Luzon

Decorations

Army Superior Unit Award, Streamer embroidered 1988–1989 (902d Military Intelligence Group cited; DA GO 15, 1990)

Philippine Presidential Unit Citation, Streamer embroidered 17 OCTOBER 1944 TO 4 JULY 1945 (902d Counter Intelligence Corps Detachment cited; DA GO 47, 1950)

1st MILITARY INTELLIGENCE BATTALION
(The Flying Eye Battalion)

HERALDIC ITEMS

COAT OF ARMS

Shield: Azure, issuant from base a lightning flash bendwise terminating in a dexter hand fesswise supporting an annulet winged to chief all or, within the annulet a human eye proper.

Crest: On a wreath of the colors, or and azure, a bundle of five arrows crossed with a hook-bladed machete in bend sinister, the arrows point down with shafts of the first barbed and flighted gules, the machete with handle to base azure all banded in center with a ribbon gold bearing three narrow stripes fesswise scarlet, all in front of a bank of clouds proper.

Motto: INFORMARE LABORAMUS (WE LABOR TO INFORM).

Symbolism: Teal blue and yellow are the colors formerly used for air reconnaissance support battalions. The annulet, symbolic of a camera lens, refers to the aerial photo interpretation mission in the unit's history. The wings allude to flight; the eye represents observation. The lightning flash alludes to the former signal element in the unit's composition and the hand commemorates the unit's mission of support.

The battalion's awards for Vietnam service, for which it received the Presidential Unit Citation (Air Force) and five Meritorious Unit Commendations (Army), are represented in the crest. The mak, or hook-bladed machete used to clear fields in Vietnam, signifies the battalion's keen reconnaissance performance, and, together with the clouds alluding to the Air Force, refers to the Presidential Unit Citation (Air Force); blue is the color of the award streamer. The five arrows, with points down signifying penetration from the air, represent five Meritorious Unit Commendations (Army), with arrowheads and feathers in scarlet, the color of the award streamers. The yellow band with scarlet stripes, suggested by the national flag of the Republic of Vietnam, also alludes to the unit's achievements in collecting aerial reconnaissance information.

DISTINCTIVE UNIT INSIGNIA

The distinctive unit insignia is the shield and motto of the coat of arms.

Lineage and Honors

Lineage

Constituted 14 December 1956 in the Regular Army as Headquarters and Headquarters Detachment, 1st Air Reconnaissance Support Battalion. Activated 1 February 1957 at Fort Polk, Louisiana. (205th Signal Company [see ANNEX 1] reorganized and redesignated 1 May 1959 as Company A; 196th Aerial Photo Interpretation Detachment [see ANNEX 2] redesignated 15 April 1959 as Company B and allotted to the Regular Army; activated 1 May 1959 at Fort Bragg, North Carolina.)

Converted and redesignated 20 March 1962 as the 1st Military Intelligence Battalion. Inactivated 15 July 1982 at Fort Bragg, North Carolina. Activated 16 January 1984 in Germany.

Annex 1

Constituted 24 January 1945 in the Army of the United States as the 205th Signal Repair Company. Activated 1 February 1945 at Fort Jackson, South Carolina. Allotted 16 May 1949 to the Regular Army. Reorganized and redesignated 15 April 1954 as the 205th Signal Company. Inactivated 28 May 1955 in Korea. Activated 1 February 1956 at Fort Bragg, North Carolina.

Annex 2

Constituted 16 June 1945 in the Army of the United States as the 196th Photo Interpreter Team. Activated 10 July 1945 at Fort Jackson, South Carolina. Reorganized and redesignated 18 May 1950 as the 196th Aerial Photo Interpretation Detachment. Inactivated 15 November 1953 at Governors Island, New York.

Campaign Participation Credit

Vietnam
  Defense
  Counteroffensive
  Counteroffensive, Phase II
  Counteroffensive, Phase III
  Tet Counteroffensive
  Counteroffensive, Phase IV
  Counteroffensive, Phase V
  Counteroffensive, Phase VI
  Tet 69/Counteroffensive
  Summer-Fall 1969
  Winter-Spring 1970
  Sanctuary Counteroffensive
  Counteroffensive, Phase VII
  Consolidation I
  Consolidation II
  Cease-Fire

Company A additionally entitled to:

Korean War
    UN Defensive
    UN Offensive
    CCF Intervention
    First UN Counteroffensive
    CCF Spring Offensive
    UN Summer-Fall Offensive
    Second Korean Winter
    Korea, Summer-Fall 1952
    Third Korean Winter
    Korea, Summer 1953

Company B additionally entitled to:

Southwest Asia
    Liberation and Defense of Kuwait

DECORATIONS

Presidential Unit Citation (Air Force), Streamer embroidered SOUTHEAST ASIA 1966–1967 (1st Military Intelligence Battalion cited; DA GO 42, 1969)

Meritorious Unit Commendation (Army), Streamer embroidered VIETNAM 1965–1966 (1st Military Intelligence Battalion cited; DA GO 17, 1968)

Meritorious Unit Commendation (Army), Streamer embroidered VIETNAM 1966–1967 (1st Military Intelligence Battalion cited; DA GO 17, 1968)

Meritorious Unit Commendation (Army), Streamer embroidered VIETNAM 1967–1968 (1st Military Intelligence Battalion cited; DA GO 42, 1969)

Meritorious Unit Commendation (Army), Streamer embroidered VIETNAM 1969–1970 (1st Military Intelligence Battalion cited; DA GO 43, 1988)

Meritorious Unit Commendation (Army), Streamer embroidered VIETNAM 1970–1972 (1st Military Intelligence Battalion cited; DA GO 5, 1973)

Republic of Vietnam Cross of Gallantry with Gold Star, Streamer embroidered VIETNAM 1965–1971 (1st Military Intelligence Battalion cited; DA GO 32, 1973)

Company A additionally entitled to:

Meritorious Unit Commendation (Army), Streamer embroidered KOREA 1950–1952 (205th Signal Repair Company cited; DA GO 94, 1952)

Meritorious Unit Commendation (Army), Streamer embroidered KOREA 1953 (205th Signal Repair Company cited; DA GO 1, 1954)

Republic of Korea Presidential Unit Citation, Streamer embroidered KOREA (205th Signal Repair Company cited; DA GO 33, 1953, as amended by DA GO 41, 1955)

2d MILITARY INTELLIGENCE BATTALION

HERALDIC ITEMS

COAT OF ARMS

Shield: Per chevron abased azure and argent, a chief dancetty of two enhanced of the last the apexes surmounted by two roundels of the first counterchanged and in base a sphinx rampant sable armed gules.

Crest: None approved.

Motto: OCULI CULTUS SECRETI (THE EYES OF INTELLIGENCE).

Symbolism: The colors, white and teal blue, symbolize the battalion's former status as an unassigned-to-branch unit. The battalion's numerical designation and mission are suggested by the two roundels or lenses directing their gaze downward. The sphinx is representative of the intelligence mission. Black alludes to the coat of arms of the old Rhineland district of Pfalz in Germany, where the unit was activated.

DISTINCTIVE UNIT INSIGNIA

The distinctive unit insignia is the shield and motto of the coat of arms.

LINEAGE AND HONORS

RA
(inactive)

LINEAGE

Constituted 18 October 1961 in the Regular Army as the 2d Air Reconnaissance Support Battalion. Activated 15 November 1961 in Germany. Converted and redesignated 16 September 1962 as the 2d Military Intelligence Battalion. Inactivated 15 November 1991 in Germany.

CAMPAIGN PARTICIPATION CREDIT

Southwest Asia
    Defense of Saudi Arabia
    Liberation and Defense of Kuwait
    Cease-Fire

DECORATIONS

Meritorious Unit Commendation (Army), Streamer embroidered SOUTHWEST ASIA (2d Military Intelligence Battalion cited; DA GO 34, 1992)

3d MILITARY INTELLIGENCE BATTALION

HERALDIC ITEMS

COAT OF ARMS

Shield: Per bend azure and checky or and gules in chief a chess piece with a griffin's head argent.

Crest: On a wreath of the colors, or and azure, a Vietnamese sunburst of the first surmounted by a bamboo cross pierced at center proper.

Motto: WINGED VIGILANCE.

Symbolism: The colors oriental blue and silver gray are used to represent military intelligence and scarlet and gold to symbolize military strength and operational excellence. The griffin, traditionally a creature of vision, alertness, and intelligence, is shown as a chess piece adjacent to a chessboard, suggesting the type of operation, requiring ingenuity and intellect, which the battalion is called upon to carry out. The squares on the chessboard represent the many engagements in which the unit participated in Vietnam.

The sunburst, taken from the Hien Nhan gate to the Imperial City in Hue, represents Vietnam and has three principal flames, suggesting the Meritorious Unit Commendations (Army) awarded to the organization. The bamboo cross stands for the Republic of Vietnam Cross of Gallantry with Palm awarded to the unit.

DISTINCTIVE UNIT INSIGNIA

The distinctive unit insignia is the shield and motto of the coat of arms.

LINEAGE AND HONORS

RA
(active)

LINEAGE

Constituted 1 June 1966 in the Regular Army as the 146th Aviation Company and activated in Vietnam. Inactivated 17 February 1973 in Vietnam. Converted and redesignated 1 July 1974 as the 146th Army Security Agency Company and activated in Korea.

Reorganized and redesignated 16 June 1982 as Headquarters, Headquarters and Service Company, 3d Military Intelligence Battalion (704th Military Intelligence Detachment [see ANNEX 1] and 542d Military Intelligence

Detachment [see ANNEX 2] concurrently redesignated as Companies A and B and activated in Korea).

ANNEX 1

Constituted 25 September 1950 in the Regular Army as the 704th Counter Intelligence Corps Detachment. Activated 6 October 1950 in Korea. Inactivated 28 March 1955 in Korea. Redesignated 28 December 1961 as the 704th Intelligence Corps Detachment. Activated 25 January 1962 in Vietnam. Inactivated 7 March 1966 in Vietnam. Redesignated 1 November 1966 as the 704th Military Intelligence Detachment. Activated 15 March 1967 in Japan. Inactivated 15 June 1972 in Japan. Activated 25 September 1976 in Korea. Inactivated 16 May 1979 in Korea.

ANNEX 2

Constituted 7 July 1945 in the Army of the United States as the 1002d Counter Intelligence Corps Detachment. Activated 25 July 1945 in France. Disbanded 24 January 1946 at Holabird Signal Depot, Maryland. Reconstituted 7 December 1950 in the Regular Army as the 442d Counter Intelligence Corps Detachment. Activated 20 December 1950 in Korea. Inactivated 25 December 1951 in Korea.

Redesignated 26 March 1965 as the 542d Intelligence Corps Detachment. Activated 7 April 1965 at Fort George G. Meade, Maryland. Inactivated 1 December 1965 at Fort George G. Meade, Maryland. Activated 19 December 1969 at Fort Bragg, North Carolina. Redesignated 29 December 1969 as the 542d Military Intelligence Detachment. Inactivated 19 November 1973 at Aberdeen Proving Ground, Maryland.

CAMPAIGN PARTICIPATION CREDIT

Vietnam
Counteroffensive
Counteroffensive, Phase II
Counteroffensive, Phase III
Tet Counteroffensive
Counteroffensive, Phase IV
Counteroffensive, Phase V
Counteroffensive, Phase VI
Tet 69/Counteroffensive
Summer-Fall 1969
Winter-Spring 1970
Sanctuary Counteroffensive
Counteroffensive, Phase VII
Consolidation I
Consolidation II
Cease-Fire

Company A additionally entitled to:

Korean War
    UN Offensive
    CCF Intervention
    First UN Counteroffensive
    CCF Spring Offensive
    UN Summer-Fall Offensive
    Second Korean Winter
    Korea, Summer-Fall 1952
    Third Korean Winter
    Korea, Summer 1953

Vietnam
    Advisory
    Defense

Company B additionally entitled to:

Korean War
    CCF Intervention
    First UN Counteroffensive
    CCF Spring Offensive
    UN Summer-Fall Offensive
    Second Korean Winter

DECORATIONS

Meritorious Unit Commendation (Army), Streamer embroidered VIETNAM 1966–1967 (146th Aviation Company cited; DA GO 17, 1968, as amended by DA GO 1, 1969)

Meritorious Unit Commendation (Army), Streamer embroidered VIETNAM 1967–1969 (146th Aviation Company cited; DA GO 2, 1971)

Meritorious Unit Commendation (Army), Streamer embroidered VIETNAM 1971–1972 (146th Aviation Company cited; DA GO 32, 1973)

Army Superior Unit Award, Streamer embroidered 1985–1986 (3d Military Intelligence Battalion cited; DA GO 30, 1987)

Republic of Vietnam Cross of Gallantry with Palm, Streamer embroidered VIETNAM 1970–1971 (146th Aviation Company cited; DA GO 6, 1974)

Company A additionally entitled to:

Meritorious Unit Commendation (Army), Streamer embroidered KOREA (704th Counter Intelligence Corps Detachment cited; DA GO 46, 1954)

Republic of Korea Presidential Unit Citation, Streamer embroidered KOREA 1950–1952 (704th Counter Intelligence Corps Detachment cited; DA GO 33, 1953, as amended by DA GO 41, 1955)

Republic of Korea Presidential Unit Citation, Streamer embroidered KOREA 1952–1953 (704th Counter Intelligence Corps Detachment cited; DA GO 24, 1954)

14th MILITARY INTELLIGENCE BATTALION

HERALDIC ITEMS

COAT OF ARMS

Shield: Per bend dove-tailed argent and azure, two whelk shells counterchanged.

Crest: None approved.

Motto: SUPPORT BY INTELLIGENCE.

Symbolism: The two shells and the dove-tailed partition line stand for the three general functions of a military intelligence unit: collecting, processing, and disseminating information. The whelk shells, which receive and transmit sound waves and vibrations, refer to the collection and dissemination of information; the fitting together of the two parts of the shield, by means of the dove-tailed line, refers to the process of interpreting and collating separate pieces of information to form an integrated whole. Oriental blue and silver gray are the colors used for military intelligence. Counterchanging the colors of the shells alludes to the counterintelligence function of the unit.

DISTINCTIVE UNIT INSIGNIA

The distinctive unit insignia is the shield and motto of the coat of arms.

LINEAGE AND HONORS

RA
(active)

LINEAGE

Constituted 4 November 1965 in the Regular Army as the 14th Military Intelligence Battalion. Activated 24 November 1965 at Fort Bragg, North Carolina. Inactivated 31 December 1972 at Fort Bragg, North Carolina. Activated 16 December 1988 at Fort Lewis, Washington.

CAMPAIGN PARTICIPATION CREDIT

None.

DECORATIONS

None.

15th MILITARY INTELLIGENCE BATTALION

COAT OF ARMS

Shield: Azure, above a base rayonné argent, a winged sphinx couchant of the last and in chief two plates partially superimposed fesswise the conjoined area sable.

Crest: None approved.

Motto: VIGILANTIA AD FINEM (VIGILANCE TO THE END).

Symbolism: Oriental blue and silver gray are the colors used for military intelligence. The winged sphinx, all-seeing and continually watchful, refers to the battalion's air reconnaissance support mission and also connotes the unit's motto. The overlapping discs simulate camera lenses and allude to the stereoscopic capabilities provided by the organization in its performance of reproduction, identification, and packaging of aerial imagery. The flames are indicative of heat sensory devices, wisdom, and zeal.

DISTINCTIVE UNIT INSIGNIA

The distinctive unit insignia is the shield and motto of the coat of arms.

LINEAGE AND HONORS

RA
(active)

LINEAGE

Constituted 6 January 1966 in the Regular Army as the 15th Military Intelligence Battalion. Activated 25 February 1966 at Fort Bragg, North Carolina. Inactivated 30 April 1972 at Fort Bragg, North Carolina. Activated 21 April 1978 at Fort Hood, Texas (Detachments A, B, C, and D concurrently consolidated to form Company A; 131st Military Intelligence Company [see ANNEX 1] and 156th Army Security Agency Company [see ANNEX 2] reorganized and redesignated as Companies B and C). Headquarters and Headquarters Company inactivated 31 May 1981 at Hunter Army Airfield, Georgia (Company C concurrently inactivated at Fort Bliss, Texas). (Company A inactivated 15 April 1982 at Fort Hood, Texas; disbanded 15 September 1983. Company B reorganized and redesignated 16 September 1983 as Company A; Company C concurrently redesignated as Company B.) Headquarters and Headquarters Company redesignated 16 October 1985 as Headquarters, Headquarters and Service Company and activated at Fort Hood, Texas (Company B concurrently activated).

ANNEX 1

Constituted 1 July 1971 in the Regular Army as the 131st Military Intelligence Company and activated in Vietnam.

ANNEX 2

Constituted 1 June 1966 in the Regular Army as the 156th Aviation Company and activated in Vietnam. Converted and redesignated 5 November 1973 as the 156th Army Security Agency Company.

CAMPAIGN PARTICIPATION CREDIT

> *Southwest Asia*
> > Defense of Saudi Arabia
> > Liberation and Defense of Kuwait

Company A additionally entitled to:

> *Vietnam*
> > Consolidation I
> > Consolidation II
> > Cease-Fire

Company B additionally entitled to:

> *Vietnam*

Counteroffensive	Summer-Fall 1969
Counteroffensive, Phase II	Winter-Spring 1970
Counteroffensive, Phase III	Sanctuary Counteroffensive
Tet Counteroffensive	Counteroffensive, Phase VII
Counteroffensive, Phase IV	Consolidation I
Counteroffensive, Phase V	Consolidation II
Counteroffensive, Phase VI	Cease-Fire
Tet 69/Counteroffensive	

DECORATIONS

Meritorious Unit Commendation (Army), Streamer embroidered SOUTHWEST ASIA (15th Military Intelligence Battalion cited; DA GO 12, 1994)

Company B additionally entitled to:

Meritorious Unit Commendation (Army), Streamer embroidered VIETNAM 1966–1967 (156th Aviation Company cited; DA GO 17, 1968, as amended by DA GO 1, 1969)

Meritorious Unit Commendation (Army), Streamer embroidered VIETNAM 1967–1969 (156th Aviation Company cited; DA GO 2, 1971)

Meritorious Unit Commendation (Army), Streamer embroidered VIETNAM 1971–1972 (156th Aviation Company cited; DA GO 32, 1973)

Republic of Vietnam Cross of Gallantry with Palm, Streamer embroidered VIETNAM 1970–1971 (156th Aviation Company cited; DA GO 6, 1974)

24th MILITARY INTELLIGENCE BATTALION

HERALDIC ITEMS

COAT OF ARMS

Shield: Azure, above a base indented or a winged eye, the wings displayed inverted of the second, emitting to base three rays throughout of the like counterchanged.

Crest: That for the regiments and separate battalions of the Army Reserve: On a wreath of the colors, or and azure, the Lexington Minuteman proper. The statue of the Minuteman, Capt. John Parker (H. H. Kitson, sculptor), stands on the Common in Lexington, Massachusetts.

Motto: OUR EYES SUPPORT.

Symbolism: Oriental blue is one of the colors used for military intelligence units. The winged eye searching the land with rays of light is symbolic of the air reconnaissance mission of the battalion.

DISTINCTIVE UNIT INSIGNIA

The distinctive unit insignia is the shield and motto of the coat of arms.

Lineage and Honors

AR
(active)

Lineage

Constituted 22 April 1959 in the Army Reserve as the 24th Air Reconnaissance Support Battalion. Activated 1 May 1959 with Headquarters at New York, New York. Ordered into active military service 15 October 1961 at New York, New York.

Converted and redesignated 13 April 1962 as the 24th Military Intelligence Battalion. Released from active military service 4 August 1962 and reverted to reserve status. Location of Headquarters changed 1 September 1962 to Staten Island, New York; changed 31 December 1968 to Fort Hamilton, New York. Battalion ordered into active military service 24 March 1970 at Fort Hamilton, New York; released from active military service 26 March 1970 and reverted to reserve status. Location of Headquarters changed 1 May 1974 to Staten Island, New York. (Detachment C ordered into active military service 17 January 1991 at Staten Island, New York; released from active military service 1 April 1991 and reverted to reserve status.)

Campaign Participation Credit

Detachment C entitled to:

Southwest Asia
    Liberation and Defense of Kuwait

Decorations

None.

101st MILITARY INTELLIGENCE BATTALION

HERALDIC ITEMS

COAT OF ARMS

Shield: Checky azure and argent in front of a sword and lightning flash in saltire a double-warded key palewise argent, on a chief invected of the like a sunburst throughout tenné.

Crest: None approved.

Motto: TRUST VIGILANCE LOYALTY.

Symbolism: Oriental blue and silver gray are the colors traditionally associated with military intelligence. The invected chief is an allusion to clouds and the atmosphere, the main field of operations for a combat electronic warfare intelligence unit. The sunburst, a symbol of Helios, the Greek sun god, is a further reference to the atmosphere. The sunburst may also denote a compass rose and the multi-directional facets of the unit's radio functions. The checky background alludes to a chessboard and symbolizes strategy and intelligence. The sword refers to the unit's military ability, the lightning flash to speed and communications, and the key to intelligence and security.

DISTINCTIVE UNIT INSIGNIA

The distinctive unit insignia is the shield and motto of the coat of arms.

LINEAGE AND HONORS

RA
(active)

LINEAGE

Constituted 16 September 1980 in the Regular Army as the 101st Military Intelligence Battalion, assigned to the 1st Infantry Division, and activated at Fort Riley, Kansas (337th Army Security Agency Company [see ANNEX 1] and 1st Military Intelligence Company [see ANNEX 2] concurrently reorganized and redesignated as Companies A and B). Inactivated 15 November 1995 at Fort Riley, Kansas. Activated 16 February 1996 in Germany.

ANNEX 1

Constituted 1 July 1952 in the Regular Army as the 337th Communication Reconnaissance Company. Activated 6 August 1952 at Fort Devens, Massachusetts. Reorganized and redesignated 16 May 1955 as Company B, 313th Communication Reconnaissance Battalion. Redesignated 1 July 1956 as Company B, 313th Army Security Agency Battalion. Inactivated 18 December

1957 at Fort Bragg, North Carolina. Activated 25 May 1962 at Fort Bragg, North Carolina. Reorganized and redesignated 15 October 1966 as the 337th Army Security Agency Company.

ANNEX 2

Constituted 12 July 1944 in the Army of the United States as the 1st Counter Intelligence Corps Detachment. Activated 16 August 1944 in France with personnel from provisional Counter Intelligence Corps detachment attached to the 1st Infantry Division. Allotted 16 February 1951 to the Regular Army. Reorganized and redesignated 25 January 1958 as the 1st Military Intelligence Detachment. Reorganized and redesignated 26 December 1969 as the 1st Military Intelligence Company. Reorganized and redesignated 15 April 1970 as the 1st Military Intelligence Detachment. Reorganized and redesignated 3 May 1971 as the 1st Military Intelligence Company. Assigned 21 July 1978 to the 1st Infantry Division.

CAMPAIGN PARTICIPATION CREDIT

> *Southwest Asia*
> Defense of Saudi Arabia
> Liberation and Defense of Kuwait
> Cease-Fire

Company A additionally entitled to:

Vietnam

Defense	Counteroffensive, Phase V
Counteroffensive	Counteroffensive, Phase VI
Counteroffensive, Phase II	Tet 69/Counteroffensive
Counteroffensive, Phase III	Summer-Fall 1969
Tet Counteroffensive	Winter-Spring 1970
Counteroffensive, Phase IV	

Company B additionally entitled to:

World War II–EAME	*Vietnam*
Tunisia	Defense
Sicily	Counteroffensive
Normandy (with arrowhead)	Counteroffensive, Phase II
Northern France	Counteroffensive, Phase III
Rhineland	Tet Counteroffensive
Ardennes-Alsace	Counteroffensive, Phase IV
Central Europe	Counterofffensive, Phase V
	Counterofffensive, Phase VI
	Tet 69/Counterofffensive
	Summer-Fall 1969
	Winter-Spring 1970

DECORATIONS

Company A entitled to:

Meritorious Unit Commendation (Army), Streamer embroidered VIETNAM 1965–1966 (11th Radio Research Unit cited; DA GO 17, 1968)

Meritorious Unit Commendation (Army), Streamer embroidered VIETNAM 1966–1967 (337th Radio Research Company cited; DA GO 17, 1968)

Meritorious Unit Commendation (Army), Streamer embroidered VIETNAM 1967–1968 (337th Radio Research Company cited; DA GO 28, 1969)

Meritorious Unit Commendation (Army), Streamer embroidered VIETNAM 1968–1969 (337th Radio Research Company cited; DA GO 51, 1971)

Meritorious Unit Commendation (Army), Streamer embroidered VIETNAM 1969–1970 (337th Radio Research Company cited; DA GO 43, 1972)

Republic of Vietnam Cross of Gallantry with Palm, Streamer embroidered VIETNAM 1965–1968 (337th Radio Research Company cited; DA GO 21, 1969, as amended by DA GO 59, 1969)

Republic of Vietnam Civil Action Honor Medal, First Class, Streamer embroidered VIETNAM 1969–1970 (337th Radio Research Company cited; DA GO 6, 1974)

Company B entitled to:

Meritorious Unit Commendation (Army), Streamer embroidered VIETNAM 1966 (1st Military Intelligence Detachment cited; DA GO 17, 1968)

Meritorious Unit Commendation (Army), Streamer embroidered VIETNAM 1968 (1st Military Intelligence Detachment cited; DA GO 7, 1970)

French Croix de Guerre with Palm, World War II, Streamer embroidered KASSERINE (1st Infantry Division cited; DA GO 43, 1950)

French Croix de Guerre with Palm, World War II, Streamer embroidered NORMANDY (1st Infantry Division cited; DA GO 43, 1950)

French Croix de Guerre, World War II, Fourragere (1st Infantry Division cited; DA GO 43, 1950)

Belgian Fourragere 1940 (1st Counter Intelligence Corps Detachment cited; DA GO 43, 1950)

Cited in the Order of the Day of the Belgian Army for action at Mons (1st Counter Intelligence Corps Detachment cited; DA GO 43, 1950)

Cited in the Order of the Day of the Belgian Army for action at Eupen-Malmedy (1st Counter Intelligence Corps Detachment cited; DA GO 43, 1950)

Republic of Vietnam Cross of Gallantry with Palm, Streamer embroidered VIETNAM 1965–1968 (1st Military Intelligence Detachment cited; DA GO 21, 1969)

Republic of Vietnam Civil Action Honor Medal, First Class, Streamer embroidered VIETNAM 1965–1970 (1st Military Intelligence Detachment cited; DA GO 53, 1970)

102d MILITARY INTELLIGENCE BATTALION

HERALDIC ITEMS

COAT OF ARMS

Shield: Per fess dancetty azure and sable, a chief invected argent, and overall a sword bend sinisterwise point to base gules surmounted by a lightning flash issuant from dexter chief bendwise overall or.

Crest: None approved.

Motto: KNOWLEDGE FOR BATTLE.

Symbolism: Silver gray and oriental blue are the colors used for military intelligence units. The divisions of the shield are symbolic of weather and terrain, with the scarlet sword representing the enemy. The unit's deployment overseas is symbolized by the wavy blue section and the black area in base refers to the steep, mountainous terrain of Korea, where elements of the battalion served during the Korean War. The lightning flash signifies the seeking, gathering, and dissemination of information relative to the areas of weather, terrain, and the enemy and further denotes the constant vigilance which is inherent in the mission of military intelligence.

DISTINCTIVE UNIT INSIGNIA

The distinctive unit insignia is the shield and motto of the coat of arms.

LINEAGE AND HONORS

RA
(active)

LINEAGE

Constituted 16 September 1981 in the Regular Army as the 102d Military Intelligence Battalion, assigned to the 2d Infantry Division, and activated in Korea (329th Army Security Agency Company [see ANNEX 1] and 2d Military Intelligence Company [see ANNEX 2] concurrently reorganized and redesignated as Companies A and B).

ANNEX 1

Constituted 23 October 1943 in the Army of the United States as the 3106th Signal Service Platoon. Activated 1 November 1943 at Fort Monmouth, New Jersey. Inactivated 10 February 1946 on Okinawa. Activated 19 November 1946 at Vint Hill Farms Station, Virginia. Redesignated 1 April 1947 as the 3d Signal Service Platoon. Reorganized and redesignated 25 March 1949 as the

53d Signal Service Company. Allotted 13 October 1950 to the Regular Army.

Converted and redesignated 1 December 1950 as the 329th Communication Reconnaissance Company. Reorganized and redesignated 25 June 1955 as Company B, 301st Communication Reconnaissance Battalion. Redesignated 1 July 1956 as Company B, 301st Army Security Agency Battalion. Inactivated 15 October 1957 in Korea. Redesignated 1 November 1975 as the 329th Army Security Agency Company and activated in Korea.

ANNEX 2

Constituted 12 July 1944 in the Army of the United States as the 2d Counter Intelligence Corps Detachment. Activated 6 August 1944 in France with personnel from provisional Counter Intelligence Corps detachment attached to the 2d Infantry Division. Allotted 3 February 1949 to the Regular Army. Inactivated 15 September 1956 at Fort Lewis, Washington. Redesignated 26 February 1958 as the 2d Military Intelligence Detachment. Activated 14 June 1958 at Fort Benning, Georgia. Assigned 30 June 1976 to the 2d Infantry Division. Reorganized and redesignated 20 February 1979 as the 2d Military Intelligence Company.

CAMPAIGN PARTICIPATION CREDIT

Company A entitled to:

World War II–AP
> Silver band without inscription

Korean War
> Second Korean Winter
> Korea, Summer-Fall 1952
> Third Korean Winter
> Korea, Summer 1953

Company B entitled to:

World War II–EAME
> Normandy
> Northern France
> Rhineland
> Ardennes-Alsace
> Central Europe

Korean War
> UN Defensive
> UN Offensive
> CCF Intervention
> First UN Counteroffensive
> CCF Spring Offensive
> UN Summer-Fall Offensive
> Second Korean Winter
> Korea, Summer-Fall 1952
> Third Korean Winter
> Korea, Summer 1953

Decorations

Company A entitled to:

Meritorious Unit Commendation (Army), Streamer embroidered KOREA 1951–1952 (329th Communication Reconnaissance Company cited; DA GO 108, 1952)

Meritorious Unit Commendation (Army), Streamer embroidered KOREA 1952–1953 (329th Communication Reconnaissance Company cited; DA GO 22, 1954)

Republic of Korea Presidential Unit Citation, Streamer embroidered KOREA (329th Communication Reconnaissance Company cited; DA GO 33, 1953, as amended by DA GO 41, 1955)

Company B entitled to:

Presidential Unit Citation (Army), Streamer embroidered HONGCHON (2d Counter Intelligence Corps Detachment cited; DA GO 72, 1951)

Meritorious Unit Commendation (Army), Streamer embroidered KOREA (2d Counter Intelligence Corps Detachment cited; DA GO 32, 1954)

Belgian Fourragere 1940 (2d Infantry Division cited; DA GO 43, 1950)

Cited in the Order of the Day of the Belgian Army for action in the Ardennes (2d Infantry Division cited; DA GO 43, 1950)

Cited in the Order of the Day of the Belgian Army for action at Elsenborn Crest (2d Infantry Division cited; DA GO 43, 1950)

103d MILITARY INTELLIGENCE BATTALION

COAT OF ARMS

Shield: Per bend azure and quarterly gules and or, on a bend engrailed argent a lightning bolt of the second and in sinister chief a wyvern's head of the fourth.

Crest: None approved.

Motto: TOP OF THE ROCK.

Symbolism: Oriental blue and silver gray are the colors associated with military intelligence units. The wyvern's head has been adapted from the device of the 3d Infantry Division, which this battalion supports. The wyvern is a heraldic creature known as a fearless guardian and thus symbolizes a major role of the intelligence mission. The lightning bolt on the engrailed bend alludes to the unit's special interest in communications of hostile and friendly forces as well as communications throughout the battalion. The scarlet and yellow quarters refer to the arms of Wurzburg in Germany, the battalion's place of activation.

DISTINCTIVE UNIT INSIGNIA

The distinctive unit insignia is the shield and motto of the coat of arms.

LINEAGE AND HONORS

RA

LINEAGE   (active)

Constituted 16 September 1981 in the Regular Army as the 103d Military Intelligence Battalion, assigned to the 3d Infantry Division, and activated in Germany (851st Army Security Agency Company [see ANNEX 1] and 3d Military Intelligence Company [see ANNEX 2] concurrently reorganized and redesignated as Companies A and B).

ANNEX 1

Constituted 29 December 1945 in the Army of the United States as the 3377th Signal Service Detachment. Activated 15 January 1946 in the Philippine Islands. Redesignated 9 June 1947 as the 50th Signal Service Detachment.

Converted and redesignated 25 October 1951 as the 851st Communication Reconnaissance Detachment and allotted to the Regular Army. Inactivated 15 August 1956 in Japan. Redesignated 3 December 1965 as the 851st Army Security Agency Detachment. Activated 15 December 1965 in the Dominican Republic. Inactivated 14 October 1966 at Fort Bragg, North Carolina. Redesignated 1 July 1974 as the 851st Army Security Agency Company and activated in Germany.

ANNEX 2

Constituted 12 July 1944 in the Army of the United States as the 3d Counter Intelligence Corps Detachment. Activated 3 September 1944 in France with personnel from provisional Counter Intelligence Corps detachment attached to the 3d Infantry Division. Inactivated 1 September 1946 in Germany. Allotted 3 February 1949 to the Regular Army. Activated 1 March 1949 at Fort Benning, Georgia. Reorganized and redesignated 25 January 1958 as the 3d Military Intelligence Detachment. Reorganized and redesignated 21 May 1972 as the 3d Military Intelligence Company. Assigned 21 April 1974 to the 3d Infantry Division.

CAMPAIGN PARTICIPATION CREDIT

Company A entitled to:

Korean War
> UN Offensive
> CCF Intervention
> First UN Counteroffensive
> CCF Spring Offensive

Armed Forces Expeditions
> Dominican Republic

Company B entitled to:

World War II–EAME

 Tunisia
 Sicily
 Naples-Foggia
 Anzio (with arrowhead)
 Rome-Arno
 Southern France (with arrowhead)
 Rhineland
 Ardennes-Alsace
 Central Europe

Korean War

 CCF Intervention
 First UN Counteroffensive
 CCF Spring Offensive
 UN Summer-Fall Offensive
 Second Korean Winter
 Korea, Summer-Fall 1952
 Third Korean Winter
 Korea, Summer 1953

DECORATIONS

Company A entitled to:

Meritorious Unit Commendation (Army), Streamer embroidered KOREA (50th Signal Service Detachment cited; DA GO 101, 1951)

Republic of Korea Presidential Unit Citation, Streamer embroidered KOREA (50th Signal Service Detachment cited; DA GO 33, 1953, as amended by DA GO 41, 1955)

Company B entitled to:

Presidential Unit Citation (Army), Streamer embroidered COLMAR (3d Infantry Division cited; WD GO 44, 1945)

Meritorious Unit Commendation (Army), Streamer embroidered KOREA (3d Counter Intelligence Corps Detachment cited; DA GO 22, 1954)

French Croix de Guerre with Palm, World War II, Streamer embroidered COLMAR (3d Infantry Division cited; DA GO 43, 1950)

French Croix de Guerre, World War II, Fourragere (3d Infantry Division cited; DA GO 43, 1950)

Republic of Korea Presidential Unit Citation, Streamer embroidered UIJONGBU CORRIDOR (3d Counter Intelligence Corps Detachment cited; DA GO 20, 1953)

Republic of Korea Presidential Unit Citation, Streamer embroidered IRON TRIANGLE (3d Counter Intelligence Corps Detachment cited; DA GO 29, 1954)

104th MILITARY INTELLIGENCE BATTALION

HERALDIC ITEMS

COAT OF ARMS

> *Shield*:   Azure an eagle's head proper in front of two swords in saltire argent hilted or and in chief a lightning flash fesswise of the like.
>
> *Crest*:   None approved.
>
> *Motto*:   WATCHFUL AND READY.
>
> *Symbolism*:   Oriental blue and silver gray are the colors associated with military intelligence. The crossed swords attest to the unit's readiness; the eagle, wide-eyed and alert, is symbolic of watchfulness. The bolt of lightning refers to the unit's electronic warfare capability. The symbols express the words of the motto and the unit's basic mission and responsibility.

DISTINCTIVE UNIT INSIGNIA

The distinctive unit insignia is the shield and the motto of the coat of arms.

LINEAGE AND HONORS

RA
(active)

LINEAGE

Constituted 16 September 1980 in the Regular Army as the 104th Military Intelligence Battalion, assigned to the 4th Infantry Division, and activated at Fort Carson, Colorado (374th Army Security Agency Company [see ANNEX 1] and 4th Military Intelligence Company [see ANNEX 2] concurrently reorganized and redesignated as Companies A and B). Inactivated 15 December 1995 at Fort Carson, Colorado. Activated 16 January 1996 at Fort Hood, Texas.

ANNEX 1

Constituted 21 November 1963 in the Regular Army as Company C, 303d Army Security Agency Battalion. Activated 20 December 1963 at Fort Lewis, Washington. Reorganized and redesignated 15 October 1966 as the 374th Army Security Agency Company. Inactivated 30 June 1972 at Fort Carson, Colorado. Activated 21 December 1977 at Fort Carson, Colorado.

ANNEX 2

Constituted 12 July 1944 in the Army of the United States as the 4th Counter Intelligence Corps Detachment. Activated 6 August 1944 in France with personnel from provisional Counter Intelligence Corps detachment attached to the 4th Infantry Division. Inactivated 23 February 1946 at Camp Butner, North Carolina. Activated 30 November 1946 in Germany. Inactivated 20 April 1947 in Germany. Allotted 5 January 1949 to the Regular Army. Activated 31 January 1949 at Fort Ord, California. Reorganized and redesignated 25 January 1958 as the 4th Military Intelligence Detachment. Reorganized and redesignated 26 December 1969 as the 4th Military Intelligence Company. Assigned 21 July 1978 to the 4th Infantry Division.

CAMPAIGN PARTICIPATION CREDIT

Company A entitled to:
Vietnam
     Counteroffensive, Phase II
     Counteroffensive, Phase III
     Tet Counteroffensive
     Counteroffensive, Phase IV
     Counteroffensive, Phase V
     Counteroffensive, Phase VI
     Tet 69/Counteroffensive
     Summer-Fall 1969
     Winter-Spring 1970
     Sanctuary Counteroffensive
     Counteroffensive, Phase VII

Company B entitled to:
World War II–EAME
     Normandy (with arrowhead)
     Northern France
     Rhineland
     Ardennes-Alsace
     Central Europe
Vietnam
     Counteroffensive, Phase II
     Counteroffensive, Phase III
     Tet Counteroffensive
     Counteroffensive, Phase IV
     Counteroffensive, Phase V
     Counteroffensive, Phase VI
     Tet 69/Counteroffensive
     Summer-Fall 1969
     Winter-Spring 1970
     Sanctuary Counteroffensive
     Counteroffensive, Phase VII

DECORATIONS

Company A entitled to:

Meritorious Unit Commendation (Army), Streamer embroidered VIETNAM 1967–1968 (374th Radio Research Company cited; DA GO 28, 1969)

Meritorious Unit Commendation (Army), Streamer embroidered VIETNAM 1968–1969 (374th Radio Research Company cited; DA GO 51, 1971)

Meritorious Unit Commendation (Army), Streamer embroidered VIETNAM 1969–1970 (374th Radio Research Company cited; DA GO 43, 1972)

Republic of Vietnam Cross of Gallantry with Palm, Streamer embroidered VIETNAM 1967–1969 (374th Radio Research Company cited; DA GO 3, 1970)

Republic of Vietnam Cross of Gallantry with Palm, Streamer embroidered VIETNAM 1969–1970 (374th Radio Research Company cited; DA GO 52, 1971)

Republic of Vietnam Cross of Gallantry with Palm, Streamer embroidered VIETNAM 1970 (374th Radio Research Company cited; DA GO 6, 1974)

Republic of Vietnam Civil Action Honor Medal, First Class, Streamer embroidered VIETNAM 1967–1969 (374th Radio Research Detachment cited; DA GO 53, 1970)

Company B entitled to:

Meritorious Unit Commendation (Army), Streamer embroidered VIETNAM 1968–1969 (4th Military Intelligence Detachment cited; DA GO 39, 1970)

Belgian Fourragere 1940 (4th Infantry Division cited; DA GO 43, 1950)

Cited in the Order of the Day of the Belgian Army for action in Belgium (4th Infantry Division cited; DA GO 43, 1950)

Cited in the Order of the Day of the Belgian Army for action in the Ardennes (4th Infantry Division cited; DA GO 43, 1950)

Republic of Vietnam Cross of Gallantry with Palm, Streamer embroidered VIETNAM 1968–1969 (4th Military Intelligence Detachment cited; DA GO 3, 1970)

Republic of Vietnam Civil Action Honor Medal, First Class, Streamer embroidered VIETNAM 1968–1969 (4th Military Intelligence Detachment cited; DA GO 53, 1970)

105th MILITARY INTELLIGENCE BATTALION
(Owls)

COAT OF ARMS

Shield: Azure, a pile to honor point argent bearing a lozenge throughout gules charged with an owl's head couped or, all above a sword and key in saltire with blade and ward to chief of the second between two lightning flashes palewise of the fourth.

Crest: None approved.

Motto: BOLD VIGIL.

Symbolism: Silver gray and oriental blue are the colors traditionally associated with military intelligence. The sword and key in the saltirewise position represent support and symbolize military leadership. The lightning flashes refer to the speed and power of electronic communications. The owl is symbolic of wisdom and watchfulness and the red diamond shape alludes to the unit's support of the 5th Infantry Division. The two lightning flashes further refer to World War II and the war in Vietnam, in which elements of the battalion served.

DISTINCTIVE UNIT INSIGNIA

The distinctive unit insignia is the shield and motto of the coat of arms.

LINEAGE AND HONORS

LINEAGE

Constituted 15 May 1967 in the Regular Army as Headquarters and Headquarters Company, 200th Army Security Agency Battalion, and activated at Fort Devens, Massachusetts. Inactivated 15 December 1967 at Fort Devens, Massachusetts.

Redesignated 1 June 1982 as Headquarters, Headquarters and Operations Company, 105th Military Intelligence Battalion, assigned to the 5th Infantry Division, and activated at Fort Polk, Louisiana (405th Army Security Agency Company [see ANNEX 1] and 15th Military Intelligence Company [see ANNEX 2] concurrently reorganized and redesignated as Companies A and B). Battalion inactivated 16 December 1992 at Fort Polk, Louisiana.

ANNEX 1

Constituted 31 May 1965 in the Regular Army as the 405th Army Security Agency Detachment. Activated 1 June 1965 at Fort Lewis, Washington. Inactivated 5 November 1965 in Vietnam. Activated 15 July 1968 in Vietnam. Inactivated 5 December 1969 in Vietnam. Activated 30 September 1971 in Vietnam. Inactivated 30 June 1972 in Vietnam. Redesignated 16 March 1979 as the 405th Army Security Agency Company and activated at Fort Polk, Louisiana.

ANNEX 2

Constituted 12 July 1944 in the Army of the United States as the 5th Counter Intelligence Corps Detachment. Activated 6 August 1944 in France with personnel from provisional Counter Intelligence Corps detachment attached to the 5th Infantry Division. Inactivated 1 April 1950 at Fort Jackson, South Carolina. Allotted 12 May 1954 to the Regular Army. Activated 15 June 1954 in Germany. Inactivated 1 July 1957 at Fort Ord, California. Redesignated 2 February 1962 as the 5th Military Intelligence Detachment. Activated 19 February 1962 at Fort Carson, Colorado. Inactivated 25 May 1969 at Fort Carson, Colorado. Activated 15 November 1969 at Fort Carson, Colorado.

Inactivated 15 December 1970 at Fort Carson, Colorado; concurrently redesignated as the 15th Military Intelligence Company. Redesignated 21 March 1976 as the 5th Military Intelligence Detachment and activated at Fort Polk, Louisiana. Reorganized and redesignated 30 September 1978 as the 15th Military Intelligence Company and assigned to the 5th Infantry Division.

CAMPAIGN PARTICIPATION CREDIT

Company A entitled to:

> *Vietnam*
>> Defense
>> Counteroffensive, Phase V
>> Counteroffensive, Phase VI
>> Tet 69/Counteroffensive
>> Summer-Fall 1969
>> Winter-Spring 1970
>> Consolidation I
>> Consolidation II
>> Cease-Fire

Company B entitled to:

> *World War II–EAME*
>> Normandy
>> Northern France
>> Rhineland
>> Ardennes-Alsace
>> Central Europe

DECORATIONS

Company A entitled to:

Meritorious Unit Commendation (Army), Streamer embroidered VIETNAM 1965 (Detachment 2, 3d Radio Research Unit, cited; DA GO 17, 1968)

Meritorious Unit Commendation (Army), Streamer embroidered VIETNAM 1968–1969 (405th Radio Research Detachment cited; DA GO 51, 1971)

Meritorious Unit Commendation (Army), Streamer embroidered VIETNAM 1971–1972 (405th Radio Research Detachment cited; DA GO 32, 1972)

Republic of Vietnam Civil Action Honor Medal, First Class, Streamer embroidered VIETNAM 1969 (405th Radio Research Detachment cited; DA GO 6, 1974)

106th MILITARY INTELLIGENCE BATTALION

HERALDIC ITEMS

COAT OF ARMS

Shield: Per chevron enhanced sable and argent, a mascle gules inter-laced by a flash bendwise and a flash bend sinisterwise azure, between four evergreen trees in pale two and two, and two evergreen trees in fess vert.

Crest: None approved.

Motto: THE NORTHERN WATCH.

Symbolism: The chevronwise division of the background together with the evergreen trees forms the illusion of a snow-covered mountain against the night sky and refers to the unit's service in Alaska as well as its around-the-clock mission and responsibilities. Black represents the covert and white is for truth. Oriental blue is one of the colors associated with military intelligence and red is symbolic of courage. The two flashes intertwined with the mascle emphasize the complexity and interrelated nature of military intelligence work. They allude to electronic capabilities, speed, and a strong defense and also represent the Gordian knot of mythology. The evergreens symbolize security and need for constant alertness; their number (six) alludes to the 6th Infantry Division.

DISTINCTIVE UNIT INSIGNIA

The distinctive unit insignia is the shield and motto of the coat of arms.

LINEAGE AND HONORS

RA

(inactive)

LINEAGE

Constituted 18 June 1987 in the Regular Army as the 106th Military Intelligence Battalion, assigned to the 6th Infantry Division, and activated at Fort Richardson, Alaska. Inactivated 15 June 1994 at Fort Richardson, Alaska.

CAMPAIGN PARTICIPATION CREDIT

None.

DECORATIONS

None.

107th MILITARY INTELLIGENCE BATTALION

HERALDIC ITEMS

COAT OF ARMS

Shield: Per fess enhanced azure and ermine the silhouette of a bayonet fesswise argent charged with a lightning flash gules and in base a fret throughout of the first.

Crest: None approved.

Motto: THROUGH KNOWLEDGE VICTORY.

Symbolism: Oriental blue and silver gray (white) are the colors traditionally associated with military intelligence units. The ermine background is a heraldic fur and alludes to a cloak symbolizing a "cloak of secrecy" and the covert activities of an intelligence organization. The fret is composed of interlaced parts showing the complexity and interconnections of intelligence information. It resembles a puzzle to be solved by finding the proper key or part, an allusion to the military intelligence mission. The bayonet signifies readiness and response. The lightning flash symbolizes the radio communications and electronics employed to make the unit prepared and effective.

DISTINCTIVE UNIT INSIGNIA

The distinctive unit insignia is the shield and motto of the coat of arms.

LINEAGE AND HONORS

RA
(inactive)

LINEAGE

Constituted 1 June 1983 in the Regular Army as the 107th Military Intelligence Battalion, assigned to the 7th Infantry Division, and activated at Fort Ord, California (601st Army Security Agency Company [see ANNEX 1] and 7th Military Intelligence Company [see ANNEX 2] concurrently reorganized and redesignated as Companies A and B). Inactivated 15 September 1993 at Fort Ord, California.

ANNEX 1

Constituted 19 March 1951 in the Regular Army as the 601st Communication Reconnaissance Detachment. Activated 4 April 1951 at Fort Jay, New York. Inactivated 15 August 1956 at Fort Jay, New York. Redesignated 21 April 1967 as the 601st Army Security Agency Detachment and activated at Fort Hood, Texas. Inactivated 20 November 1968 in Vietnam. Redesignated 21 September 1978 as the 601st Army Security Agency Company and activated at Fort Ord, California.

ANNEX 2

Constituted 12 July 1944 in the Army of the United States as the 7th Counter Intelligence Corps Detachment. Activated 7 August 1944 at Schofield Barracks, Hawaii, with personnel from provisional Counter Intelligence Corps detachment attached to the 7th Infantry Division. Inactivated 25 April 1946 in Korea. Activated 15 December 1946 in Korea. Inactivated 25 March 1947 in Korea. Activated 12 October 1950 in Korea. Allotted 8 February 1954 to the Regular Army. Reorganized and redesignated 15 May 1959 as the 7th Military Intelligence Detachment. Inactivated 30 June 1971 in Korea. Activated 21 January 1976 at Fort Ord, California. Reorganized and redesignated 21 July 1978 as the 7th Military Intelligence Company and assigned to the 7th Infantry Division.

CAMPAIGN PARTICIPATION CREDIT

Armed Forces Expeditions
    Panama

Company A additionally entitled to:

Vietnam
    Counteroffensive, Phase III
    Tet Counteroffensive
    Counteroffensive, Phase IV
    Counteroffensive, Phase V
    Counteroffensive, Phase VI

Company B additionally entitled to:

World War II–AP	*Korean War*
Leyte	UN Offensive
Ryukyus	CCF Intervention
	First UN Counteroffensive
	CCF Spring Offensive
	UN Summer-Fall Offensive
	Second Korean Winter
	Korea, Summer-Fall 1952
	Third Korean Winter
	Korea, Summer 1953

DECORATIONS

Company A entitled to:

Meritorious Unit Commendation (Army), Streamer embroidered VIETNAM 1967–1968 (601st Radio Research Detachment cited; DA GO 28, 1969)

Company B entitled to:

Meritorious Unit Commendation (Army), Streamer embroidered KOREA (7th Counter Intelligence Corps Detachment cited; DA GO 68, 1953)

Philippine Presidential Unit Citation, Streamer embroidered 17 OCTOBER 1944 TO 4 JULY 1945 (7th Counter Intelligence Corps Detachment cited; DA GO 47, 1950)

108th MILITARY INTELLIGENCE BATTALION

HERALDIC ITEMS

COAT OF ARMS

Shield: Azure, two swords crossed argent hilts to base gules, above a globe of the second gridlined of the field; on a chief sable and between two silver mullets a lightning bolt palewise or terminating upon the center of the globe.

Crest: None approved.

Motto: VICTORY THRU VIGILANCE.

Symbolism: Oriental blue and silver gray (white) are the colors associated with military intelligence. The crossed swords in the colors red and white represent the unit's military readiness and support mission. The bolt of lightning alludes to the unit's technology and to the swift and accurate use of information to thwart enemy plans. The stars and globe suggest the organization's areas of operation in search of intelligence and counterintelligence.

DISTINCTIVE UNIT INSIGNIA

The distinctive unit insignia is the shield and motto of the coat of arms.

LINEAGE AND HONORS

RA
(inactive)

LINEAGE

Constituted 16 September 1981 in the Regular Army as the 108th Military Intelligence Battalion, assigned to the 8th Infantry Division, and activated in Germany (415th Army Security Agency Company [see ANNEX 1] and 8th Military Intelligence Company [see ANNEX 2] concurrently reorganized and redesignated as Companies A and B). Inactivated 15 November 1991 in Germany.

ANNEX 1

Constituted 26 June 1967 in the Regular Army as the 415th Army Security Agency Detachment and activated at Schofield Barracks, Hawaii. Inactivated 20 November 1968 in Vietnam. Redesignated 1 July 1974 as the 415th Army Security Agency Company and activated in Germany.

ANNEX 2

Constituted 12 July 1944 in the Army of the United States as the 8th Counter Intelligence Corps Detachment. Activated 6 August 1944 in France with personnel

from provisional Counter Intelligence Corps detachment attached to the 8th
Infantry Division. Inactivated 21 November 1945 at Holabird Signal Depot,
Maryland. Activated 15 December 1946 in Korea. Inactivated 25 March 1947 in
Korea. Allotted 17 May 1954 to the Regular Army. Activated 15 June 1954 at
Camp Carson, Colorado. Reorganized and redesignated 25 June 1958 as the 8th
Military Intelligence Detachment. Reorganized and redesignated 21 February
1973 as the 8th Military Intelligence Company. Assigned 21 April 1974 to the
8th Infantry Division.

CAMPAIGN PARTICIPATION CREDIT

Company A entitled to:

> *Vietnam*
>> Counteroffensive, Phase III
>> Tet Counteroffensive
>> Counteroffensive, Phase IV
>> Counteroffensive, Phase V
>> Counteroffensive, Phase VI

Company B entitled to:

> *World War II–EAME*
>> Normandy
>> Northern France
>> Rhineland
>> Ardennes-Alsace
>> Central Europe

DECORATIONS

Company A entitled to:

Meritorious Unit Commendation (Army), Streamer embroidered VIETNAM
1967–1968 (415th Radio Research Detachment cited; DA GO 28, 1969)

109th MILITARY INTELLIGENCE BATTALION

HERALDIC ITEMS

COAT OF ARMS

Shield: Sable, between two flanches checky argent and azure a sun in splendor in chief and in base a decrescent or, overall palewise a lightning flash gules.

Crest: None approved.

Motto: SEEK AND DISRUPT.

Symbolism: Silver gray and oriental blue are the colors of military intelligence. The checkered arrangement reflects the multifaceted intelligence and electronic warfare capabilities of the battalion. The black center field suggests secrecy and symbolizes tactical operations security. The sun and moon symbols and two hemispheres denote round-the-clock tactical and global deployment capabilities. The red flash is a symbol of the offensive combat capability of electronic warfare as well as the long range electronic surveillance characteristics of the battalion.

DISTINCTIVE UNIT INSIGNIA

The distinctive unit insignia is the shield and motto of the coat of arms.

LINEAGE AND HONORS

RA
(inactive)

LINEAGE

Constituted 1 October 1981 in the Regular Army as the 109th Military Intelligence Battalion, assigned to the 9th Infantry Division, and activated at Fort Lewis, Washington (335th Army Security Agency Company [see ANNEX 1] and 9th Military Intelligence Company [see ANNEX 2] concurrently reorganized and redesignated as Companies A and B). Inactivated 15 September 1991 at Fort Lewis, Washington.

ANNEX 1

Constituted 27 March 1942 in the Army of the United States as the 112th Signal Radio Intelligence Company. Activated 18 May 1942 at Camp Crowder, Missouri. Reorganized and redesignated 1 September 1945 as the 112th Signal Service Company. Inactivated 23 December 1945 in the Philippine Islands. Allotted 20 December 1946 to the Regular Army and activated in the Philippine Islands as the 112th Signal Service Company (Philippine Scouts). Reorganized and redesignated 1 April 1947 as the 10th Signal Service Battalion (Philippine

Scouts). Reorganized and redesignated 12 June 1948 as the 112th Signal Service Company (Philippine Scouts). Inactivated 1 June 1949 in the Philippine Islands.

Converted and redesignated 17 July 1951 as the 335th Communication Reconnaissance Company. Redesignated 6 April 1966 as the 335th Army Security Agency Company. Activated 15 June 1966 at Fort Riley, Kansas. Inactivated 5 April 1971 in Vietnam. Activated 21 December 1977 at Fort Lewis, Washington.

ANNEX 2

Constituted 12 July 1944 in the Army of the United States as the 9th Counter Intelligence Corps Detachment. Activated 16 August 1944 in France with personnel from provisional Counter Intelligence Corps detachment attached to the 9th Infantry Division. Inactivated 20 April 1947 in Germany. Allotted 5 January 1949 to the Regular Army. Activated 28 January 1949 at Fort Dix, New Jersey. Inactivated 12 March 1951 at Fort Dix, New Jersey. Activated 15 June 1954 in Germany. Reorganized and redesignated 25 January 1958 as the 9th Military Intelligence Detachment. Inactivated 31 January 1962 at Fort Carson, Colorado. Activated 1 July 1966 at Fort Riley, Kansas. Inactivated 25 September 1969 at Schofield Barracks, Hawaii. Redesignated 21 December 1972 as the 9th Military Intelligence Company and activated at Fort Lewis, Washington. Assigned 21 July 1978 to the 9th Infantry Division.

CAMPAIGN PARTICIPATION CREDIT

Company A entitled to:

World War II–AP	*Vietnam*
Northern Solomons	Counteroffensive, Phase II
Luzon (with arrowhead)	Counteroffensive, Phase III
	Tet Counteroffensive
	Counteroffensive, Phase IV
	Counteroffensive, Phase V
	Counteroffensive, Phase VI
	Tet 69/Counteroffensive
	Summer-Fall 1969
	Winter-Spring 1970
	Sanctuary Counteroffensive
	Counteroffensive, Phase VII

Company B entitled to:

World War II–EAME	*Vietnam*
Tunisia	Counteroffensive, Phase II
Sicily	Counteroffensive, Phase III
Normandy	Tet Counteroffensive
Northern France	Counteroffensive, Phase IV
Rhineland	Counteroffensive, Phase V
Ardennes-Alsace	Counteroffensive, Phase VI
Central Europe	Tet 69/Counteroffensive
	Summer-Fall 1969

DECORATIONS

Company A entitled to:

Meritorious Unit Commendation (Army), Streamer embroidered VIETNAM 1967 (335th Radio Research Company cited; DA GO 17, 1968)

Meritorious Unit Commendation (Army), Streamer embroidered VIETNAM 1967–1968 (335th Radio Research Company cited; DA GO 28, 1969)

Meritorious Unit Commendation (Army), Streamer embroidered VIETNAM 1968–1969 (335th Radio Research Company cited; DA GO 51, 1971)

Meritorious Unit Commendation (Army), Streamer embroidered VIETNAM 1969–1970 (335th Radio Research Company cited; DA GO 43, 1972)

Meritorious Unit Commendation (Army), Streamer embroidered VIETNAM 1971 (335th Radio Research Company cited; DA GO 32, 1973)

Philippine Presidential Unit Citation, Streamer embroidered 17 OCTOBER 1944 TO 4 JULY 1945 (112th Signal Radio Intelligence Company cited; DA GO 47, 1950)

Republic of Vietnam Cross of Gallantry with Palm, Streamer embroidered VIETNAM 1967–1968 (335th Radio Research Company cited; DA GO 31, 1969)

Republic of Vietnam Cross of Gallantry with Palm, Streamer embroidered VIETNAM 1969 (335th Radio Research Company cited; DA GO 59, 1969)

Republic of Vietnam Cross of Gallantry with Palm, Streamer embroidered VIETNAM 1970–1971 (335th Radio Research Company cited; DA GO 6, 1974)

Republic of Vietnam Civil Action Honor Medal, First Class, Streamer embroidered VIETNAM 1967–1969 (335th Radio Research Company cited; DA GO 59, 1969)

Company B entitled to:

Meritorious Unit Commendation (Army), Streamer embroidered VIETNAM 1968 (9th Military Intelligence Detachment cited; DA GO 48, 1969)

Belgian Fourragere 1940 (9th Infantry Division cited; DA GO 43, 1950)

Cited in the Order of the Day of the Belgian Army for action at the Meuse River (9th Infantry Division cited; DA GO 43, 1950)

Cited in the Order of the Day of the Belgian Army for action in the Ardennes (9th Infantry Division cited; DA GO 43, 1950)

Republic of Vietnam Cross of Gallantry with Palm, Streamer embroidered VIETNAM 1966–1968 (9th Military Intelligence Detachment cited; DA GO 31, 1969)

Republic of Vietnam Cross of Gallantry with Palm, Streamer embroidered VIETNAM 1969 (9th Military Intelligence Detachment cited; DA GO 59, 1969)

Republic of Vietnam Civil Action Honor Medal, First Class, Streamer embroidered VIETNAM 1966–1969 (9th Military Intelligence Detachment cited; DA GO 59, 1969)

110th MILITARY INTELLIGENCE BATTALION

HERALDIC ITEMS

COAT OF ARMS

Shield: Azure, a chevronnel debased or, below two griffins' heads in fess point erased addorsed and conjoined of the like.

Crest: None approved.

Motto: SENTINELS OF THE SUMMIT.

Symbolism: Oriental blue is one of the colors associated with military intelligence. Gold is emblematic of excellence and achievement. The chevron, a symbol of strength and support, suggests a mountain peak and connotes the unit's assignment to the 10th Mountain Division. The griffins, ever vigilant and alert, appear above the mountain peak, epitomizing the unit's motto and mission.

DISTINCTIVE UNIT INSIGNIA

The distinctive unit insignia is the shield and motto of the coat of arms.

LINEAGE AND HONORS

RA
(active)

LINEAGE

Constituted 1 December 1988 in the Regular Army as the 110th Military Intelligence Battalion, assigned to the 10th Mountain Division, and activated at Fort Drum, New York.

CAMPAIGN PARTICIPATION CREDIT

None.

DECORATIONS

Army Superior Unit Award, Streamer embroidered 1994 (110th Military Intelligence Battalion cited; DA GO 14, 1997)

124th MILITARY INTELLIGENCE BATTALION

HERALDIC ITEMS

COAT OF ARMS

Shield: Sable a griffin segreant argent collared azure the collar charged with three plates all within a bordure compony of the second and third.

Crest: None approved.

Motto: INTELLIGENCE FOR VICTORY.

Symbolism: Oriental blue and silver gray (white) are the colors associated with the military intelligence branch. The checky background alludes to a chessboard and symbolizes the use of intelligence information in formulating military strategy and countermeasure. The griffin, noted for keen eyesight, symbolizes vigilance and penetration of the unknown, as suggested by the black area. The discs on the griffin's collar allude to battle engagements in which elements of the unit participated.

DISTINCTIVE UNIT INSIGNIA

The distinctive unit insignia is the shield and motto of the coat of arms.

LINEAGE AND HONORS

RA
(inactive)

LINEAGE

Constituted 1 June 1981 in the Regular Army as the 124th Military Intelligence Battalion, assigned to the 24th Infantry Division, and activated at Fort Stewart, Georgia (853d Army Security Agency Company [see ANNEX 1] and 24th Military Intelligence Company [see ANNEX 2] concurrently reorganized and redesignated as Companies A and B). Inactivated 15 February 1996 at Fort Stewart, Georgia.

ANNEX 1

Constituted 5 August 1944 in the Army of the United States as the 3323d Signal Information and Monitoring Company. Activated 15 August 1944 at Camp Gruber, Oklahoma. Inactivated 30 October 1945 in Germany. Converted and redesignated 4 September 1947 as the 310th Radio Security Detachment and allotted to the Organized Reserves. (Elements activated 16 September 1947–1 February 1949; inactivated 21 June 1949–6 June 1950.) (Organized Reserves redesignated 25 March 1948 as the Organized Reserve Corps.)

Redesignated 17 July 1951 as the 853d Communication Reconnaissance Detachment. Withdrawn 20 December 1951 from the Organized Reserve Corps and allotted to the Regular Army. Activated 10 January 1952 at Fort Devens, Massachusetts. Inactivated 1 March 1956 in Germany. Redesignated 16 March 1979 as the 853d Army Security Agency Company and activated at Fort Stewart, Georgia.

ANNEX 2

Constituted 12 July 1944 in the Army of the United States as the 24th Counter Intelligence Corps Detachment. Activated 20 August 1944 in New Guinea with personnel from provisional Counter Intelligence Corps detachment attached to the 24th Infantry Division. Inactivated 25 February 1946 in Japan. Activated 6 October 1950 in Korea. Allotted 8 February 1954 to the Regular Army. Inactivated 15 October 1957 in Japan. Redesignated 5 June 1958 as the 24th Military Intelligence Detachment. Activated 1 July 1958 in Germany. Inactivated 15 April 1970 at Fort Riley, Kansas. Activated 21 February 1976 at Fort Stewart, Georgia. Reorganized and redesignated 30 September 1978 as the 24th Military Intelligence Company and assigned to the 24th Infantry Division.

CAMPAIGN PARTICIPATION CREDIT
> *Southwest Asia*
>> Defense of Saudi Arabia
>> Liberation and Defense of Kuwait

Company A additionally entitled to:
> *World War II–EAME*
>> Central Europe

Company B additionally entitled to:

World War II–AP	*Korean War*
New Guinea	UN Offensive
Leyte	CCF Intervention
Luzon	First UN Counteroffensive
Southern Philippines	CCF Spring Offensive
	UN Summer-Fall Offensive
	Second Korean Winter

DECORATIONS

Army Superior Unit Award, Streamer embroidered 1994 (124th Military Intelligence Battalion [less Companies A and B] cited; DA GO 14, 1997)

Company B additionally entitled to:

Meritorious Unit Commendation (Army), Streamer embroidered KOREA 1950–1951 (24th Counter Intelligence Corps Detachment cited; DA GO 52, 1951)

Meritorious Unit Commendation (Army), Streamer embroidered KOREA 1953–1954 (24th Counter Intelligence Corps Detachment cited; DA GO 77, 1954)

Philippine Presidential Unit Citation, Streamer embroidered 17 OCTOBER 1944 TO 4 JULY 1945 (24th Counter Intelligence Corps Detachment cited; DA GO 47, 1950)

125th MILITARY INTELLIGENCE BATTALION

HERALDIC ITEMS

COAT OF ARMS

Shield:	Azure a pale argent overall between two mullets in fess a sword and a bayonet saltirewise or bearing a torteau charged with a heraldic rose of the third.
Crest:	None approved.
Motto:	EYES OF LIGHTNING.
Symbolism:	Oriental blue and silver gray are the military intelligence colors. The unsheathed weapons connote readiness and the heraldic rose alludes to the sub rosa mission of the organization. The stars symbolize the wartime service of elements of the unit and the color red indicates their decorations for action in World War II, Korea, and Vietnam.

DISTINCTIVE UNIT INSIGNIA

The distinctive unit insignia is the shield and motto of the coat of arms.

LINEAGE AND HONORS

RA
(active)

LINEAGE

Constituted 16 June 1983 in the Regular Army as the 125th Military Intelligence Battalion, assigned to the 25th Infantry Division, and activated at Schofield Barracks, Hawaii (372d Army Security Agency Company [see ANNEX 1] and 25th Military Intelligence Company [see ANNEX 2] concurrently reorganized and redesignated as Companies A and B).

ANNEX 1

Constituted 11 May 1962 in the Regular Army as Company A, 303d Army Security Agency Battalion. Activated 25 June 1962 at Fort Carson, Colorado. Reorganized and redesignated 15 October 1966 as the 372d Army Security Agency Company. Inactivated 6 March 1971 in Vietnam. Activated 1 July 1974 at Helemano, Hawaii.

ANNEX 2

Constituted 12 July 1944 in the Army of the United States as the 25th Counter Intelligence Corps Detachment. Activated 10 August 1944 in New Caledonia with personnel from provisional Counter Intelligence Corps detachment attached to the 25th Infantry Division. Inactivated 25 February 1946 in

Japan. Activated 6 October 1950 in Korea. Allotted 8 February 1954 to the Regular Army. Reorganized and redesignated 24 December 1958 as the 25th Military Intelligence Detachment. Reorganized and redesignated 26 December 1969 as the 25th Military Intelligence Company. Assigned 21 August 1978 to the 25th Infantry Division.

CAMPAIGN PARTICIPATION CREDIT

Company A entitled to:

Vietnam

Counteroffensive	Counteroffensive, Phase VI
Counteroffensive, Phase II	Tet 69/Counteroffensive
Counteroffensive, Phase III	Summer-Fall 1969
Tet Counteroffensive	Winter-Spring 1970
Counteroffensive, Phase IV	Sanctuary Counteroffensive
Counteroffensive, Phase V	Counteroffensive, Phase VII

Company B entitled to:

World War II–AP
    Luzon
Korean War
    UN Offensive
    CCF Intervention
    First UN Counteroffensive
    CCF Spring Offensive
    UN Summer-Fall Offensive
    Second Korean Winter
    Korea, Summer-Fall 1952
    Third Korean Winter
    Korea, Summer 1953

Vietnam
    Counteroffensive
    Counteroffensive, Phase II
    Counteroffensive, Phase III
    Tet Counteroffensive
    Counteroffensive, Phase IV
    Counteroffensive, Phase V
    Counteroffensive, Phase VI
    Tet 69/Counteroffensive
    Summer-Fall 1969
    Winter-Spring 1970
    Sanctuary Counteroffensive
    Counteroffensive, Phase VII

DECORATIONS

Company A entitled to:

Meritorious Unit Commendation (Army), Streamer embroidered VIETNAM 1966 (16th Radio Research Unit cited; DA GO 17, 1968)

Meritorious Unit Commendation (Army), Streamer embroidered VIETNAM 1966–1967 (372d Radio Research Company cited; DA GO 17, 1968)

Meritorious Unit Commendation (Army), Streamer embroidered VIETNAM 1967–1968 (372d Radio Research Company cited; DA GO 28, 1969)

Meritorious Unit Commendation (Army), Streamer embroidered VIETNAM 1968–1969 (372d Radio Research Company cited; DA GO 51, 1971, and United States Army, Vietnam, GO 690, 25 February 1971, as amended by United States Army, Vietnam, GO 1405, 25 April 1971)

Meritorious Unit Commendation (Army), Streamer embroidered VIETNAM 1969–1970 (372d Radio Research Company cited; DA GO 43, 1972)

Republic of Vietnam Cross of Gallantry with Palm, Streamer embroidered VIETNAM 1966–1968 (372d Radio Research Company cited; DA GO 48, 1971)

Republic of Vietnam Cross of Gallantry with Palm, Streamer embroidered VIETNAM 1969–1970 (372d Radio Research Company cited; DA GO 5, 1973)

Republic of Vietnam Cross of Gallantry with Palm, Streamer embroidered VIETNAM 1970–1971 (372d Radio Research Company cited; DA GO 6, 1974)

Republic of Vietnam Civil Action Honor Medal, First Class, Streamer embroidered VIETNAM 1969–1971 (372d Radio Research Company cited; DA GO 6, 1974)

Company B entitled to:

Meritorious Unit Commendation (Army), Streamer embroidered KOREA (25th Counter Intelligence Corps Detachment cited; DA GO 62, 1954)

Meritorious Unit Commendation (Army), Streamer embroidered VIETNAM 1966–1967 (25th Military Intelligence Detachment cited; DA GO 17, 1968)

Meritorious Unit Commendation (Army), Streamer embroidered VIETNAM 1967–1968 (25th Military Intelligence Detachment cited; DA GO 42, 1969)

Meritorious Unit Commendation (Army), Streamer embroidered VIETNAM 1968–1969 (25th Military Intelligence Detachment cited; DA GO 36, 1970)

Meritorious Unit Commendation (Army), Streamer embroidered VIETNAM 1969–1970 (25th Military Intelligence Company cited; DA GO 6, 1974)

Philippine Presidential Unit Citation, Streamer embroidered 17 OCTOBER 1944 TO 4 JULY 1945 (25th Counter Intelligence Corps Detachment cited; DA GO 47, 1950)

Republic of Vietnam Cross of Gallantry with Palm, Streamer embroidered VIETNAM 1966–1968 (25th Military Intelligence Detachment cited; DA GO 48, 1971)

Republic of Vietnam Cross of Gallantry with Palm, Streamer embroidered VIETNAM 1968–1970 (25th Military Intelligence Detachment cited; DA GO 5, 1973)

Republic of Vietnam Civil Action Honor Medal, First Class, Streamer embroidered VIETNAM 1966–1970 (25th Military Intelligence Detachment cited; DA GO 51, 1971)

126th MILITARY INTELLIGENCE BATTALION

HERALDIC ITEMS

COAT OF ARMS

Shield: Celeste a griffin rampant argent grasping a double-warded key with a lightning bolt shaft gules, wards to chief of the second and the bow consisting of a heraldic rose of the like and azure seeded or and slipped vert.

Crest: That for the regiments and separate battalions of the Army Reserve: On a wreath of the colors, argent and celeste, the Lexington Minuteman proper. The statue of the Minuteman, Capt. John Parker (H. H. Kitson, sculptor), stands on the Common in Lexington, Massachusetts.

Motto: VIGILANCE AND STRENGTH.

Symbolism: Oriental blue and silver gray are the colors traditionally associated with military intelligence. The griffin combines the keen eyesight and mobility of the eagle with the courage and prowess of the lion. He has acute hearing and is alert and watchful; he also epitomizes the unit's motto. The shaft of the key consists of a lightning bolt to highlight the electronic nature of the unit's mission; the bow is formed by a heraldic rose, adapted from the military intelligence branch insignia, and referring to the sub rosa functions of the unit. The key, used both to secure and unlock, underscores military intelligence as essential to total preparedness.

DISTINCTIVE UNIT INSIGNIA

The distinctive unit insignia is the shield and motto of the coat of arms.

LINEAGE AND HONORS

AR
(inactive)

LINEAGE

Constituted 16 September 1987 in the Army Reserve as the 126th Military Intelligence Battalion and activated with Headquarters at East Windsor, Connecticut. Inactivated 15 September 1993 at East Windsor, Connecticut.

CAMPAIGN PARTICIPATION CREDIT

None.

DECORATIONS

None.

128th MILITARY INTELLIGENCE BATTALION

HERALDIC ITEMS

COAT OF ARMS

Shield: Azure, a demi-griffin grasping a key, the wards upward and outward forming a keystone or; on a chief checky argent and sable, a sword and lightning flash saltirewise of the second.

Crest: That for the regiments and separate battalions of the Army Reserve: On a wreath of the colors, or and azure, the Lexington Minuteman proper. The statue of the Minuteman, Capt. John Parker (H. H. Kitson, sculptor), stands on the Common in Lexington, Massachusetts.

Motto: KEYSTONE TO VICTORY.

Symbolism: Oriental blue is one of the colors associated with the military intelligence branch. The demi-griffin stands for courage, intelligence, and vigilance and holds a key as the symbol of secrecy and security. The wards of the key form a keystone recalling the battalion's motto, its home state of Pennsylvania, and the unit's affiliation with the 28th Infantry Division. The checky chief, recalling the insignia of the 99th United States Army Reserve Command, suggests strategy, while its colors, black and white, refer to night and day operations. The sword represents military preparedness; the lightning flash suggests speed and electronic capabilities. Gold stands for excellence.

DISTINCTIVE UNIT INSIGNIA

The distinctive unit insignia is a modification of the shield and motto of the coat of arms.

LINEAGE AND HONORS

AR
(active)

LINEAGE

Constituted 18 September 1987 in the Army Reserve as the 128th Military Intelligence Battalion and activated with Headquarters at Allison Park, Pennsylvania.

CAMPAIGN PARTICIPATION CREDIT

None.

DECORATIONS

None.

134th MILITARY INTELLIGENCE BATTALION

HERALDIC ITEMS

COAT OF ARMS

Shield: Or, a griffin's head erased sable grasping in his beak a light-ning bolt gules, a bordure quarterly azure and argent.

Crest: That for the regiments and separate battalions of the Army Reserve: On a wreath of the colors, or and sable, the Lexington Minuteman proper. The statue of the Minuteman, Capt. John Parker (H. H. Kitson, sculptor), stands on the Common in Lexington, Massachusetts.

Motto: GATHER INTERPRET INFORM.

Symbolism: Oriental blue and silver gray are the colors traditionally associated with military intelligence units. Blue conveys loyalty; red is indicative of action, bravery, and courage. Gold reflects excellence, achievement, and high ideals. The griffin combines the strength and courage of a lion with the vigilance and awareness of an eagle, reflecting the mission of the organization. The lightning bolt alludes to the speed and accuracy with which the unit's mission is carried out and recalls its motto.

DISTINCTIVE UNIT INSIGNIA

The distinctive unit insignia is the shield and motto of the coat of arms.

LINEAGE AND HONORS

AR
(active)

LINEAGE

Constituted 10 February 1991 in the Army Reserve as the 134th Military Intelligence Battalion. Activated 16 September 1992 with Headquarters at Eagan, Minnesota. Location of Headquarters changed 30 June 1994 to Fort Snelling, Minnesota.

CAMPAIGN PARTICIPATION CREDIT

None.

DECORATIONS

None.

135th MILITARY INTELLIGENCE BATTALION

HERALDIC ITEMS

COAT OF ARMS

Shield: Azure a lightning flash issuant from dexter chief bendwise or, overall a fess argent bearing a bar invected sable.

Crest: That for the regiments and separate battalions of the Army Reserve: On a wreath of the colors, or and azure, the Lexington Minuteman proper. The statue of the Minuteman, Capt. John Parker (H. H. Kitson, sculptor), stands on the Common in Lexington, Massachusetts.

Motto: PIERCING THE FOG OF WAR.

Symbolism: The colors oriental blue and silver gray are traditionally associated with military intelligence units. The lightning flash is symbolic of speed in accumulating accurate information necessary to achieve total military preparedness. The stylized clouds allude to the unit's capabilities and goals to strive twenty-four hours a day to pierce enemy intelligence lines effectively and provide the information necessary for total preparedness.

DISTINCTIVE UNIT INSIGNIA

The distinctive unit insignia is the shield and motto of the coat of arms.

LINEAGE AND HONORS

AR
(active)

LINEAGE

Constituted 16 September 1988 in the Army Reserve as the 135th Military Intelligence Battalion and activated with Headquarters at Lenexa, Kansas. Location of Headquarters changed 1 April 1993 to Olathe, Kansas.

CAMPAIGN PARTICIPATION CREDIT

None.

DECORATIONS

None.

138th MILITARY INTELLIGENCE BATTALION

HERALDIC ITEMS

COAT OF ARMS

Shield: Per saltire sable and azure on a saltire argent a key and lightning flash saltirewise of the second.

Crest: That for the regiments and separate battalions of the Army Reserve: On a wreath of the colors, argent and azure, the Lexington Minuteman proper. The statue of the Minuteman, Capt. John Parker (H. H. Kitson, sculptor), stands on the Common in Lexington, Massachusetts.

Motto: FORTIOR EX VIGILIS (STRONGER AFTER VIGILANCE).

Symbolism: Oriental blue is one of the colors of the military intelligence branch. The color black represents secrecy and constancy. The saltire alludes to the joint functions of intelligence and security. The blue key is for guardianship, and the lightning flash is for electronic communications.

DISTINCTIVE UNIT INSIGNIA

The distinctive unit insignia is the shield and motto of the coat of arms.

LINEAGE AND HONORS

AR
(active)

LINEAGE

Constituted 12 March 1956 in the Army Reserve as the 314th Communication Reconnaissance Battalion; Headquarters and Headquarters Company concurrently activated at Chicago, Illinois. Redesignated 24 May–31 October 1956 as the 314th Army Security Agency Battalion. (Organic elements activated 27 August–1 November 1956.) Inactivated 21 June 1959 at Chicago, Illinois. Activated 1 October 1962 with Headquarters at Chicago, Illinois. Battalion broken up 15 August 1966 and its elements reorganized and redesignated as follows: Headquarters and Headquarters Company as Headquarters and Headquarters Company, 314th Army Security Agency Battalion; Company A as the 522d Army Security Agency Company (see ANNEX 1); Companies B and C as the 523d and 524th Army Security Agency Companies (hereafter separate lineages); Company D as the 525th Army Security Agency Company (see ANNEX 2). Location of Headquarters and Headquarters Company changed 31 March 1982 to Rosemont, Illinois.

Headquarters and Headquarters Company, 314th Army Security Agency Battalion, reorganized and redesignated 16 November 1983 as Headquarters,

Headquarters and Operations Company, 138th Military Intelligence Battalion (522d Army Security Agency Company [see ANNEX 1] and 525th Army Security Agency Company [see ANNEX 2] concurrently consolidated to form Company A; 910th Military Intelligence Company [see ANNEX 3], 121st Military Intelligence Detachment [see ANNEX 4], and 232d Military Intelligence Detachment [see ANNEX 5] consolidated to form Company B).

ANNEX 1

Constituted 12 March 1956 in the Army Reserve as Company A, 314th Communication Reconnaissance Battalion. Redesignated 19 July 1956 as Company A, 314th Army Security Agency Battalion. Activated 27 August 1956 at Chicago, Illinois. Location changed 1 June 1957 to Evanston, Illinois. Inactivated 21 June 1959 at Evanston, Illinois. Activated 1 October 1962 at Evanston, Illinois. Location changed 1 March 1963 to Chicago, Illinois. Reorganized and redesignated 15 August 1966 as the 522d Army Security Agency Company.

ANNEX 2

Constituted 23 August 1962 in the Army Reserve as Company D, 314th Army Security Agency Battalion. Activated 1 October 1962 at Milwaukee, Wisconsin. Reorganized and redesignated 15 August 1966 as the 525th Army Security Agency Company. Inactivated 31 January 1968 at Milwaukee, Wisconsin. Activated 1 February 1974 at Chicago, Illinois. Location changed 31 March 1982 to Rosemont, Illinois.

ANNEX 3

Constituted 28 July 1945 in the Army of the United States as the 536th Counter Intelligence Corps Detachment. Activated 10 August 1945 in France. Inactivated 23 February 1946 in France. Redesignated 4 September 1947 as the 910th Counter Intelligence Corps Detachment and allotted to the Organized Reserves. Activated 1 October 1947 at Chicago, Illinois. (Organized Reserves redesignated 25 March 1948 as the Organized Reserve Corps; redesignated 9 July 1952 as the Army Reserve.) Inactivated 4 December 1950 at Chicago, Illinois. Redesignated 19 May 1959 as the 910th Military Intelligence Detachment. Activated 1 June 1959 at Chicago, Illinois. Reorganized and redesignated 1 March 1972 as the 910th Military Intelligence Company. Location changed 24 February 1980 to Arlington Heights, Illinois.

ANNEX 4

Constituted 3 August 1945 in the Army of the United States as the 1020th Counter Intelligence Corps Detachment. Activated 10 August 1945 at Fort George G. Meade, Maryland. Inactivated 3 December 1945 at Camp Stoneman, California. Redesignated 16 November 1948 as the 121st Counter Intelligence Corps Detachment and allotted to the Organized Reserve Corps. Activated 31

December 1948 at Chicago, Illinois. (Organized Reserve Corps redesignated 9 July 1952 as the Army Reserve.) Inactivated 25 June 1953 at Chicago, Illinois. Redesignated 19 May 1959 as the 121st Military Intelligence Detachment. Activated 1 June 1959 at Chicago, Illinois. Location changed 24 February 1980 to Arlington Heights, Illinois.

ANNEX 5

Constituted 21 June 1944 in the Army of the United States as the 222d Counter Intelligence Corps Detachment. Activated 1 July 1944 at Camp Campbell, Kentucky. Inactivated 1 October 1945 in Czechoslovakia. Redesignated 5 June 1947 as the 232d Counter Intelligence Corps Detachment and allotted to the Organized Reserves. Activated 17 June 1947 at New York, New York. (Organized Reserves redesignated 25 March 1948 as the Organized Reserve Corps; redesignated 9 July 1952 as the Army Reserve.) Inactivated 10 November 1948 at New York, New York. Activated 18 January 1949 at Chicago, Illinois. Inactivated 4 December 1950 at Chicago, Illinois. Redesignated 5 November 1962 as the 232d Military Intelligence Detachment. Activated 11 February 1963 at Chicago, Illinois. Location changed 24 February 1980 to Arlington Heights, Illinois.

CAMPAIGN PARTICIPATION CREDIT

Company B entitled to:
> World War II–EAME
>> Rhineland
>> Ardennes-Alsace
>> Central Europe

DECORATIONS

None.

140th MILITARY INTELLIGENCE BATTALION

HERALDIC ITEMS

COAT OF ARMS

Shield: Azure within an orle argent, in base a pyramid of the like and in chief a sun in splendor issuing to base five lightning flashes or and charged with a globe of the like gridlined of the first.

Crest: That for the regiments and separate battalions of the Army Reserve: On a wreath of the colors, argent and azure, the Lexington Minuteman proper. The statue of the Minuteman, Capt. John Parker (H. H. Kitson, sculptor), stands on the Common in Lexington, Massachusetts.

Motto: SEMPER VIGIL (ALWAYS WATCHFUL).

Symbolism: Oriental blue and silver gray (white) are the colors associated with military intelligence. The sun represents the Greek god Helios, who, according to mythology, could bring all secrets to light; surrounding a globe, it represents the unit's worldwide military intelligence mission. The lightning flashes suggest electronic warfare and communication capabilities. The sun and lightning flashes are gold and allude to California, the "Golden State," the unit's home area. The pyramid personifies longevity and strength.

DISTINCTIVE UNIT INSIGNIA

The distinctive unit insignia is the shield and motto of the coat of arms.

LINEAGE AND HONORS

AR
(active)

LINEAGE

Constituted 16 July 1986 in the Army Reserve as the 140th Military Intelligence Battalion and activated with Headquarters at Bell, California.

CAMPAIGN PARTICIPATION CREDIT

None.

DECORATIONS

None.

141st MILITARY INTELLIGENCE BATTALION

HERALDIC ITEMS

COAT OF ARMS

Shield: Azure a compass rose or charged with a sword sable, grip gules surmounted by a globe argent, gridlined or bearing a lamp of knowledge of the like enflamed gules.

Crest: That for the regiments and separate battalions of the Utah Army National Guard: On a wreath of the colors, or and azure, a beehive beset with seven bees all proper.

Motto: STRENGTH THROUGH KNOWLEDGE.

Symbolism: Oriental blue and silver gray are the colors traditionally associated with military intelligence. The shield represents the unit's constant protection of the country, while the globe symbolizes its worldwide mission. The gold lamp of knowledge reflects the unit's efforts to gain knowledge to be ready and prepared to keep world peace. The black sword exemplifies its vigilance, loyalty, and readiness to defend freedom, liberty, and country. The rays of light, adapted from the military intelligence emblem, allude to a compass and symbolize the unit's readiness to respond wherever needed.

DISTINCTIVE UNIT INSIGNIA

The distinctive unit insignia is a modification of the shield and motto of the coat of arms.

LINEAGE AND HONORS

ARNG
(Utah)

LINEAGE

Organized from new and existing units and federally recognized 8 October 1988 in the Utah Army National Guard as the 141st Military Intelligence Battalion with Headquarters at Draper. Location of Headquarters changed 16 February 1995 to Provo.

Home Area: Statewide.

CAMPAIGN PARTICIPATION CREDIT

None.

DECORATIONS

None.

142d MILITARY INTELLIGENCE BATTALION

HERALDIC ITEMS

COAT OF ARMS

Shield: Celeste, a globe enhanced azure, gridlined argent above a wreath of four sego lilies proper overall a dagger palewise argent.

Crest: That for the regiments and separate battalions of the Utah Army National Guard: On a wreath of the colors, argent and azure, a beehive beset with seven bees all proper.

Motto: INTO ALL THE WORLD.

Symbolism: Oriental blue and silver gray are the colors traditionally associated with military intelligence units. The dagger symbolizes military preparedness and the globe and motto represent the worldwide capabilities and responsibilities of the unit. The sego lilies are symbols associated with Utah and reflect the unit's location in that state.

DISTINCTIVE UNIT INSIGNIA

The distinctive unit insignia consists of elements of the shield and crest of the coat of arms and incorporates the motto.

LINEAGE AND HONORS

LINEAGE

Organized and federally recognized 12 February 1960 in the Utah Army National Guard at Fort Douglas as the 142d Military Intelligence Linguist Company. Reorganized 15 May 1964 as a Table of Distribution unit. Location changed 1 December 1971 to Salt Lake City.

Reorganized and redesignated 1 April 1980 as Headquarters and Headquarters Company, 142d Military Intelligence Battalion (organic elements concurrently organized and federally recognized). Location of Headquarters changed 15 August 1982 to Fort Douglas; changed 1 January 1988 to Draper. Battalion reorganized 1 April 1988 as a Table of Organization and Equipment unit. (Company A ordered into active federal service 3 January 1991 at Bountiful; released from active federal service 2 April 1991 and reverted to state control.) Location of Headquarters changed 1 October 1995 to Salt Lake City.

Home Area: Northern Utah.

CAMPAIGN PARTICIPATION CREDIT

Company A entitled to:

Southwest Asia
    Liberation and Defense of Kuwait

DECORATIONS

None.

147th MILITARY INTELLIGENCE BATTALION

HERALDIC ITEMS

COAT OF ARMS

Shield: Checky argent and sable, on a pile argent a Viking helmet of the second detailed or, lined gules, emitting a lightning flash to base azure.

Crest: That for the regiments and separate battalions of the Army Reserve: On a wreath of the colors, argent and sable, the Lexington Minuteman proper. The statue of the Minuteman, Capt. John Parker (H. H. Kitson, sculptor), stands on the Common in Lexington, Massachusetts.

Motto: FUROR FULMINIS (FURY OF LIGHTNING).

Symbolism: Oriental blue and silver gray are the colors traditionally associated with military intelligence units. The pile reflects accuracy and the ability to pinpoint information. The blue lightning bolt emphasizes that ability while symbolizing speed and electronic warfare. The checky background alludes to strategy. The Viking helmet connotes protection and preparedness. It also signifies the unit's affiliation with the 47th Infantry (Viking) Division.

DISTINCTIVE UNIT INSIGNIA

The distinctive unit insignia is an adaptation of the shield and motto of the coat of arms.

LINEAGE AND HONORS

AR
(inactive)

LINEAGE

Constituted 18 September 1987 in the Army Reserve as the 147th Military Intelligence Battalion and activated with Headquarters at Fort Snelling, Minnesota. Location of Headquarters changed 1 July 1989 to Eagan, Minnesota. Inactivated 15 September 1992 at Eagan, Minnesota.

CAMPAIGN PARTICIPATION CREDIT

None.

DECORATIONS

None.

163d MILITARY INTELLIGENCE BATTALION
(The Blue Watch)

HERALDIC ITEMS

COAT OF ARMS

Shield: Azure on a bend checky argent and sable, overall a Philippine sun charged with a Korean taeguk in the colors of the Republic of Korea, scarlet and blue.

Crest: On a wreath of the colors, argent and azure, a trident argent interlaced with two anchors in saltire or.

Motto: KNOWLEDGE IS POWER.

Symbolism: The sun alludes to service in the Philippines during World War II and to the Philippine Presidential Unit Citation. The taeguk symbolizes the Republic of Korea Presidential Unit Citation and the unit's ten campaigns in the Korean War. The black and white checky alludes to the intelligence functions of the organization. Oriental blue and silver gray are the colors used by intelligence units.

The two crossed anchors allude to the two Presidential Unit Citations (Navy) and the trident refers to the Navy Unit Commendation.

DISTINCTIVE UNIT INSIGNIA

The distinctive unit insignia consists of elements of the shield, crest, and motto of the coat of arms.

LINEAGE AND HONORS

RA
(active)

LINEAGE

Constituted 5 April 1945 in the Army of the United States as the 163d Language Detachment. Activated 23 April 1945 in the Philippine Islands. Reorganized and redesignated 25 September 1949 as the 163d Military Intelligence Service Detachment. Allotted 19 December 1950 to the Regular Army. Reorganized and redesignated 1 September 1952 as the 163d Military Intelligence Service Platoon. Reorganized and redesignated 28 March 1954 as the 163d Military Intelligence Platoon. Inactivated 15 November 1954 in Korea. Activated 26 December 1955 in Italy.

Reorganized and redesignated 20 September 1957 as the 163d Military Intelligence Battalion. Inactivated 25 April 1964 in Italy. Redesignated 1 October 1969 as Headquarters and Headquarters Company, 163d Military Intelligence Battalion, and activated at Fort Hood, Texas (Company A concurrently constituted and activated). (Company A reorganized and redesignated 21 April 1978 as Company B; 529th Military Intelligence Company [see ANNEX] concurrently reorganized and redesignated as Company A.)

ANNEX

Constituted 14 July 1945 in the Army of the United States as the 255th Interrogation Prisoner of War Team and activated in Germany. Inactivated 30 November 1946 in Germany. Redesignated 1 October 1948 as the 529th Interrogation Team and allotted to the Regular Army. Activated 15 October 1948 at Fort Riley, Kansas. Inactivated 10 February 1949 at Fort Riley, Kansas. Redesignated 17 March 1965 as the 529th Military Intelligence Company. Activated 19 March 1965 at Fort Hood, Texas.

CAMPAIGN PARTICIPATION CREDIT

World War II
>   Luzon
Korean War
>   UN Defensive
>   UN Offensive
>   CCF Intervention
>   First UN Counteroffensive
>   CCF Spring Offensive
>   UN Summer-Fall Offensive
>   Second Korean Winter
>   Korea, Summer-Fall 1952
>   Third Korean Winter
>   Korea, Summer 1953

DECORATIONS

Presidential Unit Citation (Navy), Streamer embroidered INCHON (163d Military Intelligence Service Detachment cited; DA GO 63, 1952)

Presidential Unit Citation (Navy), Streamer embroidered HWACHON RESERVOIR (163d Military Intelligence Service Detachment cited; DA GO 38, 1957)

Navy Unit Commendation, Streamer embroidered PANMUNJOM (163d Military Intelligence Service Platoon cited; DA GO 38, 1957)

Philippine Presidential Unit Citation, Streamer embroidered 17 OCTOBER 1944 TO 4 JULY 1945 (163d Language Detachment cited; DA GO 47, 1950)

Republic of Korea Presidential Unit Citation, Streamer embroidered KOREA (163d Military Intelligence Service Platoon cited; DA GO 10, 1954)

165th MILITARY INTELLIGENCE BATTALION

HERALDIC ITEMS

COAT OF ARMS

Shield: Sable, a torch azure issuing rays from an intertwined continuous ribbon argent.

Crest: None approved.

Motto: QUALITY PRIDE SUCCESS.

Symbolism: Oriental blue is the primary color associated with military intelligence organizations. The torch is symbolic of the illumination
provided by the collection and dissemination of intelligence
data. The black background suggests secrecy and stealth. The
ribbon-like symbol, in place of a flame, folds back on itself and
is representative of the counterintelligence mission.

DISTINCTIVE UNIT INSIGNIA

The distinctive unit insignia consists of elements of the shield and motto of
the coat of arms.

LINEAGE AND HONORS

RA
(active)

LINEAGE

Constituted 27 September 1951 in the Regular Army as the 165th Military
Intelligence Service Detachment. Activated 18 October 1951 in Japan.
Reorganized and redesignated 1 September 1952 as the 165th Military
Intelligence Service Company. Reorganized and redesignated 28 March 1954 as
the 165th Military Intelligence Company. Inactivated 25 January 1958 at Fort
Bragg, North Carolina. Activated 1 June 1962 in Germany.

Reorganized and redesignated 1 July 1972 as Headquarters and Headquarters
Company, 165th Military Intelligence Battalion. Inactivated 1 July 1983 in
Germany. Redesignated 16 April 1984 as Headquarters, Headquarters and Service
Company, 165th Military Intelligence Battalion, and activated in Germany
(organic elements concurrently constituted and activated).

CAMPAIGN PARTICIPATION CREDIT

None.

DECORATIONS

None.

201st MILITARY INTELLIGENCE BATTALION

HERALDIC ITEMS

COAT OF ARMS

Shield: Argent, between in chief a terrestrial globe azure gridlined of the field and in base a helm sable lined gules upon a laurel wreath proper, a sword and lightning flash saltirewise of the fourth.

Crest: None approved.

Motto: ACCURATE FAST ALL SOURCE.

Symbolism: Oriental blue and silver gray are the colors associated with military intelligence. The helmet is adapted from the device of the 513th Military Intelligence Group, reflecting the unit's original assignment. The globe refers to the worldwide scope of the unit's mission and alludes to the "all source" emphasis of the motto. The lightning flash and sword symbolize speed and accuracy of communications. The laurel wreath denotes achievement. Black stands for strength and stability.

DISTINCTIVE UNIT INSIGNIA

The distinctive unit insignia consists of elements of the coat of arms.

Lineage and Honors

Lineage

Constituted 2 October 1982 in the Regular Army as Headquarters and Headquarters Company, 201st Military Intelligence Battalion, and activated at Fort Monmouth, New Jersey. (Organic elements constituted and activated 16 July 1987 at Vint Hill Farms Station, Virginia.)

Campaign Participation Credit

Southwest Asia
> Defense of Saudi Arabia
> Liberation and Defense of Kuwait
> Cease-Fire

Decorations

Meritorious Unit Commendation (Army), Streamer embroidered SOUTHWEST ASIA (201st Military Intelligence Battalion cited; DA GO 14, 1997)

Army Superior Unit Award, Streamer embroidered 1993 (201st Military Intelligence Battalion cited; DA GO 14, 1997)

202d MILITARY INTELLIGENCE BATTALION

HERALDIC ITEMS

COAT OF ARMS

Shield: Celeste, a lightning bolt or and torch gules fimbriated argent in saltire overall a dragon's head of the last, on a chief checky argent and sable a helm affronté garnished sable.

Crest: None approved.

Motto: CONLIGE ET PROFICE (COLLECT AND EXPLOIT).

Symbolism: Oriental blue and silver gray are the colors traditionally associated with military intelligence units. The helmet is adapted from the device of the 513th Military Intelligence Group and reflects the unit's original assignment. The helmet on the checky background symbolizes counterintelligence activities. The lightning flash denotes speed and electronic warfare. The torch symbolizes truth and alludes to interrogation. The dragon, a mythical guardian of treasure, symbolizes security and strength.

DISTINCTIVE UNIT INSIGNIA

The distinctive unit insignia consists of elements of the coat of arms.

LINEAGE AND HONORS

RA
(active)

LINEAGE

Constituted 2 October 1982 in the Regular Army as the 202d Military Intelligence Battalion and activated at Fort Monmouth, New Jersey.

CAMPAIGN PARTICIPATION CREDIT

Southwest Asia
  Defense of Saudi Arabia
  Liberation and Defense of Kuwait
  Cease-Fire

DECORATIONS

Meritorious Unit Commendation (Army), Streamer embroidered SOUTHWEST ASIA (202d Military Intelligence Battalion cited; DA GO 27, 1994, as amended by DA GO 14, 1997)

Army Superior Unit Award, Streamer embroidered 1992–1993 (DA GO 1, 1996)

203d MILITARY INTELLIGENCE BATTALION

HERALDIC ITEMS

DISTINCTIVE UNIT INSIGNIA

Description: A silver color metal and enamel device consisting of a silver gear bearing a black helmet with silver details, face forward, all centered upon a blue disc with silver grid lines encircled by a silver scroll inscribed TECHNICIANS FOR VICTORY in red letters and in base two sprigs of green laurel.

Symbolism: Oriental blue and silver gray are the colors traditionally associated with military intelligence units. The gridlined sphere represents the unit's worldwide mission and the gear refers to the technical aspect of its responsibilities. The helmet is adapted from the device of the 513th Military Intelligence Group, alluding to the unit's original assignment and symbolizing covert vigilance and preparedness. The laurel, a traditional symbol of achievement, exemplifies the motto.

FLAG DEVICE

The flag device is the same as the distinctive unit insignia.

LINEAGE AND HONORS

RA
(inactive)

LINEAGE

Constituted 2 October 1982 in the Regular Army as Headquarters and Headquarters Company, 203d Military Intelligence Battalion, and activated at Aberdeen Proving Ground, Maryland. (Organic elements constituted 16 October 1988; Company A concurrently activated at at Fort Monmouth, New Jersey.) Battalion inactivated 16 October 1989 at Fort Monmouth, New Jersey.

CAMPAIGN PARTICIPATION CREDIT

None.

DECORATIONS

None.

204th MILITARY INTELLIGENCE BATTALION

HERALDIC ITEMS

COAT OF ARMS

Shield: Azure, a double-warded key palewise with an arched lightning flash on either side connecting the ward and bow and each flash enclosing a fleur-de-lis argent and on the bow an ermine spot.

Crest: On a wreath of the colors, argent and azure, a dragon sejant with wings elevated and addorsed gules armed and langued of the second spattered with seventeen mullets and grasping in his dexter claw three lightning flashes or.

Motto: SILENTLY WE DEFEND.

Symbolism: Oriental blue is one of the colors associated with military intelligence, and a key is emblematic of authority and security. The double ward and flashes represent the unit's concern for both overt and covert security communications. The flashes also denote celerity in operation procedures and allude to the unit's signal lineage. Initially designated as the 3118th Signal Service Battalion, the unit's participation in the Northern France, Rhineland, and Central Europe campaigns during World War II is represented by the fleurs-de-lis and ermine spot. The design has been adapted from the badge of a predecessor unit, the 502d Army Security Agency Battalion.

The dragon, a mythical beast renowned as a vigilant guardian and defender, symbolizes the heritage, mission, and ideals of the unit. The red dragon alludes to the Meritorious Unit Commendation (Army) and service of elements of the battalion in Vietnam. Red emphasizes the unit's courage, determination, and valor. The stars denote military preparedness and excellence in endeavors. Service during World War II in Northern France, Rhineland, and Central Europe is represented by the three lightning flashes.

DISTINCTIVE UNIT INSIGNIA

The distinctive unit insignia is an adaptation of the shield and motto of the coat of arms.

LINEAGE AND HONORS

RA
(inactive)

LINEAGE

Constituted 4 November 1943 in the Army of the United States as the 3118th Signal Service Battalion. Activated 15 November 1943 at Camp Crowder, Missouri. Reorganized and redesignated 13 April 1945 as the 3118th Signal Service Group. Reorganized and redesignated 14 November 1945 as the 3118th Signal Service Battalion. Headquarters reorganized and redesignated 3 April 1946 as Headquarters and Headquarters Detachment, 3118th Signal Service Group (remainder of battalion concurrently disbanded). Inactivated 20 June 1947 in Germany.

Converted and redesignated 25 April 1951 as Headquarters and Headquarters Company, 502d Communication Reconnaissance Group, and allotted to the Regular Army. Activated 15 May 1951 at Fort Devens, Massachusetts. Redesignated 1 July 1956 as Headquarters and Headquarters Company, 502d Army Security Agency Group. Inactivated 15 October 1957 in Germany. Activated 3 May 1971 in Germany. Reorganized and redesignated 1 October 1981 as Headquarters and Headquarters Company, 502d Army Security Agency Battalion.

Reorganized and redesignated 16 October 1986 as Headquarters and Headquarters Company, 204th Military Intelligence Battalion (409th Army Security Agency Company [see ANNEX 1] concurrently reorganized and redesignated as Company A; 328th Army Security Agency Company [see ANNEX 2] reorganized and redesignated as Company D). Battalion inactivated 16 July 1995 in Germany.

ANNEX 1

Constituted 1 April 1966 in the Regular Army as the 409th Army Security Agency Detachment. Activated 8 April 1966 at Fort George G. Meade, Maryland. Inactivated 6 March 1971 in Vietnam. Redesignated 1 July 1974 as the 409th Army Security Agency Company and activated in Germany.

ANNEX 2

Organized 1 April 1944 in England as the 3250th Signal Service Company. (Constituted 12 April 1944 in the Army of the United States.) Inactivated 13 March 1946 in France.

Converted and redesignated 25 April 1951 as the 328th Communication Reconnaissance Company and allotted to the Regular Army. Activated 15 May 1951 at Fort Devens, Massachusetts. Redesignated 1 July 1956 as the 328th Army Security Agency Company. Inactivated 15 October 1957 in Germany. Activated 20 November 1968 in Vietnam. Inactivated 30 June 1972 in Vietnam. Activated 1 July 1974 in Germany.

CAMPAIGN PARTICIPATION CREDIT

World War II
  Northern France
  Rhineland
  Central Europe

Company A additionally entitled to:

Vietnam
  Counteroffensive, Phase II
  Counteroffensive, Phase III
  Tet Counteroffensive
  Counteroffensive, Phase IV
  Counteroffensive, Phase V
  Counteroffensive, Phase VI
  Tet 69/Counteroffensive
  Summer-Fall 1969
  Winter-Spring 1970
  Sanctuary Counteroffensive
  Counteroffensive, Phase VII
Southwest Asia
  Defense of Saudi Arabia
  Liberation and Defense of Kuwait
  Cease-Fire

Company D additionally entitled to:

World War II–EAME
  Normandy (with arrowhead)
  Ardennes-Alsace
Vietnam
  Counteroffensive, Phase VI
  Tet 69/Counteroffensive
  Summer-Fall 1969
  Winter-Spring 1970
  Sanctuary Counteroffensive
  Counteroffensive, Phase VII
  Consolidation I
  Consolidation II
  Cease-Fire

DECORATIONS

Meritorious Unit Commendation (Army), Streamer embroidered EUROPEAN THEATER (3118th Signal Service Group cited; GO 34, United States Forces, European Theater, 11 February 1946)

Army Superior Unit Award, Streamer embroidered 1991–1992 (204th Military Intelligence Battalion cited; DA GO 12, 1994)

Company A additionally entitled to:

Valorous Unit Award, Streamer embroidered LONG BINH–BIEN HOA (409th Radio Research Detachment cited; DA GO 12, 1969, as amended by DA GO 28, 1969)

Meritorious Unit Commendation (Army), Streamer embroidered VIETNAM 1966–1967 (409th Radio Research Detachment cited; DA GO 17, 1968)

Meritorious Unit Commendation (Army), Streamer embroidered VIETNAM 1967–1968 (409th Radio Research Detachment cited; DA GO 28, 1969)

Meritorious Unit Commendation (Army), Streamer embroidered VIETNAM 1968–1969 (409th Radio Research Detachment cited; DA GO 51, 1971)

Meritorious Unit Commendation (Army), Streamer embroidered VIETNAM 1969–1970 (409th Radio Research Detachment cited; DA GO 43, 1972)

Republic of Vietnam Cross of Gallantry with Palm, Streamer embroidered VIETNAM 1966–1968 (409th Radio Research Unit cited; DA GO 60, 1969)

Republic of Vietnam Cross of Gallantry with Palm, Streamer embroidered VIETNAM 1969–1970 (409th Radio Research Detachment cited; DA GO 50, 1971)

Republic of Vietnam Cross of Gallantry with Palm, Streamer embroidered VIETNAM 1970 (409th Radio Research Detachment cited; DA GO 55, 1971)

Republic of Vietnam Cross of Gallantry with Palm, Streamer embroidered VIETNAM 1970–1971 (409th Radio Research Detachment cited; DA GO 6, 1974)

Republic of Vietnam Civil Action Honor Medal, First Class, Streamer embroidered VIETNAM 1969–1970 (409th Radio Research Detachment cited; DA GO 6, 1974)

Company D additionally entitled to:

Meritorious Unit Commendation (Army), Streamer embroidered VIETNAM 1968–1969 (328th Radio Research Company cited; DA GO 51, 1971)

Meritorious Unit Commendation (Army), Streamer embroidered VIETNAM 1969–1970 (328th Radio Research Company cited; DA GO 43, 1972)

Meritorious Unit Commendation (Army), Streamer embroidered VIETNAM 1971–1972 (328th Radio Research Company cited; DA GO 32, 1973)

Republic of Vietnam Cross of Gallantry with Palm, Streamer embroidered VIETNAM 1969–1970 (328th Radio Research Company cited; DA GO 42, 1972)

Republic of Vietnam Cross of Gallantry with Palm, Streamer embroidered VIETNAM 1970–1971 (328th Radio Research Company cited; DA GO 6, 1974)

Republic of Vietnam Cross of Gallantry with Palm, Streamer embroidered VIETNAM 1971 (328th Radio Research Company cited; DA GO 6, 1974)

205th MILITARY INTELLIGENCE BATTALION

HERALDIC ITEMS

COAT OF ARMS

Shield: Azure, on pale argent a torch sable enflamed gules superimposed by a sword argent hilt or grip garnished gules, between two quills palewise argent.

Crest: On a wreath of the colors, argent and azure, a lightning flash palewise gules rising from a wreath of palm proper, overall an oriental dragon passant or armed gules and garnished azure.

Motto: PACIFIC VIGILANCE.

Symbolism: Oriental blue and silver gray are the colors traditionally associated with military intelligence units. Blue conveys devotion and loyalty, red is indicative of courage and zeal, while white portrays integrity. Gold reflects excellence, achievement, and high ideals; black reflects covert capabilities. The quills symbolize the unit's analytical functions; the torch signifies guidance, leadership, and knowledge. The sword is symbolic of military preparedness.

The lightning flash indicates speed and accuracy and alludes to the battalion's heritage and association with the Signal Corps. It is red to indicate the Meritorious Unit Commendation (Army) received by the unit during World War II. The palm fronds stand for victory, while the oriental dragon personifies vigilance and preparedness. They suggest the Pacific area and reflect the unit's motto.

DISTINCTIVE UNIT INSIGNIA

The distinctive unit insignia is the shield and motto of the coat of arms.

LINEAGE AND HONORS

LINEAGE

Constituted 1 January 1939 in the Regular Army as the 2d Signal Service Company and activated with Headquarters at Fort Monmouth, New Jersey (organic elements concurrently organized from existing units). Redesignated 14 April 1942 as the 2d Signal Service Battalion. Headquarters, 2d Signal Service Battalion, disbanded 20 April 1946 at Arlington Hall Station, Virginia. (Organic elements disbanded 15 May 1950.)

Headquarters, 2d Signal Service Battalion, reconstituted 1 October 1991 in the Regular Army as Headquarters, 205th Military Intelligence Battalion. Redesignated 31 October 1992 as Headquarters, Headquarters and Service Company, 205th Military Intelligence Battalion, and activated at Fort Shafter, Hawaii (organic elements concurrently constituted and activated).

CAMPAIGN PARTICIPATION CREDIT

None.

DECORATIONS

Meritorious Unit Commendation (Army), Streamer embroidered ARLINGTON HALL STATION 1945 (9420th Technical Service Unit, Headquarters and Detachments, 2d Signal Service Battalion, cited; GO 2, Office of the Chief Signal Officer, Army Service Forces, 1 May 1945)

206th MILITARY INTELLIGENCE BATTALION

HERALDIC ITEMS

COAT OF ARMS

Shield: Per chevron enarched reversed sable and celeste, nine rays radiating from honor point argent; in base a lion's head erased argent charged with two bars gules.

Crest: None approved.

Motto: COLLECTION FOR DEFENSE.

Symbolism: The white concentric rays represent light or knowledge gathered to a central point; they refer to the battalion's mission of collecting strategic information. The white and scarlet lion on the blue background is taken from the coat of arms of Hesse in Germany, where the unit was activated. The head of the lion is used because it is a symbol of intelligence and reason. The color of the background, oriental blue, also refers to military intelligence.

DISTINCTIVE UNIT INSIGNIA

The distinctive unit insignia consists of elements of the coat of arms.

LINEAGE AND HONORS

RA
(inactive)

LINEAGE

Constituted 15 March 1968 in the Regular Army as the 18th Military Intelligence Battalion and activated in Germany. Reorganized and redesignated 16 October 1986 as Headquarters and Headquarters Company, 18th Military Intelligence Battalion. (Organic elements constituted 16 October 1992; Company A concurrently activated in Germany.) Battalion inactivated 16 July 1995 in Germany.

Redesignated 13 February 1996 as the 206th Military Intelligence Battalion.

CAMPAIGN PARTICIPATION CREDIT

None.

DECORATIONS

Army Superior Unit Award, Streamer embroidered 1988–1989 (18th Military Intelligence Battalion cited; DA GO 15, 1990)

Army Superior Unit Award, Streamer embroidered 1991–1992 (18th Military Intelligence Battalion cited; DA GO 12, 1994)

223d MILITARY INTELLIGENCE BATTALION

HERALDIC ITEMS

COAT OF ARMS

Shield: Argent, a lightning flash palewise gules and a double-warded key and sword saltirewise sable, overall a hurt gridlined argent.

Crest: That for the regiments and separate battalions of the California Army National Guard: On a wreath of the colors, argent and gules, the setting sun behind a grizzly bear passant on a grassy field all proper.

Motto: INSIGHT THROUGH INQUIRY.

Symbolism: Oriental blue is one of the colors traditionally associated with military intelligence units. The lightning flash denotes the unit's signal intelligence. The key is emblematic of knowledge, authority, and security. The black sword is symbolic of covert operations and military preparedness; the globe reflects the unit's worldwide scope.

DISTINCTIVE UNIT INSIGNIA

The distinctive unit insignia consists of elements of the shield and motto of the coat of arms.

LINEAGE AND HONORS

ARNG
(California)

LINEAGE

Organized and federally recognized 16 January 1992 in the California Army National Guard as the 223d Military Intelligence Battalion with Headquarters at Fort Funston.

Home Area: Statewide.

CAMPAIGN PARTICIPATION CREDIT

None.

DECORATIONS

None.

224th MILITARY INTELLIGENCE BATTALION

HERALDIC ITEMS

COAT OF ARMS

Shield: Quarterly azure and argent a griffin sejant or grasping two flashes saltirewise gules.

Crest: None approved.

Motto: VIGILANCE ABOVE.

Symbolism: Oriental blue and silver gray are the colors associated with the military intelligence branch. The crosswise arrangement of the background is a reference to the Republic of Vietnam Cross of Gallantry with Palm awarded to the unit for service in Vietnam. The griffin is a heraldic creature combining the strength and courage of a lion with the vigilance and awareness of an eagle; as such, it is well suited to represent the ideals and capabilities of an intelligence unit. Its wings refer to the airborne mission, and the flashes it grasps denote the electronic data collection mission of the unit.

DISTINCTIVE UNIT INSIGNIA

The distinctive unit insignia is the shield and motto of the coat of arms.

LINEAGE AND HONORS

RA
(active)

LINEAGE

Constituted 1 June 1966 in the Regular Army as Headquarters and Headquarters Detachment, 224th Aviation Battalion, and activated in Vietnam. Redesignated 1 December 1968 as Headquarters and Headquarters Company, 224th Aviation Battalion. Converted and redesignated 19 May 1971 as Headquarters and Headquarters Company, 224th Army Security Agency Battalion. Inactivated 6 March 1973 at Oakland, California.

Redesignated 1 June 1981 as Headquarters, Headquarters and Service Company, 224th Military Intelligence Battalion, and activated at Hunter Army Airfield, Georgia (172d Military Intelligence Detachment [see ANNEX 1] concurrently reorganized and redesignated as Company A; 144th Aviation Company [see ANNEX 2] converted and redesignated as Company B and activated).

ANNEX 1

Constituted 5 April 1945 in the Army of the United States as the 172d Language Detachment. Activated 23 April 1945 in the Philippine Islands. Inactivated 15 April 1946 in Japan. Redesignated 14 January 1955 as the 172d Military Intelligence Platoon and allotted to the Regular Army. Activated 7 March 1955 in Germany. Inactivated 25 June 1958 in Germany. Activated 15 July 1959 at Fort Devens, Massachusetts. Reorganized and redesignated 25 August 1961 as the 172d Military Intelligence Detachment. Inactivated 1 September 1963 in Germany. Activated 3 May 1965 at Fort Campbell, Kentucky. Inactivated 21 August 1972 at Fort Campbell, Kentucky. Activated 21 November 1977 at Fort Wainwright, Alaska.

ANNEX 2

Constituted 1 June 1966 in the Regular Army as the 144th Aviation Company and activated in Vietnam. Inactivated 30 September 1971 in Vietnam.

CAMPAIGN PARTICIPATION CREDIT

Vietnam

Counteroffensive
Counteroffensive, Phase II
Counteroffensive, Phase III
Tet Counteroffensive
Counteroffensive, Phase IV
Counteroffensive, Phase V
Counteroffensive, Phase VI
Tet 69/Counteroffensive
Summer-Fall 1969
Winter-Spring 1970
Sanctuary Counteroffensive
Counteroffensive, Phase VII
Consolidation I
Consolidation II
Cease-Fire

Company A additionally entitled to:

World War II–AP

Luzon

Vietnam

Defense

DECORATIONS

Meritorious Unit Commendation (Army), Streamer embroidered VIETNAM 1966–1967 (Headquarters and Headquarters Detachment, 224th Aviation Battalion, and 144th Aviation Company cited; DA GO 17, 1968, as amended by DA GO 1, 1969)

Meritorious Unit Commendation (Army), Streamer embroidered VIETNAM 1967–1969 (Headquarters and Headquarters Company, 224th Aviation Battalion, and 144th Aviation Company cited; DA GO 2, 1971)

Meritorious Unit Commendation (Army), Streamer embroidered VIETNAM 1971–1972 (224th Aviation Battalion and 144th Aviation Company cited; DA GO 32, 1973)

Army Superior Unit Award, Streamer embroidered 1987–1988 (224th Military Intelligence Battalion cited; DA GO 35, 1989)

Army Superior Unit Award, Streamer embroidered 1988–1990 (224th Military Intelligence Battalion cited; DA GO 2, 1991)

Army Superior Unit Award, Streamer embroidered 1992–1993 (224th Military Intelligence Battalion cited; DA GO 27, 1994)

Republic of Vietnam Cross of Gallantry with Palm, Streamer embroidered VIETNAM 1970–1971 (224th Aviation Battalion and 144th Aviation Company cited; DA GO 6, 1974)

Company A additionally entitled to:

Meritorious Unit Commendation (Army), Streamer embroidered VIETNAM 1965–1967 (172d Military Intelligence Detachment cited; DA GO 48, 1968)

Philippine Presidential Unit Citation, Streamer embroidered 17 OCTOBER 1944 TO 4 JULY 1945 (172d Language Detachment cited; DA GO 47, 1950)

Republic of Vietnam Cross of Gallantry with Palm, Streamer embroidered VIETNAM 1968–1970 (172d Military Intelligence Detachment cited; DA GO 51, 1971)

Republic of Vietnam Civil Action Honor Medal, First Class, Streamer embroidered VIETNAM 1969–1971(172d Military Intelligence Detachment cited; DA GO 5, 1973)

229th MILITARY INTELLIGENCE BATTALION

HERALDIC ITEMS

COAT OF ARMS

Shield: Argent, on a pale wavy azure two pallets wavy of the first between two griffin heads erased in fess addorsed of the second eyes and tongues gules.

Crest: None approved.

Motto: STRENGTH FROM INTELLIGENCE.

Symbolism: Oriental blue and silver gray are the colors traditionally associated with the military intelligence branch. The griffin, noted for keen eyesight, symbolizes surveillance. The two griffins back to back represent vigilance; they also suggest the unit's original two continent and two ocean area of operations. The wavy pale refers to the Panama Canal.

DISTINCTIVE UNIT INSIGNIA

The distinctive unit insignia is the shield and motto of the coat of arms.

LINEAGE AND HONORS

RA
(active)

LINEAGE

Constituted 1 April 1985 in the Regular Army as the 29th Military Intelligence Battalion and activated in Panama. Inactivated 17 October 1991 in Panama.

Redesignated 7 December 1995 as the 229th Military Intelligence Battalion. Headquarters transferred 15 March 1996 to the United States Army Training and Doctrine Command and activated at the Presidio of Monterey, California.

CAMPAIGN PARTICIPATION CREDIT

Armed Forces Expeditions
Panama

DECORATIONS

Army Superior Unit Award, Streamer embroidered 1988–1989 (29th Military Intelligence Battalion cited; DA GO 8, 1991)

260th MILITARY INTELLIGENCE BATTALION

HERALDIC ITEMS

COAT OF ARMS

Shield: Azure, a double-warded key palewise wards to base argent, between two sphinx heads addorsed or, overall a quill and a dagger saltirewise of the second.

Crest: That for the regiments and separate battalions of the Florida Army National Guard: On a wreath of the colors, argent and azure, an alligator statant proper.

Motto: INTELLIGENTIA ET VERITAS (INTELLIGENCE AND TRUTH).

Symbolism: Oriental blue and silver gray (white) are the colors traditionally associated with military intelligence. The key is emblematic of knowledge, authority, and security. The quill over the dagger underscores the pen as mightier than the sword. The sphinx heads, one facing in either direction, signify constant vigilance and eternal watchfulness.

DISTINCTIVE UNIT INSIGNIA

The distinctive unit insignia is the shield and motto of the coat of arms.

LINEAGE AND HONORS

ARNG
(Florida)

LINEAGE

Organized and federally recognized 27 August 1990 in the Florida Army National Guard as the 260th Military Intelligence Battalion with Headquarters at Miami.

Home Area: Southern Florida.

CAMPAIGN PARTICIPATION CREDIT

None.

DECORATIONS

None.

297th MILITARY INTELLIGENCE BATTALION

HERALDIC ITEMS

COAT OF ARMS

Shield: Per bend azure and sable, in dexter base a gauntlet argent grasping a lightning flash sword bendwise blade of the like, grip gules, pommel and quillon or.

Crest: None approved.

Motto: VANGUARD.

Symbolism: The colors oriental blue and silver gray are traditionally associated with military intelligence. The armored fist represents strength; the lightning flash denotes speed. The fist seizes the blade of the sword to indicate readiness and vigilance. Black denotes dependability and suggests covert capabilities. The fist, upraised and grasping the sword, suggests leadership, highlighting the unit's motto.

DISTINCTIVE UNIT INSIGNIA

The distinctive unit insignia is the shield and motto of the coat of arms.

LINEAGE AND HONORS

RA
(active)

LINEAGE

Constituted 21 November 1962 in the Army Reserve as the 297th Army Security Agency Company. Activated 1 March 1963 at Atlanta, Georgia. Reorganized and redesignated 15 April 1966 as Headquarters and Headquarters Company, 297th Army Security Agency Battalion. Inactivated 31 January 1968 at Atlanta, Georgia.

Redesignated 1 February 1990 as Headquarters and Headquarters Company, 297th Military Intelligence Battalion; concurrently withdrawn from the Army Reserve and allotted to the Regular Army. Redesignated 17 October 1991 as Headquarters, Headquarters and Service Company, 297th Military Intelligence Battalion, and activated at Fort Monmouth, New Jersey (organic elements concurrently constituted and activated).

CAMPAIGN PARTICIPATION CREDIT

None.

DECORATIONS

None.

301st MILITARY INTELLIGENCE BATTALION

HERALDIC ITEMS

COAT OF ARMS

Shield: Azure, a dagger and lightning flash dagger saltirewise, blades argent, hilts or and sable.

Crest: That for the regiments and separate battalions of the Army Reserve: On a wreath of the colors, argent and azure, the Lexington Minuteman proper. The statue of the Minuteman, Capt. John Parker (H. H. Kitson, sculptor), stands on the Common in Lexington, Massachusetts.

Motto: THE FORCE MULTIPLIER.

Symbolism: Oriental blue and silver gray are the colors associated with military intelligence. The crossed dagger and lightning flash dagger form an X, suggesting the unit's motto. They symbolize strength, danger, speed, and the precise application of electronic warfare and intelligence to defeat the enemy.

DISTINCTIVE UNIT INSIGNIA

The distinctive unit insignia is the shield and motto of the coat of arms.

LINEAGE AND HONORS

AR
(active)

LINEAGE

Constituted 6 June 1949 in the Organized Reserve Corps as Headquarters, 301st Military Intelligence Platoon. Activated 22 June 1949 at Austin, Texas.

Reorganized and redesignated 1 September 1950 as Headquarters, 301st Military Intelligence Battalion. (Organized Reserve Corps redesignated 9 July 1952 as the Army Reserve.) Inactivated 23 February 1953 at Austin, Texas. Redesignated 16 September 1988 as Headquarters, Headquarters and Service Company, 301st Military Intelligence Battalion, and activated at Pasadena, Texas (organic elements concurrently constituted and activated).

CAMPAIGN PARTICIPATION CREDIT

None.

DECORATIONS

None.

302d MILITARY INTELLIGENCE BATTALION

HERALDIC ITEMS

COAT OF ARMS

Shield: Per fess abased argent and azure, in chief a red fox's mask proper charged on the forehead with a billet fesswise sable, and in base a key palewise between two stylized lightning flashes of the first.

Crest: On a wreath of the colors, argent and azure, a fleur-de-lis barry of ten of the second and first, the outer petals serrated, the inner charged with a bayonet or point up, and on the crosspiece of the fleur-de-lis a bar couped tenné with two barrulets argent.

Motto: LOYALTY, VIGILANCE, PRIDE.

Symbolism: The colors, white and teal blue, are symbolic of the battalion's former status as an unassigned-to-branch unit. The battalion's war service as a signal unit is shown by the colors of the fox's mask and background, while the intelligence functions of the unit are represented by the black censor's stamp. The key is for the unit's first campaign (Normandy) in World War II and also alludes to signal and intelligence functions. The stylized lightning flashes symbolize radio reconnaissance.

The fleur-de-lis represents campaign participation in Europe. The outer petals of the fleur-de-lis, suggestive of electronic flashes, reflect the unit's service in communication reconnaissance. The bar on the crosspiece is divided into five segments representing participation in five campaigns in Europe during World War II. The bayonet suggests the Army's offensive spirit and reflects the unit's association with United States Army, Europe.

DISTINCTIVE UNIT INSIGNIA

The distinctive unit insignia is the shield and motto of the coat of arms.

Lineage and Honors

RA

Lineage   (active)

Organized 1 April 1944 in England as the 3252d Signal Service Company. (Constituted 12 April 1944 in the Army of the United States.) Inactivated 24 November 1945 at Camp Kilmer, New Jersey. Redesignated 6 May 1948 as the 533d Signal Service Company. Activated 20 June 1948 in Austria. Inactivated 1 April 1949 in Austria.

Converted and redesignated 13 October 1950 as Headquarters and Headquarters Detachment, 302d Communication Reconnaissance Battalion, and allotted to the Regular Army. Activated 20 October 1950 at Camp Pickett, Virginia. Reorganized and redesignated 25 June 1955 as Headquarters and Headquarters Company, 302d Communication Reconnaissance Battalion (Companies A and B constituted 19 May 1955; Company A activated 25 June 1955 in Germany). Redesignated 1 July 1956 as the 302d Army Security Agency Battalion. Inactivated 15 October 1957 in Germany. Headquarters and Headquarters Company activated 21 December 1975 in Germany (Companies A and B concurrently disbanded).

Headquarters and Headquarters Company, 302d Army Security Agency Battalion, reorganized and redesignated 16 April 1984 as Headquarters, Headquarters and Service Company, 302d Military Intelligence Battalion (331st Army Security Agency Company [see ANNEX 1] and 327th Army Security Agency Company [see ANNEX 2] concurrently reorganized and redesignated as Companies A and B).

ANNEX 1

Constituted 26 April 1942 in the Army of the United States as the 114th Signal Radio Intelligence Company. Activated 13 July 1942 at Camp Crowder, Missouri. Reorganized and redesignated 10 January 1946 as the 114th Signal Service Company.

Converted and redesignated 25 October 1951 as the 331st Communication Reconnaissance Company and allotted to the Regular Army. Reorganized and redesignated 25 June 1955 as Company A, 307th Communication Reconnaissance Battalion. Redesignated 1 July 1956 as Company A, 307th Army Security Agency Battalion. Inactivated 15 October 1957 in Germany. Redesignated 21 September 1978 as the 331st Army Security Agency Company and activated in Germany.

ANNEX 2

Constituted 4 November 1942 in the Army of the United States as the 111th Signal Radio Intelligence Company. Activated 30 November 1942 at Camp Crowder, Missouri. Reorganized and redesignated 1 September 1945 as the 111th Signal Service Company.

Converted and redesignated 25 October 1951 as the 327th Communication Reconnaissance Company and allotted to the Regular Army. Inactivated 15 August 1956 on Formosa. Redesignated 21 October 1976 as the 327th Army Security Agency Company and activated in Germany.

CAMPAIGN PARTICIPATION CREDIT

World War II
    Normandy
    Northern France
    Rhineland
    Ardennes-Alsace
    Central Europe

Company B additionally entitled to:

World War II–AP
    New Guinea
    Leyte
    Luzon

DECORATIONS

Company B entitled to:

Philippine Presidential Unit Citation, Streamer embroidered 17 OCTOBER 1944 TO 4 JULY 1945 (111th Signal Radio Intelligence Company cited; DA GO 47, 1950)

303d MILITARY INTELLIGENCE BATTALION

HERALDIC ITEMS

COAT OF ARMS

Shield: Or, three piles, one in chief and two conjoined in base azure bearing in chief an edelweiss argent seeded of the field and issuing from base two beacons of the last enflamed tenné and gold.

Crest: On a wreath of the colors, or and azure, in front of a stylized wreath of rice or, four flashes saltirewise gules.

Motto: PRIMI NOSCERE (FIRST TO KNOW).

Symbolism: Oriental blue and silver gray are the colors associated with military intelligence. The blue piles represent the mountains of Central Europe and Korea, where the battalion's predecessor units served. The edelweiss, a small white flower prized by European mountaineers, refers to the unit's service in Central Europe. The two beacons refer to Korea's ancient and effective system of communications, which was accomplished by means of beacon fires on mountain tops, and also refer to the battalion's two unit decorations for service in Korea.

The colors red and yellow are traditionally associated with Vietnam, as is the rice wreath, a symbol of excellence and achievement. The red flashes refer to the Meritorious Unit Commendations (Army) earned while serving in Vietnam and also represent accuracy and speed.

DISTINCTIVE UNIT INSIGNIA

The distinctive unit insignia is the shield and motto of the coat of arms.

LINEAGE AND HONORS

RA
(active)

LINEAGE

Constituted 22 September 1950 in the Regular Army as Headquarters and Headquarters Detachment, 303d Communication Reconnaissance Battalion. Activated 25 September 1950 at Arlington Hall Station, Virginia. Consolidated 17 July 1951 with the 540th Signal Service Company (see ANNEX 1) and consolidated unit designated as Headquarters and Headquarters Detachment, 303d Communication Reconnaissance Battalion. Inactivated 25 June 1955 in Korea. Redesignated 11 May 1962 as Headquarters and Headquarters Company, 303d Army Security Agency Battalion (organic elements concurrently constituted).

Battalion activated 15 June 1962 at Camp Wolters, Texas. (Companies A, B, and C reorganized and redesignated 15 October 1966 as the 372d, 373d, and 374th Army Security Agency Companies—hereafter separate lineages.)

Headquarters and Headquarters Company, 303d Army Security Agency Battalion, reorganized and redesignated 21 April 1978 as Headquarters and Headquarters Detachment, 303d Military Intelligence Battalion (376th Army Security Agency Company [see ANNEX 2] and 370th Army Security Agency Company [see ANNEX 3] concurrently reorganized and redesignated as Companies A and B).

ANNEX 1

Constituted 12 April 1944 in the Army of the United States as the 3253d Signal Service Company. Activated 25 April 1944 in England. Inactivated 25 January 1946 at Camp Kilmer, New Jersey. Redesignated 6 May 1948 as the 540th Signal Service Company. Activated 20 June 1948 in Austria. Inactivated 1 April 1949 in Austria.

ANNEX 2

Constituted 20 February 1968 in the Regular Army as the 376th Army Security Agency Company. Activated 1 April 1968 at Fort Bragg, North Carolina. Inactivated 30 June 1974 at Fort Bragg, North Carolina. Activated 1 July 1974 at Fort George G. Meade, Maryland.

ANNEX 3

Constituted 10 January 1967 in the Regular Army as the 370th Army Security Agency Company. Activated 1 March 1967 at Vint Hill Farms Station, Virginia.

CAMPAIGN PARTICIPATION CREDIT

World War II	Vietnam
Normandy	Counteroffensive
Northern France	Counteroffensive, Phase II
Rhineland	Counteroffensive, Phase III
Ardennes-Alsace	Tet Counteroffensive
Central Europe	Counteroffensive, Phase IV
Korean War	Counteroffensive, Phase V
CCF Intervention	Counteroffensive, Phase VI
First UN Counteroffensive	Tet 69/Counteroffensive
CCF Spring Offensive	Summer-Fall 1969
UN Summer-Fall Offensive	Winter-Spring 1970
Second Korean Winter	Sanctuary Counteroffensive
Korea, Summer-Fall 1952	Counteroffensive, Phase VII
Third Korean Winter	
Korea, Summer 1953	

DECORATIONS

Meritorious Unit Commendation (Army), Streamer embroidered KOREA (Headquarters and Headquarters Detachment, 303d Communication Reconnaissance Battalion, cited; DA GO 22, 1954)

Meritorious Unit Commendation (Army), Streamer embroidered VIETNAM 1966–1967 (Headquarters and Headquarters Company, 303d Radio Research Battalion, cited; DA GO 17, 1968)

Meritorious Unit Commendation (Army), Streamer embroidered VIETNAM 1967–1968 (Headquarters and Headquarters Company, 303d Radio Research Battalion, cited; DA GO 28, 1969, as amended by DA GO 18, 1979)

Meritorious Unit Commendation (Army), Streamer embroidered VIETNAM 1968–1969 (Headquarters and Headquarters Company, 303d Radio Research Battalion, cited; DA GO 51, 1971)

Meritorious Unit Commendation (Army), Streamer embroidered VIETNAM 1969–1970 (303d Radio Research Battalion cited; DA GO 43, 1972)

Meritorious Unit Commendation (Army), Streamer embroidered VIETNAM 1971 (303d Radio Research Battalion cited; DA GO 32, 1973)

Republic of Korea Presidential Unit Citation, Streamer embroidered KOREA (Headquarters and Headquarters Detachment, 303d Communication Reconnaissance Battalion, cited; DA GO 33, 1953, as amended by DA GO 41, 1955)

Republic of Vietnam Cross of Gallantry with Palm, Streamer embroidered VIETNAM 1970–1971 (303d Radio Research Battalion cited; DA GO 6, 1974)

Republic of Vietnam Civil Action Honor Medal, First Class, Streamer embroidered VIETNAM 1969–1970 (303d Radio Research Battalion cited; DA GO 6, 1974)

304th MILITARY INTELLIGENCE BATTALION

Heraldic Items

Coat of Arms

Shield: Azure, a voided isosceles triangle point up sable enclosing a vine leaf or and surmounted in chief by a lozenge fesswise argent bearing a Korean taeguk all between two lightning flashes, points up gules, fimbriated or.

Crest: On a wreath of the colors, or and azure, a demi-griffin of the last armed and langued gules grasping in dexter claw a dagger or, all within a laurel wreath of the like.

Motto: HONOR VIGILANCE DUTY.

Symbolism: The diamond and taeguk simulate an eye, and the lightning flashes connote technology; together they represent the vigilance, celerity, and communication of Army Security Agency units. They also allude to the lineage and service of the organization in World War II and the Korean War. The vine leaf refers to the Rhine province and denotes the unit's participation in the Rhineland campaign. The taeguk represents Korea, where the unit participated in six campaigns. It is also used to symbolize the award of the Meritorious Unit Commendation (Army) Streamer inscribed KOREA. Black is used on the triangle to connote iron and refers to the Republic of Korea Presidential Unit Citation Streamer with the inscription IRON TRIANGLE.

Oriental blue represents the military intelligence branch. The griffin, a traditional symbol of intelligence, resourcefulness, and courage, emphasizes the qualities required of battalion personnel and recalls the European theater of operations. Its claws and tongue are scarlet, denoting courage and sacrifice. It holds a dagger, a reference to the dangers of covert activities and a symbol of preparedness. The wreath refers to all honors and achievements associated with the unit during its history. Gold signifies excellence.

Distinctive Unit Insignia

The distinctive unit insignia consists of elements of the coat of arms.

Lineage and Honors

RA

Constituted 15 April 1944 in the Army of the United States as the 590th Signal Depot Company. Activated 7 June 1944 in North Africa. Inactivated 4 December 1945 at Camp Patrick Henry, Virginia. Redesignated 17 March 1948 as the 848th Signal Radio Relay Company and allotted to the Organized Reserves. (Organized Reserves redesignated 25 March 1948 as the Organized Reserve Corps; redesignated 9 July 1952 as the Army Reserve.) Activated 2 April 1948 at Rochester, New York. Inactivated 10 November 1948 at Rochester, New York. Redesignated 11 February 1949 as the 848th Signal Service Company. Activated 10 March 1949 at Fort Myer, Virginia. Ordered into active military service 11 September 1950 at Fort Myer, Virginia.

Converted and redesignated 2 October 1950 as Headquarters and Headquarters Detachment, 304th Communication Reconnaissance Battalion. Released from active military service 25 June 1955 and reverted to reserve status. Inactivated 18 August 1955 at Fort Myer, Virginia. Redesignated 1 April 1975 as Headquarters and Headquarters Company, 304th Army Security Agency Battalion, and activated at Houston, Texas. Location changed 27 October 1976 to Pasadena, Texas. Inactivated 15 September 1988 at Pasadena, Texas.

Redesignated 1 February 1990 as Headquarters and Headquarters Company, 304th Military Intelligence Battalion; concurrently withdrawn from the Army Reserve and allotted to the Regular Army. Headquarters transferred 17 August 1990 to the United States Army Training and Doctrine Command and activated at Fort Huachuca, Arizona.

Campaign Participation Credit

World War II
    Rhineland
Korean War
    CCF Spring Offensive
    UN Summer-Fall Offensive
    Second Korean Winter
    Korea, Summer-Fall 1952
    Third Korean Winter
    Korea, Summer 1953

Decorations

Meritorious Unit Commendation (Army), Streamer embroidered KOREA (Headquarters and Headquarters Detachment, 304th Communication Reconnaissance Battalion, cited; DA GO 22, 1954)

Army Superior Unit Award, Streamer embroidered 1990–1991 (304th Military Intelligence Battalion cited; DA GO 6, 1992)

Republic of Korea Presidential Unit Citation, Streamer embroidered IRON TRIANGLE (304th Communication Reconnaissance Battalion cited; DA GO 29, 1954, as amended by DA GO 47, 1954)

305th MILITARY INTELLIGENCE BATTALION

HERALDIC ITEMS

COAT OF ARMS

Shield: Azure, a saltire argent charged with pyrotechnic projectors of the first, overall a mullet of four points tenné fimbriated of the second.

Crest: On a wreath of the colors, argent and azure, issuant from the battlements of a tower proper a fleur-de-lis or between two griffin heads respectant gules beaked or.

Motto: AD ARCANA TUTANDA (TO KEEP OFFICIAL SECRETS SAFE).

Symbolism: Teal blue and white are the colors associated with former Army Security Agency battalions. The pyrotechnic projectors allude to the signal and reconnaissance missions of the unit. The four-pointed star refers to four World War II campaigns and also symbolizes intelligence, reconnaissance, communications, and signal, all vital functions of the battalion. The color orange further alludes to its signal function. The saltire is symbolic of the southern states that made up the Third Army area, the former location of the battalion.

The tower symbolizes a strong defense and military preparedness. The griffins, personifying vigilance, stand prepared to meet all threats. Red denotes courage and zeal. The tower and fleur-de-lis commemorate the unit's World War II service in Europe.

DISTINCTIVE UNIT INSIGNIA

The distinctive unit insignia is the shield and motto of the coat of arms.

LINEAGE AND HONORS

LINEAGE

Constituted 17 November 1950 in the Organized Reserve Corps as Headquarters and Headquarters Detachment, 305th Communication Reconnaissance Battalion. Activated 23 January 1951 at Atlanta, Georgia. Consolidated 17 July 1951 with the 3255th Signal Service Company (see ANNEX) and consolidated unit designated as Headquarters and Headquarters Detachment, 305th Communication Reconnaissance Battalion. (Organized Reserve Corps redesignated 9 July 1952 as the Army Reserve.) Reorganized and redesignated 24 January 1956 as Headquarters and Headquarters Company, 305th Communication Reconnaissance Battalion (362d Communication Reconnaissance Company [constituted 18 November 1955 in the Army Reserve] concurrently redesignated as Company A and activated at Wilmington, North Carolina). Redesignated 1 October 1956 as the 305th Army Security Agency Battalion. Inactivated 15 June 1959 at Atlanta, Georgia.

Redesignated 1 February 1990 as the 305th Military Intelligence Battalion; concurrently withdrawn from the Army Reserve and allotted to the Regular Army. Headquarters transferred 18 May 1990 to the United States Army Training and Doctrine Command and activated at Fort Devens, Massachusetts.

ANNEX

Constituted 12 April 1944 in the Army of the United States as the 3255th Signal Service Company. Activated 6 May 1944 in England. Inactivated 25 October 1945 in Germany.

CAMPAIGN PARTICIPATION CREDIT

World War II
    Northern France
    Rhineland
    Ardennes-Alsace
    Central Europe

DECORATIONS

None.

306th MILITARY INTELLIGENCE BATTALION

Heraldic Items

Coat of Arms

Shield: Azure, a volcano abased argent surmounted by a pellet charged with a mullet of the second; in chief a lightning flash fesswise tenné fimbriated of the second.

Crest: On a wreath of the colors, argent and azure, a demi-griffin gules holding in its dexter claw a sword with blade in the form of a lightning flash or all in front of a wreath of palm fronds proper.

Motto: NEMO VIGILANTIOR (NO ONE MORE WATCHFUL).

Symbolism: Teal blue and white are the colors formerly used for Army Security Agency battalions. The volcano symbolizes the area in the Pacific where the unit served. The black sphere charged with a white mullet alludes to the coat of arms of Captain Cook, who discovered New Caledonia, the island on which the unit was activated. The lightning flash refers to the mission of the unit and the orange color represents its former status as a signal company.

The griffin, symbol of courage, strength, and vigilance, represents the intelligence mission of the battalion. The unit's origin as a signal company is recalled by the lightning flash sword blade, which also denotes speed of response and action. The palm wreath refers to the unit's service in the Pacific during World War II. Red signifies courage and recalls the award of the Meritorious Unit Commendation (Army). Gold stands for excellence.

Distinctive Unit Insignia

The distinctive unit insignia is the shield and motto of the coat of arms.

Lineage and Honors

Lineage

Constituted 16 December 1944 in the Army of the United States as the 3910th Signal Service Company. Activated 1 February 1945 on New Caledonia. Inactivated 19 April 1946 on Tinian. Redesignated 13 January 1948 as the 303d Signal Service Company, Army, and allotted to the Organized Reserves. Activated 23 January 1948 at Philadelphia, Pennsylvania. (Organized Reserves redesignated 25 March 1948 as the Organized Reserve Corps; redesignated 9 July 1952 as the Army Reserve.) Reorganized and redesignated 5 September 1950 as the 303d Signal Radio Intelligence Company.

Converted and redesignated 3 January 1951 as Headquarters and Headquarters Detachment, 306th Communication Reconnaissance Battalion. Ordered into active military service 1 May 1951 at Philadelphia, Pennsylvania; released from active military service 16 May 1955 and reverted to reserve status. Inactivated 20 July 1955 at Philadelphia, Pennsylvania. Activated 6 January 1956 at Philadelphia, Pennsylvania. Reorganized and redesignated 14 February 1956 as Headquarters and Headquarters Company, 306th Communication Reconnaissance Battalion. (Companies A and B constituted 13 March 1956; Company B activated 14 March 1956 at Baltimore, Maryland.) Redesignated 3 September 1956 as the 306th Army Security Agency Battalion. Inactivated 27 June 1959 at Philadelphia, Pennsylvania.

Redesignated 1 February 1990 as the 306th Military Intelligence Battalion; concurrently withdrawn from the Army Reserve and allotted to the Regular Army. Headquarters transferred 18 May 1990 to the United States Army Training and Doctrine Command and activated at Fort Devens, Massachusetts.

Campaign Participation Credit

World War II
    Asiatic-Pacific Theater, Streamer without inscription

Decorations

Meritorious Unit Commendation (Army), Streamer embroidered PACIFIC THEATER (3910th Signal Service Company cited; GO 133, Western Pacific Base Command, 11 November 1945)

307th MILITARY INTELLIGENCE BATTALION

HERALDIC ITEMS

COAT OF ARMS

Shield: Tierced in pairle reversed argent, azure, and gules, on the first and second an eagle's head erased counterchanged, and on the third, a key palewise, the ward to base, between two electronic flashes, one in bend and the other in bendsinister of the first.

Crest: On a wreath of the colors, argent and azure, in front of a wreath of laurel or an equilateral triangle point up with the points barbed gules and charged with a Philippine sun of the third.

Motto: ELECTRONIC FIREPOWER.

Symbolism: The eagles, known for swiftness, stamina, and keen vision, together with the key and electronic flashes symbolize eternal vigilance and security. All allude to the basic mission of the organization. In addition, the eagles' heads, adapted from the civic arms of the cities of Frankfurt am Main and Ludwigsburg in Germany, refer to former stations of the battalion.

The crest symbolizes unit awards received by elements of the battalion. The wreath of laurel refers to the eight Meritorious Unit Commendations (Army) for service in the Pacific during World War II, in Korea, and in Vietnam, and to the Republic of Vietnam Cross of Gallantry with Palm. The triangle and sun symbolize the Philippine Presidential Unit Citation.

DISTINCTIVE UNIT INSIGNIA

The distinctive unit insignia is the shield and motto of the coat of arms.

LINEAGE AND HONORS

RA

LINEAGE

Constituted 11 December 1951 in the Regular Army as Headquarters and Headquarters Detachment, 307th Communication Reconnaissance Battalion. Activated 27 December 1951 in Germany. Reorganized and redesignated 25 June 1955 as Headquarters and Headquarters Company, 307th Communication Reconnaissance Battalion (331st Communication Reconnaissance Company [activated 13 July 1942] concurrently reorganized and redesignated as Company A; Company B [constituted 19 May 1955] activated in Germany). Redesignated 1 July 1956 as the 307th Army Security Agency Battalion. Inactivated 15 October 1957 in Germany. Headquarters and Headquarters Company activated 1 July 1974 in Germany. (Companies A and B redesignated 21 September 1978 as the 331st and 346th Army Security Agency Companies—hereafter separate lineages.)

Headquarters and Headquarters Company, 307th Army Security Agency Battalion, reorganized and redesignated 16 October 1983 as Headquarters, Headquarters and Service Company, 307th Military Intelligence Battalion (326th Army Security Agency Company [see ANNEX 1] concurrently reorganized and redesignated as Company A; 330th Army Security Agency Company [see ANNEX 2] redesignated as Company B and activated in Germany). Battalion inactivated 15 December 1991 in Germany.

ANNEX 1

Constituted 3 April 1942 in the Army of the United States as the 126th Signal Radio Intelligence Company. Activated 14 August 1942 at Camp Crowder, Missouri. Reorganized and redesignated 1 September 1945 as the 126th Signal Service Company.

Converted and redesignated 25 October 1951 as the 326th Communication Reconnaissance Company and allotted to the Regular Army. Redesignated 1 July 1956 as the 326th Army Security Agency Company. Inactivated 15 October 1957 in Japan. Activated 25 May 1962 at Fort Bragg, North Carolina. Inactivated 14 February 1964 at Homestead Air Force Base, Florida. Activated 23 December 1968 at Fort Riley, Kansas. Inactivated 15 April 1970 at Fort Riley, Kansas. Activated 3 May 1971 in Germany.

ANNEX 2

Constituted 26 November 1943 in the Army of the United States as the 60th Signal Radio Intelligence Company. Activated 23 December 1943 at Camp Crowder, Missouri. Reorganized and redesignated 24 May 1945 as the 60th Signal Service Company.

Converted and redesignated 25 October 1951 as the 330th Communication Reconnaissance Company and allotted to the Regular Army. Redesignated 1 July 1956 as the 330th Army Security Agency Company. Inactivated 15 October 1957 in Korea. Activated 25 June 1962 at Camp Wolters, Texas. Inactivated 30 September 1971 in Vietnam. Activated 5 November 1973 in Germany. Inactivated 15 May 1979 in Germany.

CAMPAIGN PARTICIPATION CREDIT

Southwest Asia
    Defense of Saudi Arabia
    Liberation and Defense of Kuwait
    Cease-Fire

Company A additionally entitled to:

World War II–AP
    New Guinea
    Luzon
Korean War
    UN Summer-Fall Offensive
    Second Korean Winter
    Korea, Summer-Fall 1952
    Third Korean Winter
    Korea, Summer 1953

Company B additionally entitled to:

Korean War
    UN Offensive
    CCF Intervention
    First UN Counteroffensive
    CCF Spring Offensive
    UN Summer-Fall Offensive
    Second Korean Winter
    Korea, Summer-Fall 1952
    Third Korean Winter
    Korea, Summer 1953
Vietnam
    Counteroffensive, Phase II
    Counteroffensive, Phase III
    Tet Counteroffensive
    Counteroffensive, Phase IV
    Counteroffensive, Phase V
    Counteroffensive, Phase VI
    Tet 69/Counteroffensive
    Summer-Fall 1969
    Winter-Spring 1970
    Sanctuary Counteroffensive
    Counteroffensive, Phase VII
    Consolidation I

DECORATIONS
Meritorious Unit Commendation (Army), Streamer embroidered SOUTHWEST
ASIA (307th Military Intelligence Battalion cited; DA GO 34, 1992)

Company A additionally entitled to:
Meritorious Unit Commendation (Army), Streamer embroidered PACIFIC
THEATER (126th Signal Radio Intelligence Company cited; GO 166, United
States Army Forces, Pacific, 14 September 1945)
Meritorious Unit Commendation (Army), Streamer embroidered KOREA
(326th Communication Reconnaissance Company cited; DA GO 22, 1954)
Philippine Presidential Unit Citation, Streamer embroidered 17 OCTOBER 1944
TO 4 JULY 1945 (126th Signal Radio Intelligence Company cited; DA GO 47, 1950)

Company B additionally entitled to:
Meritorious Unit Commendation (Army), Streamer embroidered KOREA
1950–1951 (330th Communication Reconnaissance Company cited; DA GO 62,
1952)
Meritorious Unit Commendation (Army), Streamer embroidered KOREA
1951–1953 (330th Communication Reconnaissance Company cited; DA GO 22,
1954)
Meritorious Unit Commendation (Army), Streamer embroidered VIETNAM
1967–1968 (330th Radio Research Company cited; DA GO 28, 1969)
Meritorious Unit Commendation (Army), Streamer embroidered VIETNAM
1968–1969 (330th Radio Research Company cited; DA GO 51, 1971)
Meritorious Unit Commendation (Army), Streamer embroidered VIETNAM
1969–1970 (330th Radio Research Company cited; DA GO 43, 1972)
Meritorious Unit Commendation (Army), Streamer embroidered VIETNAM
1971 (330th Radio Research Company cited; DA GO 32, 1973)
Republic of Vietnam Cross of Gallantry with Palm, Streamer embroidered
VIETNAM 1970–1971 (330th Radio Research Company cited; DA GO 6, 1974)

308th MILITARY INTELLIGENCE BATTALION

HERALDIC ITEMS

COAT OF ARMS

Shield: Per saltire argent and azure, two griffin heads erased respectant of the first, in chief a compass rose gules.

Crest: None approved.

Motto: GUARDIANS OF AMERICA.

Symbolism: Oriental blue is the primary color associated with military intelligence. The saltire represents strength and cooperation. The griffins embody vigilance, alertness, and courage and reflect the unit's motto and mission. The compass rose alludes to the collection, analysis, and dissemination of information and the worldwide capabilities of the unit.

DISTINCTIVE UNIT INSIGNIA

The distinctive unit insignia is an adaptation of the shield of the coat of arms and incorporates the motto.

Lineage and Honors

Lineage

Constituted 31 January 1952 in the Organized Reserve Corps as Headquarters and Headquarters Detachment, 308th Communication Reconnaissance Battalion. Activated 1 April 1952 at New York, New York. (Organized Reserve Corps redesignated 9 July 1952 as the Army Reserve.) Reorganized and redesignated 23 January 1956 as Headquarters and Headquarters Company, 308th Communication Reconnaissance Battalion. Redesignated 1 September 1956 as Headquarters and Headquarters Company, 308th Army Security Agency Battalion. Inactivated 1 July 1959 at New York, New York.

Redesignated 1 February 1990 as Headquarters and Headquarters Company, 308th Military Intelligence Battalion; concurrently withdrawn from the Army Reserve and allotted to the Regular Army. Redesignated 17 October 1991 as Headquarters, Headquarters and Service Company, 308th Military Intelligence Battalion, and activated in Panama (organic elements concurrently constituted and activated). Battalion inactivated 16 September 1995 in Panama.

Campaign Participation Credit

None.

Decorations

Army Superior Unit Award, Streamer embroidered 1993–1994 (308th Military Intelligence Battalion cited; DA GO 1, 1996)

309th MILITARY INTELLIGENCE BATTALION

HERALDIC ITEMS

COAT OF ARMS

Shield: Argent, on a pale emitting in saltire four lightning flashes azure a key ward to dexter in base, the bow a bear's head, or.

Crest: None approved.

Motto: SENTINELS OF SECURITY.

Symbolism: Teal blue and white are the colors formerly used for Army Security Agency organizations. The key symbolizes the unit's mission, the guarding of security, and the golden bear's head on the key represents the state of California, where the unit was originally activated. The lightning flashes, symbolic of electricity, relate to the importance of electronic communications as part of the unit's functions.

DISTINCTIVE UNIT INSIGNIA

The distinctive unit insignia is the shield and motto of the coat of arms.

Lineage and Honors

RA
(active)

Lineage

Constituted 19 September 1952 in the Army Reserve as Headquarters and Headquarters Detachment, 309th Communication Reconnaissance Battalion. Activated 1 November 1952 at Los Angeles, California. Reorganized and redesignated 25 January 1956 as Headquarters and Headquarters Company, 309th Communication Reconnaissance Battalion (organic elements constituted 29 December 1955–4 March 1956 and activated 1 February–5 March 1956). Redesignated 1 October 1956 as the 309th Army Security Agency Battalion. Inactivated 15 July 1959 at Los Angeles, California. Activated 15 September 1962 with Headquarters at Bell, California. (Companies A, B, C, and D reorganized and redesignated 15 August 1966 as the 518th, 519th, 520th, and 521st Army Security Agency Companies—hereafter separate lineages.) Headquarters and Headquarters Company inactivated 15 July 1986 at Bell, California.

Redesignated 1 February 1990 as Headquarters and Headquarters Company, 309th Military Intelligence Battalion; concurrently withdrawn from the Army Reserve and allotted to the Regular Army. Headquarters transferred 17 August 1990 to the United States Army Training and Doctrine Command and activated at Fort Huachuca, Arizona.

Campaign Participation Credit

None.

Decorations

None.

310th MILITARY INTELLIGENCE BATTALION

HERALDIC ITEMS

COAT OF ARMS

Shield: Azure, two cramps saltirewise argent surmounted by a griffin's head erased sable, langued gules.

Crest: None approved.

Motto: ARRECTIS AURIBUS (ALWAYS ON THE ALERT).

Symbolism: Oriental blue is one of the colors associated with military intelligence. Black and white symbolize overt and covert operations and the organization's around-the-clock vigilance. The griffin embodies alertness; it is black, recalling determination and stealth. The unit's collection and exploitation mission is highlighted by the cramps or hooks. The hooks simulate flashes, representing speed and combat electronic warfare, while alluding to the ability to catch and hold.

DISTINCTIVE UNIT INSIGNIA

The distinctive unit insignia is the shield and motto of the coat of arms.

Lineage and Honors

Constituted 25 February 1954 in the Army Reserve as Headquarters and Headquarters Detachment, 310th Communication Reconnaissance Battalion. Activated 1 November 1954 at Boston, Massachusetts. Reorganized and redesignated 8 February 1956 as Headquarters and Headquarters Company, 310th Communication Reconnaissance Battalion. Redesignated 10 September 1956 as Headquarters and Headquarters Company, 310th Army Security Agency Battalion. (800th Signal Company [see ANNEX] converted and redesignated 26 July 1956 as Company A.) Battalion inactivated 1 July 1959 at Boston, Massachusetts.

Redesignated 1 February 1990 as the 310th Military Intelligence Battalion; concurrently withdrawn from the Army Reserve and allotted to the Regular Army. Activated 17 October 1991 in Panama. Inactivated 16 September 1995 in Panama.

ANNEX

Constituted 24 December 1943 in the Army of the United States as the 5th Mobile Radio Broadcasting Company. Activated 28 January 1944 at Camp Ritchie, Maryland. Inactivated 25 November 1945 in Germany.

Redesignated 14 September 1948 as the 800th Mobile Radio Broadcasting Company and allotted to the Organized Reserve Corps. Activated 27 September 1948 at Corpus Christi, Texas. Inactivated 20 September 1950 at Corpus Christi, Texas. Converted and redesignated 8 November 1950 as the 800th Signal Radio Countermeasure Company. Activated 7 December 1950 at Red Bank, New Jersey. (Organized Reserve Corps redesignated 9 July 1952 as the Army Reserve.) Reorganized and redesignated 20 March 1953 as the 800th Signal Company. Location changed 17 August 1954 to Fort Monmouth, New Jersey.

Campaign Participation Credit

Company A entitled to:
  World War II–EAME
        Ardennes-Alsace

Decorations

None.

311th MILITARY INTELLIGENCE BATTALION

HERALDIC ITEMS

COAT OF ARMS

Shield: Azure, a cross quarter-pierced argent and overall two lightning bolts in saltire or between in each quarter as many fleurs-de-lis of the second; overall a dragon passant gules.

Crest: None approved.

Motto: EYES OF THE EAGLE.

Symbolism: The checkered field in the colors used for military intelligence units, silver gray (white) and oriental blue, suggests the gathering of data to aid in the formulation of military strategy; the lightning bolts refer to the use of electronics in the gathering operation. The dragon is a reference to service in Vietnam and its scarlet color alludes to awards of the Meritorious Unit Commendation (Army). The fleur-de-lis denote service in Europe during World War II.

DISTINCTIVE UNIT INSIGNIA

The distinctive unit insignia is the shield and motto of the coat of arms.

LINEAGE AND HONORS

RA
(active)

LINEAGE

Constituted 1 June 1954 in the Regular Army as Headquarters and Headquarters Detachment, 311th Communication Reconnaissance Battalion. Activated 14 June 1954 at Fort Devens, Massachusetts. Reorganized and redesignated 16 May 1955 as Headquarters and Headquarters Company, 311th Communication Reconnaissance Battalion (336th Communication Reconnaissance Company [activated 6 August 1952] and 359th Communication Reconnaissance Company [activated 15 August 1944] concurrently reorganized and redesignated as Companies A and B). Redesignated 1 July 1956 as the 311th Army Security Agency Battalion. Inactivated 18 December 1957 at Camp Wolters, Texas. Headquarters and Headquarters Company activated 15 February 1966 at Fort Wolters, Texas (Companies A and B concurrently disbanded). Inactivated 30 June 1971 at Fort Hood, Texas. (Companies A and B reconstituted 21 September 1978 in the Regular Army as the 336th and 359th Army Security Agency Companies—hereafter separate lineages.)

Headquarters and Headquarters Company, 311th Army Security Agency Battalion, redesignated 1 June 1982 as Headquarters, Headquarters and

Operations Company, 311th Military Intelligence Battalion, assigned to the 101st Airborne Division, and activated at Fort Campbell, Kentucky (265th Army Security Agency Company [see ANNEX 1] and 101st Military Intelligence Company [see ANNEX 2] concurrently reorganized and redesignated as Companies A and B).

ANNEX 1

Constituted 2 March 1967 in the Regular Army as the 265th Army Security Agency Company. Activated 21 April 1967 at Fort Campbell, Kentucky. Inactivated 1 April 1972 in Vietnam. Activated 21 June 1976 at Fort Campbell, Kentucky.

ANNEX 2

Constituted 12 July 1944 in the Army of the United States as the 101st Counter Intelligence Corps Detachment. Activated 20 August 1944 in England with personnel from provisional Counter Intelligence Corps detachment attached to the 101st Airborne Division. Inactivated 30 November 1945 in France. Allotted 7 February 1956 to the Regular Army. Activated 25 March 1956 at Fort Campbell, Kentucky. Reorganized and redesignated 25 January 1958 as the 101st Military Intelligence Detachment. Reorganized and redesignated 26 December 1969 as the 101st Military Intelligence Company. Assigned 21 September 1978 to the 101st Airborne Division.

CAMPAIGN PARTICIPATION CREDIT

> *Southwest Asia*
>> Defense of Saudi Arabia
>> Liberation and Defense of Kuwait

Company A additionally entitled to:

> *Vietnam*
>> Counteroffensive, Phase III
>> Tet Counteroffensive
>> Counteroffensive, Phase IV
>> Counteroffensive, Phase V
>> Counteroffensive, Phase VI
>> Tet 69/Counteroffensive
>> Summer-Fall 1969
>> Winter-Spring 1970
>> Sanctuary Counteroffensive
>> Counteroffensive, Phase VII
>> Consolidation I
>> Consolidation II
>> Cease-Fire

Company B additionally entitled to:

World War II–EAME
> Normandy (with arrowhead)
> Rhineland (with arrowhead)
> Ardennes-Alsace
> Central Europe

Vietnam
> Counteroffensive, Phase III
> Tet Counteroffensive
> Counteroffensive, Phase IV
> Counteroffensive, Phase V
> Counteroffensive, Phase VI
> Tet 69/Counteroffensive
> Summer-Fall 1969
> Winter-Spring 1970
> Sanctuary Counteroffensive
> Counteroffensive, Phase VII
> Consolidation I
> Consolidation II

DECORATIONS

Meritorious Unit Commendation (Army), Streamer embroidered SOUTHWEST ASIA (Headquarters, Headquarters and Operations Company and Company A, 311th Military Intelligence Battalion, cited; DA GO 1, 1996)

Company A additionally entitled to:

Meritorious Unit Commendation (Army), Streamer embroidered VIETNAM 1967–1968 (265th Radio Research Company cited; DA GO 28, 1969)

Meritorious Unit Commendation (Army), Streamer embroidered VIETNAM 1969–1970 (265th Radio Research Company cited; DA GO 43, 1972)

Meritorious Unit Commendation (Army), Streamer embroidered VIETNAM 1971–1972 (265th Radio Research Company cited; DA GO 32, 1973)

Republic of Vietnam Cross of Gallantry with Palm, Streamer embroidered VIETNAM 1968 (265th Radio Research Company cited; DA GO 21, 1969)

Republic of Vietnam Cross of Gallantry with Palm, Streamer embroidered VIETNAM 1968–1969 (265th Radio Research Company cited; DA GO 43, 1970)

Republic of Vietnam Cross of Gallantry with Palm, Streamer embroidered VIETNAM 1970–1971 (265th Radio Research Company cited; DA GO 6, 1974)

Republic of Vietnam Cross of Gallantry with Palm, Streamer embroidered VIETNAM 1971 (265th Radio Research Company cited; DA GO 6, 1974)

Republic of Vietnam Civil Action Honor Medal, First Class, Streamer embroidered VIETNAM 1968–1970 (265th Radio Research Company cited; DA GO 48, 1971)

Company B additionally entitled to:

Presidential Unit Citation (Army), Streamer embroidered BASTOGNE (Counterintelligence Detachment, 101st Airborne Division, cited; WD GO 17, 1945)

French Croix de Guerre with Palm, World War II, Streamer embroidered NORMANDY (101st Airborne Division cited; DA GO 43, 1950)

Netherlands Orange Lanyard (101st Airborne Division cited; DA GO 43, 1950)

Belgian Croix de Guerre 1940 with Palm, Streamer embroidered BASTOGNE; cited in the Order of the Day of the Belgian Army for action at Bastogne (101st Counter Intelligence Corps Detachment cited; DA GO 43, 1950, as amended by DA GO 27, 1959)

Belgian Fourragere 1940 (101st Counter Intelligence Corps Detachment cited; DA GO 43, 1950, as amended by DA GO 27, 1959)

Cited in the Order of the Day of the Belgian Army for action in France and Belgium (101st Counter Intelligence Corps Detachment cited; DA GO 43, 1950, as amended by DA GO 27, 1959)

Republic of Vietnam Cross of Gallantry with Palm, Streamer embroidered VIETNAM 1968–1969 (101st Military Intelligence Detachment cited; DA GO 43, 1970)

Republic of Vietnam Cross of Gallantry with Palm, Streamer embroidered VIETNAM 1971 (101st Military Intelligence Detachment cited; DA GO 6, 1974)

Republic of Vietnam Civil Action Honor Medal, First Class, Streamer embroidered VIETNAM 1968–1970 (101st Military Intelligence Detachment cited; DA GO 48, 1971)

312th MILITARY INTELLIGENCE BATTALION

COAT OF ARMS

Shield: Argent, on a taeguk proper an enflamed torch palewise in front of two lightning flashes saltirewise of the first, on a chief wavy azure a chess knight argent.

Crest: None approved.

Motto: SEMPER VERITAS (ALWAYS THE TRUTH).

Symbolism: Oriental blue and silver gray (white) are the colors traditionally associated with military intelligence. The wavy partition alludes to service in the Pacific during World War II; the taeguk to service in Korea. The crossed flashes refer to the unit's origin as signal and its present combat electronic warfare and intelligence function. The torch is a symbol of truth and reflects the motto and the mission of the unit. The chess knight, a piece that can move covertly, further symbolizes the military intelligence mission.

DISTINCTIVE UNIT INSIGNIA

The distinctive unit insignia is the shield and motto of the coat of arms.

LINEAGE AND HONORS

RA
(active)

LINEAGE

Constituted 31 December 1943 in the Army of the United States as the 23d Signal Construction Battalion. Activated 10 February 1944 at Camp Pickett, Virginia. Reorganized and redesignated 24 April 1944 as the 23d Signal Light Construction Battalion. Reorganized and redesignated 21 August 1944 as the 23d Signal Heavy Construction Battalion. Inactivated 22 January 1946 at Fort Lawton, Washington. Redesignated 27 September 1951 as the 23d Signal Construction Battalion and allotted to the Regular Army. Activated 2 November 1951 in Korea. Inactivated 15 May 1953 in Korea.

Converted and redesignated 19 May 1955 as the 312th Communication Reconnaissance Battalion. Headquarters and Headquarters Company activated 25 June 1955 in Germany. Battalion redesignated 1 July 1956 as the 312th Army Security Agency Battalion. Headquarters and Headquarters Company inactivated 15 October 1957 in Germany.

312th Army Security Agency Battalion redesignated 1 October 1981 as the 312th Military Intelligence Battalion, assigned to the 1st Cavalry Division, and activated at Fort Hood, Texas (371st Army Security Agency Company [see ANNEX 1] concurrently consolidated with Company A; 191st Military Intelligence Company [see ANNEX 2] consolidated with Company B).

ANNEX 1

Constituted 11 May 1962 in the Regular Army as Company C, 313th Army Security Agency Battalion. Activated 25 May 1962 at Two Rock Ranch Station, California. Reorganized and redesignated 15 October 1966 as the 371st Army Security Agency Company.

ANNEX 2

Constituted 25 September 1950 in the Regular Army as the 191st Counter Intelligence Corps Detachment. Activated 6 October 1950 in Korea. Inactivated 24 June 1956 in Korea. Activated 15 October 1957 in Korea. Reorganized and redesignated 15 May 1959 as the 191st Military Intelligence Detachment. Reorganized and redesignated 26 December 1969 as the 191st Military Intelligence Company. Inactivated 15 August 1972 in Vietnam. Activated 21 June 1975 at Fort Hood, Texas. Assigned 2 July 1977 to the 1st Cavalry Division.

CAMPAIGN PARTICIPATION CREDIT
World War II
    Asiatic-Pacific Theater, Streamer without inscription
Korean War
    UN Summer-Fall Offensive
    Second Korean Winter
    Korea, Summer-Fall 1952
    Third Korean Winter
Southwest Asia
    Defense of Saudi Arabia
    Liberation and Defense of Kuwait

Company A additionally entitled to:
Vietnam
    Defense
    Counteroffensive
    Counteroffensive, Phase II
    Counteroffensive, Phase III
    Tet Counteroffensive
    Counteroffensive, Phase IV
    Counteroffensive, Phase V
    Counteroffensive, Phase VI
    Tet 69/Counteroffensive
    Summer-Fall 1969
    Winter-Spring 1970
    Sanctuary Counteroffensive
    Counteroffensive, Phase VII

Company B additionally entitled to:

Korean War
> UN Offensive
> CCF Intervention
> First UN Counteroffensive
> CCF Spring Offensive

Vietnam
> Defense
> Counteroffensive
> Counteroffensive, Phase II
> Counteroffensive, Phase III
> Tet Counteroffensive
> Counteroffensive, Phase IV
> Counteroffensive, Phase V
> Counteroffensive, Phase VI
> Tet 69/Counteroffensive
> Summer-Fall 1969
> Winter-Spring 1970
> Sanctuary Counteroffensive
> Counteroffensive, Phase VII
> Consolidation I
> Consolidation II
> Cease-Fire

DECORATIONS

Meritorious Unit Commendation (Army), Streamer embroidered SOUTHWEST ASIA (312th Military Intelligence Battalion cited; DA GO 27, 1994)

Company A additionally entitled to:

Presidential Unit Citation (Army), Streamer embroidered PLEIKU PROVINCE (10th Radio Research Unit cited; DA GO 40, 1967)

Presidential Unit Citation (Army), Streamer embroidered BINH THUAN PROVINCE (371st Radio Research Unit cited; DA GO 2, 1973)

Valorous Unit Award, Streamer embroidered FISH HOOK (371st Radio Research Company cited; DA GO 43, 1972)

Meritorious Unit Commendation (Army), Streamer embroidered VIETNAM 1965–1966 (10th Radio Research Unit cited; DA GO 17, 1968)

Meritorious Unit Commendation (Army), Streamer embroidered VIETNAM 1967–1968 (371st Radio Research Company cited; DA GO 28, 1969)

Meritorious Unit Commendation (Army), Streamer embroidered VIETNAM 1968–1969 (371st Radio Research Company cited; DA GO 51, 1971)

Meritorious Unit Commendation (Army), Streamer embroidered VIETNAM 1969–1970 (371st Radio Research Company cited; DA GO 43, 1972)

Republic of Vietnam Cross of Gallantry with Palm, Streamer embroidered VIETNAM 1965–1969 (371st Radio Research Company cited; DA GO 59, 1969, as amended by DA GO 43, 1970)

Republic of Vietnam Cross of Gallantry with Palm, Streamer embroidered VIETNAM 1969–1970 (371st Radio Research Company cited; DA GO 42, 1972)

Republic of Vietnam Cross of Gallantry with Palm, Streamer embroidered VIETNAM 1970–1971 (371st Radio Research Company cited; DA GO 42, 1972, and DA GO 6, 1974)

Republic of Vietnam Civil Action Honor Medal, First Class, Streamer embroidered VIETNAM 1969–1971 (371st Radio Research Company cited; DA GO 42, 1972, and DA GO 6, 1974)

Company B additionally entitled to:

Presidential Unit Citation (Army), Streamer embroidered PLEIKU PROVINCE (191st Military Intelligence Detachment cited; DA GO 40, 1967)

Valorous Unit Award, Streamer embroidered FISH HOOK (191st Military Intelligence Company cited; DA GO 43, 1972)

Meritorious Unit Commendation (Army), Streamer embroidered KOREA (191st Counter Intelligence Corps Detachment cited; DA GO 53, 1952)

Meritorious Unit Commendation (Army), Streamer embroidered VIETNAM 1967–1968 (191st Military Intelligence Detachment cited; DA GO 17, 1969)

Republic of Vietnam Cross of Gallantry with Palm, Streamer embroidered VIETNAM 1965–1969 (191st Military Intelligence Detachment cited; DA GO 59, 1969)

Republic of Vietnam Cross of Gallantry with Palm, Streamer embroidered VIETNAM 1969–1970 (191st Military Intelligence Detachment cited; DA GO 42, 1972, as amended by DA GO 11, 1973)

Republic of Vietnam Cross of Gallantry with Palm, Streamer embroidered VIETNAM 1970–1971 (191st Military Intelligence Company cited; DA GO 42, 1972)

Republic of Vietnam Cross of Gallantry with Palm, Streamer embroidered VIETNAM 1971–1972 (191st Military Intelligence Detachment cited; DA GO 54, 1974)

Republic of Vietnam Civil Action Honor Medal, First Class, Streamer embroidered VIETNAM 1969–1970 (191st Military Intelligence Company cited; DA GO 42, 1972)

313th MILITARY INTELLIGENCE BATTALION
(Snow Owl)

HERALDIC ITEMS

COAT OF ARMS

Shield: Azure, a fess checky argent and tenné, overall a mullet of six points of the second.

Crest: On a wreath of the colors, argent and azure, a dragon passant gules garnished or in front of a mount vert impaled with twelve bamboo spikes proper, the dragon's tail interlaced with the spikes.

Motto: SAVOIR C'EST POUVOIR (KNOWLEDGE IS POWER).

Symbolism: Oriental blue and silver gray (white) allude to military intelligence. The colors orange and white refer to the organization's former affiliation with the Signal Corps, and the points of the mullet allude to the unit's decorations for World War II and Vietnam.

The dragon, symbolic of alertness and readiness, denotes the unit's service as an Army Security Agency battalion in Vietnam. The mount refers to the lush terrain of that country and the spikes to the number of campaigns in which the unit participated.

DISTINCTIVE UNIT INSIGNIA

The distinctive unit insignia is the shield and motto of the coat of arms.

Lineage and Honors

RA
(active)

Lineage

Constituted 11 May 1942 in the Army of the United States as the 215th Signal Depot Company. Activated 25 September 1942 at Camp Livingston, Louisiana. Inactivated 18 November 1945 at Camp Kilmer, New Jersey.

Converted and redesignated 21 April 1955 as Headquarters and Headquarters Company, 313th Communication Reconnaissance Battalion, and allotted to the Regular Army. Activated 16 May 1955 at Fort Bragg, North Carolina (358th Communication Reconnaissance Company [see ANNEX 1] and 337th Communication Reconnaissance Company [activated 6 August 1952] concurrently reorganized and redesignated as Companies A and B). Redesignated 1 July 1956 as the 313th Army Security Agency Battalion. Inactivated 18 December 1957 at Fort Bragg, North Carolina. Activated 25 May 1962 at Fort Bragg, North Carolina. (Company A reorganized and redesignated 15 October 1966 as the 358th Army Security Agency Company [see ANNEX 1]; Companies B and C concurrently reorganized and redesignated as the 337th and 371st Army Security Agency Companies—hereafter separate lineages.)

Headquarters and Headquarters Company, 313th Army Security Agency Battalion, reorganized and redesignated 16 October 1979 as Headquarters and Headquarters Company, 313th Military Intelligence Battalion, and assigned to the 82d Airborne Division (358th Army Security Agency Company [see ANNEX 1] and 82d Military Intelligence Company [see ANNEX 2] concurrently reorganized and redesignated as Companies A and B).

ANNEX 1

Constituted 10 June 1944 in the Army of the United States as the 3191st Signal Service Company. Activated 20 June 1944 at Camp Crowder, Missouri. Inactivated 25 October 1945 in the Philippine Islands.

Converted and redesignated 25 April 1951 as the 358th Communication Reconnaissance Company and allotted to the Regular Army. Activated 15 May 1951 at Fort Devens, Massachusetts. Reorganized and redesignated 16 May 1955 as Company A, 313th Communication Reconnaissance Battalion. Redesignated 1 July 1956 as Company A, 313th Army Security Agency Battalion. Inactivated 18 December 1957 at Fort Bragg, North Carolina. Activated 25 May 1962 at Fort Bragg, North Carolina. Reorganized and redesignated 15 October 1966 as the 358th Army Security Agency Company.

ANNEX 2

Constituted 12 July 1944 in the Army of the United States as the 82d Counter Intelligence Corps Detachment. Activated 20 August 1944 in England with personnel from provisional Counter Intelligence Corps detachment attached to the 82d Airborne Division. Allotted 3 February 1949 to the Regular Army. Reorganized and redesignated 25 January 1958 as the 82d Military Intelligence Detachment. Reorganized and redesignated 11 November 1970 as the 82d Military Intelligence Company. Assigned 21 June 1978 to the 82d Airborne Division.

CAMPAIGN PARTICIPATION CREDIT

World War II
    Normandy (with arrowhead)
    Northern France
    Rhineland
    Ardennes-Alsace
    Central Europe

Vietnam
    Counteroffensive
    Counteroffensive, Phase II
    Counteroffensive, Phase III
    Tet Counteroffensive
    Counteroffensive, Phase IV
    Counteroffensive, Phase V
    Counteroffensive, Phase VI
    Tet 69/Counteroffensive
    Summer-Fall 1969
    Winter-Spring 1970
    Sanctuary Counteroffensive
    Counteroffensive, Phase VII

Armed Forces Expeditions
    Dominican Republic
    Grenada

Southwest Asia
    Defense of Saudi Arabia
    Liberation and Defense of Kuwait

Company A additionally entitled to:

World War II–AP
    Luzon
Armed Forces Expeditions
    Panama (with arrowhead)

DECORATIONS

Meritorious Unit Commendation (Army), Streamer embroidered FRANCE 1944 (215th Signal Depot Company cited; GO 10, First Army, 17 January 1945)

Meritorious Unit Commendation (Army), Streamer embroidered VIETNAM 1966–1967 (313th Radio Research Battalion cited; DA GO 17, 1968)

Meritorious Unit Commendation (Army), Streamer embroidered VIETNAM 1967–1968 (Headquarters and Headquarters Company, 313th Radio Research Battalion cited; DA GO 28, 1969)

Meritorious Unit Commendation (Army), Streamer embroidered VIETNAM 1968–1969 (Headquarters and Headquarters Company, 313th Radio Research Battalion cited; DA GO 51, 1971)

Meritorious Unit Commendation (Army), Streamer embroidered VIETNAM 1969–1970 (313th Radio Research Battalion cited; DA GO 43, 1972)

Meritorious Unit Commendation (Army), Streamer embroidered VIETNAM 1971 (313th Radio Research Battalion cited; DA GO 32, 1973)

Meritorious Unit Commendation (Army), Streamer embroidered SOUTHWEST ASIA (313th Military Intelligence Battalion cited; DA GO 27, 1994)

French Croix de Guerre with Palm, World War II, Streamer embroidered NORMANDY BEACHES (Detachments, 215th Signal Depot Company, cited; DA GO 43, 1950)

Republic of Vietnam Cross of Gallantry with Palm, Streamer embroidered VIETNAM 1970–1971 (313th Radio Research Battalion cited; DA GO 6, 1974)

Company A additionally entitled to:

Philippine Presidential Unit Citation, Streamer embroidered 17 OCTOBER 1944 TO 4 JULY 1945 (3191st Signal Service Company cited; DA GO 47, 1950)

Company B additionally entitled to:

Military Order of William (Degree of the Knight of the Fourth Class), Streamer embroidered NIJMEGEN (82d Airborne Division cited; DA GO 43, 1950)

Netherlands Orange Lanyard (82d Airborne Division cited; DA GO 43, 1950)

Belgian Fourragere 1940 (82d Airborne Division cited; DA GO 43, 1950)

Cited in the Order of the Day of the Belgian Army for action in the Ardennes (82d Airborne Division cited; DA GO 43, 1950)

Cited in the Order of the Day of the Belgian Army for action in Belgium and Germany (82d Airborne Division cited; DA GO 43, 1950)

Republic of Vietnam Civil Action Honor Medal, First Class, Streamer embroidered VIETNAM 1968 (82d Military Intelligence Detachment cited; DA GO 48, 1971)

314th MILITARY INTELLIGENCE BATTALION

HERALDIC ITEMS

COAT OF ARMS

Shield: Argent, within a cross quarter-pierced azure the device from the flag of Okinawa proper; on a chief wavy sable a dagger and a key wards up saltirewise of the first.

Crest: That for the regiments and separate battalions of the Army Reserve: On a wreath of the colors, argent and azure, the Lexington Minuteman proper. The statue of the Minuteman, Capt. John Parker (H. H. Kitson, sculptor), stands on the Common in Lexington, Massachusetts.

Motto: SAPIENTIA ET VERITAS (WISDOM AND TRUTH).

Symbolism: Oriental blue and silver gray (white) are the colors traditionally associated with military intelligence. The red and white Okinawa symbol represents the unit's service in the Pacific. The blue and white squares simulate a chessboard and allude to strategy in gathering intelligence information. Black implies covert operations, while the silver key and sword refer to securing information for military activities. Black and white also signify day and night operations.

DISTINCTIVE UNIT INSIGNIA

The distinctive unit insignia is the shield and motto of the coat of arms.

Lineage and Honors

AR

Lineage

(active)

Constituted 14 December 1944 in the Army of the United States as the 314th Headquarters Intelligence Detachment. Activated 27 February 1945 in the Philippine Islands. Inactivated 25 March 1947 in Korea. Allotted 20 April 1948 to the Organized Reserve Corps. Activated 21 May 1948 at Boston, Massachusetts. Inactivated 30 June 1950 at Boston, Massachusetts.

Redesignated 10 August 1950 as Headquarters, 314th Military Intelligence Battalion. Activated 30 August 1950 at Cleveland, Ohio. (Organized Reserve Corps redesignated 9 July 1952 as the Army Reserve.) Inactivated 1 April 1953 at Cleveland, Ohio. Redesignated 16 September 1988 as Headquarters, Headquarters and Service Company, 314th Military Intelligence Battalion, and activated at Detroit, Michigan (organic elements concurrently constituted and activated).

Campaign Participation Credit

World War II
　　Ryukyus

Decorations

None.

319th MILITARY INTELLIGENCE BATTALION

HERALDIC ITEMS

COAT OF ARMS

Shield: Per pale azure and or, a Korean temple counterchanged, a point quartered argent and sable.

Crest: None approved.

Motto: HOSTEM COGERE (CONFINE THE ENEMY).

Symbolism: Oriental blue is one of the colors used for military intelligence units; gold is symbolic of knowledge and insight. The Korean temple represents the unit's decorations and service in the Pacific area. The black and white quartered base is taken from the arms of the city of Bad Schwalbach in Germany, where the organization was activated.

DISTINCTIVE UNIT INSIGNIA

The distinctive unit insignia is the shield and motto of the coat of arms.

LINEAGE AND HONORS

RA
(active)

LINEAGE

Constituted 14 July 1945 in the Army of the United States as the 319th Headquarters Intelligence Detachment. Activated 1 August 1945 in Germany. Inactivated 31 October 1946 in Germany. Redesignated 20 December 1946 as the 319th Military Intelligence Company. Activated 30 December 1946 in Japan. Reorganized and redesignated 1 September 1952 as the 319th Military Intelligence Service Company and allotted to the Regular Army. Inactivated 28 March 1954 in Japan.

Redesignated 14 January 1955 as the 319th Military Intelligence Battalion. Activated 7 March 1955 at Fort George G. Meade, Maryland. Reorganized and redesignated 25 January 1958 as Headquarters and Headquarters Company, 319th Military Intelligence Battalion. (162d Military Intelligence Company [see ANNEX 1] reorganized and redesignated 13 July 1959 as Company A.) Battalion inactivated 15 February 1968 at Fort Shafter, Hawaii. Activated 1 April 1982 at Fort Bragg, North Carolina (336th Army Security Agency Company [see ANNEX 2] concurrently reorganized and redesignated as Company B).

ANNEX 1

Constituted 5 April 1945 in the Army of the United States as the 162d Language Detachment. Activated 23 April 1945 in the Philippine Islands.

Inactivated 10 February 1946 in Japan. Redesignated 14 January 1955 as the 162d Military Intelligence Platoon and allotted to the Regular Army. Activated 7 March 1955 at Fort George G. Meade, Maryland. Reorganized and redesignated 25 January 1958 as the 162d Military Intelligence Company.

ANNEX 2

Constituted 1 July 1952 in the Regular Army as the 336th Communication Reconnaissance Company. Activated 6 August 1952 at Fort Devens, Massachusetts. Reorganized and redesignated 16 May 1955 as Company A, 311th Communication Reconnaissance Battalion. Redesignated 1 July 1956 as Company A, 311th Army Security Agency Battalion. Inactivated 18 December 1957 at Camp Wolters, Texas. Disbanded 15 February 1966. Reconstituted 21 September 1978 in the Regular Army as the 336th Army Security Agency Company. Activated 16 September 1979 at Fort Bragg, North Carolina.

CAMPAIGN PARTICIPATION CREDIT

> *Southwest Asia*
>> Defense of Saudi Arabia
>> Liberation and Defense of Kuwait

Company A additionally entitled to:

> *World War II–AP*
>> Luzon
> *Armed Forces Expeditions*
>> Panama

DECORATIONS

Meritorious Unit Commendation (Army), Streamer embroidered KOREA (319th Military Intelligence Service Company cited; DA GO 22, 1954)

Meritorious Unit Commendation (Army), Streamer embroidered SOUTHWEST ASIA (319th Military Intelligence Battalion cited; DA GO 14, 1993)

Company A additionally entitled to:

Philippine Presidential Unit Citation, Streamer embroidered 17 OCTOBER 1944 TO 4 JULY 1945 (162d Language Detachment cited; DA GO 47, 1950)

321st MILITARY INTELLIGENCE BATTALION

HERALDIC ITEMS

None approved.

LINEAGE AND HONORS

AR
(inactive)

LINEAGE

Constituted 14 July 1945 in the Army of the United States as the 321st Headquarters Intelligence Detachment and activated in Germany. Inactivated 30 November 1946 in Germany. Allotted 12 February 1947 to the Organized Reserves. Activated 26 February 1947 at Chicago, Illinois. (Organized Reserves redesignated 25 March 1948 as the Organized Reserve Corps; redesignated 9 July 1952 as the Army Reserve.) Inactivated 31 December 1948 at Chicago, Illinois. Activated 24 March 1949 at Chicago, Illinois.

Reorganized and redesignated 24 October 1950 as Headquarters, 321st Military Intelligence Battalion. Inactivated 1 March 1953 at Chicago, Illinois. Redesignated 13 February 1996 as Headquarters, Headquarters and Service Company, 321st Military Intelligence Battalion (organic elements concurrently constituted).

CAMPAIGN PARTICIPATION CREDIT

None.

DECORATIONS

None.

323d MILITARY INTELLIGENCE BATTALION

HERALDIC ITEMS

None approved.

LINEAGE AND HONORS

AR
(inactive)

LINEAGE

Constituted 15 March 1968 in the Regular Army as the 19th Military Intelligence Battalion and activated in Germany. Inactivated 20 March 1969 in Germany.

Redesignated 13 February 1996 as Headquarters and Headquarters Company, 323d Military Intelligence Battalion, withdrawn from the Regular Army, and allotted to the Army Reserve (organic elements concurrently constituted).

CAMPAIGN PARTICIPATION CREDIT

None.

DECORATIONS

None.

325th MILITARY INTELLIGENCE BATTALION

LINEAGE AND HONORS

AR
(inactive)

LINEAGE

Constituted 14 July 1945 in the Army of the United States as the 325th Headquarters Intelligence Detachment and activated in Germany. Inactivated 30 November 1946 in Germany. Allotted 7 February 1947 to the Organized Reserves. Activated 24 February 1947 at Philadelphia, Pennsylvania. (Organized Reserves redesignated 25 March 1948 as the Organized Reserve Corps; redesignated 9 July 1952 as the Army Reserve.) Reorganized and redesignated 30 September 1949 as Headquarters, 325th Military Intelligence Platoon.

Reorganized and redesignated 21 June 1950 as Headquarters, 325th Military Intelligence Battalion. Inactivated 1 April 1953 at Philadelphia, Pennsylvania. Redesignated 13 February 1996 as Headquarters, Headquarters and Service Company, 325th Military Intelligence Battalion (organic elements concurrently constituted).

CAMPAIGN PARTICIPATION CREDIT

None.

DECORATIONS

None.

326th MILITARY INTELLIGENCE BATTALION

HERALDIC ITEMS

COAT OF ARMS

Shield: Per fess or and checky sable and argent on a pile in point party per fess azure and of the first an eagle's head couped of the third langued gules.

Crest: None approved.

Motto: FROM INTELLIGENCE ACTION.

Symbolism: Oriental blue is one of the colors used for military intelligence units. The eagle's head with piercing eye representing vigilance, keenness of vision, and swiftness of purpose symbolizes the attributes inherent in the basic mission of the organization. The checkered area alludes to secrecy and compartmentalized information and, together with the inverted triangle formed from the heraldic pile, is indicative of the penetrative methods in the gathering of intelligence.

DISTINCTIVE UNIT INSIGNIA

The distinctive unit insignia is the shield and the motto of the coat of arms.

LINEAGE AND HONORS

RA
(active)

LINEAGE

Constituted 24 November 1967 in the Army Reserve as the 826th Military Intelligence Battalion. Activated 31 January 1968 with Headquarters at Hartford, Connecticut. Location of Headquarters changed 11 October 1969 to Cromwell, Connecticut. (Company C ordered into active military service 24 March 1970 at Fort Hamilton, New York; released from active military service 26 March 1970 and reverted to reserve status.) (Organic elements inactivated 16 September 1980.) Location of Headquarters and Headquarters Company changed 1 September 1981 to East Windsor, Connecticut. Headquarters and Headquarters Company inactivated 15 September 1987 at East Windsor, Connecticut.

Battalion redesignated 1 November 1994 as the 326th Military Intelligence Battalion; concurrently withdrawn from the Army Reserve and allotted to the Regular Army. Headquarters transferred 1 December 1994 to the United States Army Training and Doctrine Command and activated at Fort Huachuca, Arizona.

CAMPAIGN PARTICIPATION CREDIT

None.

DECORATIONS

None.

337th MILITARY INTELLIGENCE BATTALION

Heraldic Items

Coat of Arms

Shield: Argent, four flashes issuant from dexter chief, sinister chief, dexter base, and sinister base convergent in fess point azure, a dagger point up proper, blade and pommel argent, grip gules, guard and garnish or winged sable.

Crest: That for the regiments and separate battalions of the Army Reserve: On a wreath of the colors, argent and azure, the Lexington Minuteman proper. The statue of the Minuteman, Capt. John Parker (H. H. Kitson, sculptor), stands on the Common in Lexington, Massachusetts.

Motto: COLLECT EXPLOIT INFORM.

Symbolism: Oriental blue is one of the colors associated with military intelligence units. The flashes, alluding to speed and electronics, converge, emphasizing the collection and assimilation of information from all sources. They underscore the electronic warfare and signals intelligence capabilities of the unit. The winged dagger symbolizes the intelligence role in total military preparedness while characterizing the diverse mission and functions of the battalion.

Distinctive Unit Insignia

The distinctive unit insignia is the shield and motto of the coat of arms.

LINEAGE AND HONORS

AR
(active)

LINEAGE

Constituted 14 May 1948 in the Organized Reserve Corps as the 337th Headquarters Intelligence Detachment. Activated 2 June 1948 at New York, New York.

Reorganized and redesignated 6 July 1950 as Headquarters, 337th Military Intelligence Battalion. (Organized Reserve Corps redesignated 9 July 1952 as the Army Reserve.) Inactivated 20 February 1953 at New York, New York. Redesignated 16 September 1988 as Headquarters, Headquarters and Service Company, 337th Military Intelligence Battalion, and activated at Charlotte, North Carolina (organic elements concurrently constituted and activated).

CAMPAIGN PARTICIPATION CREDIT

None.

DECORATIONS

None.

338th MILITARY INTELLIGENCE BATTALION

HERALDIC ITEMS

COAT OF ARMS

Shield: Argent, an oval sphere azure gridlined of the field, overall a key wards up palewise of the last superimposed by a sphinx's head or garnished sable; on a chief embattled sable two flashes saltirewise gules.

Crest: That for the regiments and separate battalions of the Army Reserve: On a wreath of the colors, argent and azure, the Lexington Minuteman proper. The statue of the Minuteman, Capt. John Parker (H. H. Kitson, sculptor), stands on the Common in Lexington, Massachusetts.

Motto: INVENI ET USURPA (FIND AND EXPLOIT).

Symbolism: Oriental blue is one of the colors associated with military intelligence. The embattled division of the shield signifies defense and military preparedness, while black and white suggest night and day capabilities. The globe denotes the far-reaching scope of the unit's mission. The key symbolizes security; the sphinx alludes to vigilance and strength. The red flashes indicate speed and action while representing electronic communications and technology.

DISTINCTIVE UNIT INSIGNIA

The distinctive unit insignia consists of elements of the shield and motto of the coat of arms.

LINEAGE AND HONORS

AR
(active)

LINEAGE

Constituted 14 May 1948 in the Organized Reserve Corps as the 338th Headquarters Intelligence Detachment. Activated 2 June 1948 at New York, New York. Reorganized and redesignated 6 July 1950 as Headquarters, 338th Military Intelligence Company. Ordered into active military service 11 September 1950 at New York, New York. Reorganized and redesignated 7 December 1950 as the 338th Military Intelligence Service Company.

Reorganized and redesignated 1 November 1951 as the 338th Military Intelligence Service Battalion. (Organized Reserve Corps redesignated 9 July 1952 as the Army Reserve.) Reorganized and redesignated 14 December 1953 as the 338th Military Intelligence Battalion. Released from active military service 7 March 1955 and reverted to reserve status. Inactivated 8 March 1955 at New York, New York. Redesignated 16 September 1988 as Headquarters, Headquarters and Service Company, 338th Military Intelligence Battalion, and activated at Fort George G. Meade, Maryland (organic elements concurrently constituted and activated).

CAMPAIGN PARTICIPATION CREDIT

None.

DECORATIONS

None.

341st MILITARY INTELLIGENCE BATTALION

COAT OF ARMS

Shield: Per bend argent and azure, a lightning bolt bendwise throughout or between a stylized representation of the Rosetta Stone of the like detailed sable and an open book of the third leathered of the fourth surmounted in saltire by a quill gold and a sword point down of the last grip sable.

Crest: That for the regiments and separate battalions of the Washington Army National Guard: On a wreath of the colors, or and azure, a raven with wings endorsed issuing out of a ducal coronet all proper.

Motto: VIGILANTIA ET VALOR (VIGILANCE AND VALOR).

Symbolism: Oriental blue and silver gray are the colors traditionally associated with military intelligence. The lightning bolt denotes swiftness of action and accuracy. The Rosetta Stone indicates the unit's role as a linguist intelligence battalion. The book and quill symbolize knowledge, and the sword represents the unit's combat role.

DISTINCTIVE UNIT INSIGNIA

The distinctive unit insignia consists of elements of the shield, crest, and motto of the coat of arms.

LINEAGE AND HONORS

ARNG
(Washington)

LINEAGE

Organized and federally recognized 2 December 1989 in the Washington Army National Guard as the 341st Military Intelligence Battalion with Headquarters at Seattle. Location of Headquarters changed 1 March 1990 to Fort Lewis; changed 1 March 1992 to Kent; changed 1 September 1993 to Poulsbo.

Home Area: Statewide.

CAMPAIGN PARTICIPATION CREDIT

None.

DECORATIONS

None.

344th MILITARY INTELLIGENCE BATTALION

HERALDIC ITEMS

COAT OF ARMS

Shield: Argent on a saltire celeste a key ward up bendwise sinister surmounted by two pikes bendwise or.

Crest: None approved.

Motto: SILENT SENTINEL.

Symbolism: Oriental blue and silver gray are the colors used for military intelligence. The key, symbol for security and secrecy, and the pikes, weapons used by sentries in the Middle Ages, symbolize the basic mission of the organization.

DISTINCTIVE UNIT INSIGNIA

Description: A gold color metal and enamel device consisting of a gold key, ward slanted upward to right behind the shafts of two pikes; all encircled by a continuous oval-shaped scroll passing through the bow of the key, behind the pike heads, keyward and over the pike staffs and bearing the inscription in black letters SILENT SENTINEL.

Symbolism: The key, symbol for security and secrecy, and the pikes, weapons used by sentries in the Middle Ages, symbolize the basic mission of the organization. The shape of the bow of the key and the two pikes further simulates the numerical designation of the organization.

Lineage and Honors

Lineage

Constituted 5 November 1962 in the Army Reserve as the 344th Army Security Agency Company. Activated 28 February 1963 at Philadelphia, Pennsylvania. Reorganized and redesignated 15 April 1966 as Headquarters and Headquarters Company, 344th Army Security Agency Battalion. Inactivated 31 January 1968 at Philadelphia, Pennsylvania.

Redesignated 1 February 1990 as Headquarters and Headquarters Company, 344th Military Intelligence Battalion; concurrently withdrawn from the Army Reserve and allotted to the Regular Army. Headquarters transferred 25 May 1990 to the United States Army Training and Doctrine Command and activated at Goodfellow Air Force Base, Texas.

Campaign Participation Credit

None.

Decorations

Army Superior Unit Award, Streamer embroidered 1990–1991 (344th Military Intelligence Battalion cited; DA GO 34, 1992)

345th MILITARY INTELLIGENCE BATTALION

None approved.

LINEAGE AND HONORS

AR
(inactive)

LINEAGE

Constituted 3 October 1950 in the Organized Reserve Corps as Headquarters, 345th Military Intelligence Battalion. Activated 24 October 1950 at Minneapolis, Minnesota. Location changed 1 May 1952 to Fort Snelling, Minnesota. (Organized Reserve Corps redesignated 9 July 1952 as the Army Reserve.) Inactivated 1 March 1953 at Fort Snelling, Minnesota. Redesignated 8 August 1995 as Headquarters, Headquarters and Service Company, 345th Military Intelligence Battalion (organic elements concurrently constituted).

CAMPAIGN PARTICIPATION CREDIT

None.

DECORATIONS

None.

368th MILITARY INTELLIGENCE BATTALION

HERALDIC ITEMS

None approved.

LINEAGE AND HONORS

AR
(inactive)

LINEAGE

Constituted 20 September 1950 in the Organized Reserve Corps as Headquarters, 368th Military Intelligence Battalion. Activated 1 October 1950 at Los Angeles, California. (Organized Reserve Corps redesignated 9 July 1952 as the Army Reserve.) Inactivated 1 February 1953 at Los Angeles, California. Redesignated 8 August 1995 as Headquarters, Headquarters and Service Company, 368th Military Intelligence Battalion (organic elements concurrently constituted).

CAMPAIGN PARTICIPATION CREDIT

None.

DECORATIONS

None.

372d MILITARY INTELLIGENCE BATTALION

HERALDIC ITEMS

None approved.

LINEAGE AND HONORS

AR
(inactive)

LINEAGE

Constituted 2 November 1950 in the Organized Reserve Corps as Headquarters, 372d Military Intelligence Battalion. Activated 15 November 1950 at Boston, Massachusetts. (Organized Reserve Corps redesignated 9 July 1952 as the Army Reserve.) Inactivated 28 February 1953 at Boston, Massachusetts. Redesignated 28 March 1996 as Headquarters, Headquarters and Service Company, 372d Military Intelligence Battalion (organic elements concurrently constituted).

CAMPAIGN PARTICIPATION CREDIT

None.

DECORATIONS

None.

373d MILITARY INTELLIGENCE BATTALION

HERALDIC ITEMS

COAT OF ARMS

Shield: Azure, a plate charged with a key ward to chief sable and a lightning flash or saltirewise upon a sunburst argent interlaced with a laurel wreath vert, overall in base a dagger, blade, hilt, and pommel or, grip gules.

Crest: That for the regiments and separate battalions of the Army Reserve: On a wreath of the colors, argent and azure, the Lexington Minuteman proper. The statue of the Minuteman, Capt. John Parker (H. H. Kitson, sculptor), stands on the Common in Lexington, Massachusetts.

Motto: COLLECT SUPPORT DEFEND.

Symbolism: Oriental blue is one of the colors associated with military intelligence. The plate, symbolizing the earth, recalls the worldwide mission of military intelligence; the sunburst behind it is adapted from the military intelligence branch insignia. The wreath stands for honor, the key for security, and the lightning flash for speed. The dagger recalls the danger of the military intelligence mission.

DISTINCTIVE UNIT INSIGNIA

The distinctive unit insignia consists of elements of the shield and motto of the coat of arms.

LINEAGE AND HONORS

AR
(active)

LINEAGE

Constituted 1 December 1950 in the Organized Reserve Corps as Headquarters, 373d Military Intelligence Battalion. Activated 20 December 1950 at Berkeley, California. (Organized Reserve Corps redesignated 9 July 1952 as the Army Reserve.) Inactivated 1 February 1953 at Berkeley, California. Redesignated 16 September 1988 as Headquarters, Headquarters and Service Company, 373d Military Intelligence Battalion, and activated at Oakland, California (organic elements concurrently constituted and activated).

CAMPAIGN PARTICIPATION CREDIT

None.

DECORATIONS

None.

376th MILITARY INTELLIGENCE BATTALION

HERALDIC ITEMS

None approved.

LINEAGE AND HONORS

AR
(inactive)

LINEAGE

Constituted 19 July 1950 in the Organized Reserve Corps as Headquarters, 376th Military Intelligence Group. Activated 1 August 1950 at Dallas, Texas. (Organized Reserve Corps redesignated 9 July 1952 as the Army Reserve.) Inactivated 23 February 1953 at Dallas, Texas.

Redesignated 28 March 1996 as Headquarters, Headquarters and Service Company, 376th Military Intelligence Battalion (organic elements concurrently constituted).

CAMPAIGN PARTICIPATION CREDIT

None.

DECORATIONS

None.

377th MILITARY INTELLIGENCE BATTALION

HERALDIC ITEMS

None approved.

LINEAGE AND HONORS

AR
(inactive)

LINEAGE

Constituted 30 August 1950 in the Organized Reserve Corps as Headquarters, 377th Military Intelligence Group. Activated 26 September 1950 at Fort Myer, Virginia. (Organized Reserve Corps redesignated 9 July 1952 as the Army Reserve.) Inactivated 1 April 1953 at Fort Myer, Virginia.

Redesignated 28 March 1996 as Headquarters, Headquarters and Service Company, 377th Military Intelligence Battalion (organic elements concurrently constituted).

CAMPAIGN PARTICIPATION CREDIT

None.

DECORATIONS

None.

378th MILITARY INTELLIGENCE BATTALION

HERALDIC ITEMS

None approved.

LINEAGE AND HONORS

AR
(inactive)

LINEAGE

Constituted 31 August 1950 in the Organized Reserve Corps as Headquarters, 378th Military Intelligence Group. Activated 3 October 1950 at Chicago, Illinois. (Organized Reserve Corps redesignated 9 July 1952 as the Army Reserve.) Inactivated 1 March 1953 at Chicago, Illinois.

Redesignated 28 March 1996 as Headquarters, Headquarters and Service Company, 378th Military Intelligence Battalion (organic elements concurrently constituted).

CAMPAIGN PARTICIPATION CREDIT

None.

DECORATIONS

None.

383d MILITARY INTELLIGENCE BATTALION

HERALDIC ITEMS

None approved.

LINEAGE AND HONORS

AR
(inactive)

LINEAGE

Constituted 8 February 1951 in the Organized Reserve Corps as Headquarters, 383d Military Intelligence Battalion. Activated 1 March 1951 at Newark, New Jersey. (Organized Reserve Corps redesignated 9 July 1952 as the Army Reserve.) Inactivated 28 February 1953 at Newark, New Jersey. Redesignated 28 March 1996 as Headquarters, Headquarters and Service Company, 383d Military Intelligence Battalion (organic elements concurrently constituted).

CAMPAIGN PARTICIPATION CREDIT

None.

DECORATIONS

None.

415th MILITARY INTELLIGENCE BATTALION

HERALDIC ITEMS

COAT OF ARMS

Shield: Azure, a fleur-de-lis or bearing a double-warded key wards up gules; on a fess sable a tiger courant proper.

Crest: That for the regiments and separate battalions of the Louisiana Army National Guard: On a wreath of the colors, or and azure, a pelican in her piety affronté with three young in nest, argent, armed and vulned proper.

Motto: PASSE PARTOUT (PASS INTO/THROUGH EVERYWHERE).

Symbolism: Oriental blue is one of the colors associated with military intelligence organizations. The tiger represents strength, readiness, and military power. The fleur-de-lis is a symbol of Louisiana, the home state of the unit. The red key symbolizes courage and vitality in the mission of unlocking information using foreign languages.

DISTINCTIVE UNIT INSIGNIA

The distinctive unit insignia is the shield and motto of the coat of arms.

LINEAGE AND HONORS

ARNG
(Louisiana)

LINEAGE

Organized and federally recognized 1 December 1989 in the Louisiana Army National Guard as the 415th Military Intelligence Battalion with Headquarters at Baton Rouge.

Home Station: Baton Rouge.

CAMPAIGN PARTICIPATION CREDIT

None.

DECORATIONS

None.

501st MILITARY INTELLIGENCE BATTALION
(Electronic Horsemen)

HERALDIC ITEMS

COAT OF ARMS

Shield: Quarterly azure and vert, in bend a lightning flash point to base gules fimbriated or and in bend sinister a cavalry saber point to chief of the like.

Crest: On a wreath of the colors, or and azure, in front of a torii gate gules a horse's head erased sable langued of the third interlaced with two lightning flashes, the one behind bendwise and one in front bend sinisterwise of the first.

Motto: OUT FRONT.

Symbolism: Blue and green refer to the air and ground assets of the battalion and further allude to the close relationship with infantry (blue) and armor (green) units of the division. The red and yellow flash connotes the prominent role of electronic signals intelligence in modern warfare. The cavalry saber, flash, and quartered field collectively suggest the blending of the traditional with the latest modern developments in intelligence, reconnaissance, security, and electronic warfare capabilities within the military intelligence battalion.

    The black horse's head, suggested by the arms of the province of Naples, refers to the participation of an element of the battalion in Italian campaigns of World War II. The torii gate alludes to the battalion's service in Korea and the flashes connote awards of the Meritorious Unit Commendation (Army) and the Republic of Korea Presidential Unit Citation.

DISTINCTIVE UNIT INSIGNIA

The distinctive unit insignia is the shield and motto of the coat of arms.

Lineage and Honors

Lineage

Constituted 13 October 1950 in the Regular Army as Headquarters and Headquarters Detachment, 301st Communication Reconnaissance Battalion. Activated 20 October 1950 at Camp Pickett, Virginia. Reorganized and redesignated 25 June 1955 as Headquarters and Headquarters Company, 301st Communication Reconnaissance Battalion (356th Communication Reconnaissance Company [activated 15 January 1946] and 329th Communication Reconnaissance Company [activated 1 November 1943] concurrently reorganized and redesignated as Companies A and B). Redesignated 1 July 1956 as the 301st Army Security Agency Battalion. Inactivated 15 October 1957 in Korea. Headquarters and Headquarters Company activated 15 December 1965 at Fort Bragg, North Carolina. Inactivated 18 June 1971 at Fort Bragg, North Carolina. (Companies A and B redesignated 1 November 1975 as the 356th and 329th Army Security Agency Companies—hereafter separate lineages.)

Headquarters and Headquarters Company, 301st Army Security Agency Battalion, redesignated 16 September 1980 as Headquarters, Headquarters and Operations Company, 501st Military Intelligence Battalion, assigned to the 1st Armored Division, and activated in Germany (202d Army Security Agency Company [see ANNEX 1] concurrently reorganized and redesignated as Company A; 501st Military Intelligence Detachment [see ANNEX 2] redesignated as Company B and activated).

Annex 1

Constituted 15 July 1967 in the Regular Army as the 202d Army Security Agency Company and activated at Fort Hood, Texas. Inactivated 19 April 1971 at Fort Hood, Texas. Activated 1 July 1974 in Germany.

Annex 2

Organized 26 August 1943 in Algeria as the 2678th Headquarters Company, Counter Intelligence Corps (Provisional). Disbanded 26 April 1944 and personnel transferred to the 6779th Counter Intelligence Corps Detachment (Provisional). Disbanded 18 August 1944 and personnel transferred to the 501st Counter Intelligence Corps Detachment (constituted 12 July 1944 in the Army of the United States). Disbanded 26 June 1945 in Italy.

Reconstituted 6 April 1951 in the Regular Army as the 501st Counter Intelligence Corps Detachment. Activated 11 May 1951 at Fort Holabird, Maryland. Reorganized and redesignated 25 January 1958 as the 501st Military Intelligence Detachment. Inactivated 31 March 1971 at Fort Hood, Texas.

CAMPAIGN PARTICIPATION CREDIT

Korean War
Second Korean Winter
Korea, Summer-Fall 1952
Third Korean Winter
Korea, Summer 1953
Southwest Asia
Defense of Saudi Arabia
Liberation and Defense of Kuwait
Cease-Fire

Company B additionally entitled to:

World War II–EAME
Naples-Foggia
Anzio
Rome-Arno
North Apennines
Po Valley

DECORATIONS

Meritorious Unit Commendation (Army), Streamer embroidered KOREA (Headquarters and Headquarters Detachment, 301st Communication Reconnaissance Battalion, cited; DA GO 22, 1954)

Meritorious Unit Commendation (Army), Streamer embroidered SOUTHWEST ASIA (501st Military Intelligence Battalion cited; DA GO 1, 1996)

Republic of Korea Presidential Unit Citation, Streamer embroidered KOREA (Headquarters and Headquarters Detachment, 301st Communication Reconnaissance Battalion, cited; DA GO 33, 1953, as amended by DA GO 41, 1955)

502d MILITARY INTELLIGENCE BATTALION

HERALDIC ITEMS

COAT OF ARMS

Shield: Argent, on a pale azure between two beacon fires in base of the second enflamed or, in chief a beacon fire of the first enflamed of the third.

Crest: On a wreath of the colors, argent and azure, issuing from a wreath of laurel or with a Korean taeguk at center proper, a griffin's head of the third langued gules.

Motto: FREEDOM BY VIGILANCE.

Symbolism: Oriental blue is one of the colors used for military intelligence units. The three beacon fires, representing Korea's ancient system of sending messages, allude to the three campaigns in which the unit served in the Korean War. The gold of the flames commemorates unit decorations received by the battalion.

The griffin is a symbol of vigilance, the essential attribute for effective intelligence work. The taeguk represents the Republic of Korea Presidential Unit Citation, and the wreath refers to the Meritorious Unit Commendation (Army) awarded to the battalion for service in Korea. Gold is used to represent excellence and achievements of the unit.

DISTINCTIVE UNIT INSIGNIA

The distinctive unit insignia is the shield and motto of the coat of arms.

Lineage and Honors

Lineage

Constituted 30 June 1952 in the Regular Army as Headquarters, 502d Military Intelligence Service Battalion. Activated 1 September 1952 in Korea. Reorganized and redesignated 28 March 1954 as Headquarters, 502d Military Intelligence Battalion. Inactivated 20 January 1955 in Korea. Redesignated 20 March 1961 as Headquarters and Headquarters Company, 502d Military Intelligence Battalion (organic elements concurrently constituted). Battalion activated 25 March 1961 in Korea. Inactivated 1 January 1978 in Korea. Activated 1 October 1986 at Fort Lewis, Washington.

Campaign Participation Credit

Korean War
  Korea, Summer-Fall 1952
  Third Korean Winter
  Korea, Summer 1953

Decorations

Meritorious Unit Commendation (Army), Streamer embroidered KOREA (Headquarters, 502d Military Intelligence Battalion, cited; DA GO 14, 1955)

Republic of Korea Presidential Unit Citation, Streamer embroidered KOREA (Headquarters, 502d Military Intelligence Service Battalion, cited; DA GO 70, 1953)

511th MILITARY INTELLIGENCE BATTALION

HERALDIC ITEMS

COAT OF ARMS

Shield: Azure, a Korean taeguk proper and issuant therefrom to chief three lightning bolts argent.

Crest: On a wreath of the colors, argent and azure, two griffins' heads addorsed and erased, that to dexter argent and that to sinister of the second both beaked and eyed or and langued gules.

Motto: PROUD AND READY.

Symbolism: Oriental blue and silver gray are the colors associated with the military intelligence branch. The lightning bolts refer to the importance of speed, electronics, and communications to all intelligence activities and represent the unit's participation in three campaigns in the Korean War and its multifaceted intelligence mission. The taeguk denotes the award of the Republic of Korea Presidential Unit Citation to the organization.

The griffin is a heraldic symbol of alertness and vigilance; the prominent eyes and ears suggest the role played by intelligence forces in support of the Army's mission. The contrasting colors and back-to-back position signify the round-the-clock and worldwide scope of the intelligence and security functions.

DISTINCTIVE UNIT INSIGNIA

The distinctive unit insignia is an adaptation of the shield, crest, and motto of the coat of arms.

LINEAGE AND HONORS

RA
(inactive)

LINEAGE

Constituted 30 June 1952 in the Regular Army as the 511th Military Intelligence Service Company. Activated 1 September 1952 in Korea. Reorganized and redesignated 28 March 1954 as the 511th Military Intelligence Company. Inactivated 20 May 1956 in Korea. Activated 1 June 1962 in Germany.

Reorganized and redesignated 1 July 1972 as Headquarters and Headquarters Company, 511th Military Intelligence Battalion. Inactivated 1 October 1983 in Germany. Redesignated 16 October 1983 as Headquarters, Headquarters and Service Company, 511th Military Intelligence Battalion, and activated in Germany (organic elements concurrently constituted and activated). Battalion inactivated 15 November 1991 in Germany.

CAMPAIGN PARTICIPATION CREDIT

Korean War
> Korea, Summer-Fall 1952
> Third Korean Winter
> Korea, Summer 1953

Southwest Asia
> Defense of Saudi Arabia
> Liberation and Defense of Kuwait
> Cease-Fire

DECORATIONS

Meritorious Unit Commendation (Army), Streamer embroidered SOUTHWEST ASIA (511th Military Intelligence Battalion cited; DA GO 34, 1992)

Republic of Korea Presidential Unit Citation, Streamer embroidered KOREA 1952–1953 (511th Military Intelligence Service Company cited; DA GO 24, 1954)

519th MILITARY INTELLIGENCE BATTALION

Heraldic Items

Coat of Arms

Shield: Or, in base a sphinx facing to dexter couchant azure detailed of the first in front of an open book of the last, fimbriated of the second, its upper edge at fess point in front of a globe overall of the like, gridlined of the field.

Crest: On a wreath of the colors, or and azure, a garb of rice of the first in front of a triangle gules conjoined at the tip with a torii sable.

Motto: STRENGTH THRU INTELLIGENCE.

Symbolism: Teal blue and yellow are the colors formerly used for Army intelligence organizations. The sphinx also symbolizes Army intelligence. Resting against the terrestrial globe is an open book, representing the knowledge made available through mastery of the languages of the world. The globe itself indicates the worldwide scope of the battalion's activities.

Red is the color for action, and the triangle, simulating a Vietnamese sun hat, alludes to service in Vietnam. The torii refers to Korea, where an element of the organization participated in seven campaigns. The rice stalks represent the unit decorations awarded during both wars.

Distinctive Unit Insignia

The distinctive unit insignia is the shield and motto of the coat of arms.

LINEAGE AND HONORS

LINEAGE

Constituted 1 October 1948 in the Regular Army as the 519th Headquarters Intelligence Detachment. Activated 15 October 1948 at Fort Riley, Kansas. Reorganized and redesignated 10 May 1949 as Headquarters, 519th Military Intelligence Platoon. Reorganized and redesignated 11 August 1949 as the 519th Military Intelligence Service Platoon.

Reorganized and redesignated 21 November 1951 as the 519th Military Intelligence Service Battalion. Reorganized and redesignated 31 December 1953 as the 519th Military Intelligence Battalion. Reorganized and redesignated 25 January 1958 as Headquarters and Headquarters Company, 519th Military Intelligence Battalion. (523d Military Intelligence Company [see ANNEX] reorganized and redesignated 15 July 1959 as Company A.)

ANNEX

Constituted 25 September 1950 in the Regular Army as the 523d Military Intelligence Service Platoon. Activated 10 October 1950 at Fort Riley, Kansas. Reorganized and redesignated 1 September 1952 as the 523d Military Intelligence Service Company. Reorganized and redesignated 28 March 1954 as the 523d Military Intelligence Company. Inactivated 15 November 1954 in Korea. Activated 25 January 1958 at Fort Bragg, North Carolina.

CAMPAIGN PARTICIPATION CREDIT

Vietnam
    Defense
    Counteroffensive
    Counteroffensive, Phase II
    Counteroffensive, Phase III
    Tet Counteroffensive
    Counteroffensive, Phase IV
    Counteroffensive, Phase V
    Counteroffensive, Phase VI
    Tet 69/Counteroffensive
    Summer-Fall 1969
    Winter-Spring 1970
    Sanctuary Counteroffensive
    Counteroffensive, Phase VII
    Consolidation I
    Consolidation II
    Cease-Fire
Armed Forces Expeditions
    Panama
Southwest Asia
    Defense of Saudi Arabia
    Liberation and Defense of Kuwait

Company A additionally entitled to:

> *Korean War*
> > First UN Counteroffensive
> > CCF Spring Offensive
> > UN Summer-Fall Offensive
> > Second Korean Winter
> > Korea, Summer-Fall 1952
> > Third Korean Winter
> > Korea, Summer 1953

DECORATIONS

Meritorious Unit Commendation (Army), Streamer embroidered VIETNAM 1968–1969 (Headquarters and Headquarters Company and Company A, 519th Military Intelligence Battalion, cited; DA GO 51, 1971)

Meritorious Unit Commendation (Army), Streamer embroidered VIETNAM 1970 (519th Military Intelligence Battalion cited; DA GO 52, 1974)

Meritorious Unit Commendation (Army), Streamer embroidered VIETNAM 1971–1972 (519th Military Intelligence Battalion cited; DA GO 6, 1976)

Company A additionally entitled to:

Meritorious Unit Commendation (Army), Streamer embroidered KOREA (523d Military Intelligence Service Company cited; DA GO 36, 1953)

Republic of Korea Presidential Unit Citation, Streamer embroidered KOREA 1950–1952 (523d Military Intelligence Service Platoon cited; DA GO 33, 1953, as amended by DA GO 41, 1955)

Republic of Korea Presidential Unit Citation, Streamer embroidered KOREA 1952–1953 (523d Military Intelligence Company cited; DA GO 89, 1953, as amended by DA GO 9, 1955)

Company C additionally entitled to:

Meritorious Unit Commendation (Army), Streamer embroidered VIETNAM 1966–1967 (Company C, 519th Military Intelligence Battalion, cited; DA GO 43, 1968)

522d MILITARY INTELLIGENCE BATTALION

HERALDIC ITEMS

COAT OF ARMS

Shield: Azure, on a bend engrailed plain cottised between a winged sphinx couchant argent and a taeguk gules and azure fimbriated of the second, a lightning flash gules.

Crest: None approved.

Motto: THE EQUALIZERS.

Symbolism: Oriental blue and silver gray are the colors used for military intelligence. The winged sphinx is symbolic of all-seeing and eternal vigilance, and the taeguk refers to the unit's Korean War service. The electronic warfare intelligence capability of the organization is represented by the engrailed bend, and the lightning flash is indicative of speed in communication and intelligence gathering.

DISTINCTIVE UNIT INSIGNIA

The distinctive unit insignia is the shield and motto of the coat of arms.

LINEAGE AND HONORS

RA
(inactive)

LINEAGE

Organized 1 September 1950 at Fort Bragg, North Carolina, as the 522d Military Intelligence Service Detachment. (Constituted 20 September 1950 in the Regular Army.) Inactivated 28 December 1951 in Korea.

Redesignated 23 June 1954 as Headquarters and Headquarters Company, 522d Military Intelligence Battalion (Companies A and B concurrently constituted). Battalion activated 27 July 1954 in Germany. Inactivated 15 August 1958 in Germany. Assigned 21 December 1976 to the 2d Armored Division and activated at Fort Hood, Texas. (373d Army Security Agency Company [see ANNEX 1] consolidated 16 October 1979 with Company A; 502d Military Intelligence Company [see ANNEX 2] concurrently consolidated with Company B.) Inactivated 15 April 1991 at Fort Hood, Texas. Activated 16 December 1992 at Fort Polk, Louisiana. Inactivated 15 January 1996 at Fort Hood, Texas.

ANNEX 1

Constituted 11 May 1962 in the Regular Army as Company B, 303d Army Security Agency Battalion. Activated 25 June 1962 at Fort Benning, Georgia. Reorganized and redesignated 15 October 1966 as the 373d Army Security Agency Company.

ANNEX 2

Constituted 21 June 1944 in the Army of the United States as the 520th Counter Intelligence Corps Detachment. Activated 1 July 1944 at Camp Campbell, Kentucky. Allotted 17 December 1948 to the Regular Army.

Reorganized and redesignated 25 January 1958 as the 502d Military Intelligence Detachment. Consolidated 28 December 1961 with the 502d Counter Intelligence Corps Detachment (see ANNEX 3) and consolidated unit designated as the 502d Military Intelligence Detachment. Reorganized and redesignated 8 January 1971 as the 502d Military Intelligence Company.

ANNEX 3

Constituted 12 July 1944 in the Army of the United States as the 502d Counter Intelligence Corps Detachment. Activated 16 August 1944 in France with personnel from provisional Counter Intelligence Corps detachment attached to the 2d Armored Division. Inactivated 14 October 1946 in Germany. Activated 10 May 1947 on Guam. Inactivated 14 March 1950 on Guam.

CAMPAIGN PARTICIPATION CREDIT

Korean War
UN Offensive
CCF Intervention
First UN Counteroffensive
CCF Spring Offensive
UN Summer-Fall Offensive
Second Korean Winter
Southwest Asia
Defense of Saudi Arabia
Liberation and Defense of Kuwait

Company B additionally entitled to:

World War II–EAME
Normandy
Northern France
Rhineland
Ardennes-Alsace
Central Europe

DECORATIONS

Company B entitled to:

Belgian Fourragere 1940 (2d Armored Division cited; DA GO 43, 1950)

Cited in the Order of the Day of the Belgian Army for action in Belgium (2d Armored Division cited; DA GO 43, 1950)

Cited in the Order of the Day of the Belgian Army for action in the Ardennes (2d Armored Division cited; DA GO 43, 1950)

524th MILITARY INTELLIGENCE BATTALION

HERALDIC ITEMS

COAT OF ARMS

Shield: Azure two chevronels fretty argent charged with eighteen pellets all within a bordure of the second.

Crest: On a wreath of the colors, argent and azure, a garb of rice or charged at base with a taeguk proper; overall a bayonet palewise, point up, blade sable and hilt argent all tied with a ribbon gules.

Motto: SILENT VIGILANCE.

Symbolism: Oriental blue and silver gray are the colors associated with military intelligence. The interlocking chevronels suggest the gathering of information from many sources processed through the unit and distributed throughout the Army, as represented by the border. The black pellets suggest the unit's ability to interpret various data and to form assessments of military situations. Eighteen refers to the number of campaigns in which the unit participated in Korea and Vietnam.

The bayonet alludes to the unit's participation in campaigns in Vietnam and Korea, represented by the garb of rice and taeguk. The black blade refers to secrecy and the unit's intelligence function. The red band of the garb refers to the Meritorious Unit Commendation (Army) awarded the unit for service in Vietnam.

DISTINCTIVE UNIT INSIGNIA

The distinctive unit insignia is the shield and motto of the coat of arms.

LINEAGE AND HONORS

RA
(active)

LINEAGE

Constituted 25 September 1950 in the Regular Army as the 524th Technical Intelligence Coordinator Detachment. Activated 10 October 1950 at Fort Riley, Kansas. Inactivated 1 December 1951 in Korea. Redesignated 22 June 1965 as the 524th Intelligence Corps Detachment. Activated 1 July 1965 at Fort Bragg, North Carolina. Redesignated 15 October 1966 as the 524th Military Intelligence Detachment. Inactivated 26 November 1970 in Vietnam.

Redesignated 16 June 1982 as Headquarters and Headquarters Company, 524th Military Intelligence Battalion, and activated in Korea. (Organic elements constituted 16 October 1988; Company A concurrently activated in Korea.)

CAMPAIGN PARTICIPATION CREDIT

Korean War
 CCF Intervention
 First UN Counteroffensive
 CCF Spring Offensive
 UN Summer-Fall Offensive
 Second Korean Winter

Vietnam
 Defense
 Counteroffensive
 Counteroffensive, Phase II
 Counteroffensive, Phase III
 Tet Counteroffensive
 Counteroffensive, Phase IV
 Counteroffensive, Phase V
 Counteroffensive, Phase VI
 Tet 69/Counteroffensive
 Summer-Fall 1969
 Winter-Spring 1970
 Sanctuary Counteroffensive
 Counteroffensive, Phase VII

DECORATIONS

Meritorious Unit Commendation (Army), Streamer embroidered VIETNAM 1966–1968 (524th Military Intelligence Detachment cited; DA GO 67, 1968)

Army Superior Unit Award, Streamer embroidered 1986–1988 (524th Military Intelligence Battalion cited; DA GO 14, 1989)

527th MILITARY INTELLIGENCE BATTALION

HERALDIC ITEMS

COAT OF ARMS

Shield: Gyronny of eight argent and sable, a pale gules voided throughout argent, surmounted by a globe azure gridlined argent, overall two swords saltirewise also argent.

Crest: None approved.

Motto: STRIVE FOR EXCELLENCE.

Symbolism: The shield, divided into dark and light sections, suggests the ever-changing methods of counterintelligence functions and the day/night vigilance of intelligence gathering. The red and white allude to the coat of arms of Kaiserslautern in Germany, where the unit has been stationed. The globe alludes to the overseas origin and duty of the unit and resembles a grid, which suggests the sifting of information through the unit to support Army goals. The crossed swords symbolize offensive and defensive counterintelligence and the defense of Europe.

DISTINCTIVE UNIT INSIGNIA

Description: A silver color metal and enamel device consisting of two silver swords in saltire, pommels to base, the lateral and base areas between the swords of black enamel and the upper area of red enamel; surmounting the swords a blue disc divided by five horizontal and vertical silver lines bearing at center a black square, point up, with a silver dot; issuing from the disc three rays to the lateral and base areas and a broad arrowhead extending beyond the top all silver; on a silver scroll issuing from under the blades and the pommels, the inscription STRIVE FOR EXCELLENCE in black enamel.

Symbolism: The square and dot simulate an observation apparatus, the disc represents a globe, and the divisions symbolize a network. The arrowhead connotes martial readiness, while the rays symbolize all facets of sound, light, and vibratory systems. All represent the collection, processing, and dissemination of information functions of a military intelligence unit. The swords refer to defensive and offensive counterintelligence methods. The white arrowhead dividing the red area suggests the coat of arms of Kaiserslautern in Germany, symbolizing service there.

LINEAGE AND HONORS

RA
(active)

LINEAGE

Constituted 18 April 1946 in the Army of the United States as the 527th Interrogation Team. Activated 1 May 1946 in Germany. Inactivated 31 October 1946 in Germany. Redesignated 6 February 1948 as the 527th Headquarters Intelligence Detachment. Activated 21 February 1948 at Fort Bragg, North Carolina. Allotted 5 May 1949 to the Regular Army. Reorganized and redesignated 23 May 1949 as Headquarters, 527th Military Intelligence Platoon. Reorganized and redesignated 4 August 1949 as the 527th Military Intelligence Service Platoon. Reorganized and redesignated 14 November 1951 as the 527th Military Intelligence Service Company. Reorganized and redesignated 31 December 1953 as the 527th Military Intelligence Company. Inactivated 25 January 1958 at Fort Hood, Texas. Activated 1 June 1962 in Germany.

Reorganized and redesignated 1 July 1972 as Headquarters and Headquarters Company, 527th Military Intelligence Battalion. (Organic elements constituted 1 October 1982 and activated in Germany.)

CAMPAIGN PARTICIPATION CREDIT

None.

DECORATIONS

Army Superior Unit Award, Streamer embroidered 1990–1991 (527th Military Intelligence Battalion cited; DA GO 34, 1992)

532d MILITARY INTELLIGENCE BATTALION

HERALDIC ITEMS

COAT OF ARMS

Shield: Checky azure and or a horse rampant sable fimbriated of the second.

Crest: None approved.

Motto: NOSCE HOSTEM (KNOW YOUR ENEMY).

Symbolism: Teal blue and yellow are the colors formerly used for military intelligence battalions. The black horse alludes to Stuttgart in Germany, the unit's place of activation. The horse and checky field combined, symbolic of a chessboard, refer to the strategic and tactical functions of an intelligence unit.

DISTINCTIVE UNIT INSIGNIA

The distinctive unit insignia is the shield and motto of the coat of arms.

LINEAGE AND HONORS

RA
(active)

LINEAGE

Constituted 16 February 1951 in the Regular Army as the 532d Military Intelligence Service Company. Activated 15 August 1951 in Germany.

Reorganized and redesignated 20 September 1951 as the 532d Military Intelligence Service Battalion. Reorganized and redesignated 20 October 1953 as the 532d Military Intelligence Battalion. Reorganized and redesignated 25 June 1958 as Headquarters and Headquarters Company, 532d Military Intelligence Battalion (521st Military Intelligence Company [see ANNEX 1], 427th Counter Intelligence Corps Detachment [see ANNEX 2], and 526th Military Intelligence Company [see ANNEX 3] concurrently reorganized and redesignated as Companies A, B, and C). Battalion inactivated 1 June 1962 in Germany. Activated 16 October 1986 in Korea.

ANNEX 1

Organized 5 September 1950 in Japan as the 521st Military Intelligence Service Detachment. (Constituted 7 September 1950 in the Regular Army.) Reorganized and redesignated 28 December 1951 as the 521st Military Intelligence Service Platoon. Reorganized and redesignated 1 September 1952 as the 521st Military Intelligence Service Company. Reorganized and redesignated 28 March 1954 as the 521st Military Intelligence Company.

ANNEX 2

Constituted 12 July 1944 in the Army of the United States as the 427th Counter Intelligence Corps Detachment. Activated 22 August 1944 on Corsica. Allotted 16 February 1951 to the Regular Army.

ANNEX 3

Constituted 18 April 1946 in the Army of the United States as the 526th Interrogation Team. Activated 1 May 1946 in Germany. Inactivated 6 November 1946 in Germany. Redesignated 6 February 1948 as the 526th Headquarters Intelligence Detachment. Activated 21 February 1948 at Fort Bragg, North Carolina. Allotted 5 May 1949 to the Regular Army. Reorganized and redesignated 23 May 1949 as Headquarters, 526th Military Intelligence Platoon. Reorganized and redesignated 4 August 1949 as the 526th Military Intelligence Service Platoon. Reorganized and redesignated 28 August 1951 as the 526th Military Intelligence Service Company. Reorganized and redesignated 20 October 1953 as the 526th Military Intelligence Company.

CAMPAIGN PARTICIPATION CREDIT

Company A entitled to:

Korean War
- UN Defensive
- UN Offensive
- CCF Intervention
- First UN Counteroffensive
- CCF Spring Offensive
- UN Summer-Fall Offensive
- Second Korean Winter
- Korea, Summer-Fall 1952
- Third Korean Winter
- Korea, Summer 1953

Company B entitled to:

World War II–EAME
- Rhineland

DECORATIONS

Company A entitled to:

Meritorious Unit Commendation (Army), Streamer embroidered KOREA 1951–1952 (521st Military Intelligence Service Platoon cited; DA GO 10, 1953)

Meritorious Unit Commendation (Army), Streamer embroidered KOREA 1952–1954 (521st Military Intelligence Service Company cited; DA GO 46, 1954)

Republic of Korea Presidential Unit Citation, Streamer embroidered KOREA (521st Military Intelligence Service Company cited; DA GO 82, 1954)

533d MILITARY INTELLIGENCE BATTALION

Heraldic Items

Coat of Arms

Shield: Per fess argent and azure two lightning flashes saltirewise counterchanged, in chief two eagles' heads conjoined erased sable and overall in pale a double-warded key, wards to base of the first.

Crest: None approved.

Motto: VIGILANCE WITH PRIDE.

Symbolism: Oriental blue and silver gray (white) are the colors traditionally associated with military intelligence. The crossed lightning flashes connote the battalion's mission as a combat electronic warfare intelligence unit. The key is a symbol of knowledge and security. The double-headed eagle symbolizes watchfulness and vigilance and alludes to the unit's former areas of service, Austria and Germany.

Distinctive Unit Insignia

The distinctive unit insignia is the shield and motto of the coat of arms.

Lineage and Honors

RA
(inactive)

Lineage

Constituted 15 February 1952 in the Regular Army as the 533d Military Intelligence Service Battalion. Activated 1 March 1952 in Austria. Reorganized and redesignated 25 May 1954 as the 533d Military Intelligence Battalion. Inactivated 8 September 1955 in Austria.

Redesignated 16 September 1980 as Headquarters, Headquarters and Operations Company, 533d Military Intelligence Battalion, assigned to the 3d Armored Division, and activated in Germany (856th Army Security Agency Company [see ANNEX 1] concurrently reorganized and redesignated as Company A; 503d Military Intelligence Company [see ANNEX 2] consolidated with the 203d Military Intelligence Detachment [see ANNEX 3] and consolidated unit reorganized and redesignated as Company B). Battalion inactivated 15 August 1992 in Germany.

ANNEX 1

Constituted 4 September 1944 in the Army of the United States as the 3148th Signal Service Platoon. Activated 25 September 1944 on New Caledonia.

Inactivated 30 January 1946 on Ie Shima. Redesignated 23 August 1948 as the 580th Signal Service Detachment and activated at Fort Greely, Alaska. Inactivated 1 June 1949 at Fort Greely, Alaska. Redesignated 7 June 1954 as the 580th Signal Detachment and allotted to the Regular Army.

Converted and redesignated 19 May 1955 as the 856th Communication Reconnaissance Detachment. Activated 25 June 1955 in Japan. Inactivated 15 August 1956 in Japan. Redesignated 6 April 1966 as the 856th Army Security Agency Detachment. Activated 15 June 1966 at Fort Benning, Georgia. Inactivated 6 March 1971 in Vietnam. Redesignated 1 July 1974 as the 856th Army Security Agency Company and activated in Germany.

ANNEX 2

Constituted 14 October 1944 in the Army of the United States as the 479th Counter Intelligence Corps Detachment. Activated 23 November 1944 on New Guinea. Disbanded 22 July 1945 in the Philippine Islands. Reconstituted 5 January 1949 in the Regular Army as the 530th Counter Intelligence Corps Detachment. Activated 28 January 1949 at Fort Knox, Kentucky. Inactivated 15 March 1951 at Fort Knox, Kentucky.

Redesignated 17 March 1955 as the 503d Counter Intelligence Corps Detachment. Activated 5 April 1955 at Fort Knox, Kentucky. Reorganized and redesignated 25 June 1958 as the 503d Military Intelligence Detachment. Consolidated 21 November 1972 with the 503d Military Intelligence Company (see ANNEX 4) and consolidated unit designated as the 503d Military Intelligence Company.

ANNEX 3

Constituted 12 July 1944 in the Army of the United States as the 503d Counter Intelligence Corps Detachment. Activated 16 August 1944 in France with personnel from provisional Counter Intelligence Corps Detachment attached to the 3d Armored Division. Inactivated 7 October 1945 in Germany. Activated 21 February 1948 at Fort Bragg, North Carolina. Allotted 25 June 1952 to the Regular Army.

Reorganized and redesignated 15 November 1954 as the 203d Counter Intelligence Corps Detachment. Reorganized and redesignated 25 January 1958 as the 203d Military Intelligence Detachment. Inactivated 5 May 1959 at Fort Hood, Texas. Activated 5 April 1962 at Fort Hood, Texas. Inactivated 20 April 1978 at Fort Hood, Texas.

ANNEX 4

Constituted 30 June 1952 in the Regular Army as the 503d Military Intelligence Service Company. Activated 1 September 1952 in Japan. Reorganized and redesignated 28 March 1954 as the 503d Military Intelligence Company. Inactivated 24 June 1955 in Japan. Activated 1 June 1962 in Germany. Inactivated 25 September 1965 in Germany.

CAMPAIGN PARTICIPATION CREDIT

Southwest Asia
> Defense of Saudi Arabia
> Liberation and Defense of Kuwait
> Cease-Fire

Company A additionally entitled to:

World War II–AP
> Ryukyus

Vietnam
> Counteroffensive, Phase II
> Counteroffensive, Phase III
> Tet Counteroffensive
> Counteroffensive, Phase IV
> Counteroffensive, Phase V
> Counteroffensive, Phase VI
> Tet 69/Counteroffensive
> Summer-Fall 1969
> Winter-Spring 1970
> Sanctuary Counteroffensive
> Counteroffensive, Phase VII

Company B additionally entitled to:

World War II–AP
> New Guinea
> Luzon

World War II–EAME
> Normandy
> Northern France
> Rhineland
> Ardennes-Alsace
> Central Europe

DECORATIONS

Company A entitled to:

Valorous Unit Award, Streamer embroidered SAIGON–LONG BINH (856th Radio Research Detachment cited; DA GO 48, 1968)

Meritorious Unit Commendation (Army), Streamer embroidered VIETNAM 1966–1967 (856th Radio Research Detachment cited; DA GO 17, 1968)

Meritorious Unit Commendation (Army), Streamer embroidered VIETNAM 1967–1968 (856th Radio Research Detachment cited; DA GO 29, 1969)

Meritorious Unit Commendation (Army), Streamer embroidered VIETNAM 1968–1969 (856th Radio Research Detachment cited; DA GO 51, 1971)

Meritorious Unit Commendation (Army), Streamer embroidered VIETNAM 1969–1970 (856th Radio Research Detachment cited; DA GO 43, 1972)

Republic of Vietnam Cross of Gallantry with Palm, Streamer embroidered VIETNAM 1968 (856th Radio Research Detachment cited; DA GO 43, 1970)

Republic of Vietnam Cross of Gallantry with Palm, Streamer embroidered VIETNAM 1968–1970 (856th Radio Research Detachment cited; DA GO 51, 1971)

Republic of Vietnam Cross of Gallantry with Palm, Streamer embroidered VIETNAM 1970–1971 (856th Radio Research Detachment cited; DA GO 6, 1974)

Republic of Vietnam Civil Action Honor Medal, First Class, Streamer embroidered VIETNAM 1966–1970 (856th Radio Research Detachment cited; DA GO 51, 1971)

Republic of Vietnam Civil Action Honor Medal, First Class, Streamer embroidered VIETNAM 1970–1971 (856th Radio Research Detachment cited; DA GO 6, 1974)

Company B entitled to:

Philippine Presidential Unit Citation, Streamer embroidered 17 OCTOBER 1944 TO 4 JULY 1945 (479th Counter Intelligence Corps Detachment cited; DA GO 47, 1950)

Belgian Fourragere 1940 (503d Counter Intelligence Corps Detachment cited; DA GO 43, 1950)

Cited in the Order of the Day of the Belgian Army for action in Belgium (503d Counter Intelligence Corps Detachment cited; DA GO 43, 1950)

Cited in the Order of the Day of the Belgian Army for action in the Ardennes (503d Counter Intelligence Corps Detachment cited; DA GO 43, 1950)

542d MILITARY INTELLIGENCE BATTALION

HERALDIC ITEMS

COAT OF ARMS

Shield: Sable, a sword and lightning flash saltirewise surmounted by a stylized chess piece with a griffin's head or, within a bordure compony argent and azure.

Crest: That for the regiments and separate battalions of the Army Reserve: On a wreath of the colors, argent and sable, the Lexington Minuteman proper. The statue of the Minuteman, Capt. John Parker (H. H. Kitson, sculptor), stands on the Common in Lexington, Massachusetts.

Motto: THE EYES OF THE BATTLE.

Symbolism: Oriental blue and silver gray (white) are the colors traditionally associated with military intelligence units. Black denotes solidity while suggesting clandestine capabilities. Gold alludes to excellence and achievement. The sword and flash represent military preparedness and speed. The border and chess piece suggest strategy and countermeasure tactics. The griffin symbolizes vigilance with its keen eyesight and acute hearing.

DISTINCTIVE UNIT INSIGNIA

The distinctive unit insignia is a modification of the shield and motto of the coat of arms.

LINEAGE AND HONORS

AR
(active)

LINEAGE

Constituted 16 September 1987 in the Army Reserve as the 242d Military Intelligence Battalion and activated with Headquarters at Staten Island, New York. Inactivated 15 September 1993 at Staten Island, New York.

Redesignated 16 September 1993 as the 542d Military Intelligence Battalion and activated with Headquarters at East Windsor, Connecticut.

CAMPAIGN PARTICIPATION CREDIT

None.

DECORATIONS

None.

549th MILITARY INTELLIGENCE BATTALION

HERALDIC ITEMS

COAT OF ARMS

Shield: Azure, a globe argent gridlined sable, overall a lightning flash issuing from dexter chief or in saltire with a sword gules in bend sinister, all within a border of the second.

Crest: That for the regiments and separate battalions of the Army Reserve: On a wreath of the colors, argent and azure, the Lexington Minuteman proper. The statue of the Minuteman, Capt. John Parker (H. H. Kitson, sculptor), stands on the Common in Lexington, Massachusetts.

Motto: MODERN WARFARE.

Symbolism: The global aspect of the mission performed by the military intelligence branch is represented by the longitude and latitude lines of the world. The lightning flash is symbolic of the electronic warfare nature of military intelligence. The sword represents the aggressive nature and dangerous missions accomplished by military intelligence personnel. The border suggests containment and alludes to intelligence gathering and its use in defense strategy.

DISTINCTIVE UNIT INSIGNIA

The distinctive unit insignia is the shield and motto of the coat of arms.

LINEAGE AND HONORS

LINEAGE

AR
(active)

Constituted 17 July 1986 in the Army Reserve as the 549th Military Intelligence Battalion and activated with Headquarters at Austin, Texas.

CAMPAIGN PARTICIPATION CREDIT

None.

DECORATIONS

None.

550th MILITARY INTELLIGENCE BATTALION

HERALDIC ITEMS

COAT OF ARMS

Shield: Argent, a lightning bolt bendwise point to base azure, all within a bordure quarterly gules and of the first.

Crest: That for the regiments and separate battalions of the Army Reserve: On a wreath of the colors, argent and azure, the Lexington Minuteman proper. The statue of the Minuteman, Capt. John Parker (H. H. Kitson, sculptor), stands on the Common in Lexington, Massachusetts.

Motto: BLUE LIGHTNING.

Symbolism: Oriental blue and silver gray are the military intelligence colors. Blue also alludes to the battalion's affiliation with the 50th Armored (Jersey Blues) Division. The colors red and white were suggested by the shoulder sleeve insignia of the 78th Division (Training), to which the battalion was attached. The lightning bolt relates to the battalion's signal security and electronic warfare mission. The quartered border signifies military strategy.

DISTINCTIVE UNIT INSIGNIA

The distinctive unit insignia is the shield and motto of the coat of arms.

LINEAGE AND HONORS

AR
(inactive)

LINEAGE

Constituted 16 July 1986 in the Army Reserve as the 550th Military Intelligence Battalion and activated with Headquarters at Pedricktown, New Jersey. Inactivated 15 September 1993 at Pedricktown, New Jersey.

CAMPAIGN PARTICIPATION CREDIT

None.

DECORATIONS

None.

629th MILITARY INTELLIGENCE BATTALION

HERALDIC ITEMS

COAT OF ARMS

Shield: Per chevron paly of six argent and azure a bend counter-changed, and of the first in base a panther's face proper grasping two lightning flashes conjoined chevronwise of the second.

Crest: That for the regiments and separate battalions of the Maryland Army National Guard: On a wreath of the colors, argent and azure, a cross bottony per cross quarterly gules and argent.

Motto: STALK THE PREY.

Symbolism: Oriental blue is one of the colors associated with military intelligence. The upper half of the shield alludes to the state flag of Maryland and identifies the home area of the battalion. The panther embodies the nickname of the unit, "Prowler," and is a predator celebrated for its stealth and patience on the hunt. It is an appropriate symbol for a tactical level intelligence unit. The lightning flashes refer to speed of operation and the dominant role of combat electronic warfare on the battlefield.

DISTINCTIVE UNIT INSIGNIA

The distinctive unit insignia is the shield and motto of the coat of arms.

LINEAGE AND HONORS

ARNG
(Maryland)

LINEAGE

Organized and federally recognized 3 May 1988 in the Maryland Army National Guard as the 629th Military Intelligence Battalion, an element of the 29th Infantry Division, with Headquarters at Greenbelt. Location of Headquarters changed 1 April 1994 to Laurel.

Home Station: Laurel.

CAMPAIGN PARTICIPATION CREDIT

None.

DECORATIONS

None.

Glossary of Lineage Terms

ACTIVATE. To transfer a constituted Regular Army or Army Reserve unit from the inactive to the active rolls of the United States Army. The unit is usually stationed at a specific location and assigned personnel and equipment at this time; however, a unit may be active at zero strength—that is, without personnel or equipment.

ALLOT. To allocate a unit to one of the components of the United States Army. The present components are the Regular Army (RA), the Army National Guard (ARNG), and the Army Reserve (AR), formerly known as the Organized Reserves and the Organized Reserve Corps. During World War II units were also allotted to the Army of the United States. An Army National Guard unit is usually further allotted to a particular state or group of states. A unit may be withdrawn from any component except the Army National Guard and allotted to another; the new allotment, however, does not change the history, lineage, and honors of the unit.

ASSIGN. To make a unit part of a larger organization and place it under that organization's command and control until it is relieved from the assignment. As a rule, only assignments to divisions and separate combined arms brigades are shown in unit lineages.

CONSOLIDATE. To merge two or more units into a single unit. The unit may retain the designation of one of the former units or it may have a new designation, but it inherits the history, lineage, and honors of all of the former units. Active as well as inactive units may be consolidated.

CONSTITUTE. To place the designation of a new unit on the official rolls of the United States Army.

CONVERT. To transfer a unit from one branch of the Army to another—for example, from signal to military intelligence. Such a change always requires a redesignation; however, there is no break in the historical continuity of the unit. Active as well as inactive units may be converted, but if the unit is active, it must also be reorganized under a new table of organization and equipment (TOE).

DESIGNATION. The official title of a unit, consisting usually of a number, a branch or function, and a command echelon. Additional descriptive terms may appear in parentheses, but such parenthetical identifications are not part of the unit's official designation.

DISBAND. To remove the designation of a Regular Army or Army Reserve unit from the official rolls of the United States Army. If the unit is active, it must also be inactivated. Disbandment is intended to be permanent and irreversible, except in extraordinary circumstances.

ELEMENT. A unit that is assigned to or is part of a larger organization.

FEDERALLY RECOGNIZE. To accept an Army National Guard unit into the force structure of the United States Army after the unit has been inspected by a federal representative and found to be properly stationed, organized, and equipped in accordance with Army requirements.

INACTIVATE. To place a Regular Army or Army Reserve unit that is not currently needed in the force structure in an inoperative status without assigned personnel or equipment for a limited period of time. The unit is transferred to the inactive rolls of the United States Army, but it can be activated again whenever needed. Upon reactivation, the unit retains its former history, lineage, and honors.

ORDER INTO ACTIVE FEDERAL SERVICE. To place an Army National Guard unit on full-time active duty under the control of the United States government. The unit remains in federal service until released by the federal government, at which time it reverts to the control of its home state or states.

ORDER INTO ACTIVE MILITARY SERVICE. To place an Army Reserve unit on full-time active duty, usually during a war or a crisis. After completing its active duty, the unit may be inactivated or it may be released from active military service, reverting to reserve status. This term does not apply to Army Reserve units on annual active duty for training.

ORGANIC ELEMENT. A unit that is an integral part of a larger organization—for example, a lettered company of a battalion.

ORGANIZE. To assign personnel and equipment to a unit and make it operative—that is, capable of performing its mission. For Army National Guard units, this term is used instead of ACTIVATE. (See above.)

RECONSTITUTE. To restore to the official rolls of the United States Army a unit that has been disbanded or one whose federal recognition has been withdrawn. The reconstituted unit may have a new designation, but it retains its former history, lineage, and honors.

REDESIGNATE. To change a unit's official title. Active as well as inactive units may be redesignated, but personnel and equipment of an active unit are not changed unless the unit is reorganized at the same time. Redesignation is a change of title only; the unit's history, lineage, and honors remain the same.

REORGANIZE. To change the structure of a unit in accordance with a new table of organization and equipment (TOE) within the same branch of the Army.

SPECIAL DESIGNATION. An official unit nickname. There are two types of special designations—a traditional designation (one that a unit has used continuously for the last thirty years or more) and a distinctive designation (one that a unit has used for less than thirty years or one with which a unit wishes to be associated). The special designation, if any, appears in parentheses after the unit's official designation.

WITHDRAW FEDERAL RECOGNITION. To remove the designation of an Army National Guard unit from the official rolls of the United States Army. Federal recognition is withdrawn when the unit no longer meets Army requirements or is no longer needed in the force structure.

Index to the Narrative